BIRTH
of a National Icon

BIRTH

of a National Icon

The Literary Avant-Garde
and the Origins of
the Intellectual in France

Venita Datta

State University of New York Press

Published by
State University of New York Press, Albany

© 1999 State University of New York

For information, address State University of New York Press,
State University Plaza, Albany, N.Y., 12246

Production by Diane Ganeles
Marketing by Anne Valentine

Library of Congress Cataloging-in-Publication Data

Datta, Venita, 1961–
    Birth of a national icon : the literary avant-garde and the
origins of the intellectual in France / Venita Datta.
        p. cm.
    Includes bibliographical references and index.
    ISBN 0-7914-4207-1 (alk. paper). — ISBN 0-7914-4208-X (pbk. :
alk. paper)
    1. France—Intellectual life—19th century—Political aspects.
2. Social change—France. 3. Avant-garde (Aesthetics)—France.
4. Intellectuals—France—Political activity—History—19th century.
I. Title.
DC33.6.D28   1999
944′.081′2′08631—dc21
                                                            98-39033
                                                            CIP

10 9 8 7 6 5 4 3 2 1

For my parents and Steve

Contents

Illustrations

Acknowledgments

This book began as the end of a dissertation on *La Revue blanche (1889–1903): Intellectuals and Politics in Fin-de-Siècle France*. Upon completing my study, I realized that for me it had raised as many questions as it had answered, namely, about the nature of political engagement and the role of the avant-garde. Yet the kind of broad study I envisioned on the avant-garde and the birth of the intellectual in France seemed extremely daunting at the time. Thanks to the encouragement of my advisors at the Institute of French Studies at New York University: Michel Beaujour, Tony Judt, and Nicholas Wahl, I pursued this new project. I will forever be grateful not only for their intellectual guidance, but also for their moral support and affection.

At Bryn Mawr College, where I taught for two years, my colleagues in the French department, in particular, Penny Armstrong and Catherine Lafarge, were among the earliest supporters of this project, as was Michel Grimaud, Chair of the French department at Wellesley College, when I arrived in the Fall of 1991. I am also indebted to my colleagues in the French and history departments at Wellesley who made helpful suggestions about the manuscript in its various stages: Anne Gillain, Andrea Levitt, Fran Malino, Vicki Mistacco, Michèle Respaut, and Andy Shennan. Special thanks goes to Stephen Bold, Catherine Masson, and Jim Petterson, who helped me steer my way through a maze of tricky translations. Other colleagues at Wellesley—Ken Winkler and Mary Lefkowitz— were extremely generous with their time and advice.

I wrote the greater part of this book while on leave, thanks to Wellesley College's Junior Faculty leave policy. In addition, the funds from the Wellesley College Faculty Grants committee allowed me not only to consult documents in France, but also to hire a wonderful research assistant, Stefanie Diaz, who worked tirelessly on the manuscript, including the compilation of the appendix. I'd like to note here that all translations, unless otherwise indicated, are my own. I also appreciate the work of Véronique Guarino, who graciously offered to help me prepare the manuscript in its final stages. I must acknowledge as well the staff of the Clapp Library—Leanne Harkness for helping me secure a study of my own, as well as Karen Jensen and Justine Crowley of the Interlibrary Loan office. They managed to track down even the most obscure sources for me.

All of the chapters of this book were presented in some form to colleagues at the Western Society for French History and French Historical Studies. Their feedback was instrumental in helping me revise my work. I would also like to thank the colleagues of the New York Area French History Seminar, especially Tip Ragan and Gene Lebovics, for allowing me to share my work with them.

My deep-felt thanks goes to friends and colleagues who read the manuscript and provided me with valuable suggestions: the anonymous readers for State University of New York Press, as well as Paul Mazgaj, Rachel Fuchs, K. Steven Vincent, Bud Burkhard, Martha Hanna, Antoinette Blum, Isabelle de Courtivron, John Cerullo, Chris Forth, Frank Murphy, Stuart Campbell, Eric Cahm, William Logue, Joy and Hines Hall, Paul Cohen, and David Wright, all of whom give real meaning to the idea of scholarly community.

My friends and former classmates from New York University: Isbabelle Genest, Harriet Jackson, Shanny Peer, and Willa Silverman offered not only scholarly advice but also moral support. My friends in Boston—Joanne Berger-Sweeney, Claire Andrade-Watkins, and Adlai Murdoch—also provided me with much encouragement.

I cannnot begin to find words to thank my parents and my husband Steve, who have always supported all my endeavors, intellectual and otherwise. This book is dedicated to them.

Introduction: Birth of a National Icon

French intellectuals have served as role models for intellectuals all over the world. In no other country does the intellectual play such an important role in society as the voice of the national conscience. Although the activist writer emerged during the Enlightenment, the notion of the intellectual was born in France during the late nineteenth century, a symbol of a modern, democratic, and secular society.

Intellectuals, as opposed to writers or *philosophes*, are part of a group. By virtue of training in their discipline, whether chemistry or literature, French intellectuals have considered it their duty to pronounce on such matters of national and international interest as the rise of fascism and communism, decolonization, the cold war, and Vietnam. Being an intellectual is a vocation, even a mission. Significantly, the intellectual in France was called at first "a cleric" (*un clerc*). Indeed, the new secular cleric supplanted the traditional priest as a source of moral authority in modern French society.

In 1880, the concept of the intellectual had not yet been defined. By 1914, it was an established category. The Dreyfus Affair is often cited as the moment at which the intellectual was born. The Affair has become a *lieu de mémoire*, enshrined in national collective memory, and the beginnings of the intellectual have consequently been veiled in a myth of origins.[1] Although it is true that the term "intellectual" as a noun gained widespread usage during the Affair, the birth of the intellectual and the subsequent establishment of intellectuals as national icons cannot be examined within the context of the Dreyfus Affair alone. Such an important development

1

must be studied within the broader cultural, political, and social context of fin-de-siècle France.

The intellectual, both as a noun and a concept, first appeared in the literary avant-garde during the years immediately preceding the Affair. The earliest Dreyfusard intellectuals came from the avant-garde as did their earliest anti-Dreyfusard counterparts. Moreover, both sides shared a common belief in the right of intellectuals to speak on matters of national importance.

The literary avant-garde emerged at the fin de siècle as an important site of French cultural life. By 1910, the avant-garde literary journal had become a hallmark of French culture.[2] A major focus of the present study, the literary journal allows us to study not only texts and ideas but also their development, circulation, and reception. Equally important is the fact that the literary journal represents a milieu. An important place of sociability of intellectuals, it is part of a network, linked to other sites of French cultural life, among them the literary salon, the café, the university, and even the political party.[3] Studying the literary avant-garde is thus not only necessary for a fuller understanding of the birth of the intellectual in France, but it also offers us the opportunity to understand better the workings of French cultural life, in particular, the way in which literature and politics overlap.

My principal aim in writing this book then is two-fold: to separate the origins of the intellectual in France from the strict confines of the Dreyfus Affair and to examine the key role played by the literary avant-garde in the emergence of this figure. Yet this book is not limited to an examination of the avant-garde, which, after all, acted not in isolation, but in conjunction with other groups in French society. My ultimate goal is to examine the emergence of the intellectual as a national figure. To this end, I concentrate on the role of ideology in the articulation of the debate surrounding the intellectual. The intellectual was first and foremost a product of rival ideologies, two opposing visions of French national identity. While such a debate cannot be reduced to a product of a sociocultural strategy, neither can it be examined in a vacuum.[4] As Jacques Julliard so pointedly put it: "Ideas do not run the streets naked."[5] Thus, it is imperative to situate the origins of the intellectual not only within the context of the contemporary intellectual milieu, but also against the backdrop of an emerging mass democracy.

The intellectual in France was born of the growing pains of modern democracy. Indeed, the notion of the intellectual implies a permanent state of crisis.[6] The Dreyfus Affair was itself a crisis of national identity which brought together a variety of related issues touching on race, class, and gender. During the late nineteenth century, French society underwent a profound transformation as traditional elites were increasingly supplanted by meritocratic ones. In such a society, intelligence and learning, rather than birth, came to represent power. The importance of intellect thus became an important object of debate in fin-de-siècle France, particularly with regard to the "virtues" of sacrifice and obedience instilled by such traditional institutions as the Catholic Church and the army. The establishment of a democratic regime that promulgated freedom of the press and compulsory primary school laws, thereby contributing to a large, literate public, was essential to the emergence of the modern intellectual.

At the same time, however, these changes inspired apprehension among certain men of thought, who were suspicious not only of traditional elites, but also of the rising masses, especially the lower-middle classes, who represented the backbone of the Third Republic. How did these men of thought feel about the democratization of society and their own role in this society? Writers and artists in particular feared being displaced in a modern society in which the marketplace ruled; they resented the commercialization of culture, even as many among them benefited from these developments. Some even looked to a golden age when writers and artists had been protected by powerful patrons. Many writers resented republican politicians and university professors, both of whom emerged as important groups at this time. To a certain degree, the banding together of writers and artists of the avant-garde was a response not only to the contemporary literary establishment, but also to the political establishment of the Third Republic.

Just as the importance of intellect in a democracy was an object of discussion, so, too, was the organization of intellect by the state, which sought to create its own elites via the system of the republican university. This led to the rise of individuals from previously excluded groups, in particular, Jews, who were increasingly associated with the new republican "state" intellectual. They became the chief targets of those writers and artists who propagated anti-Semitic theories. Anti-Semites, even those with anticlerical leanings, linked France's national identity to its Catholic past, while their opponents, many of whom were Protestant and Jewish, defined France in function of the universalist ideals of the French Revolution. In both cases, intellectuals presumed to speak for the entire nation, thereby assigning themselves an indispensable role in French society.

Questions of national identity also framed the contemporary debate on intellect and manliness. Dreyfusards and anti-Dreyfusards both articulated different notions of honor and manhood, which were embedded in conflicting ideals of the nation, seen in both moral and biological terms. Late-nineteenth-century France witnessed the emergence of an organicist discourse of national health. This discourse was reinforced by France's defeat at the hands of Germany in 1870 and the decline of the national birthrate, both of which were viewed as signs of French degeneration. In such an atmosphere, the army played a primordial role, its soldiers representing the masculine defense of a feminine national body. Any attempt to attack the army was seen as a threat to both national honor and the health of the nation, as were such figures as Jews and homosexuals, who, like critics of the army, were represented as "feminine," "emasculated" men. Anti-Dreyfusards could thus easily dismiss their opponents by lumping Jews, homosexuals, and Dreyfusard intellectuals together as enemies of a fecund France defended by virile men rooted in the traditions of the Catholic Church and the army.

Yet anti-Dreyfusards did not claim a monopoly on organicist discourse. Emile Zola, champion of the Dreyfusard cause, had popularized such ideas in his Rougon-Macquart novel series. Thus, both sides employed organicist metaphors in articulating their different visions of national identity. If intellectuals of the Left and Right differed in their vision of France, they shared a common vocabulary to express their views.

Most striking about Dreyfusard and anti-Dreyfusard intellectuals is not what divided them but rather all that they shared. Although they may have had very different visions of France, both groups believed that the intellectual should play an important role in society, thereby assuring the emerging status of the intellectual as a national icon.

As national icons in France, intellectuals have attracted a great deal of attention, especially from intellectuals themselves. They have either been glorified as heroes or vilified as traitors. Indeed, such polemical essays as Julien Benda's *La Trahison des clercs* (1927) and Jean-Paul Sartre's *Plaidoyer pour l'intellectuel* (1972) are a staple of French intellectual life. Scholarly work on the intellectual is more recent, in great part because the extreme polarization of French cultural life has long precluded dispassionate analysis.[7] Since the mid-1980s, the focus on the intellectual as an object of historical study has intensified at a rapid pace, perhaps as a result of the much lamented "decline" of the intellectual in French national life.[8] For the French, studying the intellectual is to some extent a nostalgic enterprise, an attempt to illuminate an object that is part of a national heritage that they fear may soon be relegated to the past.[9]

Recent works by Michel Winock, Pascal Ory, Jean-François Sirinelli, Jean-Pierre Rioux, Christophe Prochasson, and Christophe Charle, among many others, have not only contributed to our knowledge of the history of intellectuals, but they also attest to the vitality of the field.[10] In spite of, or more accurately, because of a deeply rooted American anti-intellectual tradition, the French intellectual continues to fascinate scholars on the other side of the Atlantic too, as the works of Robert Wohl, Alan Spitzer, and Tony Judt illustrate.[11] Nevertheless, the prehistory of the intellectual, that is, during the years immediately preceding the Dreyfus Affair—remains underrepresented among works on intellectuals, which tend to concentrate on the 1930s, World War II, and the 1950s.[12]

While the period of the Affair has attracted much attention, it has been presented as a point of departure rather than as a culmination of a process. In addition, many of those who have studied the Dreyfus Affair have concentrated on university professors and establishment writers at the expense of the literary avant-garde.[13] Furthermore, most studies of intellectuals in the Affair, whether political or sociological, tend to represent Dreyfusard and anti-Dreyfusard intellectuals as two monolithic *blocs*, each associated with a set of immutable ideals. Such a view not only ignores the great diversity that existed within each camp but also the similarities between the two groups. Finally, although a number of excellent works on nationalism and sexuality have been written, such as those by George Mosse and Robert Nye, a fundamental relation between intellect and sexuality has been ignored.[14] One of my goals is to redress this neglect by examining the events leading up to the Dreyfus Affair, along with the Affair itself, within the context of the contemporary crisis of gender identity. The construction of intellectual identity, I argue, is closely associated with representations of both masculinity and femininity.

A notable exception to the paucity of works on the origins of the intellectual is Christophe Charle's *Naissance des "intellectuels": 1880–1910* (Paris: Editions de Minuit, 1990). Charle's work is a key work for any scholar interested in the history of intellectuals. It is groundbreaking not only because of its attempt to demythologize the Affair and the involvement of intellectuals in it, but also because it clearly illustrates that the debate concerning the intellectual was in place well before the Affair. Nevertheless, Charle's research, as rich as it is, is limited and ultimately incomplete. Charle, who is a sociologist of the Bourdieu School,[15] concentrates on the sociology of intellectuals during the fin de siècle but neglects the intellectual history of the period. Furthermore, he isolates intellectuals from the rest of society by viewing them in function of their place in a literary field. When he does situate intellectuals within a wider context, it is to compare them to other elites in French society. While such an analysis is extremely instructive, it is also necessary to place intellectuals within the context of society as a whole, especially with regard to the rising masses. Intellectuals, after all, emerged fully from an affair of public opinion, indeed, the first event of the "mass media." How did they see themselves vis-à-vis the popular classes?

As for the Affair itself, Charle represents it as a confrontation pitting traditional elites, supported by anti-Dreyfusard intellectuals, against Dreyfusard intellectuals, especially those from the republican university, who sought to establish a new position for themselves in society. Charle sets the "pôle dominé" against the "pôle dominant," that is, the literary avant-garde *vs* the literary establishment as represented by the Académie française, newer disciplines *vs* older disciplines, the younger generation *vs* the older generation.[16] Although his analysis is more complex and nuanced, his work is in some measure indebted to that of leftist critic Régis Debray, who, in his *Le Pouvoir intellectuel en France* (translated into English as *Teachers, Writers, Celebrities*), described the Affair as a battle between the university and "French literature," between the Left Bank and the Right Bank, the provinces and Paris, the scholarship men and the inheritors.[17]

While much in the two presentations is persuasive, I do not find them altogether satisfactory, for such descriptions do not sufficiently account for the very real tensions due to diverging positions within each camp. For example, among Dreyfusards, university intellectuals looked at their literary avant-garde colleagues with a certain suspicion and vice versa, while among anti-Dreyfusards, such avant-garde intellectuals as Maurice Barrès and Charles Maurras viewed their more established counterparts like Ferdinand Brunetière with both scorn and exasperation. Part of the problem lies with the fact that the two camps did not correspond to a strict left/right fault line, although the ideal of the left-wing intellectual and of the right-wing counterpart emerged at this time.[18]

Finally, although Charle cites many of the works written by fin-de-siècle intellectuals on their role in society, he does not do a close reading of these texts. Such an examination is essential, as Bourdieu, who has sought a middle ground between objectivist and subjectivist history, would agree.[19]

In demythologizing the Affair—no mean feat—Charle has perhaps fallen into the opposite trap of examining ideologies and individual actions through the prism of overly rational strategies within a sociocultural "field." His analysis, although sophisticated, underestimates the power of both the Dreyfusard and anti-Dreyfusard mystiques. While a scholar should not be duped by the mythology of the Affair, neither can he or she ignore the power of this myth on the intellectuals who came of age during the Affair and after.

My own aim is to read the works of writers, professors, journalists, and artists about their self-realization as intellectuals. Such a reading does not imply an acceptance of their writings at face value; on the contrary, their words often belie their deeds. In fact, this contradiction between theory and practice lies at the heart of their struggle for identity as intellectuals.

Given the mythology of the Dreyfus Affair and the acrimonious debate that surrounded the rise of intellectuals as a recognizable group, it is not surprising that the term "intellectual" should defy easy definition. From its very origins, the term, along with the concept it implied, was contested. Nevertheless, the intellectual is a peculiarly—if not exclusively—French phenomenon, an integral part of French identity, and must be examined within the context of French history and culture.

A product of mass democracy, the intellectual, quite naturally, appeared first in France, the first nation in Europe, as well as the only major power with a republican regime during the late nineteenth century. Of course, other factors also contributed to the emergence of the intellectual in France: foremost among them, the literary nature of French culture. France is not only the home of Descartes and Pascal, a land which identifies itself with intelligence and reason, but it is also the birthplace of Voltaire and Victor Hugo, a country in which the public writer is a long-established tradition.[20] The symbiotic nature of French culture and politics facilitated the emergence of the intellectual in France. It not only produced writers who went on to become politicians, like Chateaubriand, Alphonse de Lamartine, and Léon Blum, but also politicians who could lay claim to being men of letters, like Georges Clemenceau, Jean Jaurès, and Edouard Herriot.

The centralization of the country also played an important role in the development of the intellectual. France has a long history of a strong state, whether under the monarchy or the republic. All roads, political, intellectual, or otherwise, lead to Paris, thereby facilitating both the sense of belonging to an intellectual community and contact between political and intellectual groups.

The myth of the Affair, cemented by the writings of Julien Benda and Jean-Paul Sartre, has firmly associated the intellectual with the Left in historical memory.[21] Yet the intellectual was a product of both the Left and the Right. The term "intellectual" was widely used, if not defined, in avant-garde circles, by future Dreyfusards and anti-Dreyfusards. From the start, however, the term was fraught with ambiguities and inconsistencies, with members of the two groups attaching both positive and negative connotations to the word.[22]

Immediately following the publication of Zola's "J'Accuse," the Dreyfusard newspaper *L'Aurore* printed what has become known as the "Manifesto of Intellectuals." In reality, this document was not a manifesto but a "protestation," actually two petitions, protesting the verdict of 1894. It was accompanied by the signatures of writers, professors, and students, identified as such. Nowhere was the term "intellectual" to be found. A few days later, in an editorial of 23 January 1898 in *L'Aurore*, Georges Clemenceau noted approvingly that intellectuals, of varying backgrounds, had come together in defense of a common idea: "Is this not a sign, all of these intellectuals from all corners of the horizon, united around an idea." It was only when anti-Dreyfusard Maurice Barrès, a great popularizer of the term in the 1890s, picked up on its usage by Dreyfusard Clemenceau to ridicule his opponents that the substantive entered into common usage.[23] To complete the circle, Lucien Herr, the librarian of the Ecole Normale Supérieure, responded to Barrès in *La Revue blanche*. Writing in the name of Barrès's former disciples, Herr not only excommunicated the former "Prince of Youth," he also proudly reclaimed the term "intellectual."[24]

Barrès's disavowal of the term at the time of the Affair—he would later recuperate it—should not mask the fact that intellectuals participated on both sides and that the two groups believed that the intellectual had the right and duty to intervene in public matters. Moreover, as the events of the Affair illustrate, intellectuals saw themselves not as isolated individuals but as part of a group.

These two principles, one which views intellectuals as a socioprofessional category, the other, which defines intellectuals primarily in ethical and messianic terms, are helpful in defining the term "intellectual," but are ultimately limited.[25] Just as the history of intellectuals must find a middle ground between the sociology of intellectuals and the history of ideas, so, too, must any definition of the intellectual. Socioeconomic views of the intellectual tend to be much too broad to be useful, although the distinction between producers of culture, that is, artists and savants; and mediators, in other words, journalists and professors, is an interesting one. Intellectuals can come from both groups. Pierre Bourdieu's depiction of intellectuals as the dominated fraction of the national elite is more complex and richer than a simplistic socio-professional definition, but it does not take into account the mystique associated with the intellectual.

Yet the "mystical" definition of the intellectual as an individual with a vocation, propagated largely by Dreyfusard Julien Benda, who viewed the intellectual as a secular cleric, and the latter-day Dreyfusard Jean-Paul Sartre, who also saw intellectuals as the nation's moral conscience, is perhaps too absolute. Not all intellectuals saw themselves in this way, nor did their actions correspond to this romanticized vision of the intellectual. Intellectuals, after all, are human beings; they do not limit themselves to the realm of pure ideas. Furthermore, not all historical debates are as clearly delineated as the Affair.[26]

Pascal Ory and more recently Jacques Julliard and Michel Winock, the editors of the monumental *Dictionnaire des intellectuels français*, offer a definition of the intellectual which reconciles these two different visions of the intellectual and at the same time goes beyond them. They assert that intellectuals are not defined by who they are—whether professors, writers, artists, savants, or journalists—but by what they do. Intellectuals become intellectuals at the very moment of their political involvement. Although intellectuals' authority to speak is derived from their cultural and intellectual titles as well as from their personal fame, to be considered an intellectual, one must be involved in public affairs. In other words, Sartre's notion of the "engaged intellectual" is redundant.[27] The nature of political commitment, of course, varies from individual to individual. Both practical and flexible, this definition allows for such differences and provides us a useful point of departure for our study of the emergence of the intellectual in fin-de-siècle France.

To it, I would only add that I consider as intellectuals those who saw themselves as such, thereby including Georges Clemenceau and Edouard Drumont, the first of whom was excluded by Julliard and Winock. In a work on the self-realization of intellectuals, the individuals in question, at least on this point, must be given the last word. Finally, we must remember that although many individuals disavowed the term, they certainly behaved as intellectuals, defining themselves by their actions if not their words.

Before turning our attention to the late nineteenth century, we must take time to consider the ancestors of the modern-day intellectual. Writers in the aristocratic society of sixteenth- and seventeenth-century France were tolerated, as long as they knew their place, beneath nobles and kings. François de Malherbe (1555–1628), known for his heroically independent efforts to break with the poetic tradition of the Pléiade by creating a modern and rational poetic language in France, spent almost as much effort trying to profit from another tradition: royal patronage of artists. Haughty, stoically proud Malherbe nonetheless realized that the writer's role was that of a simple entertainer: "A good poet is no more useful to the State than a good player of billiards."[28] So flattered and honored were writers by the King's attentions that some, like Racine, even gave up writing for the stage to take up state sinecures, in Racine's case, as the King's official historiographer.[29]

The repeated attempts by the Crown to curtail literary independence is perfectly illustrated by the founding of the Académie française, which originated as a secret—even illicit—meeting of bellettrists who had met (ca. 1630) to discuss literary texts and doctrine. The assembled writers were pressured by Richelieu in 1634 to accept royal sanction in exchange for cultural service to the King. Before long, membership in this official academy of writers became an end for which literature was hardly more than a means.[30] Courting the powerful, whether for money or prestige, made it generally impossible for writers to claim a true independence for their profession.

Although increasing numbers of writers were beginning to make a living solely through the pen during the first half of the eighteenth century, unless they had private means, a patron, or some occupation which left them enough leisure time for literary pursuits, they led meager existences.[31] Voltaire, for instance, was supported by numerous patrons, among them the Regent and Louis XV.[32] Montesquieu, on the other hand, achieved independence because he was both a wealthy landowner and a highly respected judge.

During the early part of the eighteenth century, writers continued to be viewed as inferior by the nobility. In 1726, Voltaire suffered an ignominious beating at the hands of the lackeys of the Chevalier de Rohan-Chabot, a nobleman he had insulted.[33] Not only did Voltaire's aristocratic friends refuse to defend him against a fellow nobleman, but when Voltaire himself attempted to challenge the Chevalier to a duel, he was put in the Bastille.[34] Only during the second half of the century did the writer's situation change significantly.

One indication of this change can be found in the development of the salon. In the earlier years of Parisian salons, beginning with the hyperrefined Chambre bleue (1618–1650) of Mme. de Rambouillet, it was the commoner-scribe who was temporarily raised in stature (if not in actual rank) by admission to these cultivated circles. Even Vincent Voiture, the first and brightest star of the Rambouillet salon, could not escape whispers that "voiture" rhymed with "roture," meaning commoner. By the end of the Ancien Régime, as John Lough has suggested, the increased leveling of ranks in Parisian salon society nearly reversed the basic function of the salon. Writers, whatever their social class or literary abilities, were given virtual unlimited entrance into salons that were otherwise inaccessible to social outsiders, whether nobles or commoners. Being part of the "beau monde" now meant being able to socialize with writers.[35] So changed was the position of the writer in French society at the end of the eighteenth century that English observer Arthur Young noted:

> The society for a man of letters, or who has any scientific pursuit, cannot be exceeded. The intercourse between such men and the great, which, if it be not upon equal footing, ought never to exist at all, is respectable. Persons of the highest rank pay an attention to science and literature, and emulate the character they confer.[36]

Conservative writers of the fin de siècle, among them Charles Maurras and Hugues Rebell, correctly identified the Enlightenment and Revolutionary period as an important turning point in the history of the writer in France. Hence, too, their nostalgia for the seventeenth century, when the writer clearly knew his place, and their consequential indictment of the *philosophes*. Fomenters of anarchy, the Encyclopédistes and their lot had contributed to the downfall of the monarchy and the Catholic Church, setting themselves up in their place.[37]

By the second half of the eighteenth century, writers had come to exercise publicly great power and prestige. No longer humble servants, they aimed to enlighten not only their fellow men, but also the government.[38] Such a change is illustrated by the apotheosis of Voltaire in 1778. The man who had summarily been beaten up some fifty years earlier returned in triumph to Paris, to be fêted and acclaimed.

Two nineteenth-century precursors of the modern intellectual include the Romantic poet and the savant. While the *philosophe* conferred on the writer the right to critique society, the Romantic prophet came to represent the aspirations of the people.[39] Victor Hugo, whose funeral in 1885 became a national event, is the most illustrious representative of this model. Finally, during the middle of the century, with the rise of the cult of science, emerged the savant, who dedicated his life to the material progress of humanity—Louis Pasteur being the most acclaimed example. Along with the *philosophe*, these two figures contributed to the notion of the modern intellectual, who combined the traits of all three.[40]

During the nineteenth century, the material condition of the writer changed substantially. Writers continued to receive state sinecures and subsidies, from the Revolutionaries, Napoleon, and successive regimes, even during the Third Republic. Indeed, this tradition continues to the present day. Nevertheless, these subsidies had decreased greatly by the mid-nineteenth century. Furthermore, it eventually became clear that writers could no longer rely on private patronage.

The gradual growth of a reading public during the century, however, contributed to the amelioration of the financial position of the writer, which was better in the eighteenth than in seventeenth century, better in the nineteenth than in the previous century.[41] An initial significant change involved the gradual development of authors' "rights." The first copyright law in France was passed during the Revolution in 1793. This right was extended by Napoleon and successive regimes.[42] So, too, did writers begin to band together in order to protect the interests of writers, as the founding in 1838 of the Société des gens de lettres, an organization later presided by Emile Zola, illustrates. At the beginning, however, many prominent writers, among them George Sand and Sainte-Beuve, ridiculed the Society, viewing it as materialistic and undignified.[43]

With the growth of a wider reading public came the development of a commercial literary marketplace, which contributed to the increased financial independence of the writer.[44] Such independence was a mixed blessing, especially for avant-garde writers of the fin de siècle, who suffered enormously from its demands.

Continuities with the past should not obscure the novelty of the modern-day intellectual, who is clearly a product of the latter half of the nineteenth century. By the fin de siècle, the intellectual had emerged as an autonomous figure, not only free to interact with the forces of the marketplace, but also liberated from government censorship and control. The advent of the Third Republic played a key role in the emergence of the intellectual; such a figure could not exist without freedom of the press. The 1881 press law not only mandated such freedom, but also reduced taxes and tariffs on printing which made possible the cheap production of newspapers.[45] Furthermore, improvements in printing technology and transportation—the construction of railways and roads—contributed to the facility of circulation. National discussions were no longer confined to the rarefied and heavily mediated atmosphere of the salon, but had moved into the more open, democratic, and infinite space of such institutions as the café, where mass-produced journalism was voraciously consumed. Félix Vallotton's famous woodcut, "L'Age du papier," published in *Le Cri de Paris* in 1898, is wonderfully illustrative of this new phenomenon.

Finally and most importantly, the 1890s marked the collective self-realization of intellectuals. No longer isolated individuals, they viewed themselves as a group with a role to play in French society. This belief was widespread among avant-garde writers of the generation of 1890, both of the Left and the Right, who expressed their opinions in a tightly knit network of literary journals—*La Revue blanche*, *Le Mercure de France*, *Les Entretiens politiques et littéraires*, *L'Ermitage*, and *La Plume*, to name the most important ones. It was here that intellectual causes first took root and spread. Many writers and artists of this time became fascinated with the anarchist movement; this involvement directly foreshadowed their engagement in the Dreyfus Affair. Moreover, anarchism provides the essential link between individuals as different as Charles Maurras, who later went on to found the right-wing Action française, and Léon Blum, the future Socialist leader.

Used judiciously, the generational approach is a good way to study a group of individuals, particularly an elite and it is here that I begin. In chapters 1 and 2 entitled, "The Literary Avant-Garde at the Fin de Siècle" and "The Generation of 1890," I present a collective biography of this intellectual generation. In the first chapter, I consider the bonds between individuals whose outlooks were formed by the same experiences and institutions. Thus, I will focus on the network of "little magazines," especially on their links with each other, with avant-garde political groups, and with the literary and political establishment.

Having placed the generation of 1890 within a sociocultural framework, I proceed in the second chapter to analyze the ideas shared by this generation, examining in particular *enquêtes* or reader surveys published in newspapers and literary magazines, in which writers and artists were asked to respond to the pressing issues of the day. I will concentrate on the most popular theme of these inquiries—the relationship between art and politics.

In chapter 3, "Aristocrat or Proletarian? Intellectuals and Elites in Fin-de-Siècle France," I situate the debate concerning the role of the intellectual in French society within the broader context of contemporary discussions on the nature of elites and their place in a democratic society. This topic was widely discussed during the fin de siècle—not only in the avant-garde but also in republican academic circles. The concept of an intellectual elite was accepted even by those who professed republican views and indeed anarchist and socialist ones.

By studying articles on "intellectual aristocracy" and "intellectual proletariat," published in avant-garde journals, along with novels and essays on this topic, I examine why such a debate emerged at this particular time with such intensity in the avant-garde. How did these writers define an intellectual aristocracy and what function should this elite serve in society? How, too, did they define an "intellectual proletariat," and what did they fear from such a proletariat?

In chapter 4: "The Jew as Intellectual: The Intellectual as Jew," as in the preceding chapter, I place the debate surrounding the role of the intellectual within the context of another contemporary problem: anti-Semitism. Although anti-Semitism was by origin a popular ideology, in its modern form it was elaborated by writers like Charles Maurras, Maurice Barrès, and Edouard Drumont, along with such artists as Adolphe Willette and Jean-Louis Forain, who feared for their status in a modern, democratic society. Their vision, which corresponded to a traditional, aristocratic order, was threatened by the new, "state" intellectual, associated with the Third Republic. For these individuals, the Jew was the ultimate symbol of modernity. Furthermore, noted Jewish scholars, in particular, Emile Durkheim of the Sorbonne and Henri Bergson of the Collège de France, were seen as pillars of the republican establishment, as "official" intellectuals who had risen to positions of power and fame via the republican university system.

For Jews, on the other hand, the emergence of the modernist intellectual, who espoused rationalism and universality, was a means by which to integrate themselves into the mainstream of French society. It allowed them to transcend their Jewishness in favor of a universal ideal.

In chapters 5 and 6, I continue the discussion of French national identity begun in chapter 4. Chapter 5, "Intellectuals, Honor, and Manhood at the Fin de Siècle," begins by exploring the contemporary debate on honor and sexuality. Next, it examines fin-de-siècle representations, both fictional and nonfictional, of the intellectual, concentrating on contemporary views of the relationship of gender and intellect. To that end, it focuses on the French reaction, in the popular press, as well as in the little magazines, to Oscar Wilde's conviction and subsequent imprisonment for homosexuality in 1895. Although many avant-garde writers, unlike most of their establishment peers, came to Wilde's defense, they did so in the name of art and humanity. Already sensitive to charges of effeminacy, these writers were reluctant to defend Wilde's homosexuality. Despite their hostility to the bourgeoisie, writers of the avant-garde shared with their opponents a common discourse of honor and masculinity.

In chapter 6: "The Sword or the Pen: Competing Images of the Hero at the Fin de Siècle," I examine two competing visions of male honor: the intellectual hero, who incarnated moral courage, and the military hero, who symbolized physical courage and the cult of the army. The chapter, which begins with discussions of the army's role in a democracy during the 1890s, culminates in a discussion of the Dreyfus Affair. Chapter 6, along with chapter 7, expands the discussion concerning intellectuals, examining both the views of members of the avant-garde and of their opponents in the political and literary establishment.

In chapter 7: "Individualism and Solidarity: Organicist Discourse in the Dreyfus Affair," I return to the debate conducted in the contemporary press between Dreyfusard and anti-Dreyfusard intellectuals. I will concentrate on the writings of leading spokesmen on both sides of the Affair, including Dreyfusards Emile Durkheim and Jean Jaurès and anti-Dreyfusards Maurice Barrès, Ferdinand Brunetière and Gustave Le Bon, to determine not only the points of difference between the two groups but especially the points of commonality. Dreyfusards and their opponents believed in "individualism" and "solidarity," although they defined them in different ways. Anti-Dreyfusard Gustave Le Bon saw himself as an "individualist" as did Dreyfusard Octave Mirbeau, who was closely associated with the anarchist movement. Similarly, both Dreyfusard Emile Durkheim and anti-Dreyfusard Ferdinand Brunetière spoke of "solidarity." New light can be shed on intellectual life in France by concentrating on the beliefs shared by Dreyfusard and anti-Dreyfusard intellectuals.

Although they came to different conclusions, intellectuals on opposite sides of the Affair viewed the problems related to the modernization of French society in remarkably similar ways. Led by the avant-garde, they shared common hopes, among them the desire to assert the importance of intellect in society and to establish an "aristocracy of intellect" that would lead the way toward national regeneration, as well as common fears, most notably, of being subsumed by the untutored masses and by the unfettered forces of the marketplace. Their struggle for self-definition paved the way for the crisis of national identity that emerged fully during the Dreyfus Affair. It is no accident that the Affair is first and foremost an "affair of intellectuals." Intellectuals occupied a central role therein, with both sides laying exclusive claim to representing the "true France." The debate about French national identity continued through the course of the twentieth century, at times, with tragic consequences. Today, it is once again the subject of profound discussion. No longer at issue, however, is the historic place of the intellectual, who is identified both as the product and the symbol of modern French culture.

1

—⁓—

The Literary Avant-Garde at the Fin de Siècle

The year 1889–1890 was a pivotal one for French history. The French observed the centennial of the French Revolution, commemorated in part by the Exposition Universelle and the construction of the Eiffel Tower, which heralded a new age of technology, industry, and progress. The anniversary afforded French men and women the opportunity to reflect both on their recent past and their future, especially in light of the Boulanger Affair, which exploded onto the national scene in 1889. The year was significant for literary history as well; it marked the founding of five avant-garde journals, publications that would become the mouthpieces of their generation. *La Revue blanche* and *La Plume* were launched in 1889, followed shortly by *Le Mercure de France*, *Les Entretiens politiques et littéraires*, and *L'Ermitage* in 1890. The year 1889 also witnessed the publication of the second novel of Maurice Barrès's *culte du moi* trilogy; for its author, *Un Homme libre* became the hallmark of his youth, and for his peers, the symbol of an entire generation. Finally, in 1891, the journalist Jules Huret's (1863) publication of "L'Enquête sur l'évolution littéraire" in the newspaper *L'Echo de Paris* introduced this new intellectual generation to its elders as well as to the public at large.

The individuals who belonged to the generation of 1890 were an elite, not only limited to men who had at least acquired the baccalaureate, if not a university degree, but also those whose ambitions—intellectual or otherwise—had brought them to Paris, the center of French political, social, economic, and intellectual life. They shared the same pedagogic education as well as a common culture and congregated together, organizing themselves around such individuals as Stéphane Mallarmé and Maurice Barrès and such literary journals as *La Revue blanche* and *Le Mercure de France*. These literary journals thus became important witnesses of a generation as well as important centers of sociability.[1]

In this chapter, I examine the generation of 1890 within a sociocultural context, concentrating on the literary avant-garde of the fin de siècle. I will study the conditions that led to the emergence of the avant-garde of the late nineteenth century and chart the development of the avant-garde network of little magazines. In the following chapter, I will continue to study the generation of 1890, examining the ideas shared by its members. From these two chapters, which combine sociological analysis and intellectual history, should emerge a collective portrait of the generation of 1890.

The cultural avant-garde, a product of liberal democracy, dates from the last quarter of the nineteenth century. Only after the Franco-Prussian War and the Commune did the term acquire its secondary, cultural meaning. Up to that time, the expression, originally a military term, was used to designate political groups. The transferral of a political term to culture, however, is of significance and is related in part to the unity of the political and the cultural avant-gardes of the mid-nineteenth century.[2]

The avant-garde of the fin de siècle was thus not the first avant-garde group. As surprising as it may seem, Zola and his fellow Naturalists were members of the avant-garde during their youth. Just as Zola went on to become the target of the avant-garde of the fin de siècle, so, too, did fin-de-siècle avant-gardistes become the next generation's old fogies; witness the trial of Maurice Barrès (1862) by Dadaists after the war. When Symbolist poet Henri de Régnier (1864) was elected to the Académie française in 1911, he and his fellow Symbolists had long ceased to be members of the avant-garde. The literary avant-garde at the fin de siècle thus corresponded closely, although not exclusively, to the generation of 1890. Not only is the avant-garde a product of youth, so, too, does there exist a cult of youth among its members.[3]

If the avant-garde at the turn of the century overlapped with the generation of 1890, it did not do so with one literary movement, although the Symbolists certainly dominated. Among the avant-garde included members of Jean Moréas's (1856) Ecole romane, a group born of opposition to Symbolism; Moréas, whose real name was Papadiamantopoulos, was a former Symbolist. The Ecole romane included such classicizers as Charles Maurras (1868), who rejected the foreign, "Germanic" influences of the Romantics and their Symbolist heirs, and called for a return to France's "true" roots in classical Greco-Roman culture. In 1895, there arrived on the scene yet another group that opposed Symbolism: the Naturists, who rejected the excessive artificiality of Symbolist poetry and its evasion of the real world. Led by Maurice Le Blond (1877) and Saint-Georges de Bouhélier (1876), the Naturists proclaimed a return to natural values and a celebration of daily life and looked upon Zola as a hero. In their admiration, they were alone among their peers—at least until the Dreyfus Affair. Yet all these groups, despite their different esthetics, shared a sense of solidarity, both spatial and temporal. They all wrote for the same little magazines. Symbolists, Naturists, and proponents of the Ecole romane often published articles in the same issues of these journals. As the future Socialist leader Léon Blum (1872), who began his career as literary critic for La Revue blanche, noted, avant-garde journals played an important role in giving young writers a sense of cohesion, of sharing common goals, if not always ideas:

> And after all, is it not in the various sincere reviews that the youth of this time has best revealed itself? . . . But their [reviews'] useful contribution has been to give some cohesion to the rather vague views of dispersed intellects. They have united a literary generation. Perhaps this union is linked more to mutual sympathies than to ideas in common.[4]

Although there existed rivalries among members of the avant-garde, they were united in their opposition to the establishment, both political and literary, along with their refusal of the forces of the marketplace. As members of the avant-garde, they shared similar views, in particular, the rejection of the bourgeois values incarnated by the Third Republic. From their different perspectives, Symbolists, Naturists, and members of the Ecole romane agreed in defining contemporary French society and parliamentary democracy as corrupt and decadent. So, too, could they agree on their desire to play an active role in contributing to the nation's regeneration.

An examination of the intellectual milieu at this time is necessary in order to understand the importance of these journals. Fin-de-siècle France—from about 1890 until 1910—witnessed a crisis in the publishing industry at the same time that it experienced a sharp increase in the numbers of writers. In the wake of the tremendous successes (1875–1885) of such writers as Emile Zola (1840) and Georges Ohnet (1848), an increasing number of individuals chose literature as their profession; from 1865 to 1899, the number of writers in France doubled.[5]

Editors had more power than ever before to control what was published. Given their need to make money, quality was often sacrificed to popularity and expedience. Some editors were so desperate that they published anything as long as the author could pay for publication. Paradoxically, editors hoping to find readers, flooded the market with books—the number of books published in 1889 reached an all time high of 14,849 titles. Given the sheer volume of production, bookstores were unable to display new works for more than a week. Window space had to be made for the newest crop.[6]

Added to the glut of the literary market was a change in consumer habits. While the 1870s and early 1880s had represented the golden age of the novel, readers during the latter half of the 1880s and during the 1890s preferred "practical," "how to" works on medicine, gardening, and etiquette. Furthermore, the general public read newspapers rather than books. The former were more easily accessible, both intellectually and in terms of immediacy and cost. Moreover, many of these newspapers published literary works in serial form; why buy a book when one could read it more cheaply in the penny press?[7]

In such an atmosphere, a new author had great difficulty finding a public and launching a career. Furthermore, the type of work written by the young members of the avant-garde, in particular, by the Symbolist poets, was not easily understood by the larger public. Unable then to get their works published by commercial presses and alienated from the cultural establishment, whose esthetics they rejected, young writers and artists banded together to form a tightly knit network of journals which could serve as a forum for their ideas, eventually even founding their own presses.[8] Poet Francis Vielé-Griffin (1864), editor of *Les Entretiens politiques et littéraires,* complained bitterly in an article published on 1 November 1890 that a hostile campaign had been waged in the press against the little magazines, referring to "this battle of calumny and insult against faith and patience. . . ." His feelings were confirmed by Henri Mazel (1864), director of *L'Ermitage,* who wrote in his memoirs of the necessity of founding an avant-garde network:

> A new generation was on the rise, which would not be satisfied by a nauseating ideal and who . . . finding moreover all the doors of the Republic of Letters closed, would be obliged, in order to sustain its intellectual life, to con-

struct its own provisional shelters, which were represented by the young reviews of the time.[9]

This exclusion was to a certain extent self-imposed. By their own rejection of commercial and official culture, these young artists sought to create a legitimacy, even an autonomy, while remaining faithful to pure artistic values.[10] Yet the avant-garde also depended on the popular press for publicity, as Maurice Barrès noted. Young writers, who wanted to become known but who found the doors of the literary marketplace closed to them, not only created a parallel universe in the little magazines, they also used such widely distributed newspapers as *Le Figaro* and *L'Echo de Paris* to launch themselves by publishing their manifestoes therein.[11]

Avant-garde writers often published *enquêtes* both in their own journals and in the popular press to forge a sense of identity. Indeed, *enquêtes* represented one of the products of the expansion of the press; along with reportages and interviews, *enquêtes* represented a new genre in French magazines and journals of the fin de siècle. Imported from the United States, they were seen as a sign of the increased professionalization of the French press, a move toward a press of information. At the same time, they represented a continued link with the traditional French press, which placed great emphasis on literature and politics, since those interviewed and polled were generally writers and politicians.[12]

Interviews and *enquêtes* contributed to the professionalization of intellectuals, as did the formation and expansion of the "new" republican university. Interviews with individual writers allowed them to reach a larger audience, but it also meant that the public acknowledged that the writer might have something of interest to say on issues of national importance. Through the *enquête*, writers and artists were grouped together, giving them a sense of cohesion. This idea of belonging to a collectivity would contribute to the emergence of the intellectual as a social category.

For young writers of the avant-garde, the *enquêtes* published in the popular press were particularly useful, for they allowed them to publicize their ideas and reach a wider audience than that of the avant-garde journals. The 1891 "L'Enquête sur l'évolution littéraire," organized by journalist Jules Huret for the newspaper *L'Echo de Paris*, was one of the first notable *enquêtes* of the period and served as a model for subsequent inquiries. Marking the emergence of a new intellectual generation, it gave young writers the opportunity to establish a dialogue with their elders, who were also polled. Indeed, a number of participants in the inquiry noted that it was a vehicle for publicizing the Symbolist poets, most of whom were unknown to the general public.[13]

Thereafter, *enquêtes* proliferated both in the popular press and in the little magazines. Huret went on to conduct *enquêtes* on a variety of topics ranging from the social question in Europe to the role of the French university in society. Such little magazines as *La Revue blanche*, *L'Ermitage*, and *Le Mercure de France* published numerous *enquêtes* during the next decade on topics including the influence of the historian-philosopher Hippolyte Taine, the impact of Scandinavian letters on French literature, the Commune, on the social question, and on cultural and political relations with Germany.[14]

The number of little magazines increased dramatically from 1885 to 1900. In a work entitled *Les Petites revues*, published in 1899, Symbolist critic Remy de Gourmont (1858) estimated that a least one hundred new little magazines were published during the years 1890 to 1898.[15] Although originally a response to the exclusion of young writers from the world of the cultural establishment as well as of the commercial press, these types of literary journals continued to flourish in the period that followed. A great number were founded during the few years preceding World War I and later, during the interwar period.[16] At least two of these little magazines, *Le Mercure de France* and *La Nouvelle Revue française* (*NRF*), became institutions. The independent literary journal itself became a fixture in French intellectual life, while such establishment literary journals as *La Revue des deux mondes*, which had dispensed general culture and conferred official consecration in the literary milieu during the fin de siècle, continued to decline, having reached their apogee from 1870 to 1914.[17] The success of the little magazines had long-term effects on intellectual life. From 1910 on, it was the avant-garde that represented real legitimacy within the intellectual milieu.[18]

Although they often shared common goals and indeed the same collaborators, the various avant-garde magazines of the late nineteenth century had distinctive personalities. *L'Ermitage*, as its name might suggest, attempted to steer clear of the various literary and political disputes reflected in the pages of its peers. If it did not engage in polemics, it did, however, reflect an interest in political and social questions. In its orientation, *L'Ermitage* was politically more conservative than *Les Entretiens politiques et littéraires* and *La Revue blanche*, both of which were closely linked to the anarchist movement. The founder of *L'Ermitage,* Henri Mazel, born in Nîmes, came from a pious Catholic family of doctors. After obtaining a *licence* in law in Montpellier, Mazel went to Paris to continue his studies at the Ecole libre des sciences politiques. He entered government service in 1889 when he began working for the Naval Ministry, a position from which he retired in 1929. Like a number of his avant-garde colleagues, critics Félix Fénéon (1861) and Remy de Gourmont among them, Mazel pursued his literary activities alongside a full-time government job.

Critic, essayist, playwright, and novelist, Mazel was a disciple of sociologist Gabriel Tarde (1843) and an admirer of Frédéric Le Play (1806), the chief representative of social Catholicism in nineteenth-century France. Mazel contributed articles to *La Réforme sociale*, the review named after Le Play's major work, including a piece comparing Tarde and Le Play. Influenced by the ideas of these two men, Mazel pursued a lifelong interest in sociological and religious questions, contributing a column on social questions to *Le Mercure de France* from 1897 to 1940.[19] Mazel, who was fairly conservative, although not conservative enough to suit Charles Maurras, protested vigorously when Maurras described *L'Ermitage* as an anarchist publication in an article on young reviews for *La Revue bleue*.[20] In his last editorial as director, Mazel proclaimed proudly that *L'Ermitage* had not indulged in the anarchist folly of its sister publications.[21]

Although Mazel was the major force behind *L'Ermitage*, he did not run the magazine by himself. At end of 1891, he asked his friends René Boylesve, whose real name was Tardiveau (1867), and Adolphe Retté (1863) to serve as members of an editorial committee. Retté, who was at the time an ardent Symbolist, accepted on the condition that the review be open to Symbolist writers.[22] When Mazel resigned as director of the review in favor of Edouard Ducoté (1870) in 1895, he could boast that during his tenure, *L'Ermitage* had published not only the works of such Symbolist poets as Stuart Merrill (1863), who also served as editorial secretary for a brief time, Francis Vielé-Griffin, and Henri de Régnier, but also the Ecole romane poetry of Jean Moréas, along with Charles Maurras's defense of this school. Nor was the work of older poets neglected; Paul Verlaine (1844) and Stéphane Mallarmé (1842) were published, along with Parnassian poet José-Maria de Heredia (1842) and Frédéric Mistral (1830), one of the founding fathers of the Félibrige movement, which celebrated Provençal culture.[23]

The colorful itinerary of Retté is not atypical of members of the avant-garde at the fin de siècle and merits a brief examination. Retté began his career as a Symbolist poet, contributing first to *La Vogue* and then to *L'Ermitage* and publishing a book of verses entitled

Le Thulé des brumes in 1891. Politicized in 1893 by a variety of events, among them the July student riots against the repression by conservative Senator Bérenger of Les Quat'z'Arts Ball, and by the strike of the Pas-de-Calais miners, Retté turned to anarchism as an outlet for his frustrations. He was even arrested in January 1894 during the government's crackdown on anarchist militants and propagandists. Later that year, he left Paris for the forest of Guermantes. The poetry he produced during the next few years was marked both by his interest in anarchism and a rejection of the Symbolist esthetic he had once espoused. A Naturist, he now called for a return to nature and castigated the Symbolists for their artificiality. He also advocated art in service of the revolution, a position he had previously criticized. Perhaps his most shocking act was to publish a diatribe against his former mentor Mallarmé in *La Plume* in 1896. His work during this period was resolutely anticlerical, although it did contain much religious imagery. His last and final transformation came in 1906 when he converted to Catholicism.[24]

Such a checkered itinerary is perfectly in keeping with the tumult and confusion of the years immediately preceding the Dreyfus Affair, before the notions of Left and Right as we understand them were crystallized. The amorphous nature of anarchism during these years allowed such confusion. Common to all of Retté's stances was his association of art and politics and an opposition to the parliamentary democracy of the bourgeois Republic.[25]

No less a colorful character was Hugues Rebell, who took over Retté's editorial duties after the latter's departure from Paris. Born Georges Grassal in 1867, Rebell was a native of Nantes. Like Mazel, he came from a pious Catholic family. Unlike Mazel, however, he execrated Christianity, while praising Catholicism and the Catholic Church. A self-styled paganist and admirerer of Nietzsche, Rebell was a member of the Ecole romane group and later went on to join the Action française. Not only was he closely involved with *L'Ermitage*, he also wrote for *La Plume*, *La Revue blanche,* and *Le Mercure de France*, in which he wrote a resounding defense of Oscar Wilde in 1895.[26]

Any review is more than a mere collection of its collaborators; it also represents a milieu. The collaborators of *L'Ermitage* met regularly at the Café Vachette, popular among students and writers during the late nineteenth century. Mazel himself hosted Wednesday evening gatherings at 26, rue de Varenne, the headquarters of *L'Ermitage* as well as his personal residence.

The relations of *L'Ermitage* with *La Plume* and *Le Mercure* were good; as for *Les Entretiens*, its collaborators Paul Adam (1862),

Henri de Régnier, and Francis Vielé-Griffin all published in *L'Ermitage*—despite the protestations of Rebell, who opposed the presence of writers associated with the anarchist movement. Links with the *La Revue blanche* appear to have been limited. Mazel ironized in his farewell editorial that *La Revue blanche* had ignored *L'Ermitage* until the present, when it had "kindly" offered to take over its subscriptions.[27] After Mazel's departure, the review, which appeared until 1906, oriented itself toward a modern classicism. Unlike the classicism of Maurras, it sought to integrate the contributions of Symbolism. Henri Ghéon (1875) and André Gide (1869) were regular collaborators before going on to found the *NRF*.

Like *L'Ermitage*, *Le Mercure de France* maintained a certain distance from the political quarrels of the day. It was founded by a group of eleven friends, among them Jules Renard (1864), Ernest Raynaud (1864), Remy de Gourmont, and Alfred Vallette (1858), who served as its director for a great many years. These friends included Symbolists (Gourmont) as well as members of the Ecole romane (Raynaud). Like the other reviews, *Le Mercure* was born of school friendships and collaborations on other little reviews. Raynaud, who had met Renard at the Lycée Charlemagne, introduced the latter to Vallette. The others had contributed to *La Pléiade*, the precursor of *Le Mercure*. Among the collaborators of *La Pléiade* were Stuart Merrill, Francis Vielé-Griffin, Pierre Quillard (1864), Henri de Régnier, Laurent Tailhade (1854), Rachilde (1860), and Alfred Vallette, all of whom were associated with *Le Mercure* at one time or another. Vallette himself had served as editor of another little magazine called *Le Scapin* to which a number of the eleven founders of *Le Mercure* had contributed. Finally, a great many of them had frequented the same cafés and salons. Indeed, several of the future founders of *Le Mercure* had met at Rachilde's Tuesday evening gatherings.[28]

The opening declaration of *Le Mercure*, written by Vallette, closely resembles those of the other avant-garde journals: "Of the three goals that a literary journal may choose—to make money, to unite a literary group around a common esthetic . . . or to publish purely artistic works . . . not accepted by journals which must cater to a clientele, it is the latter that we have chosen."[29] Like its sister publications, *Le Mercure*, in opposition to commercial values, presented itself as a defender of art. If the editorial committee initially rejected adherence to one literary movement, it did subsequently become—around 1895—the semiofficial organ of Symbolism. Although the review was weak in its publication of prose, it excelled in its publication of poetry, not surprising given its predilection for Symbolism. The review also became the *grande dame* of the avant-garde journals, not only because of its longevity, but also as a result of its near-encyclopedic coverage of the literary and artistic movements of the period. At one time or another, almost all the members of the literary avant-garde of the fin de siècle published in its pages. *Le Mercure* is also known, along with *La Revue blanche*, for its promotion of foreign literatures. A number of its collaborators were the translators of foreign writers, especially of Nietzsche and Ibsen.

According to Vallette, *Le Mercure*'s transformation from a modest little journal to a serious review came in 1896–1897, with the inauguration of a rubric called "Revue du mois," which carefully catalogued contemporary literary and artistic movements. By this time, *Le Mercure* was associated with its own press, founded in 1894. It was also during this period that *Le Mercure*, which had hitherto remained distant from the literary quarrels of the day, became embroiled in them. Adolphe Retté's attack on Mallarmé in *La Plume* elicited a number of responses in *Le Mercure*, as did the discussion that pitted Naturists against Symbolists.[30]

Unlike *Les Entretiens politiques et littéraires* and *La Revue blanche*, which were financed by wealthy young men and their families, *Le Mercure* was launched by the monetary contributions of its eleven founders, most of whom came from modest families. The review's success and longevity are entirely to the credit of its director Alfred Vallette. Vallette, like Léon Deschamps (1863), the founder of *La Plume*, was an excellent administrator rather than a talented litterateur. Born in Paris, Vallette, the son of a typographer, ran his own printing shop. Unlike the majority of the founders of avant-garde magazines, Vallette had a firm knowledge of the printing metier.[31]

Vallette's wife Marguerite Eymery was the novelist Rachilde. In 1890, Rachilde was already a successful writer whose novel *Monsieur Vénus* had earned her the title "queen of the decadents" and the praise of Maurice Barrès, who wrote the preface to this novel. Rachilde played an important role at *Le Mercure*, serving as the review's literary critic for novels from 1892 to 1926. She claimed that she had been relegated this task by *Le Mercure*'s other founders, who felt that reviewing novels—as opposed to poetry—was unworthy of their literary talents. Rachilde also published short stories in *Le Mercure* and submitted her novels to the review's press. Her influence was also felt in other, less easily quantifiable ways. She dispensed creative advice to her husband and attracted the literary lights of the period to her salon on the rue des Ecoles, before her marriage, and after, rue de l'Echaudé and finally, rue de Condé.[32]

As a woman in a predominantly male milieu, Rachilde represents a notable exception. The avant-garde, born of friendships forged at the *lycée* and/or the university, was a male-dominated world that consciously rejected the presence of women or tolerated them when they were the wives of review directors. Women often played the role of *salonnière* or muse as did Misia (1872), the wife of *Revue blanche* director Thadée Natanson. In their views toward women, members of the avant-garde were no more revolutionary than the bourgeois gentlemen they criticized. If their memoirs are any indication, Rachilde appears to have won the grudging respect of her male colleagues at *Le Mercure*.[33]

Another personality closely associated with *Le Mercure* was Remy de Gourmont, the finest and best-known of the critics associated with the Symbolist movement. Born of a noble Norman family, he came to Paris to study in 1884. He worked at the Bibliothèque Nationale until he was fired in 1891 for his publication in *Le Mercure* of an "anti-patriotic" article entitled "Le Joujou patriotisme." Although Gourmont was also a novelist and playwright, he is best-known for his criticism, especially his brief sketches of Symbolist writers in *Le Livre des masques* and *Promenades littéraires*. Gourmont's temperament, both aristocratic and individualist, led him to anarchism.[34] During the 1890s, he was among the most ardent of the literary anarchists, even writing an article in which he likened Symbolism to anarchism. His anarchism, however, was more individualist and esthetic than political and social. He subsequently adopted a more conservative, indeed, reactionary political stance.

La Plume was directed by Léon Deschamps until his death in 1899. The review continued to appear until 1914, with a long interruption between 1905 and 1911. Deschamps, whose astute business sense contributed to the success of *La Plume,* maintained excellent relations with all the other avant-garde magazines not only with the more politically active *Les Entretiens* and *La Revue blanche,* but also with the more circumspect *Le Mercure* and *L'Ermitage.*

The most eclectic of the avant-garde journals, *La Plume* published the works of members of the Ecole romane—Moréas, Maurras, and Rebell—for whom Deschamps had a personal preference, but also those of Symbolists Stuart Merrill and Francis Vielé-Griffin, and the Naturists, including the newly converted Adolphe Retté (who published his diatribe against Mallarmé here), not to mention of older writers, among them Zola, Mallarmé, and the Parnassian poet François Coppée (1842). This mixture of generations, literary movements, and political foes was the hallmark of *La Plume*.[35] Where else, remarked former collaborator Ernest Raynaud, could Charles Maurras rub elbows with anarchist militants.[36]

Although Deschamps admired certain of his elders, he did seek especially to promote the work of members of the avant-garde. It is for this reason that he founded a press, entitled Bibliothèque artistique et littéraire, which published Verlaine's *Dédicaces* as its first title, along with the works of young writers, including those of Hugues Rebell and Adolphe Retté. The collaborators of *La Plume* were quick to come to the aid of fellow artists. They launched subscription campaigns for a Baudelaire monument and for the destitute Verlaine. In 1895, Deschamps, along with *La Plume* collaborator Stuart Merrill, initiated a petition in favor of Oscar Wilde, convicted of "crimes of gross indecency" and condemned to two years of "hard labour." They did so out of artistic solidarity for Wilde, whom they viewed as a fellow member of the avant-garde.

La Plume is best known for its special issues devoted to various literary movements: Naturism, Symbolism, and the Félibres, specific authors, among them Moréas and Barrès, as well as social and political questions: anarchism, socialist literature, and even an issue on "aristocracy," guest edited by Henri Mazel. It is also remembered for the soirées and banquets it organized, presided by the likes of Zola, Mallarmé, and Paul Adam. In addition, Deschamps expanded *La Plume*'s contacts to the world of art, when he published a special issue on 15 November 1893 devoted to the history of the French illustrated poster. Included were the works of such artists as Jules Chéret (1836), Adolphe Willette (1857), Henri-Gabriel Ibels (1867), and Toulouse-Lautrec (1864). Subsequently, Deschamps offered a special deluxe edition of issues of *La Plume*, which were accompanied by an original print, photogravure or watercolor. Deschamps also organized art exhibitions in the review's offices at 31, rue Bonaparte. The exhibitions, known as "Le Salon des cent," presented the work of both established artists as well as of their unknown peers.[37] The publicity which these banquets, exhibitions, and campaign drives attracted not only for *La Plume* but for the avant-garde in general is perfectly in keeping with the avant-garde desire for attention.

Les Entretiens politiques et littéraires was founded by Francis Vielé-Griffin, Henri de Régnier, and Paul Adam. In 1891, they were joined by Bernard Lazare (1865), newly arrived to Paris from his hometown in Nîmes. Vielé-Griffin came from a wealthy family. Born in Norfolk, Virginia, he came to Paris with his mother after his parents' divorce in 1872. He attended the Collège Stanislas in Paris, where he met fellow *Entretiens* collaborator and poet Henri de Régnier.[38] Born in Honfleur, Régnier descended from an aristocratic family. If Vielé-Griffin is among the most independent and original of the Symbolists, Régnier is among the best known. Like Vielé-Griffin, Régnier studied law but never practiced it. Although Régnier was an ardent Symbolist, he did have connections with Parnassian José-Maria de Heredia, having married one of his daughters, the poet Gérard d'Houville (1875).

The tone of *Les Entretiens*, both in literary and political matters, was more polemical than that of the other reviews. Vielé-Griffin, who served as the review's editor-in-chief, regularly published diatribes against members of the preceding generation, particularly against Zola, execrated by the Symbolist members of the avant-garde. During its brief life, the review published the work of a great many young writers, including André Gide, Paul Valéry (1871), and Paul Claudel (1868).

As its name indicates, *Les Entretiens politiques et littéraires* followed contemporary politics closely. In 1891, it published excerpts of the *Communist Manifesto*; it later published texts by Engels as well by anarchist theoreticians, among them Mikhail Bakunin, Pierre-Joseph Proudhon, and Jean Grave. In addition, it gave free rein in its pages to literary anarchists. The most notorious of these writings was an article by Paul Adam in which he eulogized the recently executed terrorist Ravachol. Members of the *Entretiens* staff, especially Adam and Lazare, had ties with anarchist publications. Both men, along with Lucien Descaves (1861), Jean Ajalbert (1863), Camille Mauclair (1872), Victor Barrucand (1866), Félix Fénéon, and Octave Mirbeau (1848), wrote for Zo d'Axa's (born Gallaud in 1864) *L'Endehors*, the most literary of the anarchist journals. In addition, Lazare was an ardent admirer of anarchist militant Jean Grave (1854). When Grave was tried in 1894, Lazare came to his defense, publishing articles in the mainstream press and even testifying on his behalf, as did Adam.

Les Entretiens ceased publication in December 1893, in part, because the review, financed by Vielé-Griffin, was costly, but also because Lazare and Vielé-Griffin disagreed on its future orientation. Lazare, whose interest in anarchism had become increasingly political and social, rather than merely literary, wished to move in this direction. In fact, after *Les Entretiens* folded, Lazare founded his own briefly lived journal, first called *L'Action* and then *L'Action sociale*.[39]

Although Lazare is best known as the first defender of Alfred Dreyfus, he began his career in avant-garde circles, publishing not only in *Les Entretiens* but also in *La Revue blanche* and *L'Ermitage*. During the course of the 1890s, Lazare expanded his reach beyond the avant-garde, writing for such mainstream newspapers as *Le Figaro, L'Echo de Paris,* and *Le Journal.* His vigorous defense of the Symbolists and his anarchist sympathies made him a controversial figure in this bourgeois milieu. By the time members of the Dreyfus family asked him to came to their aid in 1896, he was already a journalist of note.

The other name closely associated with *Les Entretiens* is Paul Adam. Adam's itinerary is no less colorful than that of Adolphe Retté. Indeed, it can easily be argued that Adam was involved in nearly every literary and political trend of the late nineteenth century. The grandson of an officer in the Napoleonic army, Adam came from a well-to-do family that had fallen on hard times. Henceforth, Adam was obliged to earn a living, which explains the frenetic rate of his production. Adam began his career as a Naturalist, publishing a novel called *Chair molle* in 1885. He also wrote two Symbolist novels during the next few years with Moréas, and contributed to a number of avant-garde journals, *La Revue indépendante, La Vogue,* and *Le Symboliste,* which he helped to found.[40]

It was also at this time that Adam joined Barrès in presenting himself as a Boulangist candidate from Nancy; although he lost, Barrès won. From Boulangism, Adam moved on to anarchism, becoming one of the writers most closely associated with the anarchist movement. He inaugurated a column called "Critique des moeurs" in *Les Entretiens* that he continued upon joining the staff of *La Revue blanche.* The novels he wrote during these years can best be described as social commentary, including one entitled *Le Mystère des foules* (1895) on Boulangism. His fascination for the man on horseback, which continued through his involvement in the anarchist movement and the Dreyfus Affair, and even beyond, illustrates the link between political extremes during the 1890s. Indeed, during the Affair, Adam, an ardent supporter of the army, found himself in an awkward situation as a Dreyfusard. In the years leading up to World War I, Adam, who was a fervent believer in *revanche* against Germany, was once again able to take up the cause of the French army. During the war (in 1916), he founded the Ligue de la Fraternité intellectuelle latine, which proclaimed the superiority and the defense of the "Latin races."

If *La Plume* was the most publicity conscious, *La Revue blanche,* directed by the Natanson brothers, was easily the most unique and the best strategically placed of the avant-garde magazines of the fin de siècle. It served as mediator between the avant-garde and the establishment as well as between the literary and political avant-gardes. *La Revue blanche* further distinguished itself from its rivals in that it was a major center for Jewish intellectuals, although it never saw itself as such. Its directors, along with an important number of its collaborators, were Jewish, among them Léon Blum, Tristan Bernard (1866), Bernard Lazare, Gustave Kahn (1859), Lucien Muhlfeld (1870), Romain Coolus (born René-Max Weil in 1868), Pierre Veber (1869), Julien Benda (1867), Daniel Halévy (1872), and Marcel Proust (1871). During the Dreyfus Affair, it played a key role as a meeting place for Dreyfusard politicians and intellectuals. Given its historical importance, it is surprisingly little-known by most American scholars and thus merits close attention.[41]

Founded in 1889 in Belgium, *La Revue blanche* emigrated to Paris in 1891. The review's directors were the Natanson brothers, who came from a wealthy Jewish family in Warsaw that had emigrated to France during the early years of the Third Republic. The elder brothers Alexandre (1866) and Thadée (1868) were naturalized Frenchmen, while the youngest, Alfred (1873), was born in France. Their father Adam, a wealthy businessman, financed the review during the years of its operation. Since avant-garde journals in general tend to lose money rather than make it, this financial support was an important factor in the longevity of *La Revue blanche*, which lasted until 1903.

La Revue blanche's opening manifesto, like that of *La Plume*, *L'Ermitage,* and *Le Mercure*, proclaimed an openness of spirit and a dedication to pure artistic values. A later statement, which reflected the influence of Barrès and the *culte du moi*, proclaimed the right of *La Revue blanche*'s authors to freely express their opinions and "develop themselves."[42] Again, like *La Plume* and *L'Ermitage, La Revue blanche* followed a policy of eclecticism, publishing the works of Symbolists and Naturists alike, according special attention to the works of young authors. In addition, its collaborators expressed a desire to found a review that would rival such establishment publications as *La Revue des deux mondes*, but from a youthful, less conformist perspective.[43]

La Revue blanche paid special attention to poetry, publishing the works of Mallarmé and Verlaine, as well as those of Stuart Merrill, Henri de Régnier, Francis Viélé-Griffin, Camille Mauclair, Saint-Pol Roux (1861), and Emile Verhaeren (1855). In 1897, the review's poet-in-residence, Gustave Kahn, inaugurated a column

exclusively devoted to the review of poetic works. *La Revue blanche*'s
literary criticism was also comprehensive; its first literary critic,
Lucien Muhlfeld, was succeeded by Léon Blum in 1896, when the
former left to write drama criticism for the mainstream newspaper
L'Echo de Paris. Blum's successor was André Gide.

  La Revue blanche maintained close contact with the theater
world. Pierre Veber, Romain Coolus, Alfred Athys (Natanson), and
Alfred Jarry (1873), who all served as *La Revue blanche*'s drama
critics over the years, were themselves playwrights. Coolus, Veber,
and their *Revue blanche* colleagues Tristan Bernard and Victor
Barrucand had their works staged not only in avant-garde theaters, notably the Théâtre de l'Oeuvre, founded by Aurélien Lugné-
Poë (1869), but also in the boulevard theaters. Lugné-Poë is best
known for popularizing Ibsen and his fellow Scandinavians in
France, along with his presentation of Alfred Jarry's *Ubu roi*, which
created a scandal when it was performed in 1896. Not only did
Revue blanche collaborators subscribe to Lugné-Poë's theater, the
review artists, notably, Edouard Vuillard (1868), Pierre Bonnard
(1867), Henri de Toulouse-Lautrec (1864), and Maurice Denis (1870),
all designed theater programs and sets for his productions.

  Through Fénéon and Thadée Natanson, both of whom were art
critics, *La Revue blanche* maintained contacts with young artists.
Not only did it publicize their work, but its editors also invited
artists to submit their drawings for publication in the review. Vuillard,
Denis, Bonnard, Toulouse-Lautrec, Ker-Xavier Roussel (1867), Paul
Ranson (1864), and Felix Vallotton (1865) were all asked to submit
lithographs as frontispieces for the review, which were eventually
published by the *Revue blanche* press in album form. Illustrations
regularly appeared in *La Revue blanche*, especially those of Vallotton,
the most assiduous of the review's artist collaborators. Naturally, art
criticism was a regular feature. Among those who published articles
on this topic included such artist-critics as Maurice Denis, Paul Signac
(1863), and Jacques-Emile Blanche (1861).

  Although *La Revue blanche* never covered music as fully as it
did literature and art, it did publish articles by Wagnerian special-
ist Henri Gauthiers-Villars (1859), better known as Willy, of Colette
fame, as well as by Claude Debussy (1862). *La Revue blanche*,
unlike the more sober *Mercure* and *Ermitage*, also gave free rein to
the comedic talents of the best humorists of the day. Tristan Bernard, Jules Renard, Romain Coolus, and Pierre Veber wrote articles and contributed to the journal's humoristic supplements.

  After Muhlfeld's departure, his editorial duties were taken over
for a short period by Marcel Barrière (1868), former secretary to

the Duc d'Orléans, before the arrival in 1895 of Félix Fénéon. A key figure connecting the Parisian cultural and political milieus of the fin de siècle, Fénéon was simultaneously involved in three different movements: Symbolism, Post-Impressionism, and anarchism. The first and foremost champion of the artist Georges Seurat (1859), he also helped launch the careers of such writers as Jules Laforgue (1860), Arthur Rimbaud (1854), André Gide, and Alfred Jarry. For many years, Fénéon was by day an employee of the War Ministry; at the same time, he was closely involved with the anarchist movement. When Fénéon, along with a number of anarchist propagandists and militants, was brought to trial in 1894, he attracted the attention of Thadée Natanson, who was serving as assistant to Fénéon's lawyer Maître Demange (who later became Alfred Dreyfus's lawyer). Thadée immediately invited Fénéon to join the *Revue blanche* staff. When the review folded in 1903, Fénéon began writing for *Le Figaro* and *Le Matin* and later joined the staff of the Bernheim art gallery. Fénéon maintained left-wing sympathies throughout his life, even becoming a Communist in his later years.[44]

Fénéon's arrival coincided with a turning point for *La Revue blanche*, which established a number of new rubrics at this time: columns on politics and contemporary manners, history, foreign literatures, and even sports. It was at this time that *La Revue blanche* made the transition from a relatively unknown little magazine to a publication that was read even outside the avant-garde milieu. Its circulation reached perhaps ten thousand.[45] The publicity provided by the now celebrated Bonnard and Lautrec posters of *La Revue blanche*, the advertisements published in the boulevard publication, *Le Cri de Paris*, also owned by the Natansons, and the phenomenal success of *Quo Vadis*, published by the *Revue blanche* press, made the journal highly visible.

Fénéon, who was seriously interested in contemporary political and social movements, unlike his predecessor Muhlfeld, elicited the approval of anarchist leader Jean Grave when *La Revue blanche* began devoting in-depth articles to the anarchist and socialist movements, along with the writings of such thinkers as Peter Kropotkin and Leo Tolstoy. Other articles included a study on anti-Semitism during the Middle Ages by Bernard Lazare and a series on German socialism by Charles Andler (1866). A noted Germanist, Andler was a friend of Lucien Herr (1864), the librarian of the Ecole Normale, who is best-known for having converted several generations of *normaliens* to socialism, including Socialist leaders Jean Jaurès (1859) and Léon Blum.

At the time of the Dreyfus Affair, Herr sent other *normaliens* to write for the review, among them François Simiand (1873), the future disciple of Emile Durkheim (1858), and Charles Péguy (1873), who wrote a special column on contemporary politics. During the Affair, the review published a series of antimilitarist articles by Urbain Gohier (1862), which were later reprinted in book form as *L'Armée contre la nation*. For publishing these articles, the *Revue blanche* press and Gohier were accused of defaming the army and the navy and brought to trial. Among the witnesses for the defense was the distinguished historian Charles Seignobos (1854) of the Sorbonne. His testimony not only contributed to the acquittal of the defendants, but it also suggested that *La Revue blanche* was highly regarded in certain academic circles—at the Sorbonne as well as at the Ecole Normale.[46]

During the Affair, *La Revue blanche* threw itself into the fray with "Protestation," a companion piece to Zola's "J'Accuse." Although the Affair represented a major triumph for *La Revue blanche*, it also signaled its demise. Thadée Natanson, a founding member of the Ligue des Droits de l'Homme, lost a considerable portion of the family fortune in an ill-fated scheme to raise money for the new cause he had adopted. In addition to such financial difficulties, review collaborators increasingly disagreed on its purpose and mission. While the more politically active collaborators—Léon Blum, Tristan Bernard, and Jules Renard—went on to join the staff of Jean Jaurès's socialist newspaper *L'Humanité*, others, like André Gide, retreated to the realm of pure literature, founding *La NRF*.

Because of the variety of its contacts, *La Revue blanche* stood at the crossroads of important political, social, and cultural currents, mediating not only between the avant-garde and the establishment, but also between the literary and political milieus. Although an exhaustive study of *La Revue blanche*'s role in contemporary political and cultural life is not possible here, a brief examination of its networks of sociability offers us an important glimpse into the workings of the avant-garde, in particular, the social solidarity it represented.

If we are to chart the meeting places for members of the avant-garde, the best place to begin is the Parisian *lycée*. Condorcet, Henri IV, and Louis-le-Grand were among the best *lycées* in France. During the late nineteenth century, the *lycée* was still the bastion of the elite, a place where bourgeois families sent their sons to become cultured. Here, a select group of young men formed lifelong friendships—women did not yet attend *lycées* with men—that would prove decisive for their future.[47] Condorcet, unlike its more austere counterparts, was located in the bustling streets of the Ninth *arrondissement* and accepted day pupils. It is perhaps for this reason that the school produced such an impressive number of writers and artists, including a great many Symbolist writers like Pierre Quillard and Stuart Merrill. The Symbolist connection extends even to Mallarmé, who taught English there for many years.

The Natanson brothers all attended Condorcet; the two older brothers were especially friendly with Lugné-Poë, Maurice Denis, Bonnard, Vuillard, and Ker-Xavier Roussel, along with Pierre Veber, Tristan Bernard, and Romain Coolus. The second group of Condorcet graduates at *La Revue blanche* consisted of a group of men slightly younger: Daniel Halévy, Jacques Bizet (1872), Marcel Proust, Fernand Gregh (1874), and Alfred Natanson. These men founded the review *Le Banquet*, which survived only a few months. When it folded, the *Revue blanche* editorial board invited the staff of *Le Banquet* to join them.

Other Parisian *lycées* also contributed to the staff of *La Revue blanche*; Gide and Blum both attended Henri IV. Through Gide, Blum met Pierre Louÿs (1870), founder of another little magazine *La Conque*. Blum published several poems here before submitting texts to *Le Banquet* and then moving on to *La Revue blanche*.

A number of members of the literary avant-garde had ties with the republican university. Indeed, the literary milieu at this time was in part fed by disenchanted members of the university population who could not find other jobs.[48] Alexandre and Thadée were lawyers. Blum possessed a *licence* in law as did Tristan Bernard, Henri de Régnier, and Lucien Muhlfeld. For much of the nineteenth century and a good part of the twentieth, obtaining a law degree was a common option for sons of the bourgeoisie. Even if the holder never practiced law, he acquired the cachet of an educated man.

A number of *Revue blanche* collaborators were *normaliens*: Léon Blum, Romain Coolus, Charles Péguy, Charles Andler, and Lucien Herr. In fact, Herr was chosen by the *Revue blanche* group to excommunicate Barrès on behalf of an entire generation in the pages of the review after the latter declared his anti-Dreyfusard stance. The Sorbonne was another meeting place for review collaborators. Proust, Gregh, Halévy, Blum, and Muhlfeld all took classes here. Muhlfeld even served as the Sorbonne's assistant librarian.

As must be increasingly obvious, there existed a multiplicity of links between reviews. Writers wrote concurrently for several magazines. Jules Renard, Rachilde, Remy de Gourmont, Henri de Régnier, Pierre Quillard, Stuart Merrill, Hugues Rebell, and Saint

Pol-Roux, all of whom were associated with *Le Mercure de France,*
and some with *L'Ermitage, La Plume,* and *Les Entretiens,* also wrote
articles for *La Revue blanche.* Jarry was first a member of the
Mercure staff, but left in 1896 to write drama criticism for *La
Revue blanche.* Among the older members of the *Revue blanche*
group, Fénéon, Kahn, and Adam had already participated in other
avant-garde ventures together. Fénéon and Kahn had collaborated
on *La Vogue,* founded by the latter, and on *Le Symboliste,* which
the two had founded with Jules Laforgue and Jean Moréas, as well
as on *La Revue indépendante.* Paul Adam, Bernard Lazare, Vielé-
Griffin, and Henri de Régnier had worked on *Les Entretiens
politiques et littéraires* together before contributing to *La Revue
blanche.*

Family relations also tied various members of the avant-garde
together. Muhlfeld and Adam were married to two sisters. Ker-
Xavier Roussel and Pierre Veber were wedded to the sisters of
Vuillard and Tristan Bernard respectively. Régnier and Pierre Louÿs
were brothers-in-law. The Blums were friendly with the Bernards,
who knew the Natansons. Like the other avant-garde journals, *La
Revue blanche* also constituted a milieu. Thadée's wife, Misia, received visitors to her home on Thursday afternoons; when the
Natansons summered in Valvins, they invited their *Revue blanche*
friends, among them Mallarmé, Mirbeau, Toulouse-Lautrec, Vuillard,
Bonnard, and Coolus.[49]

As for the location of *La Revue blanche,* while most of the
avant-garde journals were tucked away on quiet streets of the Left
Bank, *La Revue blanche*'s offices were located in the busiest parts
of the Right Bank. Its first home was located on the rue des Martyrs, where it was close both to the cabarets of Montmartre as well
as to the offices of various anarchist publications. In 1895, *La Revue
blanche* moved to the rue Laffitte, known as the street of artists
because some twenty art galleries were located here. In its last
headquarters on the boulevard des Italiens, *La Revue blanche* was
in the company of the major newspapers, which were located on
the *grands boulevards.* In fact, it shared offices with its sister
publication *Le Cri de Paris.*[50]

This brief examination of the avant-garde journals, their collaborators, and their relations reveals a small world of dense and
multiple contacts. Yet by no means was the avant-garde, despite its
rhetoric, cut off from other groups, both political and literary. A
number of members of the avant-garde belonged both to it and to
the larger world of the popular press. Maurras and Barrès are the
most obvious examples, but certain members of the *Revue blanche*

group—Paul Adam and Bernard Lazare—could also be included in this category. As for the avant-garde reviews—*La Revue blanche*'s links with the Ecole Normale, the Sorbonne, the boulevard press and the theater; *La Plume*'s association with older writers, and the relations of *La Plume, La Revue blanche* and *Les Entretiens politiques et littéraires* with the anarchist journals belie the myth of an isolated avant-garde.

Some members of the avant-garde themselves yearned for the success and popularity they decried. Indeed, their anti-establishment rhetoric and their celebration of pure artistic values was to a certain extent fueled by their anger at being rejected by these forces. The little magazines of the fin de siècle provided a comfortable space for members of the avant-garde, a solidarity that extended beyond their different esthetics and political opinions. Here they shared a common sense of purpose born of their opposition, not only to the rule of the marketplace, but also to the bourgeois values associated with parliamentary democracy. This cohesion was further reinforced by demographic factors, in particular, by the notion of belonging to the same age group and facing similar experiences as a result of their youth. Thus, the avant-garde journals represented a perfect outlet for the voices of a new generation.

2

—◦∿◦—

The Generation of 1890

The literary avant-garde of the fin de siècle represented a solidarity that was not only spatial but also temporal. The members of this generation were self-conscious of their identity as distinguished from that of their elders and they expressed their feelings repeatedly in their writings of the period.

One of the most ardent generationalists of the nineteenth century was the self-styled "Prince of Youth," Maurice Barrès. In his *Un Homme libre*, dedicated to the youths of Paris and the provinces, Barrès declared that he wrote specifically for the young. Their elders, who had already been formed by the experiences of their youth, would find his work superfluous.[1] One of Barrès's admirers, Léon Blum affirmed that different generations must maintain a distance from each other,[2] and moreover, that the rising generation was the "natural judge" of its predecessors.[3]

Enmity toward one's elders is often a way of positioning oneself. The words avant-garde and generation both imply combat. Writing in his last issue as editor of *L'Ermitage* in December 1895, Henri Mazel spoke of "these three or four first years that we all spent in the beautiful fire of battle."[4] Similarly, Adolphe Retté referred to the year 1893 as "a year of combat" in *La Plume*'s 15 December 1893 issue.[5]

Yet despite their opposition to their elders, these young men, anxious to make their presence known on the intellectual scene, also resented being ignored by their older colleagues.[6] Some young writers reproached Octave Mirbeau for favoring young Belgian artists like Maurice Maeterlinck (1862) at the expense of French artists, while Bernard Lazare admonished Anatole France (1844) for taking so long to recognize the talents of the young generation.[7]

If a rising generation by definition opposes its elders, it also represents itself as the standard-bearer of truth, as the following declaration of Francis Vielé-Griffin illustrates: "Were we to find that this generation had only discovered the right path and, worn from the effort, had simply been able to show it to those who followed, still how great its dignity would appear to future generations."[8] His ideas were shared by Retté, who viewed the young intellectuals of the avant-garde as the only ones worthy of the name.[9]

The generation of 1890 was the first official "intellectual" generation, the first generation of intellectuals to view itself as a sociological group with a role to play in French society. Its history is inextricably linked to the cultural and political history of the period. A generational portrait of the young men of 1890, who were highly self-conscious of their historical role at a pivotal time in French history, sheds light on the workings of the intellectual milieu and its relation to the world of politics. It also illuminates the origins of the Dreyfus Affair and the engagement of intellectuals in it, and most importantly, the emergence of the intellectual as a figure in the age of mass democracy. While the last chapter placed the generation of 1890 within a sociological context, this chapter seeks to examine it against the backdrop of the political and cultural movements of the day. To this end, I will examine the ideas of the members of the generation of 1890 via three *enquêtes* which trace the evolution of their thought during the course of the 1890s. I begin with the 1891 Huret inquiry, which introduced them to the public at large, and then proceed to chart their increased politicization in the 1893 social referendum published by *L'Ermitage*, and the 1895 *Mercure de France* survey, which presented their views not only toward Germany, but more importantly, toward France and their own relationship to the nation. Through the course of these three *enquêtes* emerges the unifying theme of the generation of 1890: the belief in the writer's role in national life.

Before continuing further, I would like to define briefly the notion of intellectual generation and its place in French history. While a number of observations about generational theory would be in order, I have no intention of reproducing the debate on the validity of the generational concept in studying history, a subject that has been amply developed elsewhere.[10] When used judiciously, generational theory offers historians a valuable tool for the study of elites, particularly of modern European intellectual elites, who tend to think in generational terms.[11] As a *lieu de mémoire*, situated between memory and history, the concept of generation represents no small contribution to the history of mentalities. It presents insight into the way a concrete group thought about itself and its place in history, since the generational concept is a "device by which people conceptualize society and seek to transform it."[12] The use of the generational concept may be used as a political tool not only to attack enemies, but also to forge identities.

The concept of generation is a product of modernity, of the rise of democracy, and the acceleration of history.[13] Although generationalism is not uniquely a French phenomenon, it has perhaps found a special home in France. Not only is France historically predisposed to seeing itself in terms of a series of binary oppositions (father *vs* son; Paris *vs* the provinces; unity *vs* diversity), it is also a traditionalist country, so rooted in the past that change can only come through revolution. Such a tendency toward revolt seems natural, given the hierarchical and authoritarian nature of French society. All of these characteristics favor the type of conflict engendered by the concept of generation.[14]

Moreover, in a country that so values "Culture," the literary and political are inextricably linked.[15] Indeed, the intermingling of these two elements has made the generational concept such a powerful one in French history. It is not surprising then that the notions of avant-garde and generation are parallel phenomena, united in playing a subversive role in both the political and literary milieus.[16]

How does one define a historical generation? Karl Mannheim, one of the pioneers of generational theory, spoke not of age cohorts but of an ensemble of common experiences.[17] Age does not necessarily define generation but rather the consciousness of belonging. The members of the generation of 1890 were born during the waning years of the Second Empire and the first years of the Third Republic—roughly from 1858 to 1872.[18] The first republican generation, its members came of age during the mid-1880s and 1890s. The time at which an individual came of age publicly is more important than the date of birth, thereby rendering rigid demarcations impossible. For example, Dreyfusard intellectual Charles Péguy, born in 1872, belonged to the generation of 1890, while his compatriot Henri Barbusse, born a year later, was a member of the generation of 1914 because he emerged as a national figure during World War I.[19]

A set of common experiences, however, does not necessarily mean the same ideas but rather a similar way of looking at those ideas.[20] Given the overlapping of generation and avant-garde, it is possible to view the generation of 1890 as a social network, since it was this network that created a common set of experiences.[21]

A generation whose members are as different as Maurice Barrès, Charles Maurras, Léon Blum, Julien Benda, and Charles Péguy defies facile generalizations and is not easily categorized. Its ideas, however, have been distorted for posterity by members of the succeeding generation, in particular, by Henri Massis (1886) and Alfred de Tarde (1880), the authors of the "Agathon" inquiry. The two authors have been roundly criticized for their portrait of the "generation of 1912," but they must also be taken to task for their distortion of the preceding generation. Agathon not only used a limited sample to make gross generalizations about their own generation, they also oversimplified and exaggerated the traits of their predecessors to better define themselves in opposition to them. Thus, they depicted the generation of 1890 as a "sacrificed generation," obsessed with decadence, paralyzed by its dilettantism, pessimistic, overly intellectual, anti-patriotic, defeatist, and unable to act as a result of all these factors. In contrast, the members of the generation of 1912 were sure of themselves, reconciled with their faith, patriotic and inclined toward action.[22]

The reality is of course much more complicated; not only was there more diversity within each of these generations than Agathon acknowledged, but there was also greater continuity between the two generations. Moreover, certain members of the generation of 1890 were themselves partly responsible—both for the characterizations of the new generation and the distortion of their own generational portrait.[23] Their commentary on the new generation was in part determined by their views at maturity of their own youth. Those who sought to distance themselves from their youthful positions did so by juxtaposing a stereotype of the new generation with an equally stereotyped counter-image of their youth.[24] It is essential then to examine the generation of 1890 during its youth via its own *enquêtes* and other contemporary writings.

Cultural Crisis and the Revolt against Positivism

The young men of 1890 were France's first republican generation as well as children of the defeat, the first generation to come of age in a Europe no longer dominated by France. Although the defeat of the Franco-Prussian War was viewed with distance, as the affair of their elders, the war and the ensuing events of the Commune had an impact on them, as it did with all French men and women of that era. The young men of 1890 grew up in a country preoccupied with revenge against Germany and its own feelings of inadequacy.

In his classic study *La Crise allemande de la pensée française, 1870–1914*, Claude Digeon points out that the "German question" dominated French national discourse from the Franco-Prussian War to World War I.[25] After 1870, French men and women, especially intellectuals, struggled to define French national identity, often doing so via their representations of Germany.[26] Thus, Germany served as a gauge by which France was measured; its successes were viewed not in and of themselves but rather as corollaries of French failures or shortcomings. Especially worrisome was the relative stagnation of the French population, particularly in light of the German population explosion. From 1872 to 1911, the French population increased by a modest 10 percent while Germany, whose birthrate was double that of her western neighbor, witnessed a population increase of 58 percent.[27] Similarly, although France's industrial output had increased significantly, it still lagged far behind Germany's impressive advances.

The defeat, along with the coming of mass democracy and the increasing industrialization of French society, contributed to a sense of moral crisis among many French intellectuals at this time, both young and old. The belief in French decadence was expressed not only by literary intellectuals but also by social scientists and politicians.[28] Such malaise was not necessarily at odds with the material progress of the age; to a certain extent these feelings were the result of fears of modernity.[29]

During the 1880s and 1890s, French medical researchers, in particular, Jean-Martin Charcot, developed a pathology of nervous disorders, whose causes were attributed to the degeneration of the nervous system. Of special interest was the condition of neurasthenia. Defined as a state of nervous exhaustion, characterized by mental hypersensitivity and physical debility, neurasthenia was linked to the rigors of modern, urban life. A number of writers, among them Emile Zola, Joris-Karl Huysmans, and Paul Bourget, translated the clinical states of neurasthenia and degeneration into literary form and then applied the findings concerning individuals to the nation. The publication in 1894 of the French translation of Max Nordau's *Degeneration* (in French *Dégénerescence*), which became a best-seller, marked the apogee of this type of analysis. In his book, Nordau first defined in medical terms the decadent esthete and then proceeded to extend this metaphor to the national body, thereby elaborating a social and cultural critique of French society.[30] Thus, late-nineteenth-century France witnessed the emergence of an organicist discourse of national health, common to both the Right and Left, which gave rise to what Robert Nye calls "a medical model of cultural crisis."[31]

The "obsession with decadence," ascribed to the generation of 1890 by Agathon, was therefore not limited to the members of their generation but was widespread among all their contemporaries during the fin de siècle. Two of the most prominent diagnosticians of national decline were Hippolyte Taine (1828–1893) and Ernest Renan (1823–1892), both of whom had a deep impact on their fellow citizens of the late nineteenth century, including the members of the generation of 1890.[32] Shaken by the events of the Franco-Prussian War, Renan and Taine maintained their faith in science and progress but harnessed it to a pessimism about humankind, and specifically, about the future of France.[33] Their historical writings played an important role in shaping the political philosophies of the time.

Unlike Taine, whose historical writings were wholeheartedly adopted by future right-wing historians, Renan meant different things to different people. Among the members of the generation of 1890, individuals as different as Daniel Halévy, Romain Rolland (1866), Charles Maurras, and Maurice Barrès appreciated Renan. Conservative Roman Catholics condemned Renan as an opponent of religion, but Maurras, whose Catholicism was more tactical than religious, praised his elitist ideas and saw in him a monarchist. While he rejected Renan's pronouncements on the origins of Christianity, Maurras welcomed his acerbic comments on the Revolution.[34] Léon Blum, on the other hand, felt that Renan's writings after 1871, especially on democracy, were misguided. The shock of the war and Commune, he declared, had shaken the dearest lifetime convictions of both Renan and Taine.[35] As for Barrès, although he discarded most of the liberal aspects of Renan's thought early in his career, his idea of a nation borrowed heavily from the *maître's* cult of ancestors.[36] Despite certain pronouncements against democracy, members of the republican establishment found in Renan's work the justification for the Ferry School Laws and accorded him an official state funeral in his native Brittany.

Taine's observations on the crowd had a great impact on all contemporary perceptions of the "masses." Even those with republican sympathies like Emile Zola were influenced by the master's depiction of unruly mobs as dangerous to the health of the nation. Indeed, Taine's writings on the crowds during the French Revolution and the Commune gave birth to the development of crowd psychology during the late nineteenth century.[37]

Taine's influence, however, was greatest on Barrès and Maurras. Maurras admired Taine as the diagnostician of the ills that had befallen France, agreeing with him that it was the fault of the Revolution.[38] Barrès objected to Taine's vituperations against the Revolution, particularly against the Jacobins, whom he admired for their "heroism." Responding to an inquiry on the influence of Taine in *La Revue blanche* in August 1897, Barrès declared that Taine was "no professor of energy." Nevertheless, despite his shortcomings, Taine, along with historian Fustel de Coulanges (1830), had made Barrès feel the "reality of the history" of his country.[39] Barrès used Taine's ideas on "race," "milieu," and "moment" in elaborating a critique against Kantian universalist principles, especially in *Les Déracinés*, in which one of his characters actually met with the philosopher. Leftist intellectuals like Blum, however, rejected the idea of "race, milieu, and moment," as did such liberals as Henri Mazel, who felt that the three categories overlapped.[40]

Although they may have borrowed certain political ideas from Renan and Taine, the members of the generation of 1890 rejected their teachers' excessive faith in science. As both Maurice Barrès and Léon Blum pointed out, Renan's belief in the future perfectibility of science was in itself a faith.[41] Members of the 1890 generation were not anti-scientific nor were they anti-rational but rather anti-positivist. They rejected the self-satisfied cult of progress which accorded science the ability to solve all of society's problems[42]—science, noted Blum, had the power to do good or evil.[43] They also objected to the literal application of the principles of natural sciences to literature, art, and the social sciences. Barrès complained that science had invaded all areas of thought: "For vulgar minds and for a few shrewd customers, it is called 'realism,' 'naturalism.' Politicians easily satisfied with one-word definitions call it 'Progress.' "[44]

To call the members of this generation irrational or mystical would constitute a gross exaggeration; this was after all the generation of Charles Maurras, Léon Blum, Emile Durkheim (1858), and Julien Benda, all of whom assumed the mantle of rationality. Even Henri Bergson (1859), who pushed the limits of science in his work, did not oppose science but attempted to reconcile science with faith and intuition.[45] Nor was this reaction limited to the avant-garde or even to members of this generation. Their nemesis Ferdinand Brunetière (1849), who was literary critic of *La Revue des deux mondes*, published an essay on the "bankruptcy of science" in 1895 and their immediate predecessor Paul Bourget (1852) penned a scathing indictment of Taine in his 1889 novel *Le Disciple*.

In literature, the revolt against positivism manifested itself as a rejection of the Naturalist novel as well as of Parnassian poetry. Jules Huret's *Enquête sur l'évolution littéraire*, which polled sixty-four writers, is an invaluable document on the literary tendencies of the time.[46] It revealed the existence of what Barrès called "a Republic of letters."[47] The writers, who were engaged in a dialogue with their peers, clearly felt a sense of belonging to a sociological group. For Huret, who was influenced by Darwinian theories, the ferocity of the quarrels in the literary milieu revealed by the *Enquête* was proof of the "struggle for life" in art.

The inquiry illuminated not only the quarrels between different literary schools and generations, but it also illustrated the diversity and rivalries among members of the same generation.[48] The young generation included Symbolists as well as partisans of the Ecole romane like Jean Moréas, neorealists like Jean Ajalbert and Abel Hermant (1862), and even the "scientific" poet René Ghil (1862), some of whom criticized each other as much as they did their elders. Indeed, the Naturists, many of whom were younger than the Symbolists, violently opposed Symbolism. There was a great deal of variety even among the Symbolists. Indeed, the term "Ecole Symboliste" was a misnomer according to Henri de Régnier, who observed that the so-called Symbolist school was a provisional refuge for all literary newcomers who opposed the Parnassians and Naturalists.[49] Thus, despite their internecine quarrels, members of the young generation saw themselves as a unit in opposition to the establishment.

Rejecting the "materialism" of the Parnassians and Naturalists, Symbolists believed that "reality" was neither objective, nor was it shaped by external stimuli. Instead, it was subjective, determined by an individual's perception of the outer world.[50] Indebted to German idealist philosophy, Symbolists posited the predominance of the "Idea" over material fact. They also sought to redefine artistic language. The object of the Symbolist poem, as Charles Morice (1861) observed in the Huret inquiry, was to evoke or suggest, not name an object.[51]

Like Symbolism, Barrès's *culte du moi*, which was adopted by a number of educated fin-de-siècle youths as their design for living, represented a rejection of positivism. It, too, relied on German idealist philosophy. In justifying the *culte du moi*, Barrès declared that in an uncertain world, the only reality was the Self and that a "generation weary of all systems" found solace in the quest for self-knowledge.[52] Barrès himself became a cult figure for many of his peers and more than one literary journal was founded in his honor.[53]

Given such views, it is not surprising that members of the young generation, while they may have respected the Parnassians for their technical perfection, found the content of their poetry arid, lacking in feeling. If the majority of the members of the generation of 1890 merely disliked Parnassian poetry, admiring instead the work of Mallarmé and Verlaine, their feelings toward Naturalism were akin to loathing. Symbolist critic Remy de Gourmont was emphatic in his opposition to Naturalism: "There is no doubt about the tendencies of the new literary generations: they are rigorously anti-Naturalist . . . we have distanced ourselves with horror from a literature whose baseness turned our stomachs."[54] Even a young neorealist like Abel Hermant criticized Zola for translating literally scientific theories in his novels. Among members of the young generation, only the Naturists admired Zola's work.[55]

Members of the generation of 1890 opposed Zola's Social Darwinism. Referring to an article in which Zola had spoken of the necessity of war—one must eat or be eaten—Vielé-Griffin stated that in depicting the "struggle for life" and in looking at human beings in Darwinian terms, Zola had denied the noble sentiments of humankind that separated human beings from animals. He also criticized *Germinal* for depicting revolution as brutal and destructive; the miners, he claimed, were struggling for justice, not vengeance, as Zola stated.[56] Zola, he declared, was no socialist, especially in light of his aspirations to the Academy and the sales of his novels, which earned him a great deal of money.[57]

As the most eminent and prolific representative of the Naturalists, best-selling author Zola was the target of the young generation. The pages of the little magazines were filled with diatribes against both the man and his work; in fact, *Les Entretiens* was founded to combat his influence. Zola himself contributed to such tensions, carrying on a running dispute with his young colleagues in the press. In the Huret *Enquête*, Zola broke the unspoken code, which forbade talk of money, by bragging about the sales of his most recent novel. He was criticized by both the avant-garde and the literary establishment for his esthetics as well as for his unseemly interest in financial gain and moreover for his appeal to the rising middle classes. Not until the Dreyfus Affair would the feelings of certain young writers toward Zola be attenuated.[58]

The Social Question and the Body Politic

For many young writers of the avant-garde, their disdain of the cultural establishment and of the literary marketplace predisposed them to a similar rejection of the political establishment of the Third Republic. In retrospect, the three decades preceding the

Great War seem calm, yet for contemporaries, these years, especially between the Boulanger and Dreyfus Affairs, were a time of
great political and social upheaval, of "endless crisis."[59] The Republic seemed constantly under attack from both ends of the political
spectrum.

The numerous political scandals in which the Opportunist republicans were implicated only heightened the contempt of young
intellectuals for all politicians, whom they viewed as both inept and
corrupt.[60] One such scandal led to the rise of General Boulanger, who
posed a particularly acute threat to the Republic since he united
disparate forces from the Left and Right.[61] Boulangism, however, did
not inspire much enthusiasm among members of the generation of
1890, although some of its older cohorts, notably Maurice Barrès and
Paul Adam, viewed Boulanger as the potential savior of France. On
the whole, the youth of the *grandes écoles* was almost uniformly
anti-Boulangist, as Romain Rolland pointed out in his memoirs.[62]
Despite its failure, Boulangism made a great impact on contemporaries, marking the emergence of new "radical" nationalism, which
increasingly acquired authoritarian, militarist, antiparliamentary, and
racist tendencies during the course of the 1890s.[63]

One of Boulanger's disgruntled followers, Edouard Drumont,
(1844) used the Panama scandal, in which parliamentary politicians were suspected of accepting bribes, to resurrect his failing
newspaper *La Libre Parole*.[64] Drumont, the author of the best-
selling *La France juive* (1886), fanned anti-Semitic sentiments,
capitalizing on the fact that one of the chief financiers of the Panama
Company was Baron Reinach, a Jewish entrepreneur. Some members of the generation of 1890, notably Maurice Barrès and Charles
Maurras, like Drumont, would also employ anti-Semitism, albeit of
a different variety, to combat their political and intellectual foes.

For the parliamentary republic, the threat from the Left was
even greater than that from the Right. The heightened nature of
social tensions was illustrated by a wave of strikes during the
1880s, among them the Anzin (1884) and Decazeville (1886) strikes,
the first of which served as a model for Zola's fictional portrayal in
Germinal (1885).[65] These strikes, along with an incident in which
nine people, mostly women, were killed by national guardsmen at
Fourmies during the second May Day celebration in 1891,
exemplified for many French men and women the indifference and
heartlessness of the government to the plight of the working class.
For others, it was "proof" of the brutality of the crowd, whom they
viewed with great alarm. The entry of fifty socialists in the Chamber of Deputies after the 1893 elections only aggravated their fears.

The early 1890s were no less calm, as a wave of anarchist bombings shook Paris. Along with the strikes and the emergence of the socialists, they assured the dominance of the "social question" in French national life during this time. Not all the violent attacks against "bourgeois" institutions and public officials during these years were the acts of anarchist militants—anarchist leaders like Jean Grave and Peter Kropotkin rejected such violence—but many of the individuals who committed these acts cited anarchist theory. Thus, the association of anarchists with "propaganda by deed" was cemented in the public imagination.

These attacks culminated in the assassination of President Sadi Carnot in June 1894. Following the president's death, the government passed a series of repressive laws known as "les lois scélérates," which condemned both the perpetrators of the deeds as well as the propagandists who apologized for them. The resulting *Procès des Trente*, in which several anarchist leaders and intellectuals were charged with criminal conspiracy, along with a number of common thieves, was one of the most famous trials of the period. Although most of the anarchist militants and intellectuals tried were acquitted, the trial marked the end of the era of "propaganda by deed" and the decline of intellectual support for the anarchist movement.

These events made an impact on the young intellectuals of the avant-garde, as it did on all of their fellow citizens. In 1892, Léon Blum wrote that disillusionment with the regime and its politicians had led the French to lose their sense of national identity: "Political passion is dead . . . Apoliticism has broken the link between the individual and the nation."[66] Indeed, the 1893 national elections in which nearly 30 percent of the electorate refused to vote would seem to confirm this trend.

The Huret *Enquête* of 1891 would also appear to bear this out; literary questions, almost without exception, were examined in a vacuum. Yet just two years later, writers were "politicized," as an 1893 *Ermitage Enquête*, in which litterateurs were asked to comment on the "social question," indicated. Such a change, however, could not have taken place in this short period of time. Unlike the earlier proponents of "art for art's sake," the Symbolists and other members of the avant-garde were "politicized" because of their marginalized position in the cultural milieu, by simply belonging to the avant-garde. Furthermore, their rejection of the cultural establishment fueled their opposition to the political establishment and their attraction to the anarchist movement.

Avant-garde intellectuals were not "apolitical" but rather anti-political, with a particular aversion to parliamentary politics. Witness the following declaration, published in *La Revue blanche*: "The social question is one in which young people cannot be disinterested . . . Make no mistake, however . . . Political debates leave us highly indifferent."[67] As opponents of bourgeois culture and society, they were "political" in the larger, Geertzian sense of the term.

The year 1892–1893, however, was viewed as a turning point by contemporaries, no doubt because of the anarchist bombings that shook Paris during these two years. Adolphe Retté noted in December 1893 that the efforts of his generation, which had heretofore been strictly literary, were henceforth also political and social:

> Up to this year, our efforts were sparse, limited to esthetic evolution and, as a result, the emancipation of young minds . . . only occurred in the realm of art. Given, however, our objective: the free synthesis of faculties essential to man, and our means: the destruction of representations of Authority, we have expanded our reach. Through an instinctual agreement, we have attacked not only esthetic Authority but moral Authority as well . . . our work was above all that of demolition and purification.[68]

L'Ermitage's "Référendum artistique et social," published in its July 1893 issue, offered clear proof of the growing interest of writers in the social question. Avant-garde writers may already have been "politicized" in the Huret inquiry, but they had not spoken of the contemporary social situation. Ninety-nine young writers (those under the age of thirty-five) from France and abroad were polled in the *Ermitage* inquiry. Participants were first requested to choose the best condition for "social good"—a "disciplined and methodical" organization or a "spontaneous and free" one—and then to elaborate on which of the two the artist should prefer.[69]

Although the words politics and government are missing from the question—writers were not asked the form of government they preferred but rather what organization represented the best condition for social good—the aim of the survey, as the title "Un Référendum artistique et social" indicated, was political. The intellectuals who organized this inquiry perhaps rejected politics per se, but they were proposing themselves as an alternative parliament to that of corrupt politicians.[70] The Referendum of 1893 was thus a confirmation of a new trend in the intellectual milieu. Writers and artists of the young generation, even the Symbolists, were henceforth aware of both the necessity of becoming involved in their time and the expedient of doing so.

In part because of their rejection of politics *qua* politics, young intellectuals of the generation of 1890, almost without exception, were seduced by the anarchist ideal, as both Léon Blum and his nemesis Charles Maurras, future leader of the right-wing Action française, noted.[71] Even those who deplored the attraction of anarchism for members of their generation, like Maurras, Henry Bérenger (1867), Hugues Rebell, and Henri Mazel—the latter two among the authors of the *Ermitage* inquiry—were still shaped by it. Anarchism may be seen then as a major issue that polarized a generation. As such, the intellectual generation of 1890, often referred to as the generation of the Dreyfus Affair, might more accurately be called the "anarchist generation." Young intellectuals' involvement in the anarchist movement paved the way for their engagement in the Dreyfus Affair.

Strictly speaking, anarchism at the fin de siècle was a political movement, situated within the context of the socialist movement, but despite its firm grounding as a movement of the Left, anarchism served as a bridge between intellectuals of the Left and Right.[72] Avant-garde intellectuals shared with anarchists a common sense of revolt against the bourgeois order. Like the artisans who constituted the rank and file of the anarchist movement, they saw themselves as victims of the increased industrialization and commercialization of French society. Intellectuals attracted to anarchism may not have all opposed the state in principle, but they did share a disdain for the state as represented by the Third Republic.

Anarchism was not a coherent system of thought and was by its very nature diverse and diffuse. If all anarchist militants called for the destruction of society, they neither agreed on the way in which the present order should be destroyed nor on what kind of economic order should replace it. Such confusion was exacerbated by the existence of five different socialist parties. This was a time when Maurice Barrès could call himself a socialist. Moreover, his brand of socialism closely resembled certain strands of anarchism—he did, after all, see himself as a disciple of Proudhon. The POSR (Parti ouvrier socialiste révolutionnaire) of Jean Allemane, which advocated economic rather than political solutions, had more in common with the anarchists than it did with Jules Guesde's POF (Parti ouvrier français), which pursued a parliamentary strategy.

For intellectuals, anarchism became a catchall term for discontent; hence its appeal for men as different as Maurice Barrès, Bernard Lazare, and Maurice Pujo (1872), future founding member of the Action française. Anarchism was valued above all by young avant-garde intellectuals for its celebration of the individual. Although most historians, as Richard Sonn has observed, have ignored the role anarchism played in shaping the early career of Maurice Barrès, his fellow litterateurs saw Barrès as the champion of literary anarchism after the publication of his *culte du moi* trilogy and of *L'Ennemi des lois*.[73]

For many young writers, the *culte du moi* coincided with anarchist theory; in their minds, both called for the unfettered development of the individual. In November 1891, Ludovic Malquin (born Louis Malaquin), a literary anarchist, published an article entitled "L'An-archie" in *La Revue blanche*.[74] In this article, which began with a quotation from Barrès, Malquin stated that men would naturally be inclined toward good if unencumbered by the machinery of the state and by other traditional authorities. He did not define, however, the means by which a new society would come about. In another *Revue blanche* article "Notes sur obéir," Malquin defined action as "satisfying one's passions."[75] Such a view did not correspond to the anarcho-communism of Jean Grave and Peter Kropotkin, who distinguished between negative and positive liberty, but as literary critic Lucien Muhlfeld noted in his review of Kropotkin's *La Conquête du pain*:

> Dare I say that the constructive aspects interest me little? It is without doubt the nihilist turn of my mind that decrees that only the destructive role of Anarchy seduces me. Anarchy seems to me to be an admirable and necessary demolition of contemporary laws . . . It is foremost a state of mind that is less communist than individualist. We protest against the constraints of future socialisms as much as against those of past governments. I see the anarchism of contemporary writers as being above all a desire for relaxation [of manners].[76]

For Muhlfeld, as for many of his literary colleagues, anarchism was strictly an individualist, nihilist doctrine.[77]

Seen in this light, the act of the bomb thrower was the supreme act of individualism, a heroic deed which showed not only utter scorn for society but also for death. Ravachol, Vaillant, and Emile Henry were Wagnerian heroes who defied all laws and not only disdained death but invited it.[78] Paul Adam wrote an "Eloge de Ravachol" in *Les Entretiens politiques et littéraires*, calling him a martyr and a saint; his colleague Victor Barrucand likened Ravachol to Jesus Christ.[79] Just as anarchist leaders did not ap-

prove of this violence even if they did not always disavow the
terrorist acts, neither did all intellectuals.

If the early writings of Barrès represented one type of literary
anarchism, then Symbolism represented another. While Barrès
emphasized the liberty of the individual in society, Symbolists referred specifically to the liberty of the artist to create. In an article
entitled "Le Symbolisme," published in *La Revue blanche* in its
June 1892 issue, Remy de Gourmont outlined the parallels between anarchism and Symbolism.[80] For Symbolists like Remy de
Gourmont, one was a Symbolist in art just as one was an anarchist
in politics. Symbolism represented an attempt to liberate French
poetry from its formalized structures in the same way that anarchism constituted an attempt to free society from its socioeconomic
chains. In the most obvious terms, Symbolism was liberating because of its experimentation with free verse and syntax, but it also
represented a freedom of ideas since the Symbolists invited the
artist to create a world in which symbols were endowed with personal meaning.

These writers did not necessarily ignore social issues; nevertheless, their primary concern lay in the changing status of the artist
in a materialist society and in using anarchism as a metaphor for
esthetic revolution. Paul Adam suggested that the fascination of
writers and artists for anarchism was partly due to a desire for
harmony in the world which matched their desire for beauty in art:

> In fact, the literary attraction for active altruism is born
> of a purely esthetic consideration. The disharmony of the
> moral world is shocking because it is an artistic mistake.
> The extreme complacency of certain fat cats and the suf-
> fering that one believes to be familiar to the laboring
> masses outrage writers, as would disproportion in archi-
> tecture, a maddening opposition of tonalities, cacophony
> in an orchestra.[81]

Adolphe Retté, one of the litterateurs most closely associated
with anarchism, spoke of the avant-garde's "violent affirmation" of
"a liberated esthetics" as well as its members' belief in humankind.
Concern for humankind, however, was linked to their own quest for
liberty: "We believe in Man, we do what we want. . . ."[82] Most of
these intellectuals were attracted to anarchism rather than socialism because they could reconcile anarchist theories with their own
elitist beliefs, although a few approached anarchism globally rather
than specifically in terms of artistic liberty, among them Bernard

Lazare, Léon Blum, and Victor Barrucand. In the wake of the *Procès des Trente*, these intellectuals turned increasingly to social issues and examined them in a constructive way, with an eye toward finding a solution to the inequalities in French society.

The conflation of anarchist liberty with the freedom of the artist to create is evident in the *Ermitage* Referendum, and a closer examination of this inquiry offers us the opportunity to gauge intellectual interest in the social question. The aim of an *enquête* is often to shape opinion rather than measure it. The authors of the *Ermitage* Referendum, Henri Mazel and Hugues Rebell, both of whom were hostile to anarchism and socialism, sought to present their cohorts as moderates and minimize the importance of "radical" movements for their generation. To that end, they presented a summary in the epilogue which classified the responses of those polled. Opinions were divided into three categories: those who favored constraint; those who chose liberty, and finally, an intermediate group of individuals who sought a compromise between "communist constraint" and "anarchist liberty."[83]

These three categories reflect a refusal of the traditional opposition of Left and Right. Since socialists, authoritarians, and aristocrats were lumped together under the category of restraint, they were all seen as partisans of order. Thus, the aristocratic, antidemocratic Hugues Rebell, who favored a "union of three aristocracies" (birth, wealth, and intellect),[84] which he was willing to establish by force, was grouped with the socialist Stuart Merrill.[85] Similarly, anarchists, who normally would have been associated with their socialist peers, were grouped with liberals, some of whom were antidemocratic and extremely hostile to the anarchist movement. Henri Mazel, who opposed anarchism, was placed in the same overall category as Camille Mauclair, Maurice Beaubourg (1866), and Pierre Quillard, all of whom were sympathetic to the anarchist movement.

Furthermore, by subsuming anarchism in the liberal category, the authors underestimated its impact on members of their generation. They, however, inadvertently reinforced the very image they sought to avoid in another issue when they polled members of the older generation. The results indicated that only one or two among their elders, notably, Octave Mirbeau, were sympathetic to the anarchist movement, thereby pointing to the popularity of anarchism among those of their own generation.[86]

It is striking that some of the most visible partisans of anarchism were placed in the intermediate category as hesitating between liberty and constraint, yet they, like Grave and Kropotkin, saw themselves as anarcho-communists. Such a classification reflects a misunderstanding, whether deliberate or accidental, of anarchism since the authors denied the idea of anarcho-communism, which presupposed some form of organization. Instead, they opposed structured organization to anarchism, which then became a narrowly individualist doctrine devoid both of organization and a social conscience. Furthermore, strictly literary anarchists were not distinguished from those who were concerned with social responsibility.

The categorization of socialists as partisans of constraint also testified to the anti-socialist predilections of the authors and reflected the general distrust among intellectuals of political parties which might limit their independence.[87] Even those who were interested in social justice feared that socialism would crush the individual, specifically the superior artist and rejected socialism as too "scientific" and "materialist."[88] The Socialists, under the leadership of Jules Guesde, were also unsympathetic to young iconoclast intellectuals because of their dogged pursuit of a parliamentary strategy. No doubt Maurice Beaubourg, who was classed as an anarchist, spoke for the majority when he declared that art and socialism were polar opposites.[89]

The independence of the artist was affirmed by the majority, whether apolitical (Gourmont) or political; anarchist (Beaubourg), liberal (Mazel), aristocratic (Joseph Declareuil, 1863) or socialist (Quillard). This then is the clearest message of the *Enquête*: the members of the generation of 1890 were by and large partisans of liberty. As writers, they naturally emphasized the freedom of the artist to create, independent of all constraints.

If the inquiry rejected distinctions of Left and Right, so, too, did it eschew "political" and "apolitical" distinctions. Those who were "indifferent to politics" were placed in the intermediate category, while the advocates of "art for art's sake," generally thought to be apolitical, were listed as partisans of liberty. Moreover, there was little to distinguish between the answers of those categorized as "indifferent" and those listed as partisans of "art for art's sake."[90] This confusion illustrates that contemporaries often meant different things when they spoke of "art for art's sake" and "social art." Moreover, individual artists were themselves inconsistent in their usage. As Gustave Kahn noted, it was more important to define the terms used than to determine the relative value of two opposing theories.[91]

Yet historians have long juxtaposed the partisans of "art for art's sake," meaning those who showed no interest in their time, with the adherents of "social art," defining them as social realists who would subordinate art to the revolution. In reality, most of the partisans of "social art" at this time were opposed to industrial and utilitarian art.[92] Furthermore, the stance of most writers of the time fell somewhere in between these two poles. A brief examination of these varying positions is illuminating.

Remy de Gourmont, classified as "indifferent" in the *Ermitage* inquiry, comes closest to the "art for art's sake" stereotype. A self-styled idealist, he proclaimed the complete liberty of the individual, which he equated with anarchism.[93]

Adolphe Retté, placed in the intermediate category, represents a somewhat more complicated and inconsistent position. Although he believed that artists must not remain in an ivory tower and that they must combat "Authority," he felt they had to choose.[94] In "L'Art et l'anarchie," Retté told artists interested in anarchism that no compromise was possible. Either they were anarchist militants and had to act, even taking up propaganda by deed—at this point, they would no longer be artists—or they were artists whose sole goal was the defense and the glorification of art. Retté denounced "social art," which he viewed as utilitarian art. Such art was a "monstrous antinomy."[95] While Maurice Barrès, listed as a partisan of liberty, agreed that the aim of art should be pleasure, and thus independent of the conditions of time or milieu, he noted in his response to Retté's article that art could be both "pure" and "social," pointing to Plato's *Republic* and Shakespeare's *The Tempest*. Barrès could not resist needling Retté; in criticizing "social art" wasn't Retté falling in his own trap, by serving as propagandist?[96]

A position more consistent than Retté's was that of Vielé-Griffin, classified as a partisan of liberty. Dismissing "art for art's sake" as an outmoded Parnassian illusion, he declared that art could no more constitute an end in and of itself than could chewing: "Art is thus a natural function of man, the ultimate form of universal prayer. . . ." Instead of "art for art's sake," he proposed "art for beauty's sake":

> The artist, by the sole fact that he professes the cult of Beauty, proclaims Justice and Truth . . . Certainly, artists, your duty is to persist in your very being to preserve it from circumstances that would diminish it, to lift it toward the Absolute, and in doing so, you duly glorify humanity of which you are an elite.[97]

Fellow poet Gustave Kahn, who was not polled, adopted a similar idea: the ultimate aim of art was form—not the ideas presented but the way in which they were presented.[98] This did not mean that

the artist should ignore social questions or that art should be egotistical. Kahn rejected the narrow definition of "art for art's sake" as
represented by Théophile Gautier and Charles Baudelaire. Like
Barrès, Kahn believed that an artist could examine social and political questions as long as art and beauty, not propaganda, remained
the ultimate goal. Great artists like Voltaire, Rousseau, Ibsen, and
Tolstoy were concerned with the world around them but examined
such questions globally rather than presenting specific arguments
for or against a certain position.[99] Both Kahn and Vielé-Griffin, who
were sympathetic to the anarchist movement, found no contradiction
between their pursuit of beauty in art and their political beliefs.[100]

In 1893, future Dreyfusard Bernard Lazare, who was also not
polled, declared that the debate that pitted the adherents of "art
for art's sake" against partisans of "social art" was a false one since
the adversaries spoke at cross-purposes. Responding to Pierre
Quillard (one of the few to be listed as a socialist in the *Ermitage*
survey), who rejected "social art," Lazare declared that one must
not condemn art that was educative, by dismissing it as "useful."
Quillard's error, as well as of all those who rejected "social art,"
according to Lazare, was their belief that such art had been expressly written as propaganda. The artist must not write for his
own pleasure but should be an educator in the most noble sense of
the word. This did not mean that he was a dogmatic pedagogue:
"The writer, the artist truly worthy of this name must not misuse
his status for his own personal satisfaction, he should be an
educator . . . he should instruct us in a lofty manner. . . ."[101] Such
universal art was the only kind worthy of the name.[102] Lazare's
position as outlined here closely resembled Barrès's view that art
could be at the same time "pure" and "social."[103]

Despite the different ways in which they expressed themselves
and defined their terms, all of these writers, with the exception of
Gourmont, believed that the writer should be involved in national
life. Involvement in society was inevitable, in spite of vehement
proclamations in favor of "art for art's sake," given the symbiotic
relationship between culture and politics in France. Yet the confusion of the "political" and "apolitical" in the *Ermitage Enquête* also
testified to avant-garde intellectuals' desire to establish via their
inquiry a sense of cohesion based not on political grounds, but on
generational loyalty and the solidarity of artists who shared certain ideals of beauty and art. Two of the authors, Mazel and Rebell,
subsequently published works advocating an intellectual aristocracy, which would unite like-minded individuals and transcend
divisions of class and politics.[104]

Although the Referendum of 1893 stopped short of asking what the role of the artist in society should be, it certainly implied that artists should be involved in their time, thus marking an important step in the politicization of intellectuals. The next stage would be to affirm the right and the duty of the writer and artist to make pronouncements in the national arena. The Referendum of 1893 announced the 1895 *Mercure de France Enquête*, in which writers were asked to comment on social, economic, and cultural relations with Germany.[105]

Of Germany and Germans

Not only was Germany used as a gauge by which to measure France; so, too, were German thinkers, especially Richard Wagner, Nietzsche, and Kant, appropriated by different groups in defense of or in opposition to competing visions of Frenchness. After 1870, Kant was heralded by republican educators who wanted to replace Catholic morality in schools with lay morality, while in the wake of the Dreyfus Affair, Nietzsche was used by nationalists to spearhead the attack against Kantianism.

The image presented of the generation of 1890, and not only by Agathon, is that of a group of "anti-patriots." Remy de Gourmont's article, "Le Joujou patriotisme," published in *Le Mercure de France* in April 1891, is often cited by contemporaries and historians alike as "proof" of the "anti-patriotic" sentiments of this generation, along with antimilitarist novels published by Abel Hermant, Georges Darien (1862), and Lucien Descaves.[106] Antimilitarism was not necessarily anti-patriotic. Moroever, a closer reading of Gourmont's article reveals that he, like many of his avant-garde colleagues, was not necessarily anti-patriotic. Instead, they opposed the jingoistic, exclusive nationalism of Paul Déroulède and his followers.[107] An examination of the 1895 *Mercure de France Enquête*, which polled intellectuals about cultural and social relations with Germany, and a comparison of this inquiry to a subsequent one published in *Le Mercure* in late 1902 and early 1903 is helpful in determining the evolution of French intellectual opinion toward Germany during these years.[108]

In the first survey, conducted jointly by *Le Mercure* and by the *Neue deutsche Rundschau* in Germany, those polled were asked the following: "Politics aside, do you favor closer intellectual and social relations between France and Germany, and what would be the best means of furthering these exchanges?"[109] Although the question seemed straightforward, it presupposed that one could discuss intellectual and social relations without regard to political issues. Such an assumption could easily be challenged (and it was by certain respondents), but on the whole, participants seemed to accept it as a given. Such a premise reflected the same anti-politics bias expressed in the *Ermitage* inquiry.

Given such an attitude, it is not surprising that most of those polled were intellectuals, in particular, of the avant-garde. Alfred Vallette, the review's editor, mentioned in his introduction to the inquiry that there was no point in even polling politicians since they were responsible for the enmity between the two peoples.[110] Despite the lacunae of the survey—the obvious bias toward avant-garde intellectuals and the absence of such classicizers as Jean Moréas and Charles Maurras—the survey did reflect the contemporary mood of cooperation with Germany prevalent even among intellectuals of the mainstream.[111]

Internationalism was the most salient feature of the survey responses. Most of those polled did not view Germany as an entity in and of itself but rather within an internationalist perspective. Remy de Gourmont represented himself as a "citizen of the world" who dealt only with individuals, while others, among them Bernard Lazare, mentioned cooperation not only with Germany but also with England and Italy.[112] Some of the participants, in particular, those most serious about their involvement with the anarchist movement, opposed war in principle.[113]

Much of the "anti-patriotic" bluster of intellectuals like Gourmont, Joséphin Péladan (1859), and Laurent Tailhade was directed toward their enemies at home, both cultural and political. The survey thus became a means by which to settle scores with their own countrymen. Déroulède and his followers were their favorite targets. Thus, Gourmont stated, "I am not the crowd; the metaphysics of patriotism is unknown to me," while Péladan declared that nationalist sentiment had served as a pretext for great crimes.[114] As for Laurent Tailhade, he denounced both "this old cannibalistic idol the 'Nation'" and the "inept rabble it oppresses."[115]

The elitist sentiments expressed by both Gourmont and Tailhade, whose attraction to anarchism was born of esthetic concerns, should not go unnoticed. Indeed, Tailhade is best-known for his offhand defense of propaganda by deed: "What do the victims matter as long as the gesture is beautiful," a statement that is ironic in light of his loss of an eye during the anarchist bombing of the Restaurant Foyot shortly thereafter. Tailhade, Péladan, and Gourmont used Germany as an excuse to criticize bourgeois society and culture, thereby combining cultural and political critique. Tailhade lumped statesmen, entrepreneurs, magistrates, academicians, and soldiers together, representing them as the enemies of "intelligence," and held Déroulède responsible for "the assassination of Beauty."[116] Péladan stated that he had more in common with Greek monks than he did with popular playwright Victorien Sardou (1831) or with conservative critic Francisque Sarcey (1827), whom he designated as his enemies.[117] In his article "Le Joujou patriotisme," written four years earlier, Gourmont had railed against his fellow countrymen and women, who ignored the merits of the French avant-garde, advising them to show their patriotism by supporting French art: "There is a patriotism within reach of all those who possess three francs fifty [the price of a book], that is, to buy the books of talented men and not let them die in misery."[118]

Specific Germans were only infrequently mentioned in the survey; among those cited most often were Goethe, Kant, Hegel, Nietszche, and Wagner. Paul Adam viewed himself and his contemporaries as "the spiritual heirs of Goethe and Hegel," while Barrès spoke of the "sacred river of learning spread by Kant via Hegel."[119] Both Symbolist theories and the *culte du moi* owed a great deal to the German idealists.

Most of those polled believed in the reciprocity of intellectual influences between the two countries, also citing the influence of French thinkers on German ones. Lazare mentioned the impact of the Naturalists and Symbolists on German writers and Barrès cited Heinrich Heine as a perfect example of the "clarity" and "order" embodied by the French spirit.[120] Yet only Barrès among those of the young generation implied an opposition between the French genius and its German counterpart, a theme that would prevail in the second survey.

Internationalist sentiments did not necessarily preclude "patriotic" sentiments toward France, if patriotism were to be defined as pride in French culture and traditions. While Gustave Kahn believed in defending "against all military attack, the totality of ideas, traditions, and even interests that constitute the French nation," he much preferred peaceful evolution which would render such defensiveness unnecessary.[121] Even Gourmont had claimed in "Le Joujou patriotisme" that he would defend France against war with Germany—albeit reluctantly since he opposed war.[122] Moreover, he believed in the superiority of French art and culture, which was equated with that of the avant-garde, but recognized the contributions of Germany in philosophy and the sciences.[123]

Evident in the responses of the 1895 *Mercure* survey is a sense of solidarity with other intellectuals. Most of those polled, both young and old, believed that cultural and intellectual exchanges between the two countries would prove fruitful.[124] As in the *Ermitage* Referendum, these writers proposed themselves as alternatives to the politicians. Paul Adam suggested the creation of a Franco-German league of "artists, merchants and socialists," stating that this new "intellectual elite" could bring about European peace, while Bernard Lazare mentioned the establishment of a triple alliance, both moral and intellectual, with Germany and England via the creation of a vast association of sociologists, poets, artists, novelists, critics, and savants.[125] Finally, Gustave Kahn called on thinkers and poets to be the voice of reason against force.[126] The 1895 survey thus announced both the banding together of intellectuals in the Affair and their engagement in national and international issues.

A comparison of the 1895 *Mercure* survey with a subsequent one published in 1902 reveals both elements of continuity and rupture. Despite the shortcomings of the second survey—it did not poll several leading Dreyfusard intellectuals and it was worded in such a way as to appeal to injured French pride—it clearly showed an evolution in French intellectual opinion toward Germany. Intellectuals, even those not known for their "nationalist" sentiments, manifested a wariness of Germany and of German culture. Germany was no longer viewed in an internationalist perspective but in and of itself; moreover, it was viewed as both a political and cultural entity.[127] The complementary nature of the two cultures was no longer emphasized but rather their opposition. Indeed, France was held up as the heir to classical Western culture.

The shift in intellectual opinion was partly due to a shift in the political atmosphere on both the foreign and domestic fronts. Until the first years of the new century, England was as likely as Germany to be seen as a threat to French interests, as the 1898 Fashoda incident so aptly demonstrated. By 1902, although the entente with Britain was still two years away, French Foreign Minister Théophile Delcassé had already decided to play the British card and was making overtures to the British Foreign Office. As for Germany, it came to be viewed as increasingly bellicose; witness the emperor's speech on German cultural superiority cited at the beginning of the second survey. The French looked to their eastern neighbor with a mixture of apprehension and envy.

The Barrès who had praised Kant and Hegel in the first *Mercure* survey denigrated the influence of Kant in the second.[128] Similarly, "citizen of the world" Gourmont, who in another survey, published in 1897, had denounced the followers of Nietzsche as puerile, celebrated the German philosopher as an antidote to the pernicious influence of Kant in 1902.[129] One should note, however, certain continuities. In 1895, Péladan had exalted Wagner while rejecting Kant and Hegel, whom he held responsible for contemporary anarchy. By the same token, Téodor de Wyezwa (1862), a regular contributor to *La Revue wagnérienne*, had seen no point in pursuing cultural relations with Germany, with the exception of Wagner.[130]

The defense of French culture which is so clearly manifest in the second survey was already present, to a much lesser degree, in an 1897 *Revue blanche* survey on the influence of foreign literatures, specifically of Scandinavian literature, on French letters.[131] Most respondents stressed the cross-cultural nature of exchanges, with a good number emphasizing French contributions to other cultures. Despite a desire for international exchanges, many French writers of this generation still felt a sense of pride in their own culture.

The evolution of intellectual opinion toward Germany, although significant, is perhaps not as dramatic as would seem at first glance. The 1897 *Revue blanche* survey points to a gradual change in attitudes toward foreign cultures, an evolution leading to greater defensiveness about French culture. Furthermore, given the avant-garde's need to exalt Germany in order to denigrate their enemies at home in the first *Mercure* survey, one questions the sincerity and the depth of their regard for Germany. Therefore, the impact of the shift in attitudes toward Germany in the second survey is somewhat attenuated.

The Dreyfus Affair represented a significant turning point in the evolution of French intellectuals' opinions of Germany. Factors internal to France played as important a role as external factors in determining the change in attitudes. The realignment of the intellectual milieu, specifically the split of the avant-garde, gave anti-Dreyfusard intellectuals reason to criticize Germany as the country of Kant in the second survey. Similarly, the same intellectuals, who depicted Nietzsche as anti-German, used the German philosopher to spearhead their opposition to Kant, or more precisely, to French neo-Kantians, who were associated with the Dreyfusards and the republican university.[132] Gourmont's change in opinion of Nietzsche between 1897 and 1902 may be viewed in this context. Dreyfusard intellectuals could and did defend Kantianism in the second survey, but given the political situation, they did not have many reasons to defend Germany as a cultural entity, and even fewer as a political one.

Conclusion

This examination of the generation of 1890 should illustrate the inaccuracy of the Agathon portrait. The members of the generation of 1890 were no more "sacrificed" than previous generations; they were certainly less so than their successors who died in the Great War. In addition, they were no more "obsessed with decadence" than their elders. Unlike their elders, they sought positive solutions to France's problems. Indeed, they viewed themselves as "men of action" and sought to combine their intellect with deeds. This is a far cry from their depiction as "passive" by Agathon.

Their "anti-patriotism" too should not be exaggerated, even if the changes that took place on both the national and international scene between 1890 and 1905 contributed to the differences in outlook of youths of the generation of 1890 and of 1912. Their sometimes outlandish statements against the nation were directed toward the political and cultural establishment that ignored them. If they stressed international cooperation rather than jingoistic patriotism, they were no less patriotic than other generations. Their pride in French culture, as represented by their own achievements, was evident in both *Mercure* surveys and in the *Revue blanche* inquiry on Scandinavian literature. Finally, the revolt against positivism, launched by the generation of 1890, assured a sense of continuity between the two generations and distinguished them from previous generations.

Marked by great change, the fin de siècle was a time of cultural crisis. The works of writers and artists of this period reflect the contemporary fear of the manifestations of modernity, which included the emergence of mass democracy, the growth of cities, the rise of the working class, and the entry into public life of Jews and women. France in particular was haunted by the loss of national honor, in light of both the defeat in the Franco-Prussian War and the precipitous decline of the national birthrate.

It is within this context that the intellectual emerged as a national figure, specifically, within the generation of 1890, whose members went on to engage themselves in the Dreyfus Affair, on both sides. The *Mercure de France* survey of 1895, along with the 1893 *Ermitage* Referendum, and the 1891 Huret inquiry, all reveal a preoccupation with national identity and the social question, in particular, with the role of the writer and artist in society. The birth of the intellectual was thus a part of a larger quest for national identity in a modern world. The competing visions of national identity and of the intellectual as a standard-bearer of that identity would manifest themselves during the 1890s before their direct confrontation during the Dreyfus Affair.

The strong sense of generational solidarity present among members of the generation of 1890 was shattered by the events of the Dreyfus Affair. As such, the Affair marked the coming of age of these intellectuals. From their lifelong opposing vantage points, Léon Blum and Charles Maurras could agree that the Dreyfus Affair represented both the defining moment in the history of their generation and in the history of the Third Republic.[133]

3

—◦◦◦—

Aristocrat or Proletarian?
Intellectuals and Elites in Fin-de-siècle France

During the years preceding the Affair, the debate concerning the nature of elites, particularly of intellectual elites, and their place in a democratic society assumed an intensity unparalleled in French history.[1] The concept of an intellectual elite was not limited to conservatives but was accepted by those who professed republican views and even those with anarchist and socialist ones. The need for a "moral and intellectual elite" was thus emphasized across the spectrum of political opinion.[2]

Such a debate was not limited to the political sphere; it was also prevalent in the literary milieu. The venerable *Revue bleue* devoted a series of articles from 1896 to 1898 to the "intellectual proletariat" and in the wake of the Affair published an *enquête* entitled "L'Elite intellectuelle et la démocratie."[3]

Intellectual elites, both within the university and literary milieus, had become increasingly isolated from political and economic elites during the latter part of the nineteenth century. This isolation and accompanying sense of frustration at not being properly recognized led to the elaboration of independent political positions in the name of intellectual authority as distinct from that of other elites.[4]

Such alienation was particularly acute in the literary avant-garde. The scandals which shook the Third Republic at this time served to confirm intellectual opinion of politicians as both corrupt and inept. Writers and artists of the avant-garde became increasingly politicized, many of them adhering to the anarchist and socialist movements.[5] As

65

a turning point in this progressive political awakening, the 1894 *Procès des Trente* forced these writers and artists to examine further not only the implications of their political affiliations but also their own role in society.

In June 1894, Henri Mazel guest edited an issue of *La Plume* on "L'Aristocratie." In November, he devoted an entire issue of his own *Ermitage* to the same topic. During the same year, Hugues Rebell, future anti-Dreyfusard, published *Union des trois aristocraties*, a work that shared common themes with future Dreyfusard Henry Bérenger's *L'Aristocratie intellectuelle*, which appeared a year later.

Of particular importance is *La Cocarde*, a formerly Boulangist publication, edited by Maurice Barrès from 5 September 1894 to 7 March 1895.[6] Billed as "a republican opposition newspaper to which socialists and intellectuals will contribute," it included among its staff members an equal number of future Dreyfusard and anti-Dreyfusard intellectuals.[7] Henry Bérenger, Gustave Kahn, and Camille Mauclair became Dreyfusards, while Hugues Rebell and Charles Maurras, along with Barrès, became anti-Dreyfusards. Yet these future foes, despite their political differences, all believed in the sacred mission of the writer. Moreover, they viewed themselves as part of an intellectual elite.

Accompanying their belief in an intellectual elite was the fear of the proletarianization of intellectuals, a fear for the status of intellectuals in a modern, democratic society. Indeed, this was the theme of Barrès's novel *Les Déracinés*, published in 1897, and that of Henry Bérenger's *La Proie*, also published the same year.

In order to understand why such a debate took place at this time and why with such intensity in the literary avant-garde, it is first necessary to examine the profound political, social, and cultural changes which took place in France during these years. The democratization of French society, as represented by the establishment of the Third Republic, led to the explosion of the press and the development of a literate public. Although the public writer had long been established as a cultural icon, only during the 1880s and 1890s did there emerge in the cultural milieu a general discussion of the role of the writer and artist in society.[8] This discussion, as Stephen Wilson tells us, was largely inspired by "an anxiety about the role and status of the intellectual in democratic society, for the traditional concept of civilization depended on a thoroughgoing cultural elitism."[9]

The coming of mass democracy and the rapid pace of industrialization made a great impact on all writers, not just those of the avant-garde. As many litterateurs of varying political persuasions observed, the status of the writer had changed profoundly during the course of the nineteenth century. Liberated from the restrictions of the patronage system, the writer was henceforth subject to the demands of the marketplace. Many felt overwhelmed by the newly democratized public which set tastes and fashions that had long been the province of a small minority. The fear of overcrowding in the literary field and the perceived "industrialization" of literature led some writers to adopt anti-Semitic ideas.

Anti-Semites or not, avant-garde intellectuals all agreed with poet Adolphe Retté that of all the individuals who suffered in contemporary society, poets suffered the most. Society hated and feared them because they were ahead of their time. By pretending that writers, "practically speaking," were not useful, society forced poets to earn their living and thereby betray their principles.[10] Another litterateur, Alphonse Germain (1861) wrote that the rise to power of the Voltairian bourgeoisie had relegated intellectuals to the margins of society and that in losing religious faith a race had lost the notion of Art and Beauty. Lamenting the indifference and hostility of the public, he declared that France did not appreciate her art.[11]

The debate concerning the role of the writer must be viewed not only against the backdrop of the new democratic society, but also in light of contemporary discussions concerning the heritage of the French Revolution. The early Third Republic, after all, marked the establishment of the legacy of the Revolution.[12] Among writers and artists of the avant-garde, attitudes toward democracy and as a result toward the Revolution varied. Some accepted democracy, others did not, but all agreed with future Dreyfusard and Radical Senator Henry Bérenger that the coming of democracy was the most important social development of the time: "The democratic spirit is in the process of changing the world: it transforms the present and leads the way to the future."[13]

Although he is forgotten today, Bérenger—not to be confused with the conservative moralist with the same last name—along with Paul Bourget and Maurice Barrès, did a great deal to popularize the term intellectual at the fin de siècle.[14] He wrote for a number of avant-garde journals, chief among them L'Art et la vie, directed by future anti-Dreyfusard and Action française founding member Maurice Pujo. Bérenger also collaborated regularly on La Revue bleue, for which he conducted a number of important enquêtes, including one in 1897 on the responsibility of the press.[15] Like a number of members of his generation, he had a foot in both the avant-garde literary milieu and in the republican university, where he served as president of the Students' Association.[16] He was thus an important if not typical figure in the literary avant-garde.

His avant-garde colleagues Hugues Rebell and Charles Maurras both deplored the advent of democracy, which they held responsible for all contemporary ills—including the decline of the status of the writer. Even at this early date, Maurras held a noteworthy position both in and outside the avant-garde. Known as a literary critic and journalist, he wrote regularly for *La Gazette de France*; in 1895, he began writing for the royalist *Le Soleil*. A friend of both Henri Mazel and Maurice Barrès, he contributed to *L'Ermitage* as well as to *La Cocarde*. The major critic of the classicist Ecole romane, he was also one of the principal animators of the federalist campaigns launched by the Provençal Félibrige group.

As a respected novelist and one of the major collaborators of *L'Ermitage*, Rebell, too, occupied an important position in the avant-garde. Although Rebell went on to join the Action française, his admiration for Nietzsche distinguished him from Maurras.[17] In *Union des trois aristocraties*, Rebell wrote that the principles of 1789 had destroyed traditional elites and ideas in the name of the illusory principle of equality, which translated into the triumph of the masses and the reign of mediocrity.[18] According to Rebell, the Revolution exalted the rights of the individual at the expense of public good.[19] Rebell feared the domination of the minority by the majority. The superior man, in particular, the intelligent man, could not survive in a democracy because it denied him his rightful superior position.[20] In place of a democracy, Rebell advocated an absolute government in which he proposed to unite the aristocracies of birth, wealth, and intellect.[21]

Henri Mazel shared a disdain for the parliamentary government of the Third Republic with his avant-garde cohorts Maurras and Rebell.[22] Mazel, like Bérenger, is little-known today, but as editor of *L'Ermitage* during its early years and the author of *Le Mercure de France*'s column on social issues, he occupied a significant place in the avant-garde. Along with Rebell and Maurras, he blamed the Revolution for the birth of democracy. For Mazel, as for Rebell, the superior man could not survive in a democracy. Mazel, too, contested the idea of absolute equality. Finally, in common with Maurras and Rebell, Mazel viewed socialism and anarchism as two systems of thought that masked envy and hatred through the guise of a love of justice.[23] Although he also condemned the Revolution, unlike Rebell, he did not view the Revolution as an excess of individualism but of collectivism.[24] For Mazel, civilization was the prod-

uct of strong individuals, not of numerous groups. Despite the ve-
hemence of his pronouncements, Mazel was not as ardent an opponent of democracy as Rebell and Maurras; he did not oppose its
numbers but rather its decadence.[25] Mazel advocated gradual
change, pointing to England as a model.[26] He believed that all the
good that came out of the Revolution would have come gradually—
without the violence.[27] Moreover, he showed little nostalgia for the
absolute monarchy. In fact, by destroying traditions and usurping
the rights of elites, the absolute monarchy was directly responsible
for the destruction of the Revolution.[28] A liberal, Mazel claimed
that true liberalism was compatible both with the idea of an aristocracy and the rights of the individual, thereby echoing his friend
and mentor sociologist Gabriel Tarde.[29]

Like the others, Henry Bérenger deplored the violence and
destruction of the Revolution.[30] He, too, rejected the idea of absolute equality, stating that the great error of the Revolution had
been to deny the existence and necessity of hierarchies.[31] Finally,
he also attacked anarchism and socialism for being inspired by
envy and hatred.[32]

Unlike the others, however, Henry Bérenger was a democrat
who believed in the democratic ideals of universal suffrage and
instruction. The goal of a democracy, he felt, was to assure a maximum of liberty with a maximum of fraternity.[33] Like Mazel, Bérenger
had little sympathy for the King and for the Ancien Régime, but
unlike Mazel, he believed in the necessity of the Revolution to put
an end to an unjust government. Bérenger spoke of a modification
of universal suffrage; in its present state, it contributed only to
parliamentary mediocrity and corruption.[34] In many ways, he agreed
with Maurice Barrès, who simultaneously inspired and irritated
him and was, like him, a democrat disenchanted with parliamentary democracy.[35]

While Mazel spoke of the excesses of collectivism and Rebell of
individualism, Bérenger sought to reconcile the two.[36] Although he
rejected the label socialist, associating it with Marxist theories as
interpreted by Jules Guesde, he clearly sympathized with what he
called "French idealist socialism," whose representatives included
Benoît Malon, Georges Renard, Eugène Fournière, Jean Jaurès,
and Maurice Barrès.[37] Their brand of socialism united solidarity
and individualism: "To be simultaneously *oneself and others*, there
can be no ideal more magnificent to propose to the individual!"[38]
Bérenger detested the "plutocracy," which consecrated the oppres-
sion of one man by another.[39] Although he felt sympathy for socialists, who sought to ameliorate working conditions, he disapproved

of their strictly economic and political solutions, claiming that until socialism accepted the moral necessity of an aristocracy, it was doomed.[40]

Not only did literary intellectuals of the avant-garde fear both overcrowding in the literary field and the tastes of the new public, which resulted from the establishment of democracy, but they also feared competition from the republican university, which sought to create its own intellectual elites. Traditional hierarchies in French society were challenged and displaced as the new republican regime sought to supplant old elites based on birth and wealth with its own university-trained, meritocratic elites. In such a society, knowledge increasingly became equated with power, thereby contributing to a heightened concern for the role of the intellectual, along with an interest in the institutions that formed the intellectual and dispensed "culture."

The 1880s and 1890s were "shaken by acute social conflict in education," in large part as a result of sweeping changes that took place in the educational system, not only in the primary schools, but also at the secondary and university levels.[41] Inspired simultaneously by a genuine desire for national renewal and a fear of social disorder, republican politicians and their academic allies sought to provide civic education for all, including the masses, and to form and train republican elites.[42]

While democratic liberals believed in equality of political and civic rights, they did not at all envision a leveling of social, economic, and intellectual differences, although they did seek to increase social mobility and promote social solidarity. No less than conservatives, they believed in the necessity of moral and intellectual elites in society. Unlike their traditional counterparts, however, republican elites were more broadly based, if not completely open. Philosopher Alfred Fouillée, whose ideas were extremely influential in republican circles, felt that competition and natural selection would lead to the formation of natural elites of talent.[43]

When republicans spoke of training elites, they thought of the minority of students who attended the secondary schools and the university, not of the lower classes. Indeed, it was disunity within the elite which most worried liberals of the late nineteenth century rather than disunity between the masses and the elite.[44] Although they made some concessions to social mobility within the secondary system, including the introduction of a modern option for the baccalaureate, they maintained the traditional separation between the primary and secondary systems. Enrollments in secondary education thus remained relatively stable during the late nineteenth century.[45]

The most dramatic of the republican reforms affected university education. A series of laws enacted between 1885 and 1896 led to the emergence of something like the modern research university as we know it. For most of the nineteenth century in France, the faculties of letters and sciences were used for grading baccalaureate exams; they had no curriculum of their own, nor did they have their own students. The republican reforms, which led to the creation of the "new Sorbonne," reorganized the faculties into sixteen universities, which were then given increased financial and curricular independence. Such measures led to the development of closed courses and the enrollment of students.[46] Indeed, the republicans sought to increase enrollments and promote social mobility by providing scholarships to students from the *nouvelles couches* [newly emergent social groups] of Gambetta fame—from the commercial and industrial middle classes as well as from the lower middle classes.[47] Thus, although secondary enrollments remained relatively stable at this time, France witnessed a phenomenal growth in university enrollments, especially in sciences and letters, the rate of increase being the greatest from 1876 to 1901.[48]

For some, these reforms went too far, while for others, they did not suffice since by isolating primary-level education from secondary and higher education, they fell far short of the open, meritocratic society of republican rhetoric. The dramatic increase in enrollments, however, was viewed with alarm by critics on both sides of the political spectrum. Barrès and Bérenger deplored the fact that the state school system turned out students at such an alarming rate that many, who were obliged to earn a living, were unable to find jobs. Instead of dispensing learning, the state educational system had become a bureaucratic machine, which had no purpose but to perpetuate itself.[49] Students, obsessed with competitive examinations (*concours*), were fit only for jobs in the bureaucracy. Rigid uniformity stifled creativity, and created arid individuals, isolated from both their social origins and regional roots. Thus, the state school system had failed to live up to its mission to enlighten and educate.

Les Déracinés told the story of seven young *bacheliers* from Barrès's native Lorraine and their experiences in Paris, where they had come to seek their fame and fortune. The novel explicitly stated that those who did not possess sufficient economic capital should not attempt to gain access to the bourgeoisie through the acquisition of

cultural capital. The poorer students in Barrès's novel constituted
not a "democracy on the rise" but a "degraded aristocracy."[50] Those
best equipped to deal with the uprooting influences of philosophy
teacher Bouteiller's teachings, along with life in Paris, came from
well-to-do families. Given such a conservative message, Barrès could
no longer claim the label "socialist." His path had clearly diverged
from that of disciples like Léon Blum, who reluctantly acknowledged this distance in his review of *Les Déracinés*, published in *La
Revue blanche* in 1897.[51]

Although Bérenger's writings on the "intellectual proletariat"
seem to echo Barrès, a closer examination of his work reveals a
clear distinction between his views and those of Barrès.[52] In his
article on the "intellectual proletariat," Bérenger was careful to
distinguish between bohemians and *déclassés*, who were outcasts
of bourgeois society, and an intellectual proletariat, which was
comprised of men born poor (the sons of peasants, workers, and
petty civil servants), who sought to enter the ranks of the bourgeoisie via the university system. These men, whose economic resources
were not commensurate with their cultural capital, ended up as
"candidates for hunger."[53] Bérenger feared that these men would
either be subjugated by the "plutocracy," as was the case of his hero
Raoul Rozel in *La Proie*, or become dupes of such revolutionary
movements as anarchism. He pointed to bomb-thrower Emile Henry
as the real life example of the latter case.[54]

Bérenger, who believed that the "intellectual proletariat" was
an international problem, viewed it as a by-product of modern
democracy. The French Revolution, which abolished corporatism,
had opened the liberal professions to the people by establishing a
competitive, meritocratic system. Such a system created a bureaucratic mentality and accounted for the overproduction of *diplômés*,
which resulted in an "intellectual proletariat."[55]

Bérenger did not advocate turning back the clock by abolishing
this system; such a solution, he claimed, would be far worse than
the problem itself.[56] Indeed, he believed in the continued mission of
the university in a free society. Moreover, unlike Barrès, he advocated continuing the practice of scholarships in order to insure that
France's intellectual aristocracy remained an open one.[57] Finally,
he lamented the fact that the salaries of occupants of the liberal
professions had not kept up with the cost of living during the
course of the century such that only those with sufficient independent means could afford to accede to the liberal professions. He
castigated the government for creating false hopes and expecta-
tions it could not meet by granting scholarships without assuring

that enough jobs would be available after students completed their studies. The people were being duped into believing that the university system was truly open.[58]

Bérenger proposed to discourage mediocre students who entered the university to escape military service since an 1891 law granted dispensation from military service to holders of university degrees.[59] Under this law, these men were required to serve only one of three years of obligatory military service. Bérenger claimed that this dispensation encouraged many who would have entered other professions into "hiding" out in the university milieu in preparation for careers for which they were ill-suited.[60] Unlike Barrès, he criticized the militarism which made army service obligatory.[61]

Bérenger's suggestion to abolish this dispensation would perhaps limit the numbers of students entering the university, but it is not clear how he would actually prevent "mediocre" students from attending since the university was open to all those who had completed the baccalaureate. Although the fear of an "intellectual proletariat" was shared by intellectuals on both the Left and Right, their remedies differed markedly.

One thing they could agree on, despite their differing political opinions, was a belief in the superior man. In his 20 December 1894 editorial for *La Cocarde*, Barrès spoke of the "usefulness of heroes," whom he called "sublime educators." According to Henri Mazel, only heroes had made the world progress. Hugues Rebell, a great admirer of Nietzsche, agreed.[62] Even the republican Henry Bérenger insisted on the need for superior men, especially in the midst of a democracy, since the hero only combated democracy in order to improve it.[63]

One should not think that intellectuals associated with the anarchist and socialist movements eschewed a belief in an intellectual elite. In an article entitled "L'Art et l'anarchie," Adolphe Retté warned against sacrificing Art to the masses, to whom he referred as "a massive brute," since their triumph meant the end of any aristocracy, especially an intellectual aristocracy.[64] Retté also spoke of the duty of the poet to affirm the only legitimate aristocracy, that of the "Idea."[65] Moreover, he called on Poets to act as both Hercules and Prometheus.[66] This idea of an elite was echoed by poet Francis Vielé-Griffin, who told artists they formed part of an elite whose mission it was to serve humanity. As for Paul Adam, whose diatribes against the bourgeoisie were frequent, he advocated the reign of an intellectual aristocracy.[67] The idea of an elite was thus not always viewed in opposition to equality; equality meant an equality of access, not necessarily of abilities or talent.

While all of these individuals spoke of the need for an elite, specifically an intellectual elite, they did not all define the word in the same way—neither its composition nor its recruitment. They disagreed, too, on its relationship to other groups in society as well as to the state. The words elite and aristocracy had undergone a transformation in the late nineteenth century; they had not necessarily lost their traditional meanings, but henceforth, one could also speak of a republican "elite" or "aristocracy." The term elite, in particular, was devoid of the class connotations of such older expressions as "enlightened classes," "notables," and "ruling classes."[68] Moreover, the vagueness of the term elite accounted for its ubiquity as well as for the confusion of usage.

Most of the writers examined here used the words "aristocracy" and "elite" interchangeably, the notable exceptions being Maurras, who preferred elite to aristocracy, and Maurice Barrès, who rejected the term "intellectual aristocracy," while advocating aristocratic principles in both society and art.[69] Barrès did not criticize the idea of an intellectual elite but rather the belief that such an "intellectual aristocracy" was morally superior to the common man.[70]

Since Rebell called for a union of the aristocracies of birth, wealth, and intellect, he thereby acknowledged the legitimacy of certain traditional elites. Similarly, Charles Maurras believed that one could not become a hero; heroes, poets, and aristocrats were born, not made.[71]

Like Rebell, Mazel delineated three types of aristocracies, but he defined them as follows: "*aristes* [a special term of his] of will," kings and warriors; "*aristes* of love," saints, and finally, "*aristes* of intellect," who included savants, artists, poets, and thinkers.[72] On the other hand, Mazel, along with Bérenger, defined aristocracy in a more broad sense, making clear that theirs was an open aristocracy with open recruitment. Mazel was careful to distinguish his meaning of aristocracy from its traditional definition:

> Is it necessary to repeat that we view the word Aristocracy in its heroic sense and not in its noble or governmental one? ... there are many types of aristocracies, of race, of birth, of religion, of political sect, and even of the soul ... However ... we conceive of aristocracy only as a heroism, as a super-humanity of the soul, an exaltation of the heart, of the mind or of will.[73]

Bérenger, too, dismissed the traditional aristocracies of birth and wealth as completely out of step with the times,[74] proclaiming that the future aristocracy would be above all open: "constantly renewed," it would "admit no other heredity than that of intelligence, no other privileges than those of genius."[75] For Bérenger, the only legitimate aristocracy was an intellectual aristocracy:

> The Best today are neither the best armed, nor the richest, nor the most pious: they are the most intelligent. It is they who lead the world and change nature. They constitute the sole legitimate aristocracy.[76]

Bérenger's colleague on *La Cocarde*, the art critic Camille Mauclair agreed that the aristocracy of thought was the only one worthy of the name.[77]

These writers placed their faith in an intellectual aristocracy as an antidote to what they described as contemporary decadence due to the lack of energy in society. Writers from both ends of the political spectrum—anarchists and socialists, as well as conservatives—shared a belief in the decline of France and sought to restore the honor and dignity of their country. Although they differed on the manner in which this regeneration should be accomplished, they all felt that in her quest for political freedom and material comforts, France had lost sight of a national ideal. Indeed, Alphonse Germain ventured that French society was "putrified" by a "moral syphilis."[78]

In one of the first issues of *La Cocarde*, Barrès wrote that Karl Marx was right to signal the importance of economic emancipation but wrong to affirm that this constituted total emancipation. Human beings also needed ideas to live.[79] Rebell agreed with the necessity of an ideal, declaring that the union of three aristocracies had no meaning without a guiding principle.[80]

Mazel and Bérenger, both Catholics who criticized the contemporary state of the Catholic Church, nevertheless deplored the loss of religious spirit during the course of the nineteenth century. Mazel, who admired Frédéric Le Play and Gabriel Tarde, agreed with Bérenger that the social question was a moral one.[81] All of these writers agreed on the necessity of an ideal as well as on who should be responsible for this ideal. "This ideal, generator of vast works and which unites in one and the same undertaking the multitude of humans, this necessary ideal, it is the intellectual who will one day present it to the world," wrote Rebell.[82] Camille Mauclair felt that artists were the guarantors of national honor; they represented the nation's conscience.[83] Barrès, who was somewhat equivocal, agreed nevertheless that the goal of the intellectual was to raise all of humanity to an intellectual state:

If by "intellectual" one means a man who has had the good fortune to receive a complete education, let us remember that the real problem is to elevate all of humanity to intellectuality, to make all participate in a civilization which, up to this time, in our harsh society, has only been open to the happy few....[84]

Similarly, Adolphe Retté called on poets to combat the "Authority" of traditional society and secure for all of humanity the material, moral, and intellectual benefits which accrued only to a minority at the present time.[85]

Bérenger designated the great artist as the supreme aristocrat because he spoke in the name of humanity; this "man of genius," declared Bérenger, would become the "new priest of the soul."[86] Moreover, he thought that the university should be the primary place of recruitment and formation of an intellectual aristocracy, calling it "the repository and creator of a national ideal."[87] Bérenger, unlike many literary intellectuals, especially conservative ones, did not contest the state's right to form elites but rather the way in which they were recruited and formed.

A strong sense of generational loyalty linked all of these writers, who appealed to their cohorts to restore France to her glory. In an article entitled "Sursum Corda," Mazel exhorted his peers to action:

We wanted to send out a warning cry, an urgent appeal to all the rising young generation . . . Let us be men, let us arm our peers and share a common self-respect . . . let us each exalt our own being and allow our fellow man to exalt his own![88]

Camille Mauclair spoke in similar terms:

During the last ten years, there has appeared in France a generation of free minds, of individuals resolved to protect the aristocracy of thought . . . that one must defend against egalitarianism. . . .

According to Mauclair, this generation, unlike its predecessors, was concerned about moral issues: "This generation too was preoccupied with its moral liberation, attempting to maintain the dignity of its esthetic, and to create consciences."[89] As for Maurras, although he deplored the anarchist tendencies of certain members of his generation, he also felt that France's moral salvation could come from other members of this generation. Finally, Henry Bérenger, who saw Barrès as a predecessor rather than as a contemporary, also appealed to his generation to find a solution to France's ills.[90]

Implicit or explicit in all of these declarations was a sense of cohesion, of belonging not only to an intellectual generation, but also to a sociological group: of intellectuals. Writing in *La Cocarde*, Mauclair called upon his intellectual peers to unite:

> Think of the strength at your disposal, and do not act in isolation. Your language, your expression will be your own, but the time has come for the desire for intellectual individualism and independence to become universal: attach yourself spiritually to those who can help you.[91]

Mauclair was not alone; fellow litterateur Alphonse Germain called on "intellectuals," whom he defined as writers and artists, to form "a solid alliance . . . a Hanseatic league."[92] Such cohesion is not surprising, especially among avant-garde collaborators of the "little magazines."

These writers all concurred that the intellectual must act, even such future anti-Dreyfusards as Maurras and Rebell. The name of Maurras's group was after all "L'Action française." For Rebell, the model intellectual was involved in the national life of the time, not isolated in an ivory tower, a view echoed by literary anarchist Adolphe Retté.[93] Bérenger specifically stated that intellectuals should directly involve themselves in politics, pointing to the heroic examples of Lamartine and Hugo.[94] Barrès, as a litterateur who had entered politics, was an example (albeit flawed—for Bérenger) of Bérenger's ideal.

What form should action take? Did it involve direct involvement in politics, running for public office, as Bérenger suggested, or should the artist serve as propagandist? Although answers varied on this point, writers during this time sought to reconcile thought and action. As Bernard Lazare observed in a lecture on the writer and social art: "For some time now, one has had little choice but to recognize that the writer should play a role in society."[95]

In an interview with Jules Huret, published in 1893, Barrès claimed that literature and politics were not contradictory; moreover, he felt that politics should be conducted by men of thought. He did acknowledge, however, that his presence at the Palais Bourbon would not suffice to change the "disastrous inferiority of the parliamentary world."[96] Two years later, perhaps in light of his defeat in the 1893 legislative elections, Barrès continued to marry thought and action, but this time, he suggested that the artist could best "act" by inspiring ideas and shaping thought. Indeed, this constituted real action as opposed to the elaboration of electoral programs by professional politicians:

> In fact, to draft programs is not to act. To act is to modify, by an artistic work, the sensibilities of two or a thousand of one's contemporaries; better still, it is to bolster and join together agents of change, to help and to precipitate events.[97]

In an editorial "L'Intellectuel et la politique," published in *La Cocarde* on 24 February 1895, Barrès cited the examples of Hugo, Lamartine, and Chateaubriand, claiming that they had served their party as well as any politician—in fact, even better:

> They have served their parties far better, better than the most meticulous politicians who agitate daily. Herein lies their service. They give ideas the power to move people. Their words pulsate through crowds, make possible great days—and allow little men to rise to power.[98]

Mauclair shared similar sentiments although he expressed them in slightly different terms. He had once thought that artists should become "men of action" but now realized that by representing a national ideal, artists constituted a more powerful force and were more in tune with reality than the "men of action" who scorned them.[99] This concept of action is an important element of male identity at the fin de siècle and explains the pains writers took to illustrate that they in their own fashion were also men of action; witness Bernard Lazare's declaration: "To act is not only to act physically: to manipulate a rifle, a dagger or dynamite; there is also intellectual action. . . ."[100]

Although these writers wished to engage themselves in some form in politics, they all disdained professional politicians for their machinations; most of these writers, with the exception of Barrès, who had served as Deputy from Nancy, had no political experience and vowed resolutely to practice a form of "pure" politics. Representative of these writers were Emile Zola and Paul Adam, who declared themselves ready to enter the Chamber of Deputies, but maintained their intention to remain above politics—the former referring to "the ignoble political intrigues of professionals," the latter proclaiming: "I would try especially *to prevent such politicking.*"[101]

Even Barrès was somewhat equivocal, as the above statements illustrate. Although he viewed writers as superior to politicians, in a review of Henry Bérenger's *L'Aristocratie intellectuelle*, which he damned by describing as an idealistic work of a young man (he referred to Bérenger as one of "the brothers of Bernadette of Lourdes"), Barrès clearly distinguished himself from such "idealistic" intellectuals. Politics required discipline and cooperation:

> In order to engage in politics, one must submit to a certain discipline, accept a tradition, follow tactics, gather support. Experience in such matters is decisive. In politics, one cannot afford to be a solitary man.[102]

Barrès obviously saw himself as a man of letters with principles vis-à-vis his fellow deputies and a practical man of politics with regard to his literary colleagues.

Evident in all these statements, made by writers of different political persuasions, is jealousy of politicians, who wielded so much power in the new democratic society. Writers sought to rival this power, even while disparaging it. An indignant Henry Fèvre (1864), writing about the candidacy of litterateur Henry Becque, could not understand why the public mocked the candidate, whom he viewed as intelligent, honest, and serious. Why should the public prefer an industrial to a man of thought, he wondered?[103] Such apprehension reinforced the exaltation of words and ideas by writers; in this way, they could present themselves as an alternative to politicians—by emphasizing their role as public spokesmen. They were conscious, too, of representing a new moral authority which would supplant that of the priest.[104]

These writers were sincere about the mission of the intellectual. They agreed on the moral "disinterestedness" of the intellectual as well as on the duty of the intellectual to assure what Bérenger referred to as "the health of the social body."[105] They differed, however, on the nature of the ideal to be defended. Rebell called on intellectuals to raise their voices against democracy in order to convince the aristocracies of birth and wealth to ally themselves with the intellectual elite.[106] Maurras and Mazel both objected to the alliance of intelligence and money, fearing that intelligence would be subjugated by wealth. Mazel believed that the intellectual, far from appealing to an aristocracy of birth and wealth, should appeal to all people. For Maurras, before a nation could be aristocratic or democratic, it had to exist. He felt that the French nation had not yet been born and exhorted intellectuals to unite to restore the monarchy and purify the nation of its foreign elements.[107] Barrès, too, exalted the preservation of the nation above all but disagreed with Maurras's belief in the necessity of a monarchy. Bérenger, who called for the reconciliation of science, religion, and democracy, was for this reason the most unusual of all of the writers examined here.[108] In an era in which republican anti-clericals were pitted against clerical anti-republicans, such a task was well near impossible.

Although the differences between intellectuals who went on to become Dreyfusards and anti-Dreyfusards were visible beforehand, they did not crystallize until the Dreyfus Affair. What is striking in these texts on aristocracy, written by writers of varying political tendencies, is not so much their differences but rather their similarities. Conservative intellectuals and their anarchist and socialist counterparts agreed on the decadence of contemporary French society. Both groups opposed parliamentary democracy as incarnated by the Third Republic, criticizing its inefficacy and corruption.

Some intellectuals opposed the advent of democracy itself and/ or its attempt to create new elites. Many writers—not exclusively conservatives—were highly suspicious of the new state intellectuals, in particular, university professors. Such a division corresponds neither with left/right distinctions nor with the various sociological analyses of the Dreyfus Affair.

In *Teachers, Writers, Celebrities*, Régis Debray has argued that the debate which culminated in the Dreyfus Affair pitted the new republican university against the world of letters, the scholarship boys against the "héritiers," the Left Bank against the Right Bank.[109] Such a dichotomy is much too neat; it implies the presence of two clearly delineated groups. Christophe Charle's analysis, which consists of a "pôle dominé," "pôle dominant," and an intermediate group, is more satisfying. In this scenario, the avant-garde is opposed to the establishment, newer disciplines to older, more consecrated ones. Neither of these two analyses, however, adequately accounts for the heterogeneity within the Dreyfusard and anti-Dreyfusard camps, nor for the points of commonality between various members of the two groups.[110]

The literary avant-garde provides the key to a better understanding of the Dreyfus Affair. Although a major portion of the literary avant-garde joined forces with the republican university— especially with those who espoused new disciplines like sociology—to combat the literary establishment, a significant minority of these individuals, including Barrès and Maurras, allied themselves with their former literary foes against the Dreyfusards. Within the Dreyfusard camp, there existed a tension between litterateurs and university professors while in the anti-Dreyfusard camp, this tension was essentially, although not exclusively, one that pitted younger litterateurs of the avant-garde against older members of the literary establishment.[111]

It must be remembered that there were not two groups which laid claim to intellectual legitimacy at this time, but three, not only the university professors and the literary establishment, but also the literary avant-garde. All three groups proclaimed themselves the true "intellectual elite," castigating the other two as false elites.[112]

Intellectuals associated with the anarchist and socialist movements, who called for a more open and just society, were disgruntled with the regime because of the contradiction between republican meritocratic theory and practice. Yet paradoxically, even among those who clamored for a more democratic society, there was a rejection of certain consequences of such a society: overproduction of literary works, the influx of mediocre writers who produced on a mass scale for financial gain, and the rise of an "intellectual proletariat." Writers from both sides of the political spectrum lamented the degradation of the status of the writer and sought to restore the dignity and grandeur of this figure in society—hence the preoccupation with an intellectual elite. Despite their differing political perspectives, they shared a common belief in an elitist culture. Their rejection of the commercial marketplace and mass culture was in keeping with their desire to maintain "pure" and aristocratic values.

All believed in the notion of the intellectual not only as a sociological concept, but also as a vocation. They saw themselves as part of a group, which had both the right and obligation to make pronouncements concerning issues of national importance.[113] Indeed, they looked to the intellectual elite to lead France toward salvation and regeneration. Despite declarations to the contrary during the Affair, even anti-Dreyfusard writers like Maurras and Barrès accepted and used the term "intellectual" as a substantive regularly before the Affair.

Pronouncements in the national arena represented a means by which intellectuals could carve out a position for themselves in a modern, democratic society. They sought to marry thought and action to demonstrate that they were not obsolete and that they could play a role in the new society. The ideal of an intellectual elite was a way of affirming their independence from political and economic elites, from which they were increasingly isolated. Avant-garde writers, as the most marginalized group, had the most to gain and lose in the new society. It is no accident that they led the way for intellectual involvement in the Dreyfus Affair, on both sides.

The dream of an "intellectual aristocracy" was also a means by which to assert their position vis-à-vis the rising masses. Conservative writers often defined themselves in opposition to the masses, whereas those associated with the anarchist and socialist movements insisted on their role as educators of these masses. Literary anarchist Adolphe Retté's comments in this matter are especially illuminating; he encouraged anarchist writers to devote themselves to "soothing" and educating the masses in order to protect them from the machinations of the bourgeoisie and also to defend the interests of writers.[114] Thus, both groups felt the need to control "the people" in some way, either by opposing or co-opting them.

Intellectuals did not always define "the people" in the same way. Eugen Weber notes that "the people" for Barrès meant the *nouvelles couches*, the upstarts who sought to accede to the bourgeoisie through the republican university.[115] Others clearly feared the proletariat.[116] Common to all, however, was the fear of a tyranny of the majority, of being overtaken by the "crowd", be it proletarian or lower middle class.[117]

The Dreyfus Affair may thus be viewed not only in function of the internal struggle for position and power in the intellectual milieu but also as an opportunity for intellectuals to assert their place in society with regard to other social groups. For similar reasons—in order to assure their own position in society—Dreyfusard and anti-Dreyfusard intellectuals chose to oppose or defend the parliamentary government. Conservative intellectuals felt their cause could best be served either by another "pure" Republic (as was the case for Barrès) or the monarchy (Maurras), while more progressive intellectuals, despite their quarrels with the bourgeois Republic, realized their only hope was to come to the aid of the beleaguered regime.

The involvement of intellectuals in the Affair, however, must not be viewed merely in function of their struggle for power both within and outside the intellectual milieu. The belief in an intellectual elite also represented, paradoxically, a desire to transcend divisions of class and rise above political parties, by rejecting distinctions of Left and Right in the name of intelligence. These writers sincerely believed in the exalted mission of the intellectual as a voice of the national conscience. The split that occurred during the Dreyfus Affair within the literary avant-garde had less to do with whether an artist should be involved in the life of the city than with what constituted appropriate action, along with the nature of the ideal to be defended. The Dreyfus Affair is thus revelatory not so much of the differences among intellectuals but instead an affirmation of their common belief in the power and authority of intellectuals to speak and act in the national arena. During the years leading up to the Affair, avant-garde writers had already advocated this position.

4

—◠◠◠—

The Jew as Intellectual, the Intellectual as Jew

Anti-Semitism was by origin a "popular" ideology, but in its modern form, it was elaborated by writers, journalists, and artists. While they were articulating general grievances, these anti-Semites were also expressing grievances peculiar to intellectuals.[1] Writers like Charles Maurras, Maurice Barrès, and Edouard Drumont, along with such artists as Adolphe Willette, Jean-Louis Forain, and Caran d'Ache feared for their status in a modern, democratic society. Their vision, which corresponded to a traditional, aristocratic order, rooted in a profoundly Catholic culture, was threatened by the new state intellectual, associated with the hated Third Republic.

These "traditionalists," who sought to maintain traditional Catholic values artificially, may more accurately be called neo-traditionalists. Given that they expressed their traditionalism in a thoroughly modern manner, they themselves represented a movement of modernism on a cultural level. For neo-traditionalists, however, it was the Jew who represented the ultimate symbol of modern, democratic society. Jewish successes were equated with the triumph of the new republican order. As many anti-Semites noted, with the advent of the Third Republic, more Jews than ever were visible in the fields of art, literature, journalism, and academe. Furthermore, noted Jewish intellectuals, in particular, Emile Durkheim of the Sorbonne and Henri Bergson of the Collège de France, were seen as pillars of the republican establishment, as "official" intellectuals who had risen to positions of power and fame via the republican university system.

Although the fin de siècle was a period of dechristianization—measured by a decline in Church attendance—France still remained for many French men and women, as it had for centuries, a Catholic society. With the establishment of the Third Republic came to power a secular regime which created new politico-administrative elites, doing so moreover through a state-run educational system. This new regime sought to "de-Christianize" public space, not only through the passage of the Jules Ferry school laws, which supplanted religious moral authority, but also through the establishment of civil marriage and the legalization of divorce—all of which led ultimately to the separation of church and state. Intolerant of social and political diversity, the republican state laid sole claim to national legitimacy and encroached increasingly on the lives of its citizens.

Supporters of the radical right-wing nationalism that emerged out of the Boulanger Affair viewed the republican state and its allies, which included a significant number of Protestants and Jews, as the avowed enemies of the "true France."[2] They resented and feared the efforts of the Third Republic to diminish the influence of the Catholic Church not only in the political sphere, but also in the social and cultural realms.

Anti-Semitism, as Pierre Birnbaum has forcefully argued, was most widespread in countries like France and Germany which had strong states. Fin-de-siècle France witnessed the development of a new type of political anti-Semitism that targeted Jews, who increasingly assumed functions of the state. In a sense, Drumont was a transitional figure, linking the older, nineteenth-century, economic strain of anti-Semitism, to the new political anti-Semitism of Barrès and especially of Maurras, which targeted both the republican, meritocratic, centralized state, and Jews, whose integration was a symbol of that state.[3] The French example, notes Birnbaum, is almost unique, not only because of the precocious development of a strong state in France, but moreover of one which adopted a universalist model of citizenship and relegated all particularisms, ethnic and religious, to the private sphere.

On the other hand, for Jews, whose integration into the national community rested precisely on this universalist model, the emergence of the state intellectual, who espoused rationalism and universality, was a means by which to integrate themselves into the mainstream of French society. It allowed them to transcend their Jewishness in favor of a universal ideal, thereby allowing them to reconcile their identities as Frenchmen and Jews. Jewish intellectuals like Léon Blum, Emile Durkheim, and Julien Benda were quick to seize upon the universal attributes of the state intellectual.[4] For both sides then, the birth of this modernist intellectual was emblematic of the quest for identity, both individual and national. For Jews, the modernist intellectual was a way to escape their marginality; for neo-traditionalists, this figure was a symbol of a new order which threatened to marginalize them.

The rise of anti-Semitism in France and the birth of the state intellectual are concomitant developments, both products of the emergence of a modern, democratic society. The two are inextricably linked, for in France especially, anti-Semitism was articulated first and foremost by writers and artists, who did a great deal to popularize its message. In no other country where anti-Semitism was present did it possess such a strong literary character. Anti-Semites in France were more interested in responding to political, social, and cultural developments than in developing racial theories.[5] Examined together, the development of anti-Semitism and the birth of the state intellectual shed light on the construction of French national identity during the late nineteenth century.

The aims of this chapter are twofold: first, to examine the ways in which neo-traditionalists viewed the state intellectual, and second, to study the manner in which assimilated Jews associated themselves with this new figure. To that end, "The Jew as Intellectual" will explore the attitudes of anti-Semitic writers toward the modernist intellectual. What were the concerns of writers and journalists, especially those of anti-Semites, with regard to the status of the writer, and how did they translate their fears of a modern, democratic society into a diatribe against Jews?

The "Intellectual as Jew" focuses on the writings of such assimilated Jewish intellectuals as Emile Durkheim, Bernard Lazare, Léon Blum, and Julien Benda. In what ways did they perceive themselves? How did they associate themselves with the modernist intellectual and reconcile their Jewish heritage with the universalist values articulated by this new figure? To what extent did anti-Semitic discourse shape the ideas of these intellectuals, and how did that construction have discursive parallels with certain anti-Semitic formulations? Such a study points not only to the inherent contradictions of assimilation, but also to the irony that anti-Semitism gained momentum at the height of the assimilation of French Jews.[6] Finally, this examination of the response of assimilated Jewish intellectuals to anti-Semitism presents the historian with valuable information on how anti-Semitism was experienced, thereby providing an index of its importance—not merely as an ideology—but as a social and cultural phenomenon in fin-de-siècle France.

The Jew as Intellectual

A great many writers, not only of the avant-garde, feared the decline in status of the writer and the rise of an "intellectual proletariat." Many resented the emergence of a new elite, promoted by the republican university. For some, this fear led to anti-Semitism. According to historian Robert Byrnes, the determining factor of the anti-Semitism of professional men was economic: "The depression which struck the French publishing industry in 1890 left behind also a generation of 'frustrated aesthetes,' of men who had grown to manhood in the 1870s and 1880s with visions of following the paths of Zola, Verne, Sainte-Beuve, Taine . . . to fame and fortune." In his view, these men, some of whom were driven to hack work, became anti-Semites (either sincere or purchased) while others became anarchists and socialists.[7]

Aside from the fact that being anarchist or socialist and anti-Semitic were not mutually exclusive—at least before the Affair—the impact of the crisis in the publishing industry, however real, constituted only one element in the development of anti-Semitism among writers and artists. Anti-Semites counted among their number not only Edouard Drumont, who could perhaps be characterized as marginal, but also successful, established individuals like Barrès and Maurras. More to the point, Maurras and Barrès were outside the new intellectual establishment. Economics certainly played a key role in the anti-Semitism of certain intellectuals, but equally important was the fear of neo-traditionalists of being displaced by the new state intellectual. To a great extent then, the anti-Semitism of neo-traditionalist writers and artists was the jealousy of one set of intellectuals for another.[8] Although their anti-Semitism intensified during the height of the Affair, it did exist beforehand and indeed helped to shape their own emerging consciousness as intellectuals during the 1890s, as the "true" voices of the nation, in opposition to those who spoke in the name of a France, which they viewed as both decadent and false.

Hugues Rebell's *Union des trois aristocraties*, examined in the last chapter, provides a good point of departure for a further exploration of contemporary attitudes concerning the status of the writer, since although he was a future anti-Dreyfusard, some of his views were shared by those who went on to become Dreyfusards. Furthermore, despite the fact that Rebell was a neo-traditionalist, he was not an anti-Semite, yet his views could easily be turned to anti-Semitic ends.

Rebell, like many writers of the time, deplored the current status of writers in French society. In *Union des trois artistocraties*, he wrote that the contemporary writer had become a "fabricant," an industrial producer. The more he produced, the more he was admired by his contemporaries.[9] Rebell felt that quality work was lost in the surfeit of published materials. Charles Maurras shared these ideas, which he developed in *L'Avenir de l'intelligence*, a collection of essays written for various newspapers during the 1890s and published in book form in 1905. He, too, lamented the "industrialization" of literature and the concomitant loss of literature as an "artisanal" endeavor:

> Well before the middle of the [nineteenth] century, they [writers] realized that one could set up a business, and so-called industrial literature was born. One made use of one's pen and one's thoughts, as one would his wheat or wine, copper or charcoal. To live by writing became "the sole motto. . . ."[10]

For Maurras, as for Rebell, the ideal was the aristocratic writer of the sixteenth and seventeenth centuries, when the prestige of the writer remained considerable yet was still subordinate to that of kings and princes.[11]

Maurice Barrès, too, deplored the degradation of the status of the writer in French society:

> During the course of this century . . . we have not witnessed a period whose intellectual misery is comparable to that in which we now live. We are impoverished in all the literary genres, or if you prefer, less rich, than were our fathers, except perhaps in journalism. . . .[12]

Only journalism, according to Barrès, lived up to the standards of the past. Yet even a journalist like Drumont, who viewed himself as a man of letters with a sacred trust, bemoaned the current status of the writer, observing indignantly that M. de la Rochefoucauld received the industrial Rothschild without inviting a writer like d'Hervilly, whose play was being staged at one of his *soirées*.[13] He also felt that new writers did not live up to the standards of old writers.[14]

According to all of these writers, the dominance of money in the literary world constituted the primary reason for this decline of the status of the writer. Drumont believed in the incorruptibility of the journalist, but deplored the venality of the manipulating, calculating editor: "The casual disregard of liquid capital vis-à-vis intellectual capital surpasses all that one could imagine."[15] He and his fellow litterateurs noted a debasement of the status of the writer not only because of an overproduction of materials, but also because the new writer, unlike the aristocratic writer, was not a *rentier* who dabbled in literature but an individual who earned his living from his pen. No wonder then that Emile Zola attracted the ire not only of the literary establishment, but also of members of the avant-garde, since both groups opposed the control of literature by the marketplace.[16]

Many writers resented what they saw as the degradation of contemporary manners by the demands of economics. Maurras declared that never had such coarseness defined daily life:

> A certain crudeness has entered into daily life. The moral situation of the French man of letters in 1905 is no longer what it was in 1850. The writer's reputation is lost. Writing everywhere, signing everything, assuming responsibility only for what one signs, working to give the impression that one is not the mouthpiece of a newspaper but of one's own thoughts. . . . Either too high or too low, the writer is the most displaced [*déclassé*] of beings.[17]

Drumont complained about the current disinterest for books and ideas: "The French no longer think, no longer have time to think, no longer know how to think; they only think via their newspaper, they have a brain made of paper."[18] He particularly deplored the disdain for books and ideas among the "gens du monde": "After books, what they hate the most are the men who write them. They understand the writer only as a well-informed illiterate. . . ."[19] Rebell, like the majority of writers, both conservative and progressive, lamented the tyranny of the bad taste of the "people king and judge—the people whose artistic ideal is café-concert songs and whose intellectual sustenance consists of newspapers that recount political scandals."[20] This statement could easily have been made by Paul Adam or Octave Mirbeau, two writers associated with the anarchist movement. Both sides criticized parliamentary democracy— most neo-traditionalists opposed democracy in principle while those professing anarchist/socialist views rejected bourgeois democracy.[21]

According to Rebell, the artist needed a public but he must not let it dictate his art. Moreover, he needed a cultivated public—

something that modern democracy could not offer him.[22] Maurras, too, felt that the contemporary writer, unlike the aristocratic writer, who was protected by a salon, an important personage or by an entire [aristocratic] class, was prey to the dictatorship of the people.[23] Drumont especially lamented the fact that the aristocracy, which had supported the writer during the Ancien Régime, had now become lazy, and more importantly, had been corrupted by its association with rich Jews. In his view, the aristocracy could no longer play the role of patron of the arts.[24] Although Rebell did not share Drumont's anti-Semitism, he blamed the advent of modern democracy for the dictatorship of the people in guiding public opinion and taste:

> The nineteenth century has thus realized the plebeians' dream: the triumph of individuals and the ruin of intellects. From the moment that all hierarchy disappears, from the moment that everyone has the right to express his opinion . . . all discernment is lost. Freedom of the press means slavery of thought, strength of all men means oppression of the best. In light of this explosion of democratic stupidity, it would be foolish to speak of a public because it does not exist.[25]

Such progressive writers as Adam and Mirbeau shared with neo-traditionalists the disdain of modern, parliamentary democracy, which they believed crushed individual liberty and creativity. They also feared the idea of the tyranny of the proletariat, proposed by Guesdist Socialists. They would not have agreed, however, with the idea of a hierarchical society proposed by Rebell. Nor would they have accepted Rebell's criticism that modern democracy had forsaken the public good in favor of the triumph of the individual.[26] For Mirbeau and Adam, the Revolution had not accomplished enough, whereas for neo-traditionalists, it had destroyed the organic order of French society.

Maurras took some of Rebell's arguments one step farther, developing an elaborate critique of French society since the Revolution and attributing what he viewed as the decline of France to the advent of mass democracy. He blamed in particular writers for this state of affairs, stating that the writer had usurped the role of both the aristocrat and the priest. Indeed, he believed that currently writers were overrated and overadulated in French society. Maurras especially deplored the role of the *philosophes*, whom he saw as outlaws and revolutionaries. Not only had they assumed the role of kings and priests, but they were also responsible for the destruction of the French Revolution. The real successor to the Bourbons, wrote Maurras, was the man of letters.[27]

From a generalized critique of the role of writers in a modern, democratic society, Maurras, Barrès, and other neo-traditionalists proceeded to attack the relationship of the modernist intellectual and the state. Maurras began *L'Avenir de l'intelligence* with a diatribe against the mediocre but representative writer who was flattered by the honors accorded him by the republic.[28] Maurras believed that while the state decorated intellectuals, these honors were also a means by which to control them: "The monied-State administers, gilds and decorates Intellect but it also muzzles and hypnotizes it." One could not remain impartial if one were directly responsible to the state; such a position only encouraged obsequiousness.[29]

Barrès and Maurras may have disagreed on the form the state should take—republic or monarchy—but both agreed on the pernicious influence of state centralization on local culture, as their decentralization campaign in *La Cocarde* in 1894–1895 illustrates. Given their view of the state, it is not surprising that Maurras and Barrès should oppose state control of education, specifically the republican school system, which they felt served as a conduit to high functions in the state. Control of education, which meant the power to mold future citizens and to shape a certain vision of national identity, was of great interest to both republicans and their opponents. In Maurras's view, the *grandes écoles* dominated French society: "Letters and Sciences lead to all things. Count how many graduates of the Ecole Normale, the Ecole des chartes and of the Ecole des hautes études have become parliamentary presidents, government ministers."[30]

Barrès claimed that a republican education, a product of centralization, took youths away from their "patrie" and deprived them of the support of their local community. Writing in *La Cocarde* of 8 September 1894, he compared the plight of the worker, oppressed by the industrial, to that of bourgeois youths, forced to study the "mechanistic" school programs at the *lycée* and the university, developing this premise more fully in *Les Déracinés*, published three years later. Such sentiments also found echo in his *Cahiers*:

> We must watch over the university. It contributes to the destruction of French principles, to our intellectual ruin [*décérébrer*]; on the pretext that it makes of us citizens of humanity, it also uproots us from our soil, from our national ideal.[31]

Barrès and Maurras both challenged the contemporary domination of Kantian thought in the school system, an influence they
depicted as alien, specifically German, and therefore pernicious.
They developed this anti-Kantian theme repeatedly in their writings, both public and private, before, during, and after the Affair.
The essence of their remarks was subsequently developed into a
systematic attack against the entire republican university system
by Action française member Pierre Lasserre in *La doctrine officielle
de l'Université*, published in 1913.[32]

Barrès and Maurras both opposed Kantian thought for its
promotion of excessive "individualism." The two men believed that
Kantianism contributed to the "uprooting" of French youths. For
Maurras, Kantianism led first to their espousal of anarchism—
which he equated with anarchy and cosmopolitanism—and then of
Dreyfusism.[33] In *Scènes et doctrines du nationalisme*, Barrès wrote
that he was lucky to have escaped the anarchical influence of
Kantianism, given that he had been corrupted by its humanist
teachings at the university.[34]

Such neo-traditionalists as Barrès and Maurras also opposed
the universality and abstraction of Kantian thought. In *Les
Déracinés*, Barrès's target was the philosophy teacher Auguste
Burdeau, model for the fictional Bouteiller of the novel, who taught
his students the Kantian principle: "to act in such a fashion so that
one's actions could serve as a model for all men in the same situation."[35] Such a claim contradicted Barrès's belief in relativity. How
could one speak of "The Rights of Man?" wondered Barrès. Which
rights of which men, at what time? During the time of the Dreyfus
Affair, he asked: "What is Justice? There are just relations at a
given time, between given objects."[36]

Just as man was not a universal being, so, too, was there no
one "Truth." According to Barrès, there were many truths; indeed,
what men defined as Truth was their own personal truth, born of
their way of seeing the world, which in turn was shaped by their
background and milieu:

> What we call truth is really a way of seeing that we inherit
> from our parents, our childhood, and from various educa-
> tive settings and which as a result possesses such a senti-
> mental value that we attribute to it the look and feel of
> simple fact.[37]

One must judge, concluded Barrès, in relative terms.[38] From this
perspective, Barrès attacked republican philosophy professors who

sought to inculcate their pupils with a sense of absolute Truth. Rather they should teach French Truth, a version of the truth which would be the most useful to the French nation.[39]

Barrès also criticized the abstraction of Kantian philosophy. In the place of abstractions, university professors should deal with reality. Writing about *Les Déracinés* in his *Cahiers*, he remarked: "In my first chapter, 'Bouteiller in Nancy,' have I not shown that this abstract man who wishes to create *social elements* creates *individuals*." Barrès also criticized Lucien Herr, librarian of the Ecole Normale, for propagating an abstract vision of the "patrie."[40]

Charles Maurras developed an even more elaborate critique of Kantian philosophy, basing it on his theory of the decline of France since the Revolution. Unlike Barrès, Maurras was not a republican; he viewed the Revolution and the advent of democracy as having contributed greatly to France's current plight. He differed from his mentor Taine in that he saw the French Revolution not as an excess of the classical, rational spirit, but rather as an excess of the foreign, German influence of Romanticism.[41]

Maurras deplored the fact that his own generation had been nourished on German thought, even in the wake of the French defeat in the Franco-Prussian War. One of the manifestations of this Romanticism was the teaching of Kant in the *lycée* and in the university.[42] Indeed, Maurras, like Barrès, viewed Kantianism as the official "religion" of the Third Republic and held the republican state responsible for the propagation of Kantian theories.[43]

Barrès not only linked Kantianism to the university, and thus the state, he also accused this philosophy of creating the state intellectual, a figure which he defined as an enemy of French society:

> This schoolroom Kantianism of ours claims to gauge universal man, abstract man without consideration of individual differences. . . . The philosophy that the state teaches is primarily responsible if people find it intellectual to disdain the national unconscious and exercise intellect in pure abstraction, detached from the real world. A verbalism that distances children from any reality, a Kantianism that uproots them from the land of their dead, an overproduction of diplomas . . . this is what we have criticized the University for, this is what makes its product, the "intellectual," an enemy of society.[44]

Not only did the state intellectual advocate the Kantian principles of individualism, abstraction, and universality, he was a "déraciné" who threatened the organic order of the nation.

From the intellectual and the state, specifically the republican state, the idea of the Jew as representative of this modernist intellectual was but one step away. Maurras lamented the fact that the republican state was dominated by foreign elements, which he defined as follows: "Masonic organization, foreign colony, Protestant society, Jewish nation, such are the four elements that have increasingly developed in modern France since 1789."[45] Maurras claimed that these "alien" elements had created a new elite which had supplanted the traditional, aristocratic, Catholic elites of France.[46] Indeed, just as Jews were criticized for pretensions to being the "chosen" people, so, too, were state intellectuals accused of establishing themselves as a new elite. During the Affair, Barrès accused Dreyfusard intellectuals, many of whom were university professors, of comprising an "obscure elite."[47]

These new elites, according to neo-traditionalists, reigned over Paris, in all centers of intellectual and cultural activity, not only in the university but also in the salons, in publishing and in the press.[48] Drumont expressed his fear for a society in which "intellectual powers" were obliged to defend themselves from "shady dealings," thereby linking economic concerns with intellectual ones.[49] He and other neo-traditionalists were obsessed by the "domination" of Protestants and especially Jews in French society.

For Maurras, Jews and Protestants were the pillars of the republican regime. Indeed, both Jews and Protestants were highly visible not only in the republican school reforms, but also in legislation involving divorce and girls' schooling, thus supplying Maurras and others with ample ammunition.

Anti-Semitism, of course, had little to do with the actual numeric strength of Jews in French society, since Jews represented a small minority of the French population of the time—roughly eighty thousand individuals out of a population of thirty-nine million, thereby representing less than 1 percent of the entire population.[50] There were far fewer Jews in France than in neighboring countries—180,000 in England and 600,000 in Germany.[51] Moreover, there were a great many more Protestants, whose numbers equalled roughly 500,000, than Jews in France. Under the lay republic, however, many Jews rose to prominent positions in the army, politics, and high civil service, as well as in the arts and academe. The number of eminent Jews in these fields was much greater than their relative number in the French population. The turn of the century was in many respects a golden age for French Jews. While earlier generations had pursued careers in commerce and industry, the members of the generation which came of age during the fin de siècle increasingly chose careers in the liberal professions, in literature, the arts, the theater, and the press.

Jews were particularly prominent as cultural middlemen, that is, as reviewers, critics, and art collectors.[52] Indeed, the critic Albert Thibaudet observed that the literary generation of 1890 was the first in which Jews occupied such an important place, citing the young Jews of the Lycée Condorcet, the Ecole Normale, and *La Revue blanche*.[53] Moreover, significant numbers of Jews were at the forefront of avant-garde movements, not only in the literary and artistic avant-garde—witness the role of *La Revue blanche*—but also in academic disciplines, as the examples of Emile Durkheim and Lucien Lévy-Brul illustrate. Although these Jews represented exceptions within the French Jewish community, they were represented as the "typical," "radical" Jew in the popular imagination.[54]

Increasing numbers of Jews entered politics and civil service as well. Léon Blum, André Spire, and Paul Grunbaum-Ballin were among the first Jews to enter the prestigious Conseil d'Etat; under the Third Republic, there were many more Jewish soldiers in the army. Significant numbers of Jews attended the *grandes écoles*: the Ecole Normale, the Ecole Polytechnique, and especially the newly created Ecole pratique des hautes études. Neo-traditionalists felt threatened by the new society which privileged learning and competition over heredity. Jews with their long tradition of intellectual pursuits were adept at the system of competitive exams. Indeed, Emile Durkheim claimed that historically Jews were much more interested in education than Catholics or Protestants not only because it enabled them to be better armed for struggle, but also because it was a means of offsetting the unfavorable position imposed on them by society.[55] Jews like the Reinach brothers, who were derisively depicted by anti-Semites as "bêtes à concours" (competitive workhorses), were held up as examples both in the Jewish community and in anti-Semitic circles.[56] Jews were highly visible at the Sorbonne as well, among them Léon Brunschvicg, Lucien Lévy-Bruhl, Victor Basch, and Emile Durkheim.

The higher visibility of Jews served to exacerbate anti-Semitic passions. Such sentiments ran especially high in Paris. Not only did more Jews live here than anywhere else in France, especially after the influx of Jews from Alsace and Lorraine in the wake of the German occupation, but Paris, as the center of French cultural, political, and social life, was also the headquarters of the national press.[57]

It must be noted that manifestations of anti-Semitism increased dramatically during the 1880s and 1890s not only in the popular press but in novels and other books as well. According to Robert Byrnes, literature attacking Jews rose from an annual average of less than one from 1879 to 1885, to fifteen in 1886, the year of *La France juive*'s publication, fourteen in 1887, nine in 1888, and twenty in 1889.[58] Although the Jewish moneylender was a stock figure in nineteenth-century fiction, as was the "seductive Jewess," the numbers of novels published in the 1890s with such anti-Semitic depictions were much greater than before. Among them were Georges Ohnet's *Nemrod et Cie* (1892), Paul Bourget's *Cosmopolis* (1893), and Eugène-Melchior de Vogüé's *Les Morts qui parlent*, (1899).[59] Anti-Semitic sterotypes could also be found in the works of Léon Bloy, the Goncourt brothers, and of course in the best-selling popular novels of Gyp, who undoubtedly carried these representations to new depths.

Anti-Semitism was more prevalent in certain socio-professional groups in French society, not only among those belonging to the liberal professions, including writers and journalists, but also among the aristocracy and upper bourgeosie, in the army, among small shopkeepers and among practicing Catholics.[60] Although several of the major republican newspapers condemned the book, among them *Le Figaro*, *Le Temps*, and *Le Journal des débats*, Drumont's *La France juive* did a great deal to spread the anti-Semitic message. Sentiments were so widespread by the 1890s that they even found their way into the works of those who were sympathetic to Jews like Emile Zola, who represented the Jewish moneylender in his novel *Paris* (1898) and Paul Adam, a member of the *Revue blanche* circle, married to a Jewish woman, whose novel *Le Mystère des foules* (1895) depicted avaricious Jews whose venality eventually led to a war with Germany.

One must not, however, judge by modern-day standards. There existed much inconsistency in attitudes; witness the example of Barrès. Despite his anti-Semitism, which predated the Dreyfus Affair—as his articles in *Le Courrier de l'Est* or even in *La Cocarde*, to which a number of Jewish intellectuals contributed, attest—Barrès was friendly with the Jewish members of the *Revue blanche* circle. Such inconsistency was undoubtedly confusing for his Jewish admirers, among them Léon Blum, who was still shocked by Barrès's anti-Dreyfusard stance, even though the latter had published *Les Déracinés* a year earlier. It took the Dreyfus Affair for attitudes to harden and for the battle lines to be more clearly drawn.

Anti-Semitic writers and artists concentrated on the "pernicious" influence of certain highly visible Jews and Protestants, who served as magnets for their ire just as the Rothschilds and Péreires had done in the economic realm. Inveterate observers of the Parisian cultural scene, the Goncourt brothers accused young Jews, particularly those of the avant-garde journal *La Revue blanche*, of taking over the national literary scene:

> We were speaking today of N . . . [Natanson], where le Tout-Paris goes to dinner. . . . At a certain moment, when the theatre was the only branch of literature where one could make money, the only Jewish writers were playwrights: for example, Dennery and Halévy. . . . But now the young generation of Jews has understood the all-powerful weight of criticism and the kind of blackmail that critics can exert on theatres and publishers and has founded the *Revue Blanche*, which is a real nest of "Yids." One can well imagine that with the help of their elders, who provide the money for almost all newspapers, they will control French literature within twenty-five years.[61]

Such vitriolic sentiments were prevalent in the anti-Semitic press; when *La Revue blanche* was founded, Drumont's *Libre Parole* denounced it as a "Jewish publication." Predictably, Drumont's attacks against the review and its collaborators only escalated during the Dreyfus Affair.[62]

Indeed, even a relatively moderate anti-Dreyfusard like Ferdinand Brunetière could claim at the time of the Affair:

> Freemasons, Protestants and Jews, all of whom had the advantage of having no links to the past, rushed *en masse* through the door opened to them; they entered; they took over politics, civil bureaucracy, schools; they reign therein.

For Brunetière, anti-Semitism was simply the acute desire to dispossess Jews of these functions.[63]

Attacks against Jewish and Protestant intellectuals in the University system thus were widespread. According to Maurras, the Protestant Gabriel Monod was a "German sentry within the university. His patriotism, already subordinated to the admiration of the enemy, was also subordinated to the republican form of the state."[64] Another target was the president of the Ligue des Droits de l'Homme, Victor Basch, depicted as "A pillar of this [Kantian] religion and of this regime."[65] Emile Durkheim was especially vilified; as the leading exponent of the republican model of citizenship, he

Figure 4.1 "Page d'histoire: Baptême intellectuel," *Psst!* 12 February 1898. Re-edition of: "'Let us save the nation in danger!' Only, it is the exact opposite." Illustration by Caran d'Ache. Reproduced courtesy of the Trustees of the Boston Public Library, Rare Books.

was held responsible for the decline of a traditional national identity. For Maurras, Durkheim would obviously be inspired by Germany; after all, "Monsieur Durkheim [is] a Jewish metic, a Dreyfusard and naturally a high-ranking official in our 'University.' "[66]

In other writings, Maurras vented his spleen against Bergson, another so-called pillar of the republican regime. There is a certain irony in the enmity Maurras felt for Bergson since the latter was himself anti-Kantian. Moreover, Bergson was the object of attacks not only by the Action française but also by co-religionist Julien Benda.[67] To further complicate the situation, Bergson's ideas inspired certain intellectuals close to the Action française like Henri Massis who saw in him a leader in the anti-intellectual movement, while members of the Sorbonne establishment were wary of his stature among youths like Massis who used Bergson in support of their attack against the "nouvelle Sorbonne." Since Bergson was difficult to categorize, to assimilate into one camp or the other, he was subject to attacks from both sides.[68]

The association of intellectuals as diverse as Durkheim and Bergson was linked to their status as representatives of the new state intellectual, their loyalty to democracy, and moreover to the fact that they were Jews.[69] After all, Bergson was *the* philosopher and Durkheim *the* sociologist of early-twentieth-century France. Neo-traditionalists could not let these "false" Frenchmen represent the nation.[70]

For neo-traditionalists, Jews and Protestants were lumped together; both were seen alien to the French tradition of a Catholic state. In *Trois Idées politiques*, Maurras advocated the teaching of theological studies at the university, not for religious reasons, but for the intellectual discipline Catholic theology taught. Even Barrès, who professed republican views, admitted that the French tradition was equated with the Catholic tradition.[71]

The anti-Semitism of both Maurras and Barrès was thus deeply rooted in their idea of a monolithic Frenchness defined by Catholicism. Barrès's later work bears the imprint of the racial theories of Jules Soury, but before the Affair, the influence of "Catholic republican" Drumont dominated.[72] Barrès, like Drumont, believed that Jewish intelligence differed from French intelligence so that a peasant could understand Racine and Corneille by instinct in a way that a Jew with his "foreign" intelligence never could.

A discussion of "Jewish" and "Protestant" intelligence—deemed dangerous to the health of the nation—would be particularly useful at this point, for the very traits associated with these two religions were also associated with the modernist intellectual. Just as the

words "Jew" and "bourgeois" had previously become interchange-
able, so, too, did the word "Jew" come increasingly to be associated
with the state intellectual and vice versa. Like the state intellectuals, Jews were "déracinés." According to Barrès, Jews had no
country in the physical, organic sense. For them, as for such intellectuals as Lucien Herr, the notion of "la patrie" was an idea, an
abstraction:

> Jews do not have a country in the sense that we under-
> stand it. For us, the country is the soil and our ancestors;
> it is the land of our dead. For them, it is the place where
> they find their greatest profit. Their "intellectuals" thus
> arrive at their famous definition: "The nation is an idea."[73]

The theme of Jews as alien to the nation was common among
anti-Semites, but Barrès and other neo-traditionalist writers added
an intellectual dimension to this portrait by leveling the same
charges of universalism and abstraction they associated with
Kantianism at Jews. In their view, Kantianism was an alien, German philosophy propounding excessive individualism, abstraction,
and universalism, promoted by the state. Since Jews were closely
associated with that state, Jewish intelligence was associated with
Kantianism. Indeed, Jews and Protestants were responsible for
promoting Kantianism.

Neo-traditionalists claimed that Jews and Protestants were
responsible for "germanizing" French culture.[74] Writing about *Les
Déracinés* in his *Cahiers*, Barrès specifically made the link between
Jews and their "corrupting" influence on French intelligence as
well as on the French national ideal.[75] The decline of France was
the natural result of leaving teaching in the hands of the "déracinés,"
[read Protestants and Jews] remarked Maurras to Barrès.[76]

In opposing the ideas of neo-traditionalist writers to those of
the modernist intellectuals, one should be wary of facile generalizations which would categorize the first group as "anti-intellectual"
or even "anti-scientific" and the second, as "scientific." Both sides
proclaimed an allegiance to science and intelligence. How they
defined science and intelligence, however, differed markedly. Moreover, as Barrès pointed out, "belief" in science was a type of faith.[77]
Indeed, in a letter written to Barrès by Jules de Gaultier, the latter
claimed that of all the individuals commenting on the Dreyfus
Affair, only Barrès based himself on purely "intellectual" concerns;
it was the Dreyfusards who prided themselves on their rational,
scientific values who were fervent believers.[78] Both sides defined

"intellectual" in opposing ways; moreover, one person's rationality was another person's belief.[79]

As this brief examination illustrates, the status of the writer in society was an important issue for writers of all political persuasions. While most writers were elitist to a certain extent, for some, their fear for their status led to a neo-traditionalist desire for a return to an idealized and aristocratic past. The "triad" of Drumont-Barrès-Maurras was instrumental in developing anti-Semitic discourse in France.[80] It is easy to see how the ideas of Rebell could be expanded by Maurras and Barrès to include a critique of the republican intellectual and from there turned to anti-Semitic ends. As in other European countries, the politics of these anti-Semitic men of thought were born of what Fritz Stern calls the "politics of cultural despair."[81] Both Jews and the state intellectuals were symbols of modernity who threatened to displace neo-traditionalists whose ideals were based on long-established hierarchies.

The primordial role of Drumont, Barrès, and Maurras in the propagation of anti-Semitic discourse points to the overlap of the literary and political which characterizes French anti-Semitism. These three men were first and foremost literary figures whose esthetics shaped their political theories. Barrès's *culte du moi* evolved into his integral nationalist theories, while Maurras's critique of Romanticism and his association with the Ecole romane and the Félibrige movement became an indictment of French society since the French Revolution.[82] Without discounting the importance of esthetics in the shaping of political theories in other countries,[83] it is important to note that only in France have writers occupied such an important position in society. Only France possesses a literary culture that imbues them with the power to speak for the entire nation.[84]

Indeed, the anti-Semitism of these men helped to forge their own identities as intellectuals during the 1890s. It was the Dreyfus Affair, however, that allowed their full emergence as nationalist intellectuals. Viewed in this context, it is not surprising that the battle for French national identity should be articulated by two opposing groups of intellectuals, both of whom saw themselves as representatives of the national ethos. Each group in its own way propagated a monolithic vision of the nation. Having examined the views of anti-Semitic writers, it is time now to turn to the writings of assimilated Jews, who sought to identify the cultural legacy of Judaism with the ideals of Frenchness as exemplified by the modernist intellectual.

The Intellectual as Jew

As we have just seen, anti-Semitism became an important element of the debate surrounding the role of the state intellectual in France. Both the state intellectual and the Jew, who was associated with this figure, were represented by neo-traditionalists as the antithesis of what was French. Jews, on the other hand, sought to integrate themselves further into the mainstream of French society by equating their own Jewishness with the universality, abstraction, and rationality of the state intellectual. Certainly, there were exceptions. Jewish writers like Edmond Fleg, André Spire, and even Bernard Lazare were influenced by the nationalist theories of Barrès, while Henri Bergson sought to integrate rationality and instinct. In general, however, the attempt to reconcile Jewish traits with French ones, specifically those promoted by the French Revolution, was entirely in keeping with the tradition of Franco-Judaism.

In the second half of this chapter, I will examine the writings of certain key Jewish intellectuals, most of whom could be considered "state Jews." Although I shall cover both the periods preceding and following the Dreyfus Affair, I plan to concentrate on the time of the Affair itself since in many instances, it was the Affair and the anti-Semitism it engendered that forced them to grapple simultaneously with their identities as Frenchmen, Jews, and intellectuals.

It is essential to begin by placing these Jewish intellectuals not only within the context of French society during the early Third Republic, but also within the context of the French Jewish community of this time. From the start, the admission during the Revolution of Jews to citizenship and thus to participation in the national community was contingent upon their assimilation, as summarized in Clermont-Tonnerre's often-cited dictum: "To the Jews as individuals—everything; to the Jews as a group—nothing."[85] Jews were first and foremost to be Frenchmen; their religion was their private concern. Jews were certainly not singled out in this regard. The Revolutionaries sought to destroy all intermediary, corporate bodies and establish a direct relationship between the individual and the state. Legislation enacted under Napoleon set the standard of behavior for the French Jewish community until the separation of church and state in 1905.

In establishing a consistory system, similar to that of French Protestants, Napoleon created an official administrative body for French Jewry that was directly responsible to the state. The dual duty of the consistories was to serve the nation and to administer to the French Jewish community. Early on then, to be a good Jew also meant being a good Frenchman. In fact, "Fatherland and Religion" became the official slogan of the Central Consistory.[86]

It was natural for French Jews to adopt the values of the Enlightenment and the Revolution—not only the universalist model of citizenship—but also democratic ideals, along with a belief in reason and progress. They easily gravitated toward the Republic and eagerly espoused its secular vision of nationhood.[87] Yet these were the very ideas which anti-Semites viewed as alien to French identity.

One of their major targets was the avant-garde journal, *La Revue blanche*, an important center for Jewish intellectuals at the fin de siècle. *La Revue blanche* will provide the focus for our examination of assimilated Jewish intellectuals not only because of its significance within the avant-garde, but also because of its role as a leading *centre dreyfusard*, a meeting place for revisionist intellectuals and politicians. The example of the *Revue blanche* group offers further proof of the active involvement of individual Jews in the Affair; perhaps more important and less typical, however, is that in the *Revue blanche*, certain Jewish intellectuals were involved as a group.[88]

During the Dreyfus Affair, a significant part of the literary avant-garde joined forces with the republican university. The *Revue blanche*, however, was unique in that even before the Affair, it maintained close ties with the Ecole Normale Supérieure and the Sorbonne through its collaborators, many of whom had attended these two institutions. Although two of the Jewish intellectuals we will examine here—Durkheim and Bergson—were not immediate members of the *Revue blanche* group, they had ties with the review, through the Ecole Normale. Durkheim and Bergson, who had graduated a few years earlier than the *normaliens* who belonged to the *Revue blanche* group, were friendly with each other and with classmate Jean Jaurès, who was a frequent visitor to the review. Furthermore, François Simiand, a contributor to Durkheim's *Année sociologique*, wrote a number of articles for the review. Another obvious connection was of course Lucien Herr. Ties between Durkheim and the *Revue blanche* group were strengthened during the Affair. Both the Natansons and Durkheim were founding members of the Ligue des Droits de l'Homme.

The *Revue blanche* was much more than a journal; it was also a milieu and a group of friends linked by school ties and family relations. Many of them studied together at the Lycée Condorcet, a school with a reputation for a high proportion of Jewish students.[89] Indeed, membership in the Jewish community played an important, although by no means exclusive, role in the development of the *Revue blanche* circle. For example, the Natansons were acquainted with the Blums, who attended the same synagogue as the Bernards. Others met later at the Sorbonne or at the Ecole Normale.

Although the review viewed itself as a staunch defender of the underdog and of the downtrodden before the Affair, it rarely published articles on anti-Semitism and Jews, the exception being Lazare's article "L'Antisémitisme au Moyen Age," published in the April 1894 issue.[90] Indeed, the *Revue blanche*'s literary critic Lucien Muhlfeld, who was himself Jewish, did not know what to make of Lazare's *L'Antisémitisme, son histoire et ses causes historiques*, published in 1894; his review of June 1894, somewhat ambiguous, at times flippant, amply illustrates his discomfort.[91] Similarly, Blum's analysis of Daudet's *Voyage de Shakespeare*, which appeared in *La Revue blanche* in May 1896, ignored the book's anti-Semitism. Not until the Dreyfus Case became the "Affair" in late 1897 was this reticence overcome. Henceforth, *Revue blanche* collaborators, Jews, as well as Gentiles, were obliged to address anti-Semitism.

Jewish collaborators represented roughly half of the review's staff and a much higher proportion of its editorial board.[92] Although the *Revue blanche* never presented itself as such, even before the Affair, friends and foes alike saw it as a "Jewish" publication. The critic Henry Bérenger called the review's cohort a "groupe judéo-universitaire," declaring: "All the latent sophistry of the Sorbonne education, all the bilaterality of Israelite brains, you will find them here in this review."[93]

For their part, members of the group saw themselves as "French Israelites." They were French first and "Israelite" second. All of these individuals were assimilated, their Jewishness cultural, rather than religious—even Durkheim, the unbelieving son of a rabbi.[94] For Léon Blum, his Jewishness was a matter of culture rather than religious faith:

> I have never met a people so free from religious notions or traditions. So much so that it is impossible . . . to formulate Jewish dogma. Among the people, religion is but an ensemble of familial superstitions which are obeyed, without any conviction whatsoever, only out of respect toward one's ancestors . . . for the enlightened, it no longer means anything.[95]

Such a statement is presumptuous, to the say the least. Blum arrogantly dismissed centuries of Judaic traditions and beliefs. In his effort to divorce himself from the "primitive," religious aspects of Judaism, he made gross generalizations about Judaism on the basis of his own personal experience. His view would obviously not be accepted by practicing Jews in Eastern Europe, nor even by the leader of French Jews, Rabbi Zadoc Kahn, for Blum opposed "enlightenment" to religious belief. Yet Blum was not alone; his sentiments were echoed by his Jewish colleagues at the *Revue blanche*, who also spoke of a secular upbringing.

In his memoirs, Julien Benda wrote of his family providing an atmosphere of total liberty with regard to religion:

> Naturally, my parents did not teach me to respect the Jewish religion, from which they were entirely detached, and of which they observed not the slightest rite. They did not speak to me of religions. For them, they [religions] constituted relics, destined . . . soon to disappear.[96]

If the Jewish children of this generation and milieu grew up in a secular atmosphere, it must be noted that they were brought up to respect the lay Republic. Even Durkheim, who came from an orthodox, practicing background, was raised in a family that held the republican values of effort, rationality, and moral duty in great esteem.[97] Benda's father, who believed in the cult of science, taught his children the ideals of laicity, civic equality, and individual liberty. Benda also wrote of his father's attachment to the Revolution: "I often heard him say that it was scandalous that a Jew should oppose it [the Revolution], given that without it he would still be in the ghetto."[98] To link the fate of Jews to that of the Republic was typical and automatic for Jews of an older generation, but it was taken for granted by their highly assimilated children. For them, the gains of the Revolution were a given.[99]

How did assimilated French Jews view anti-Semitism, and how did it shape their own sense of identity? Many saw it as a foreign import, specifically a German one. Durkheim felt that anti-Semitism in Germany and Russia was chronic and traditional, whereas in France it was sporadic, "the consequence and the superficial symptom of a state of social malaise."[100] Blum saw French anti-Semitism in theoretical terms rather than as a real threat. Like Durkheim, he believed that anti-Semitism could become dangerous in Poland or Rumania, but minimized its importance in France, viewing it primarily as a *phénomène mondain*.[101] Benda claimed that in the well-to-do circles frequented by a small minority of extremely wealthy and socially prominent Jews, it was a point of honor to hate the Republic. Since Jews, on the contrary, identified with the Republic, they were seen as traitors to their class:

> [H]ow very naturally the Jewish ideal—at least for Jews at that time—fit in with the spirit of the Revolution, how easily, how harmoniously they adopted its dogmas, [ones] that so many Frenchmen found repugnant. I understand that those who hate this spirit can curse my race.[102]

Because French Jews of the late nineteenth century frequently equated their fate with that of the Republic, they easily and understandably explained anti-Semitism in terms of the opposition engendered by the Ferry School Laws, nonreligious marriage ceremonies (le mariage civil), and divorce.[103]

Anti-Semitism could also be understood in terms of jealousy of Jewish successes within the Republic. Gustave Kahn, the poet-in-residence of the *Revue blanche*, described anti-Semitism as a generalized form of envy.[104] Benda added that the problem was exacerbated by the desire of the Jewish community to "prove" itself:

> Because the modern state was opening all its doors to us, admitting us to all its competitive exams, we had to take advantage of this opportunity which was finally offered us to prove that we were not the inferior race that our detractors claimed we were, but on the contrary, a race of the first order by reason of its great capacity for work and by its intellectual gifts.[105]

Benda concluded that this impulse provided one of the primary causes of the Affair.[106] Léon Blum concurred, thereby seeming to validate the stereotype of Jewish "pushiness." Like Benda, he seemed to advocate restraint:

> Too many Jews had rushed headlong toward the civil service at the same time; it is not a bad idea for them to distance themselves from it, if only for their own protection; the condition of the civil servant was ill-adapted to the fundamental characteristics of their race. . . . The superior gifts of intelligence . . . are of no service to the bureaucrat, civilian or military, rather, they would be detrimental.[107]

Was Blum, himself one of the first Jews to enter the Conseil d'Etat, speaking of his own case? Did he feel constrained by his position as a high civil servant?[108] No doubt Blum's statement was in part motivated by a desire to steer Jews toward their "true" destiny—socialism.[109] But Blum, like Benda, perhaps felt not only family pressure to succeed, but also the anti-Semitism Jewish success provoked.[110]

Linking anti-Semitism to envy was a way of minimizing its strength. Yet it also indicated that assimilated Jews had taken at face value certain aspects of anti-Semitic discourse. French Jewish identity, as Paula Hyman has suggested, was in no small measure influenced by general public opinion.[111] Instead of denying the truth of such allegations, Blum, Benda, Kahn, and others tried to rationalize what was essentially an irrational discourse. They seemed to suggest that if Jews succeeded less often, anti-Semitism would go away. Blum, on one occasion, even advocated ignoring anti-Semitism, albeit as a deliberate strategy:

> I have heard some Jews in France complain about persecution. Poor people! How had they not understood that it depends entirely on an individual, on a race to be persecuted or not? What constitutes persecution is not this or that vexatious measure, but the spirit with which it is received and accepted. If the Jews are courageous, if, far from exaggerating the effect of acts which are detrimental to them, they absorb and attenuate it, if instead of lamenting their fate, they smile about it, if they are tranquilly confident, like their ancestors, that all injustice is precarious and that civilization never takes a step backwards, then no one will be able to say that they are a persecuted people.[112]

More farseeing, the sociologist Durkheim not only saw Jews as scapegoats for societal disasters, he also advocated a firm stance against anti-Semites and state intervention through education.[113] Even if Blum and Benda felt somewhat uncomfortable about their close association as Jews with the state, they, like Durkheim, espoused a progressively liberal view of the state and its role in society. Furthermore, they were diametrically opposed to such neo-traditionalists as Barrès and Maurras, who advocated decentralization.[114] While for Maurras, the state was simply an organ of society, its "civil servant," for "state Jews" Blum and Durkheim, the state played a primordial role as the conscience of society. Blum, writing a review of *Les Déracinés* in *La Revue blanche*, declared that individuals were only free in a centralized nation. Although Blum subsequently moved away from this stance, he returned to the quasi-Jacobin concept of an emancipating state after World War II.[115] Durkheim went even farther, stating that the state's function was to think for its citizens; it should not merely follow in their wake.[116]

The case of Durkheim merits special attention; not merely a product of the republican state, he also became one of its most eloquent spokesmen. The successor to Ferdinand Buisson as *chargé de cours* in the Science of Education at the Sorbonne, he was in a position to shape national education and thus the future of the country. For this reason, he became the special target of anti-Semites. First of all, Durkheim equated the republican state with the nation and justified increased state activity in modern society. Durkheim felt that the individual's interests were better protected by a strong state. Moreover, such a state assured a united community.

In part as a result of his experience of France's defeat in the Franco-Prussian War, Durkheim, like most Alsatian Jews, was especially patriotic, without being chauvinistic. Destined for the rabbinate, he instead directed his efforts toward nothing less than the regeneration of France. According to his friend Georges Davy, Durkheim saw sociology as the "philosophy which would contribute to giving the Republic a basis and inspiring in it rational reforms while giving to the nation a principle of order and a moral doctrine."[117]

Durkheim approved of a meritiocratic society and believed that equality of access to education in the modern world replaced the ideal of charity in the religious world of the past.[118] He was thus a great proponent of a secular, moral education, viewing schoolteachers as the nation's new priests.

Given their secular, even anticlerical, perspective, the review's Jewish writers were somewhat contemptuous of certain features of traditional Judaism. Before his conversion to Zionism, Bernard Lazare wrote an article entitled "Juifs et israélites," in which he claimed that French Jews were the latter, and thus assimilated, while the former, mostly eastern Europeans, remained bound by Jewish tradition.[119] He also wrote of his indifference to religious Jews in other countries: "What do they matter to me, Israelite of France: Russian usurers, Galician cabaret owners, Polish horse traders, middlemen of Prague and money-lenders of Frankfurt?" In a similar vein, Benda indicated that his family found certain Judaic practices distasteful, even "barbaric."[120]

In this spirit, *Revue blanche* collaborators sought to equate the anti-Semitism of certain Catholics with the earlier exclusivity of Jews. Thus, they wrote in "Protestation," the article which marked their entry into the battle of the Affair:

> There is in this anti-Jewish clamor a judaic character of religious exclusiveness which brings the anti-Semites down to the level of the Jews of the early centuries. There is in this racial persecution a judaic superstition of the origins that takes us back to the time when Jews still believed in the Talmud.[121]

The *Revue blanche* collaborators placed themselves firmly in the lay camp; for them, anti-Semitism gave expression to an age-old zealotry to be condemned wherever it might appear.[122] Similarly, they and other assimilated Jewish intellectuals like Durkheim joined the Ligue des Droits de l'Homme, thereby associating their defense of Dreyfus with the defense of the Republic.

On the other hand, ample evidence existed that even among secular Jews a strong sense of Jewish identity and pride existed. Tristan Bernard tells us about his father, who did not practice his faith, but insisted that the family was completely Jewish:

> My father, who observed none of the rites of our Israelite religion, who, in his relations, made no distinction between Jews and Christians, obeyed nevertheless, in accordance with a sacred trust, the wishes of his ancestors. They, like Papa himself, refused to reveal that they were not 100 percent Jewish.[123]

Bernard does not use the term "race" in this passage, but he and other assimilated French Jews often spoke of their cultural heritage in terms of race since they could not speak of religious solidarity. Likewise, in his response to Henri Dagan's 1899 *Enquête* on anti-Semitism, Durkheim referred to his own "Jewish origin," while maintaining that Jews lost their "ethnic characteristics" with great rapidity—hardly two generations sufficed.[124] This reasoning provided a means of reconciling a Jewish heritage with a sense of French patriotism. By speaking of a "Jewish race," secular Jews could express their sense of community without resorting to religious identification.[125] Anti-Semites, of course, also used the word "race." As Michael Marrus has shown, the term was widespread and possessed a fluidity of meaning during the late nineteenth century. It could be used in a biological, racial sense, or could carry essentially cultural and historical meanings.[126]

Even if Durkheim did not specifically refer to Judaism, his discussion of the "sacredness" of the individual in society seems to be an attempt to come to terms with his Jewish background, although he believed that individualism was part of a French tradition, inherited from the Revolution and rooted in Christian morality.[127] His view of Christianity, it must be noted, appears more Protestant than Catholic.[128] Some members of the *Revue blanche*, including Lazare, Blum, and Kahn, associated the Jew not only with the Revolution but also with socialism.[129] Bernard Lazare's "L'Esprit révolutionnaire dans le judaïsme," published by *La Revue bleue* in 1893 and later included in his book on anti-Semitism, expressed such sentiments. Blum was apparently influenced by the writings of Lazare, who was in turn influenced by Ernest Renan and James Darmesteter.[130] Lazare's book marked a turning point in his evolution from assimilated "israélite" to Jewish nationalist. Although he eventually disavowed many of the statements made in the book, notably his contention that anti-Semitism would disappear with assimilation, he continued to build upon the theme of the revolutionary spirit of Judaism.[131]

In their attempt to reconcile Judaism with their socialist beliefs, Lazare, Blum, and others were especially critical of bourgeois Jews.[132] At the time of the Affair, Blum berated Jewish military officers, stating that if they wanted to be judged on their individual merits, they should have chosen another career.[133] Writing from the same Marxist perspective in the 1930s, this time as leader of the Socialist Party, he excoriated the French Jewish bourgeoisie for protecting its class interests:

> One should certainly not think that in the Jewish milieus I then frequented . . . there was the slightest predisposition toward Dreyfusism. As a general rule, Jews had accepted the condemnation of Dreyfus as definitive and just. Jews did not wish for others to think that they were defending Dreyfus because he was a Jew.[134]

As men of the Left, Lazare and Blum had to deal with the question of Jewish capitalists. For them, the real Jewish spirit was not to be found among bankers and financiers such as the Rothschilds, but among members of the proletariat.[135] The former, by pursuing wealth, had forgotten the teachings of their religion. Blum stated that Jewish capitalists, once persuaded of the inevitability of a social revolution, would cede to the inevitable because of their clairvoyance.[136] As for Gustave Kahn, he warned against associating Jewish capitalists with all Jews, citing the importance of Jews in the socialist movement, notably Marx and Lassalle.[137]

Lazare, Blum, and Kahn all spoke of the revolutionary spirit that defined the Jew. For Blum, "the collective force" of their race, their "critical spirit," their "need to destroy any idea, any tradition that did not coincide with the facts, that could not be justified by reason" pushed Jews toward revolution.[138] Lazare was careful to point out that they were agents of progress, and that a communist in a capitalist system was as revolutionary as a capitalist in a communist state.[139]

Benda recalled his rational upbringing, while Blum and Lazare spoke of the "rational faith" of the Jew.[140] According to Blum and Lazare, Jews believed in the here and now. It is thus that they were proponents of justice on earth; unlike Christians, they could not wait for an afterlife to right wrongs. Blum wrote that the need for justice would lead Jews to socialism: "The Bible says: a just man where the Gospel says a saint."[141] Lazare, too, believed that piety for Jews was equated with justice while injustice was equated with impiety and crime: "The man whom the Jew praises is not the saint, it is not he who is resigned: it is the just man . . . . To know justice is to know God."[142]

According to Lazare, the Jewish conception of divinity also contributed to a revolutionary ethic. It led Jews to believe in human equality. For Jews, Yaweh was the one and only source of authority, with all men equal before this authority.[143] For the same reason, Jews had a highly developed sense of individual liberty (as distinguished from political authority). Any temporal power that attempted to usurp divine authority necessarily engendered opposition.[144] The privileging of Judaism over Christianity, specifically over Catholicism, is implicit in the arguments made by both Blum and Lazare. According to them, Judaism, unlike Christianity, was a more just religion; moreover, this quality meant that Judaism was better adapted to the needs of a secular society. In this way, Blum and Lazare were "guilty" of what anti-Semites accused them: of representing Jews as a superior people, as an elite.

These self-characterizations presented by the assimilated leftist Jews of the *Revue blanche* provide an interesting comparison with anti-Semitic depictions of Jews. Indeed, my reading of these texts points to striking parallels between the two discourses, which at times represent mirror images of each other. These similarities arose from a shared historical context in which assimilated Jews as well as anti-Semites linked their fate to the Revolution of 1789. According to the latter, reactionaries and even some socialists, Jews were responsible for the Revolution of 1789. No other group had supposedly benefited more from the Revolution than Jewish capitalists, who were thought to dominate French society. Echoing Alphonse Toussenel, who called Jews "les rois de l'époque" (the kings of the era), Drumont wrote in *La France juive*: "The only one to have profited from the Revolution is the Jew; everything comes from the Jew; everything comes back to the Jew."[145]

Blum, on the other hand, called Jews the great victims of history, yet this claim was based on dubious, indeed, equivocal premises: "They have imagined the very prophetism that turned against their race; they have created the very capitalism which today seeks their ruin." By asserting that Jews had created capitalism, Blum only confirmed anti-Semitic suspicions. Moreover, he perpetuated the stereotype of Jews as the creators of capitalism. Lazare, on the other hand, had taken great pains to indicate that there existed Protestant and Catholic capitalists as well. Finally, anti-Semites like Charles Maurras saw Jews as part of an international-socialist conspiracy against the present order. Again, Blum's declaration that "Jews inaugurated the internationalism that the socialists will tomorrow realize" merely confirmed anti-Semitic fears.[146] And in fact, Maurras noted with great satisfaction the list of revolutionary Jews cited by Lazare.[147] For Blum, Jews were farseeing, ahead of their time, but for neo-traditionalist anti-Semites, this translated into revolutionaries, agents of modernity, who destroyed the organic national order, whether by capitalism or socialism.

Drumont and others criticized Jews for their materialism, that is, their acquisitive nature; for Blum, this materialism, defined in a Marxian sense, assumed a positive character. While such anti-Semites as Maurice Barrès and Jacques Bainville criticized Jewish intelligence for its abstract clarity, Durkheim, Benda, and Blum praised these same rational qualities. Furthermore, anti-Semites depicted Jews as rootless and alien to the national community, while young leftist Jews associated Judaism with a universalist perspective. Benda, for example, spoke of his family's heritage of "spiritual values conceived in the absolute, in the nonhistorical."[148] Indeed, these two different visions of the world—the one rational, abstract, and universal, and the other instinctual, relative, and national—found expression in the competing Dreyfusard and anti-Dreyfusard discourses.

Despite the great divide of the Dreyfus Affair, assimilated Jews and anti-Semites nonetheless shared a remarkably similar understanding of the developments of their day. How does one explain such parallels? Did anti-Semitic discourse shape the ideas of the assimilated Jews of *La Revue blanche*? Instead of influence, it is perhaps more accurate to speak of a convergence of ideas. Given the historical association of French Jews with the Republic, assimilated leftist Jews naturally claimed this heritage without any prompting from anti-Semites. They did, however, engage in a dialogue with anti-Semites. Charges made by one side were refuted by the other. This dialogue points paradoxically to a symbiotic relationship between the two sides. Rather than simply denying anti-Semitic allegations, writers from *La Revue blanche* frequently turned anti-Semitic discourse on its head. At the same time, by adopting universalist, rational values, they remained within the mainstream of French culture, thereby reconciling their identities as Frenchmen and Jews. For most anti-Semites, however, such values ran counter to their vision of a traditional order rooted in the past and based on the values of particularism and instinct. For them, Jews were symbols of modernity and a democratic order which threatened to marginalize older national values associated with a rural, hierarchical and Catholic order. The parallels between assimilated Jews of the Left and anti-Semites indicate that Jewish identity and assimilation were part of a larger question of French national identity.

The anti-Semitism of the fin de siècle, which reached its apogee with the Affair, had a profound effect upon the Jewish intellectuals of *La Revue blanche*. It forced them to deal with, if not necessarily come to terms with, their Jewish identities. The writings of Blum, Lazare, and others betray an uneasiness and even confusion. Assimilated, they were both attracted to and repelled by the traditions of Judaism. They faced the dilemma of all secular Jews: of reclaiming the cultural aspects of their heritage while rejecting its religious character. On the one hand, they drew strength from an abstract, intellectual vision of Judaism in harmony with their universal, republican beliefs. Yet as anticlericals and modernists, they were repulsed by Judaism's religious practices and rites, which they viewed as backward and even barbaric. Furthermore, their attempt to equate Jews with socialist ideals seems at times forced, and they never fully came to terms with the socialist tradition of anti-Semitism.[149]

The example of the assimilated Jews of *La Revue blanche* illustrates that assimilation constituted a contradictory stance, fraught with inconsistencies. As secular Jews, they could never feel comfortable with religious Jews; nor obviously would they associate with practicing Catholics. Yet there existed a certain uneasiness in their alliance with non-Jewish anticlericals, who targeted all forms of religion, including Judaism. In attempting to disassociate Jewish identity from Judaism as a religion, they skated perilously close to a Jewish anti-Semitism. It was thus that they sometimes occupied a spiritual and ethical limbo, a "no-man's-land."[150]

A gap also existed between the way these intellectuals saw themselves and the way in which others, anti-Semites or not, viewed them. While they tended to minimize their Jewishness, defining themselves first as Frenchmen, then as Jews, this was often the first thing noticed by others.[151] Finally, their optimistic faith in progress led most of these writers (the exception was Lazare) to believe that anti-Semitism would one day disappear and that the pogroms found in other countries could never take place in France.[152] For those who would read history backward, this faith seemed entirely justified even though some must have been aware that the government condemned anti-Semitism not so much because it was directed against Jews but because it represented a threat to the lay Republic.

The experience of anti-Semitism, especially during the Dreyfus Affair, obliged the intellectuals of *La Revue blanche* to reshape their discourse in such a way as to acknowledge and valorize their Jewish identity. They were forced to rethink their understanding not only of themselves, but also the world, and indeed, their politics. For Durkheim, the secular thinker, the Dreyfus Affair made him realize the importance of religion in social life.[153]

The Affair led Blum to a lifelong political commitment to socialism. Lazare abandoned assimilation for Jewish nationalism. As for Benda, he was awakened to the strength of religious passions and hatred in French society and concluded that his mission as an intellectual was to combat such forces. Indeed, Benda's involvement in the Affair prepared the way for his fierce devotion to antifascist movements in the 1930s. For many leftist assimilated Jews, the Dreyfus Affair was thus not only a first step toward becoming intellectuals, but also Jewish intellectuals.

For neo-traditionalist writers, many of whom were anti-Semites, the Affair also represented a key moment in their development. Although their anti-Semitism predated the Affair and helped to shape their consiousness as intellectuals during the 1890s, only during the Affair did they fully emerge as nationalist intellectuals. Maurras launched the Action française during the height of the Affair and Maurice Barrès's nationalist "masterpiece," *Scènes et doctrines du nationalisme*, published in 1902, was largely a reworking of articles written during the Affair. Although the Affair cannot and should not be reduced to a left/right paradigm, leftist intellectuals and their right-wing counterparts did emerge as a result.

Writing in 1935, Léon Blum declared: "The Affair was a human crisis, less widespread and shorter lived but as violent as the French Revolution or the Great War."[154] Seen by contemporaries as a turning point in French history, the Affair has been viewed by some historians as a defining moment in a series of civil wars over national identity.[155] These wars involved what constituted national identity as well as which group had the power to speak for the nation. The "Jewish question" in France was thus inextricably linked to the issue of national identity not only because the Republic and the integration of Jews in it were seen as alien to a French, Catholic tradition by anti-Semites, but also because assimilated Jewish intellectuals themselves helped to propagate the republican, Revolutionary vision of national identity.[156] Each group purported to represent the "true" vision of France. No wonder then that these two visions increasingly came into conflict through the course of the twentieth century.

5

—◈—

Intellectuals, Honor, and Manhood
at the Fin de Siècle

The fear of Jews as a threat to established hierarchies and to national identity was often expressed in sexual terms. Like homosexuals and the "New Woman," Jews were associated with excessive or "abnormal" sexuality.[1] This fear was especially acute during the late nineteenth century, a time which witnessed deep-rooted gender anxiety, specifically, a crisis of male identity.[2] France at the fin de siècle had difficulty accepting the political and cultural domination of the industrial middle classes so that aristocratic notions held sway even in an age of increasing democracy.[3] One of the cornerstones of French fin-de-siècle society, particularly that of the Parisian middle and upper classes, was the firm belief in honor, represented as strength in men and virtue in women.[4] The decline of the national birthrate was viewed as a symptom of French degeneration and, more specifically, as a sign of male impotence. Indeed, French demographers and scientists believed that the general physiological vigor of the father was a decisive factor in the production of healthy children and in particular the production of male children.[5] The fear of the loss of virility was exacerbated by the defeat of 1870. French men, notes Edward Berenson, returned from the Franco-Prussian War "feeling dishonored and lacking in the virtues of strength, action, and will so central to long-standing notions of masculinity...."[6]

This chapter begins by exploring the contemporary debate on honor and sexuality. To that end, it examines fin-de-siècle

117

representations, both fictional and nonfictional, of the intellectual, concentrating on contemporary views of the relationship of gender and intellect. It focuses on the French reaction, in "la grande presse," as well as in the little magazines, to Oscar Wilde's conviction and subsequent imprisonment for homosexuality in 1895. Although many avant-garde writers, unlike most of their establishment peers, came to Wilde's defense, they did so in the name of art and humanity. Already sensitive to charges of effeminacy, these writers were reluctant to defend Wilde's homosexuality. Despite their hostility to the bourgeoisie, writers of the avant-garde shared with their opponents a common discourse of honor and masculinity.

Honor, Sexuality, and Intellect in Fin-de-Siècle France

Gender issues at the fin de siècle in France and elsewhere were intertwined with political and social ones.[7] The struggle to control sex and sexuality—the attempt to distinguish between "normal" sexuality and its "abnormal" counterpart—represented a means by which to stem the tide of modernity, as exemplified by political upheaval, industrialization, the increasing prominence of the working classes, and the advent of the "New Woman."[8] Without the powerful ally of nationalism, bourgeois ideals of respectability could not have spread to all groups in society. The contemporary discourse on sex and reproduction became so compelling precisely because it was linked to the health and well-being of the nation.[9]

Thus, France was not unlike its neighbors in looking at gender issues within the context of the nation, but the fear of a loss of masculinity was more acutely felt in France, given its defeat in the Franco-Prussian War and the precipitous decline in the birthrate. Writer Hugues Le Roux warned that French men were becoming the "women of Europe."[10] The fact that they could not control their destinies abroad made French males even more adamant in their stand against those who transgressed societal norms. Although notions of masculinity and femininity were inextricably linked, order and stability in such a world were based on the traditional separate spheres of men and women. Women occupied domestic, private space, while men occupied public space. The "New Woman" thus challenged French men's ideas of their own role; the "masculinization" of women necessarily meant the "feminization" of men.[11]

Contemporary medical research like Jean-Martin Charcot's development of a pathology of nervous disorders, in particular, the condition of neurasthenia, made a deep impact on writers, social scientists, and politicians of the time. Although neurasthenia was thought to afflict both males and females, it did not revise the commonly held belief that women's bodies were the site of nervous excitement but rather projected femininity onto new bodies.[12]

Avant-garde writers, despite their opposition to the bourgeois order, shared with their opponents a common fear of the "masculine" woman, as is evidenced in their writings, which warned against the effects of sport and education on the "weaker" sex.[13] In an article entitled "Le Féminisme et le bon sens," published in *La Plume*, writer Victor Joze stated that it was not by sending women to the Chamber of Deputies and to the municipal councils that one could make them happy but rather by giving them the means to raise their children.[14] Moreover, he denounced bluestockings, including George Sand, and declared that the majority of literary works written by women were intellectually inferior to those written by men, because a woman "is a kind of big, nervous child, incapable of judging things calmly, with accuracy and good sense."[15] The nervousness of women was viewed as a defining characteristic of their sex by Michel Provins, author of a series of articles on women in France, published in *Le Gaulois* in 1895.

Even a politically progressive writer like Octave Mirbeau shared such beliefs. Women, he claimed, were defined by their sex; their principal role in life was to reproduce—children, not works of art. Only a few, unnatural women could create works of art but their work was unoriginal, a pale copy of *male* creation.[16] The representation of women as children and the use of the term "nervous" are significant. In the context of the fin de siècle, nervousness was a sign of intellectual and physical disability. Women were not capable of competing intellectually with men. Furthermore, in attempting to use their intellectual powers, they denied their femininity and thus presented a threat to the family and the nation.

Significantly, Joze concluded his article with a call against both "androgynes" and "eunuchs."[17] Crossing gender border lines was viewed as dangerous.[18] George Mosse has suggested that "sexual perversion" was seen as a greater threat to the social order than the restlessness of the lower classes.[19] While this is true, these fears often went hand in hand, specifically the association of the "feminine" with the subversive.[20] As Debora Silverman, Susanna Barrows, and others have demonstrated, feminists and socialists were lumped together; witness the depiction of unruly crowds by writers as different as Taine and Zola.[21] Indeed, any threat to the social order, including the artistic revolt of the avant-garde, was represented as "feminine."[22]

While the women's movement was gaining increasing attention and momentum during the 1880s and 1890s, it was divided
among Catholics, moderate republicans, and socialists. Moreover,
women in France at the turn of the century still lagged behind
their English and American sisters—in large part because France's
religious, legal, and political structures created obstacles to a
women's rights movement more severe than those in the United
States and Britain—although the fear of these women in France
appears to be more acute than in neighboring countries.[23]

Intellectual women did exist, but they often operated outside
the mainstream of the literary world. Even in the avant-garde,
women were the exception. Rachilde, a member of the *Mercure de
France* circle, owed her position largely to her marriage to Director
Alfred Vallette. Although Barrès wrote a preface to her novel *Monsieur Vénus* (1884), he indicated in it that her work had no artistic
merit but was the work of a young woman expressing her animal
instincts. Rachilde herself was no feminist, despite the fact that
she published seemingly daring novels, some of which depicted a
reversal of male/female sexual relationships. These works indulged
rather than criticized male masochistic fantasies.[24] Novelist Gyp
(born in 1849, her real name was the Comtesse de Martel de
Janville), a ubiquitous figure in nationalist circles, offers a similar
example. Like Rachilde, she was ambivalent about women and,
indeed, about her own identity as a woman, preferring to describe
herself as a man. Again, in common with Rachilde, she denigrated
women, whom she viewed as responsible for the social disorganization of contemporary society. In fact, one male reviewer of her
Autour du mariage (1883) noted that it was the "cruelest indictment ever leveled against women."[25]

Not all women intellectuals exhibited such misogyny. Journalist Séverine (born Caroline Rémy in 1855), who wrote for the feminist, Dreyfusard newspaper *La Fronde*, felt that women, like the
accused Jewish Captain Dreyfus, were the scapegoats of an increasingly bloodthirsty, militarist society. In order to escape their
status as victims, she exhorted women to exhibit "feminine heroism" by combating reactionary forces in society.[26]

The crisis of manhood at the fin de siècle must be viewed in
light of the contemporary crisis of intellect. The use of the expression "crisis of intellect" may seem surprising to describe an age in
which technology and progress were the watchwords of the republican regime, whose representatives, among them Ernest Lavisse,
celebrated intelligence and learning. The "crisis of intellect" does
not mean a denigration of intelligence but rather a recognition of

its limitations, particularly with regard to emotion, and a wariness of its excesses.[27]

Men, as opposed to women, were viewed as the rational, intellectual sex. Women, who were placed lower on the evolutionary scale, were represented as overly emotional and nervous. Although intellect was valorized in distinguishing between males and females, among males, an excess of intellect was deplored, especially by literary intellectuals who opposed the positivism of university professors. This theme is present in the works of a variety of authors, more often in the works of conservative writers, but also in the writings of some progressive ones. Such a reaction can be explained in part by a revolt against positivism, but it was also the result of the effects of modern, urban life.

Middle-class men had lost contact with the land and with physical activity. In fact, elite urban males at this time were represented as inactive and effete as opposed to active males of the popular classes. Just as intellect was opposed to instinct and emotion, so, too, was it contrasted with physical activity.[28] Max Nordau described modern city dwellers as "degenerates," who were overly stimulated intellectually but physically weak and inactive.[29] The popularity of sports at this time, including dueling, was thus part of an effort by elite males to reassert their manhood. In justifying their column in La Revue blanche on sports, Léon Blum and Tristan Bernard distinguished between the noble, antique ideal of sports, which they viewed as a battle between heroes, a representation of "life for struggle," and the modern mercantile concept of sports for profit.[30] Octave Mirbeau, on the other hand, denigrated the cult of sports, which he felt exalted a barbaric and outmoded culture of honor.[31]

The ideal of manliness meant not only physical strength but also moral conduct and manners. Moreover, this ideal translated into the nation's spiritual and material vitality.[32] The culture of honor cut across ideological lines; individuals as different as republican Charles Péguy and conservative critic Emile Faguet could agree on the necessity of dueling as an integral part of that culture. For Péguy, the duel represented the defense of truth and justice, while Faguet saw in it the bulwark of social order.[33] Indeed, many social commentators of the period believed that dueling prepared men for the field of battle.

One exception was journalist Gaston Jollivet, who wrote for Le Gaulois. As a practicing Catholic, Jollivet deplored the shedding of blood. Another exception, from the other side of the political spectrum, was writer Octave Mirbeau, who warned against duels, which he believed, privileged animal instincts and brute force over intellect and reason. The duel, he stated, represented little more than an occasion for untrammeled aggression. It pitted the honorable man against the so-called man of honor, who used the duel to advance his own personal interests. Why should a man be obliged to reestablish his honor at the risk of his life? Moreover, why should society celebrate as a hero a man who had challenged another to a duel on a trumped-up excuse and had then won? Mirbeau lamented the spread of such nefarious aristocratic ideals to the rest of society.[34] His position is interesting in light of his future defense of Colonel Picquart as an intellectual hero, rather than as a military man during the Dreyfus Affair.

It is within this context that novels like Bourget's *Le Disciple*, Barrès's *Les Déracinés*, and Bérenger's *L'Effort* and *La Proie* must be viewed. Barrès and Bérenger both called for a return to regional roots and contact with the soil. Barrès's seven *bacheliers* in Paris were like the leaves of an old plane tree, part of a larger, organic whole.[35] In the same vein, Zola's *Fécondité* sang the praises of its hero, a farmer with a wife named Marianne (the significance of her name would have been obvious to contemporary readers) who bore him numerous children. As Zola's title suggests, contact with the land, rather than life in the modern city, could regenerate French men and through them, the nation.

In *Les Déracinés*, Barrès called for real men with rifles, not half-men bureaucrats.[36] Again, denigrating the manhood of one's opponents, in this case, state intellectuals, was a way of depicting them as subversive and dangerous to the health of the nation. Similarly, when Bérenger described the rise of an "intellectual proletariat," he claimed that the physiological consequences of such a proletariat were grave not only for the individuals in question, but also for the health of the nation or the "race," to use Bérenger's terminology. Members of the intellectual proletariat, because of pecuniary necessity, would take on too many sedentary occupations. Such an overtaxing of the intellect would create nervous individuals who were physically weak. A less healthy body would in turn create weak children. Indeed, members of the intellectual proletariat would be forced into unnatural liaisons—he mentioned prostitution and implied homosexuality—since they could not afford to marry and have children, thereby further contributing to France's declining birthrate.[37]

Barrès's description of the seven *bacheliers* in *Les Déracinés* in this regard is telling. The healthiest men in the novel are solidly bourgeois, firmly implanted in society, and true to the land and their regional roots. Roemerspacher, based in part on Charles Maurras, and Sturel, who serves at times as Barrès's own double, are saved by their contact with Lorraine. Roemerspacher is described as strong and well-built; his physiognomy is harmonious.[38] Although Sturel is delicate, he maintains a vitality through his ancestors and is thus able to ward off pernicious foreign influences.[39]

On the other hand, Mouchefrin and Racadot, the most disadvantaged of the group, are without regional roots and adrift in Parisian society. Both are depicted as physically grotesque. Mouchefrin is described as a "gnome," with the honeyed voice of a eunuch.[40] Racadot, son of a serf, looks old for his age; moreover, his physiognomy announces the violence which has been the mainstay of his family's history.[41] Finally, Racadot and Mouchefrin are also morally deformed; they kill Sturel's former mistress Mme. Aravian in order to sell her jewels and obtain money for their failing newspaper.

The character of Mme. Aravian, like Marina in L' Ennemi des lois, is foreign, "exotic," and exercises a fascination over Barrès's hero. In the earlier work, Marina, who represents instinct, is valorized; she is as necessary to André's happiness as is his cerebral wife Claire. At the end of the novel, André is living in a state of bliss with the two women, having joined his head and his heart, reason and instinct. Mme. Aravian, on the other hand, is depicted largely in negative terms. She represents the danger of the foreign, the uprooted, which threatens to engulf, indeed, to "poison" the young impressionable Sturel and through him, the health of the nation. A creator of disorder—like her murderers Racadot and Mouchefrin—she is a woman born to be assassinated, writes Barrès.[42] Barrès's portrayal of women is complex; although the feminine in his writings could represent the subversive, he also depicted the "feminine" trait of instinct in a positive fashion.

In common with Bourget and Barrès, Bérenger manifested a fear of "intellectualism," which he defined as a "perversion of the intellect that reduces us in life to seeking the spectacle of life, and in the realm of emotions, to seeking abstract ideas of emotions."[43] Bérenger, like other critics of "intellectualism," did not oppose intelligence but rather its excessive use which killed all emotion—both love and instinct—and created a dried out individual:

> The "intellectual" of our generation is a being more complex and more tormented . . . every trend of the century is realized in him, from the ages of eighteen to twenty-five. He has exhausted all the alternatives of modern thought

and has found satisfaction in none. A lucid dryness has
slowly crystallized his soul. Yet he suffers, and, on occasion,
he even dies from it, and therein lies his nobility.[44]

In *L'Effort*, Bérenger depicted Georges Lauzerte whom he described as "this thirty-year old intellectual, with a used up intellect, a withered heart, weary senses . . . this sick man."[45] His mother,
explained Bérenger, was an intellectual, too occupied by her intellectual activities to devote time to her son. Although Bérenger was
progressive in his view of male/female relations—he deplored the
dowry system and denounced a society that separated men and
women—he clearly attributed Lauzerte's inability to love and feel
to an "unnatural" mother, incapable of nurturing. His portrait of
Mme. Lauzerte is largely the product of his suspicion of excessive
"intellectuality," but it also seems to reflect the contemporary male
fear of a woman who did not know her place. Georges Lauzerte, the
unnatural son of an unnatural mother, grew up to become an "intellectual," who was either incapable of real action or a man who acted
in order to act, like a "neurasthenic [who] takes showers and plays
sports."[46] This reference to neurasthe. a is significant; in the context
of the fin de siècle, it implied nervousness and thus femininity.

It is difficult not to see in Bérenger's work a direct critique of
Barrès's heroes in the *culte du moi* series. Action for action's sake,
which Barrès's hero takes up in *Le Jardin de Bérénice*, was according to Bérenger, as sterile as "art for art's sake." Such an intellectual was doomed to extinction, destined for suicide, as was the case
with Lauzerte. Bérenger favored activity among intellectuals, as
opposed to passivity, advocating "art for life," action with a view to
understanding. Intellect, he claimed, was not an end in itself but
a means. Like Barrès in *L'Ennemi des lois* and *Les Déracinés*, he
called for the unity of head and heart.[47]

Bérenger, in common with other literary intellectuals of his
time, notably future anti-Dreyfusards Bourget and Barrès, deplored
not only the excessive scientific spirit that marked the age but also
the influence of Kant that accompanied it. Positivism, he believed,
was a by-product of Kantianism. Along with Barrès and Bourget,
the future Dreyfusard Bérenger opposed the absolutism and universality of Kantianism. His position contradicts the stereotypical
image of the Dreyfusard. Literary intellectuals in the Dreyfusard
camp were not always in agreement with their allies from the
republican university.

The case of Charles Maurras also challenges traditional
classifications of Dreyfusards and anti-Dreyfusards. Unlike fellow

anti-Dreyfusards Bourget and Barrès, Maurras was a firm believer in reason and deplored the overly sentimental. In *L'Avenir de l'intelligence*, he not only castigated women writers but represented the Romantic tradition and its Symbolist heirs as both feminine and foreign—specifically German. The "real" French tradition, incarnated by classicism, was virile. Responding to the contemporary preoccupation with "degeneration," he stated that instead of speaking of the degeneration of modern art, one could speak of its effeminacy: "Rather than saying that Romanticism has contributed to the degeneration of French intellects, wouldn't it be better to admit that it has feminized them?"[48] How could Hugo, represented as a virile male, be seen as anything other than a nervous, effeminate male? Romantic literature, which emphasized the *moi* and privileged sensibility over intellect and action, was resolutely feminine.[49]

In his thinking, Maurras was more in line with Max Nordau, who attacked modern art as degenerate and hysterical; both were accompanied by extreme emotionalism.[50] The excess of intellect was thus associated with nervousness, which in turn was linked with excessive emotion and physical inactivity. In *Degeneration*, Nordau denounced not only the Symbolists, the Wagnerians, and the Decadent-Esthetes, but also the Parnassians and the Naturalists, and devoted separate chapters to Ibsen, Tolstoy, and Nietzsche. The contemporary representation of artists as "degenerate" and "hysterical" paralleled the portrait of the invert, who was similarly represented; both were linked with effeminacy.

The anxieties about the health and numbers of the population, along with bourgeois ideals of the family, and the "crisis" of masculinity played an important role in determining the boundaries between "normal" and "abnormal" male sexuality. Indeed, the homosexual male posed an even greater danger to the social order than the "New Woman" because of the thin line separating male collegiality and friendship from male same-sex desire.[51] In France, as in other European countries, the medical community was instrumental in the definition of sexual "others;" the work of these doctors shaped the cultural construct of homosexuality for years to come.[52] France, however, differed from its neighbors in a number of important ways. England and Germany had harsher legislation concerning homosexuality—it was under the 1885 Criminal Law Amendment, which criminalized all homosexual acts, both public and private, that Oscar Wilde was convicted. France's Napoleonic Code, on the other hand, ignored homosexuality and distinguished between the public and the private, but French attitudes, both medical and cultural, were much more hostile to homosexuals than elsewhere in Europe. Moreover, French medical writings on homosexuality were out of step with the work of researchers in other countries like Richard von Krafft-Ebing and Havelock Ellis.[53]

The French persisted in equating sexuality with sex and moreover tended to view homosexuals not as a "third sex" but rather as effeminate males.[54] It is partly for this reason that the French could not accept the Greek ideal of masculine, virile homosexuals. In fact, the French discourse on homosexuality was largely developed in the absence of the word. The term "invert" was popular, but inverts were not seen as expressing the opposite of heterosexual desire but rather as exhibiting a weaker, incomplete version thereof. French researchers believed that the invert's weakened state left him vulnerable to "cerebral passions" which might lead to "unnatural" attachments. Inverts were seen as sexually inferior, impotent, and incomplete men. Moreover, they were represented as timid, cowardly, and even wicked, for dishonor was seen as the natural consequence of sexual perversion.[55] Even Gide, who penned a defense of homosexuality in *Corydon*, relied on this model to distinguish "real, manly pederasts" from "feminine" inverts.[56]

The Homosexual as Esthete: Defending Oscar Wilde

Despite the parallel discourses on avant-garde artists and homosexuals, it was not until the Wilde trial that the "decadent-esthete" was explicitly associated with the homosexual. By 1898, Krafft-Ebing could assert that there existed a medically proven connection between "homosexual decadence" and artistic feeling; both implied a heightened sensibility.[57] The Wilde trial, like other sexual scandals of the fin de siècle, contributed to a greater awareness of sexuality and moreover served to reinforce and encode gender roles.[58]

On 25 May 1895, Oscar Wilde was convicted under the British penal code for crimes of "gross indecency" and sentenced to two years of imprisonment with "hard labour." In the wake of Wilde's conviction, the French press rushed to condemn the author, whom they had lionized only four years earlier. In the years immediately preceding his conviction, Wilde had been the toast of the Parisian world of letters, even frequenting the famous *mardis* of Mallarmé.

Many of his fellow litterateurs on the other side of the English Channel abandoned Wilde, each outdoing the other to deny any relationship with the fallen artist. When journalist Jules Huret referred in *Le Figaro littéraire* to Catulle Mendès (1842), Marcel

Schwob (1867), and Jean Lorrain (born Paul Duval in 1856) as the "intimates" of Oscar Wilde during the latter's trial in April 1895, all three protested vigorously and Mendès even fought a duel with Huret.[59] The fact that Lorrain himself was a homosexual did not change matters. In fact, both Jean Lorrain and Marcel Proust fought duels against those who described them as homosexual, with Proust challenging Lorrain to a duel after one such incident! In the atmosphere of fin-de-siècle France, even to be called "effeminate" was a serious charge, a threat to a man's honor and to be avoided at all costs.

Gide himself claims to have been surprised by the allegations against Wilde: "Nothing, since I had been associating with Wilde, could have ever made me suspect a thing," he writes.[60] This is not as implausible as it sounds. As Alan Sinfield indicates in *The Wilde Century: Effeminacy, Oscar Wilde and the Queer Movement*, up until the first Wilde trial, being a "decadent-esthete" may have implied a certain "overrefinement," even an "effeminacy," but no *explicit* connection with homosexuality had yet been made.[61]

Indeed, Nordau made no mention of homosexuality with regard to Wilde in his first edition of *Degeneration*, instead denigrating his art: "The ego-mania of decadentism, its love of the artificial, its aversion to nature, and to all forms of activity and movement, its megalomaniacal contempt for men and its exaggeration of the importance of art, have found their English representative among the 'Aesthetes,' the chief of whom is Oscar Wilde."[62] Moreover, he criticized Wilde for his desire to "épater le bourgeois" and call attention to himself with his outlandish dress and manners. Nordau did note that "Oscar Wilde apparently admires immorality, sin and crime," but in his work, like that of his mentor Cesare Lombroso, avant-garde artists were associated with crime and madness.[63] Homosexuality was not necessarily an important component of this picture, but with the Wilde trials, the connection which had hitherto been implied, was now clearly drawn, as the reports in the major newspapers of the day illustrate.

The public in England and in France was disturbed by Wilde's nonchalant, indeed, facetious attitude on the stand, and his flaunting of conventions in the name of art. His firm belief in the superiority of the artist and his view that art was neither moral nor immoral disconcerted conventional sensibilities, as did his association with men of the lower classes.

The French popular press was somewhat bewildered by the criminal proceedings against Wilde and mocked the prudery of the English; humorist Alfred Capus wrote in *Le Figaro* of 11 April 1895 that in France such notoriety would increase an author's sales rather than close down his plays, as was the case in England. Finding the Marquess of Queensberry nearly as distasteful as Wilde himself, Gaston Jollivet wrote in *Le Gaulois* that the Wilde Affair struck a blow to British pride, to the aristocracy as well as to the middle classes.[64] In another article, he wrote that France had luckily narrowly escaped—Wilde had threatened to become a French citizen a few years earlier after his play *Salomé* was prevented from being staged in England.[65]

Still other articles cast aspersions on Wilde's sexuality, depicting him as effeminate. One of these, published in *Le Figaro* on 9 April, referred to Wilde as "a fat boy" (in English) and emphasized the fact that he had no facial hair. In France at this time, most men, especially republican men, sported abundant facial hair, a sign of virility. The same article, which depicted Wilde as "ce fantoche vicieux" (this vicious puppet), indicated that he applauded with small motions with his "mains mortes" (lifeless hands). The word "fantoche" refers figuratively to a man controlled by others. The expression "mains mortes" of course evokes the image of the effeminate "limp-wristed" homosexual. Wilde was thus no longer seen as a man of substance; he had lost his honor and could no longer be taken seriously. In this vein, the author of the article concluded by stating that Wilde was not an artist but a simple "fumiste" (phony).

In the 10 April issue of *Le Gaulois*, Paul Roche interviewed Max Nordau on Wilde. Nordau repeated textually the description of Wilde in *Degeneration* and added that he had predicted such a fate for the Irish writer. Nordau's influence was evident in the press reports on Wilde. Jollivet deplored Wilde's "monstrous vice," which he described as the result of a "fatality of physiological constitution."[66] In the following entry from *Le Figaro* of 7 April 1895, the author indicated that the Wilde trial offered a lesson in the dangers of "esthetic art." Such art could lead to overly refined sensualism, which could then exert a nefarious influence on the intelligence and manners of talented individuals:

> The English treat us to . . . lessons of esthetics which are not only spicy but which are also extremely instructive. . . . This is the natural, physiological outcome of a [certain] literary and esthetic effort. . . . It shows us the effect that the deviation of certain literary faculties toward a refined sensualism can exercise on the mind and manners of men who are surely gifted. . . . There are fatal degenerations that

result when one makes intellectual effort the product rather than the guide to sensations. Depravity follows shortly thereafter. . . .

He continued his diatribe against "esthetic" art by warning French artists against the influence of foreign literatures, which were represented as being dangerous to the health of the French nation: "Thus must we prevail upon our esthetes to show some moderation. We pardon them for Ibsen, albeit with difficulty. . . . But we would be appalled by the equivalent of Monsieur Wilde. . . ."

The well-thinking (bien pensante) French press, which saw itself as the defender of French culture, used the trial to criticize the esthetic school of art and castigate the avant-garde as subversive not only because it challenged traditional morality and conventions, but also because it favored foreign art. Indeed, a columnist for L'Echo de Paris, who wrote under the pseudonym of "Nestor," believed that the English magistrature in condemning Wilde, had served notice to "esthetes" that they could no longer act with impunity.[67]

Only a few journalists, chief among them Octave Mirbeau in Le Journal and Henry Bauër in L'Echo de Paris, came to Wilde's defense in the major newspapers. Both Mirbeau and Bauër denounced the barbarity of the sentence and castigated the hypocrisy of a culture that had condemned Wilde not on criminal grounds but on religious and moral ones.[68] As for Wilde's sexual preferences, they only mentioned them to dismiss them as Wilde's personal business and a source of disgust, although Bauër did recognize that homosexual liaisons were accepted when they occurred in classical literature but not in contemporary times.[69] Bauër further noted that men such as Wilde were subject to an "organic fatality;" they had little choice in the matter.[70] Thus, even those who defended Wilde distanced themselves from his sexual preferences.

The major avant-garde journals—La Plume, Le Mercure de France, and La Revue blanche—all published articles defending Wilde. Many criticized English morality and prudery. Writing in La Plume, Louis Lormel pointed out that the crime of which Wilde stood accused was not even recognized by French law. He defended Wilde in the name of individual liberty. Society, he stated, had no right to intervene unless the act were public or if a minor were involved.[71] His colleague at La Plume, Adolphe Retté agreed; Wilde's personal life was his own business.[72] Most of these writers felt that Wilde had not committed a crime and that the punishment far exceeded the transgression (faute). Moreover, they asked, given that the "crimes" for which Wilde had been charged had taken place in private, how could one prove he had committed them?[73] In his defense of Wilde, Hugues Rebell launched a diatribe against narrow, base Calvinist morality:

> They strike at Wilde first because he has violated the laws of this petty Calvinist morality, indulgent of all baseness of the soul and severe only toward passions, a morality that diminishes the beautiful and noble classical sense of the word virtue (*virtus*, courage) and which considers as crimes acts which in reality only offend he who commits them.[74]

Although these writers used the Wilde trial to criticize the hypocrisy of bourgeois morality, they themselves had difficulty in addressing Wilde's homosexuality. They either ignored Wilde's supposed crime or deplored his personal habits while defending his art. Paul Adam, writing in *La Revue blanche*, was one of the rare individuals who couched his defense of Wilde as a defense of homosexuality. He declared that French patriots, far from denouncing Wilde, should praise him for military reasons, since in antiquity the best armies were made up of soldiers who were lovers, an argument later taken up by Gide in *Corydon*.[75]

Adam used the opportunity to criticize contemporary French morals, which condoned heterosexual adultery—indeed, it was the subject of boulevard theater—but which viewed homosexuality as an anathema. Although the public was more tolerant of heterosexual adultery, it denounced all non-procreative sex, heterosexual and homosexual, as a threat to the health of the nation, a fact noted by Adam. Men were not supposed to waste their "vital forces," which they owed to the nation.[76] Adam found the passion shared by Lord Alfred Douglas and Wilde to be of the most noble sort; it depended neither on instinct nor on money.[77]

Lord Alfred Douglas himself published a defense of Wilde and of homosexuality in *La Revue blanche* on 1 June 1896. He noted that although the Catholic Church condemned sodomy, it praised chaste love between two friends of the same sex.[78] Denouncing the writings of Max Nordau and the tyranny of public opinion, he declared that he would gladly be in the company of such "degenerates" as Verlaine, Rosetti, and Wilde. Douglas also claimed that homosexuals, whom he described as the "salt of the earth," were often intellectually superior to other men and even better athletes.[79] Later in life, Douglas was to deny authorship of this article and maintain that his friendship with Wilde had been purely platonic.

Among the defenders of Wilde, Adam's was a lone voice. His avant-garde colleague Hugues Rebell spoke for the majority when he stated that he could not approve of such a defense.[80] These writers then were at some pains to distance themselves from Wilde's supposed manners. Stuart Merrill emphatically declared that the petition he and the editor of *La Plume*, Léon Deschamps, had launched in favor of Wilde was not a defense of Wilde's morals but rather a defense of his art and an appeal to humanity, describing Wilde as a madman, whose offense was lessened by the fact that it only afflicted those, who like him, were madmen.[81] Similarly, Retté claimed that if Wilde were indeed a "pederast," his "uncleanliness" only affected his conscience.[82] Even the paganist Rebell declared that he had no intention of defending acts of perversity, any more than the puritans.[83]

Even if they accepted that Wilde had committed homosexual acts, these writers saw them as individual acts, as signs of perversity perhaps, but not of perversion. Although they shared a belief in a common honor code with their fellow countrymen, their thinking was more liberal and more in keeping with that of sexual reformers in other countries. Wilde, who had lost his honor, was a fallen hero, "this sad hero," in Lormel's words. He was to be pitied rather than punished.[84]

If they were somewhat reticent with regard to Wilde's sexual proclivities, avant-garde writers were more forthcoming on Wilde's art. They felt, rightly so, that Wilde the artist, more than Wilde the man, had been on trial. Rebell viewed the trial as a crime of democracy, a crime of the "crowd" against the artist, the superior man: "the population of London which no longer has any gratitude for the man who entertained and charmed them but only hatred for the writer who has humiliated them by his talent. In attacking Wilde they attack success, wealth, intelligence. . . ."[85] A hallmark of Rebell's writings, this belief in the superior man and the hatred of democracy was echoed by other writers. Merrill railed against the false egalitarianism of present day society and spoke bitterly of the "Barbares," who had no right to destroy a poet, no matter his crime. He regretted the days when the Pope could forgive the artist Cellini even for murder, with the explanation that such men of talent were above the law.[86]

Most of those who defended him, Camille Mauclair, Adolphe Retté, Hugues Rebell, and Stuart Merrill believed that Wilde's art had been condemned. Rebell was furious that Wilde's writings, in particular, *The Portrait of Dorian Gray*, had been cited as "proof" of his immorality: "They have dared to destroy all the works of a writer whose morality no one had hitherto questioned."[87] Camille Mauclair commented that Wilde's disdain of bourgeois tastes and morals had worked against him: "The author has paid dearly for his disdain, his aristocratic tendencies, his refinement, his free-wheeling commentary on England; to have used his novel to condemn him is akin to condemning M. Huysmans upon the publication of *A Rebours*."[88] The comparison to *A Rebours*, also made by others, is significant since *A Rebours* was viewed as the principal text on homosexuality and decadence at this time.

Retté spoke for the majority when he reiterated Wilde's belief that art was neither moral nor immoral, and that the ultimate goal of the artist was the creation of beauty: "In times like ours, marked by excess and fatigue, should not Beauty be allied with Intensity? For souls . . . overburdened with disparate emotions, to feel deeply is practically a necessity."[89] In direct response to Nordau, Retté exalted the heightened sensibility of the artist and the Symbolist ideal of art. The avant-garde view of art, then, celebrating as it did an intensity of emotion, contradicted the contemporary ideal of manhood, which eschewed extreme emotionalism.

When Merrill and Deschamps circulated their petition for Wilde in the name of art and humanity, they expressly sought the signatures of well-known writers, realizing their own imprimatur would hardly persuade Queen Victoria to lessen Wilde's sentence.[90] Most of these writers, including Bourget, Coppée, Zola, Lemaître, and Barrès, however, refused to sign and thus the petition had to be abandoned. Unlike the Lucien Descaves trial, which united avant-garde and establishment authors against government censorship— fifty-four writers signed a petition in *Le Figaro* in favor of Descaves—the Wilde case pitted the avant-garde against the establishment. Well-known writers refused to sign, in large part because of Wilde's sexuality. They feared association with the "effeminate." Stuart Merrill expressed a great deal of bitterness toward established writers, whom he accused of betraying the example of Victor Hugo. Hugo, he felt, would have signed immediately, without worrying about his own reputation.[91]

While avant-garde writers may have shared the fears of established writers, they obviously felt they had more to gain than lose in defending Wilde. In coming to the beleaguered writer's aid, they manifested the solidarity of the avant-garde and defended at the same time a certain ideal of art, not shared by all of their elders. Finally, they not only defended themselves, they also lobbied for the liberty of the artist to create. These young writers clearly stated that fellow writers who abandoned Wilde to his fate were traitors to their calling.

Members of the avant-garde, much more than their established peers, felt a sense of common purpose with other artists. Seen in this light, the avant-garde's early, although by no means unanimous, defense of Emile Zola three years later seems less surprising. Once again, they came to the aid of a fellow writer, albeit one who did not share their esthetic ideals. The Affair, of course, assumed the proportions of a national event. It led to the involvement of writers and artists as a group, not just members of the avant-garde, and it went beyond the defense of one writer (Zola) by his peers. In a certain sense, the Wilde case was a dress rehearsal—albeit incomplete—for the Dreyfus Affair not only because writers banded together to intervene publicly, but also because it illustrates the ambivalence of contemporary attitudes vis-à-vis manliness.[92] The tensions already visible during the Wilde trial would explode onto the national scene during the Dreyfus Affair.

Eventually, Dreyfusards would exalt moral courage over physical courage, action by the pen rather than by the sword, but within each camp, there existed a great deal of diversity, as is evidenced by the pronouncements of intellectuals during the years before the Affair. On the one hand, Max Nordau, who was progressive in many ways, denigrated modern art as both excessively intellectual and emotional and praised strong, virile, and active men. Indeed, the future Zionist leader preferred "muscle Jews" to "coffeehouse" Jews.[93] Within the literary milieu, intellectuals hostile to the republican university's positivism, deplored the excess of intellect and called for the return of instinct and emotion. Not all of these intellectuals were future anti-Dreyfusards. Members of the literary avant-garde, especially the Symbolists, exalted emotion and heightened sensibility. On the other hand, even among future anti-Dreyfusards could one find individuals who celebrated reason over emotion. The fault line was thus by no means clearly demarcated. Historians of the Dreyfus Affair largely ignore this diversity within each camp when they designate Dreyfusards as "rational" and anti-Dreyfusards as "instinctual."

Despite their different definitions of manhood, intellectuals of the fin de siècle agreed on the ideal of manliness and designated their enemies, both male and female, as "effeminate." Caught between men of action on the one hand, as represented by politicians, workers, and military men, and university professors, on the other, whom they viewed as overly intellectual, literary intellectuals, particularly of the avant-garde, sought to defend themselves against charges of effeminacy and illustrate their manliness by asserting that one could act with the mind. Bernard Lazare's declaration that the pen was as worthy a weapon as the shotgun is telling.[94] Both conservative and progressive writers of the avant-garde called for heroes and men of action and will to regenerate the country—Bérenger's "effort" is paralleled by Barrès's "energy." Furthermore, they believed that they themselves could fulfill this function. In an article published in 1896, Bérenger called for a literature of action, announcing "the place of writers at the vanguard of social action."[95]

Bérenger's "intellectual heroes" included not only future Dreyfusards Zola and Clemenceau but also future anti-Dreyfusards Barrès and Léon Daudet. Barrès's hero was also a man of action; he could be a man of letters like poet Victor Hugo, symbol of an entire people, but he could also be a military hero like Napoleon or Boulanger. Nevertheless, Barrès's desire for an "intellectual Bonaparte" was indicative of his desire to unite thought and action.[96] As for Maurras, who denigrated Hugo as "effeminate," he, too, called for a virile literature of action. Both sides then exalted the ideal of action, but the nature of these ideals differed.

6

—ᴗᴧᴧ—

"The Sword or the Pen: Competing Visions of the Hero at the Fin de Siècle"

During the years that followed the French defeat in the Franco-Prussian War, the cult of the hero gained great popularity in France. The contemporary exaltation of the army and of sports, especially dueling, promoted the heroic ideal. This heroic cult manifested itself in all aspects of national life, from the curriculum of the primary schools to literature and the arts.[1] Indeed, writers and artists, along with the architects of the republican school reforms, did a great deal to promote the cult of the hero—not only popular writers like Paul Déroulède, Alphonse Daudet, Erkmann-Chartrian, and G. Bruno but also Charles Péguy, Maurice Barrès, and Romain Rolland. Among the most beloved plays of the period was Edmond Rostand's *Cyrano de Bergerac.*

The celebration of heroes was part of a concerted effort toward national redressment. France may have been defeated in the Franco-Prussian War but she had not been vanquished. Indeed, she possessed a strong heroic race which had contributed to the grandeur of the French nation. The use of heroes not only cemented national solidarity, but it also served to legitimize the new Republic and illustrate that it was rooted in tradition. Heroes of the distant past like Vercingétorix and Joan of Arc were celebrated, along with the heroes of the recent past, of the Revolution and the Empire.

Although the military hero was an especially powerful symbol at this time, an integral component of *revanche*, by no means did he represent the only type of heroic ideal. The leaders of the Third

Republic also encouraged the cult of civilian heroes. In an era of dechristianization, the rise of secular heroes was accompanied by a decline in religious ones. Political leaders Danton and Mirabeau were celebrated by republicans, as were writers Voltaire and Diderot. During the early years of the Republic, poet Victor Hugo and savant Louis Pasteur emerged as contemporary national heroes. Even syndicalist and socialist groups joined in, creating their own "Pantheon" of heroes, choosing among the leaders of 1848 and the Commune. The democratic creed of the Republic also encouraged the belief that anyone could become a hero, even the ordinary man or woman. The Académie française discerned annual *prix de vertu*, in order to celebrate the heroism of "daily acts of courage."[2]

Despite the different types of heroes exalted, heroism, whether incarnated in a single act or in an exemplary life, was founded, above all, on courage, both physical and moral. Heroism also implied self-control and scorn of danger, both male qualities (*une mâle vertu*.) Although heroes were not limited to men, as Joan's popularity suggests, heroic virtues were viewed as specifically male. Heroes, who exhibited an exceptional strength of will, were defined by their strong sense of self, honor, and duty, along with their belief in discipline and sacrifice. Furthermore, heroes sacrificed themselves not for egotistical reasons but for the greater good of the collectivity, in most cases, the nation. Finally, heroic qualities could be innate but more often were the result of religious or civic and moral instruction, hence the importance of the church, school, and army in the formation of different types of heroes.[3]

The search for national heroes at the fin de siècle was the consequence of a widespread sense of national inferiority vis-à-vis Germany, indeed, a perceived loss of national honor, as well as the product of collective guilt with regard to the egoism and selfishness of modern consumer culture.[4] Both these fears fed directly into the contemporary crisis of masculinity in France, which was further exacerbated by the emergence of feminist movements and the decline in the national birthrate. Frenchmen feared the loss of honor not only on the field of battle but also in their daily lives, both at work and at home. The specter of modern, industrial, consumer society threatened traditional notions of male and female separate spheres and of social distinction, producing instead men whom they viewed as enervated, overly intellectual, and "effeminate."

Given such an atmosphere, it is not surprising that there emerged conflicting ideals of the hero during the Dreyfus Affair, with each side laying exclusive claim to honor and manhood. Dreyfusard and anti-Dreyfusard intellectuals, I will argue, represented two competing visions of male honor: the Dreyfusard intellectual hero privileged moral and intellectual courage over physical courage, while the anti-Dreyfusard military hero celebrated physical courage and the cult of the army.[5]

New light can be shed on the Affair by viewing it as a battlefield for conflicting views of intellect, honor, and manhood. An examination of Dreyfusard and anti-Dreyfusard heroes is also a means by which to recover the mystique of the Dreyfus Affair, lost in most sociological analyses of the events. Before examining this issue within the context of the Affair, it is necessary to first study the army and its role in French society during the years preceding. The place of the army in a modern, democratic society became a source of heated debate, which was closely linked to the importance of intellect and learning in this society.

In the wake of the Franco-Prussian War, the army represented the repository of national honor, specifically of male honor. According to nationalist Paul Déroulède, the army was the guardian of "male sentiments" and of "virile habits."[6] Similarly, the Marquis de Chasseloup-Laubat, one of the members of the Assemblée Nationale of 1872–1873, referred to the "virile education" provided by the army. Through the army, France would regain her lost honor and glory.[7]

During these years, the idea of universal military service became increasingly popular. In 1873, substitution for military service was abolished; heretofore, an individual could buy a substitute to serve in his place. The well-to-do often did so, as did peasants, who needed their sons to work the land. Military service of five years was also established at this time, although those who drew a good number in the draft lottery were only required to serve for a year (this two-tiered system continued until 1889). The government, however, established a number of dispensations, mostly for the educated, including service for a year on payment of 1,500 francs. In 1889, when service was reduced to three years, the 1,500 franc exemption was abolished, as were dispensations for those previously exempt, namely, students, seminarians, and teachers. Henceforth, these individuals were obliged to serve, although only for a year.[8]

In light of such reforms, the relationship of the army to the nation underwent a profound change. Not only was the army instrumental for military reasons, but it also had acquired important social functions. The early leaders of the Third Republic, of varying political persuasions, viewed the army as "the great school of future generations."[9] It would provide social and moral discipline, especially important in a democracy, but would also promote national reconciliation and the fraternity of social classes. While monarchists and other traditionalists associated the soldier's role with that of the priest, republicans associated it with that of the *instituteur*. Both groups, however, obviously viewed the army as a means by which to educate the common man and inculcate in him the love of country, the sense of honor and dignity, and the necessity for sacrifice, along with obedience and respect to and for hierarchy, order, and authority.[10]

The military cult reigned supreme during the first years of the Third Republic, as is evidenced by the popularity of the school battalions in which young boys dressed in military uniforms were taught gymnastics and the manipulation of arms. The spectacular rise of General Boulanger may also be seen in light of the exaltation of the military hero as savior.[11] The army thus became the "holy arch" (*l'arche sainte*), a sacred institution inextricably linked to the well-being of the nation. Any attack on the army was therefore viewed as an attack on national honor. Moreover, it called into question the virility and heroism of the French soldier, who, according to a writer for the patriotic *Le Gaulois*, represented "the most beautiful incarnation of national honor."[12]

If the army had represented a source of national unity during the early years of the Republic, it no longer did so from 1890 onwards. The decline of *revanche*, the rise of socialism and anarchism, and the coming of age of a new generation of bourgeois writers obliged to serve the flag all contributed to a reexamination of the army and its role in a democracy. These writers published numerous works attacking the army; among the best known included Abel Hermant's *Le Cavalier miserey* (1887), Lucien Descaves's *Les Sous-offs* (1889), and Georges Darien's *Biribi* (1890). Their writings provoked a heated national debate, and the army became, not a source of cohesion, but of great division.

By its supporters and its detractors alike, the army during the late nineteenth century was depicted as an institution in conflict with modernity and specifically with the development of a democracy. In truth, this conflict did not just pit civilian society against military society; it was present inside the army itself. The Dreyfus Affair revealed and exacerbated a crisis within the army, which had undergone a number of changes in recruitment and service that altered its composition, especially its mode of advancement.[13]

France's defeat in the Franco-Prussian War revealed a backward army lacking in technology, strategy, and leadership. In order to address these failings, the Ecole de Guerre, based on the Prus-

sian model, was founded in 1876 and organized in 1880. Its function was to furnish and train future officers of the General Staff in
the formulation of new methods of waging war.[14] Entry into the
Ecole de Guerre was based on competitive examination which favored intellectual abilities. Those most likely to succeed had attended one of two *grandes écoles* for the military, Saint-Cyr or the
Ecole Polytechnique. The privileging of meritocratic, intellectual,
and technocratic values was denigrated by traditional army officers,
including those from the aristocracy, who viewed this new method
of promotion as German and foreign to French tradition. Intelligence, they felt, hardly qualified as a martial quality. The traditional French soldier had been a man promoted through the ranks
by virtue of his wartime exploits; he had paid for his advancement
with his own blood and courage. By 1894, this model had all but
disappeared. From 1880 on, the level of academic instruction of
army officers rose significantly, as an increasing number of Saint-
Cyr and Polytechnique graduates filled the officer corps. The new
emphasis on technology thus created a corps of elite officers. Graduates of one of the *grandes écoles*, they were most likely to be members of the artillery, which had became the preferred path to high
leadership.[15]

In light of the new type of recruitment based on meritocratic
and intellectual criteria, an increasing number of bourgeois families, including Jewish families, sent their sons into the army.[16]
Alfred Dreyfus and Armand Mayer, who was killed in a duel by the
anti-Semitic Marquis de Morès in 1892, were two such individuals.
Both were not only Jews, but also artillery officers and graduates
of the Ecole Polytechnique; in addition, Dreyfus was a member of
the General Staff. Seen as upstarts, they represented the new army
and were viewed with suspicion and resentment by traditionalists,
who were especially numerous in the upper echelons of the army
bureaucracy. The rise of anti-Semitism among army officers during
the 1880s and 1890s may be seen as part of a general phenomenon
in French society, but it was also specifically related to the army
and corporatist in nature.[17]

During the Affair, opponents of the army depicted it as the last
stronghold of the aristocracy and of practicing Catholics, denouncing the army as a "jésuitière," that is, filled with former students
of the Jesuits. Yet the true situation of the army offers a more
complex and nuanced picture. Although the proportion of nobles in
the officer corps increased slightly after 1870 (to 11 percent), it
never attained the all time high level of the years of Charles X's
reign. Nobles occupied an especially important place in the cavalry,

up to 38 percent in 1885, while their numbers in the infantry and the artillery were relatively modest (in the single digits); in the artillery, their numbers even decreased after 1870.[18] The proportion of nobles did increase as one went up in the ranks; 17 percent of colonels were noblemen, as were 35–39 percent of the generals.[19] In fact, the proportion of students from Jesuit institutions was small compared to those from public institutions.[20] It is true, however, that in the wake of the defeat and the Commune, an increasing number of officers returned to their Catholic faith as a guarantor of order, and the numbers of practicing Catholics in the army increased.[21]

The army at the fin de siècle was profoundly divided into individuals from different social categories who expressed vastly different cultural outlooks. Members of the traditionalist aristocracy, feeling isolated in a democratic, capitalist society in which money and intelligence played an increasingly greater role in social promotion, sought refuge in the army as the last bastion of aristocratic privilege. For them, it represented the aristocratic values of tradition, hierarchy, honor, and courage. Yet the army itself was undergoing the same types of social changes that were occurring in the rest of society. The new means of promotion, which emphasized intellectual attributes, acquired through the state university, seemed to shut them out of the army as well.

As for uneducated soldiers of the popular classes like Colonel Henry of *faux patriotique* fame, the new system meant that promotion through the ranks of petty officers was no longer possible. The author of "Nos Petits Pioupous," a journalist for the ultra-patriotic *Le Gaulois*, noted that the new system of intellectual merit excluded soldiers of the poor classes, just as the old aristocratic system of promotion through one's name and alliances had, perhaps even more. They saw sons of the bourgeoisie bypassing them in rank, simply because they possessed a cultural and intellectual capital inaccessible to them.[22] Such a critique, expressed here in a right-wing newspaper, was echoed by the Left. Finally, in peacetime, advancement was extremely slow; indeed, the role of the officer in peacetime was a question of discussion. Besieged from within and without, the army was politicized during the late nineteenth century. Its soldiers became both actors and objects of a national drama that would explode onto the national scene during the Dreyfus Affair.

The debate that pitted the intellectual hero against the military hero during the Affair, however, was not a new one. It was already in place during the 1890s, launched by the publication of a number of antimilitarist writings. Antimilitarism was by no means a homogeneous phenomenon. Different individuals and groups opposed the army for a variety of reasons. While pacifists like Leo Tolstoy opposed the army because they held all war in horror, many anarchists rejected the idea of a nation itself and denounced the army as a pillar of that nation. As for workers, most of them feared the army as a strikebreaker. Many of the bourgeois intellectuals who wrote about the excesses of the army during the 1890s did not necessarily oppose the army itself but rather the conditions inside the army and its brutal treatment of conscripts. Furthermore, a good number of Dreyfusard intellectuals viewed themselves as patriots whose love of the army obliged them to denounce its manipulation of justice and its claim to be above civilian law, although the antimilitarism of a number of their fellow intellectuals was born of their anarchist sympathies.[23]

Among opponents and defenders of the army, there existed individuals who believed that the values of the army were incompatible with those of a modern democratic society. Indeed, some of the populist attacks launched against the army by Dreyfusard Urbain Gohier are echoed by anti-Dreyfusard Edouard Drumont. Part of the problem lay in the contradiction between the establishment of universal military service, which brought civilians in great numbers into the army, and the maintenance of a professional army. The goals of the two groups conflicted with one another.

Le Cavalier miserey (1887), one of the first of the antimilitarist works of the period, did not expound a specific thesis. Instead, it told the story of a simple solider corrupted and destroyed, both physically and emotionally, by the hardships he experienced in the army. He was a cog in a system he barely understood. Hermant did not question the institution of the army itself but rather conditions within it. Nevertheless, the book provoked a strong reaction among defenders of the army, including Anatole France, who forbade any questioning of a sacred institution.[24]

Lucien Descaves's *Les Sous-offs*, published two years later, elicited an even stronger reaction. Dedicated to "those whose blood the nation takes, not to shed it, but in order to submit it, in the absurd peace of the military wine cellar, to the taints of dilution and of sophistication," it thus held the nation responsible for the sufferings of its soldiers.[25] *Les Sous-offs* traced the paths of two young conscripts, Favières and Tétrelle, and their careers as petty officers. The portrait painted by Descaves was somber. Army life corrupted young, innocent men, and encouraged them to lead lives of debauch and dishonor. The official army rhetoric of honor was juxtaposed with the private lives of its officers. When Favières learns that a fellow officer lives off the earnings of his prostitute mistress, he is shocked by such behavior. Through the course of his military service, however, he, too, is corrupted. He and Tétrelle frequent a bordello. Favières impregnates his lover and then abandons her upon learning of her pregnancy. The book culminates with the suicide of Tétrelle and the end of Favières's term of service.

As he heads for home, Favières, who feels that he is recovering from a long illness, reflects on the immorality and brutality of life in the army. Not only had his civilian clothes been taken away from him when he entered the army, but he also had been deprived of his conscience and his soul: "it was his entire being which had been transformed. . . . He was obliged as well in order to put on the moral uniform of the establishment, to leave behind his conscience."[26] The army created brutalized automatons, deprived of their humanity:

> And he thinks of the immense hoax, of the prodigious duplicity of this exemplary repetitive machine . . . he is incensed by the monstrosities rendered possible, natural, normal by the bearing of the sabre; of the kind of immunity he creates in favor of cowardice of the heart, of intelligence, of abuses of power, of things in life which are stripped of heroism. Heroism! . . . He asks himself why this cultivated hothouse flower requires so much fertilizer from the dunghill.[27]

For his audacity, Descaves, along with his publisher, was tried for defamation of the army and its officers, as well as for an affront to public decency in 1890. The government was particularly indignant that the book had provoked the *Berlin Gazette* to note that the French were tiring of their military regime. Supporters of the army argued, as they would during the Dreyfus Affair, that criticism of the army was dangerous to the national defense. The intellectual community, too, was profoundly disturbed by the charges brought against one of their own, launching a petition in Descaves's favor in the 24 December 1889 issue of *Le Figaro*.

The text, which included the names of fifty-four signataries, began with the following declaration:

> For twenty years now, we have become accustomed to liberty. We have acquired the right to honesty. In the name of the independence of the writer, we raise ourselves up with energy against all attacks against the liberty of written expression. In solidarity, when art is at issue, we urge the government to consider [its actions].

Although most of the authors who signed were young, avant-garde writers like Descaves, a significant number included established writers who belonged to the older generation. Among the signataries included such future Dreyfusards as Emile Zola, Jean Ajalbert, and Gustave Geoffroy (1855), but also supporters of the army like Alphonse Daudet, Edmond de Goncourt, Paul Bourget, and Maurice Barrès. Although Bourget and Barrès became anti-Dreyfusards, as did Jean Lorrain, another signatary, (Goncourt and Daudet died before the height of the Affair), here, they defended the right to liberty of expression of a fellow writer.

Since the liberalization of the press laws in 1881, writers had become accustomed to their freedom of speech and claimed their independence vis-à-vis all forms of authority. This petition, as Christophe Charle notes, which did not attempt to comment on Descaves's book, allowed writers of different political tendencies to band together in defense of a fellow writer.[28] Descaves was acquitted the following month, perhaps in part because of the petition. By the time of the Affair, tensions ran so high that such a petition uniting supporters and critics of the army was no longer possible.

Finally, Georges Darien's *Biribi*, published a year later, recounted the sufferings of soldiers in the colonial army, who were tormented by their superior officers and subjected to excessively harsh punishment. The authors of the antimilitarist literature of the period depicted the brutal conditions of army life. These critics of the army deplored the unnecessary cruelty of officers toward their soldiers and the immorality and debauchery promoted by life in the barracks. The army, they believed, deprived a man of his manhood, as defined by his ability to think and act freely. It took his conscience and his humanity away from him and created a robot, capable only of following orders blindly.

Such themes were continued in much of the Dreyfusard literature on soldiers. In "Conscrits," Dreyfusard Laurent Tailhade referred to young recruits as "pantins" (puppets), the same image used to deride Oscar Wilde.[29] In "Valets de Picque," Tailhade described soldiers as "the darlings of Sodom."[30] He also wrote that the army contributed to the brutalization of young men; deprived of the right to think for themselves, they would be forever devirilized.[31] Similarly, Urbain Gohier wrote that life in the barracks was responsible for "brutal vices" and "ignoble perversions."[32] Like other Dreyfusards, who criticized both the army and the Catholic Church, Tailhade wrote that Catholicism, in suppressing pride and honor, "these two supreme manifestations of sexual life and of intelligence," suppressed manhood as well.[33]

Women were often depicted as subversive forces, by both Dreyfusards and anti-Dreyfusards. Gohier's series "Les Femmes," for *L'Aurore*, was particularly misogynist. Gohier criticized women— mothers, daughters, sisters, and wives—for perpetuating the military cult: "From the females of the caves to . . . the beautiful Mesdames of the Horse Races, women are responsible in large part for the warlike histrionics of males."[34] Many men, according to Gohier, became soldiers because they felt they could attract women with their uniforms and moreover make a good marriage. If women raised their sons to despise the military, they would not become soldiers. In a subsequent article, Gohier held women responsible not only for the ills of militarism, but also for those of clericalism.[35] This was yet another way of undercutting the manhood of soldiers, by describing them as the pawns of women. In all of these works then, the soldier was deprived of his manhood; either a victim or a torturer, he was no hero.

"L'Appel au Soldat" or the Anti-Dreyfusard Hero

Like critics of the Left, many conservatives decried the debauchery of life in the barracks, among them Etienne Lamy, who published a lengthy article on "Les Ennemis de l'armée," in *La Revue des deux mondes* in 1894.[36] Lamy suggested that money be spent to create a friendlier and more hospitable atmosphere in the barracks, so that soldiers would not be tempted to seek their pleasures elsewhere.[37] Unlike left-wing critics of the army, however, most conservatives did not believe that the depiction of conditions in the army was accurate. Lamy felt that the abuses of which they wrote were either the exceptions to the rule or had disappeared in the new army by the time they wrote about them.[38] Truth be known, the army suffered not from cruelty due to excessive discipline, but rather a lack thereof.[39]

Carle des Perrières, writing in *Le Gaulois,* shared these opinions, believing that the French had gotten both too soft and too sentimental. The excesses inflicted on soldiers, such as those described in Darien's *Biribi*, were to be condemned, but at the same time, one should continue to support officers and recognize the importance of discipline in the army.[40] Another commentator, René Vallery-Radot deplored the increasingly violent and polemical tone of the antimilitarist novels of the period, in particular of Descaves's *Les Sous-offs*, but cautioned military leaders to treat their soldiers with humanity. Obligatory military service could seem unnecessary and onerous to a new generation for whom the Franco-Prussian War represented ancient history.[41]

Supporters of the army clearly recognized the changes wrought by universal military service. Lamy believed that antimilitarist literature was born of obligatory military service. He castigated these writers for criticizing the army without recognizing its grandeur, like their illustrious predecessor, Romantic poet Alfred de Vigny. They had not been motivated by national interest, but rather by their own personal needs. Moreover, they wrote not as soldiers but as civilians. While these writers were inspired by their own imaginations and egos, the army's goal was self-sacrifice.[42] As another defender of the army put it, imagination, which was the prerogative of the artist, contradicted the goal of the soldier.[43]

In "L'Officier et l'intellectuel," published in La Libre Parole during the height of the Affair, the military spirit was defined as a spirit of obedience and sacrifice. The military hero was a "disinterested soldier" who suffered for the common good, in contrast with egotistical intellectuals who cared only for their Moi and conspired with foreigners.[44] In his famous article "Après le procès," published in La Revue des deux mondes, anti-Dreyfusard Ferdinand Brunetière opposed the spirit of solidarity of the army to the "individualism" and "anarchy" of intellectuals.[45]

Just as the disinterestedness of the soldier was opposed to the egotism of intellectuals, so, too, was the soldier's virility juxtaposed with the intellectual's weakness. In a series of articles on the army and the nation, Jules Lemaître deplored the decline of patriotism among young people who had never known France's grandeur. Born after the defeat of 1870, these "pale intellectuals" undermined the army with their antimilitarist writings.[46] Lemaître described the army as a "sacred tribe," which constituted a "virile baptism" for young men, praising soldiers' courage, energy, and physical endurance.[47]

The virility and honor of the army corresponded to a critique of the increasing importance of commerce, industry, and money in society. In "Patrie, armée, discipline," sometimes Dreyfusard René-François-Armand Sully-Prudhomme argued that any country that wished to preserve its independence had to keep its military spirit intact, protecting it from the softening effects of modern life, particularly in a mercantile democracy.[48] He deplored the "refined and soft manners of modern society," which conspired to emasculate the army, the sole remaining virile force in society.[49] Once again, that which threatened the status quo was represented as feminine. Commerce and industry, according to Sully-Prudhomme, contributed to a lessening of the military spirit.

Such sentiments were echoed by his *Revue des deux mondes* collaborator Ferdinand Brunetière, who wrote that a nation's grandeur did not depend on its commerce and industry but rather on its military might and diplomacy.[50] Brunetière lauded the soldier's disinterestedness and his rejection of material goods, citing the low commissions of army officers, who could barely make ends meet. Soldiers sacrificed their personal ambition to serve their country.[51] The author of the *Libre Parole* article "L'Officier et l'intellectuel" shared this conviction, contrasting the soldier's scorn of riches to the pursuit of wealth and recognition by intellectuals. Just as Jews were denied the right to honor because of their association with money, so, too, in this instance were intellectuals. Anti-capitalism was a powerful theme in anti-Dreyfusard literature, but it was echoed by socialists and anarchists in the Dreyfusard camp.

Although not all of them were antidemocratic, most anti-Dreyfusards praised the army as the last bulwark against the anarchy and disorder disseminated by the advent of democracy. Charles Maurras believed that democracy contributed to the destruction of the army. In an article published in *Le Soleil* on 29 October 1895, he denounced the law of 1889, which had established universal military service. This law, he believed, had introduced anarchy and disorder in the army by obliging young, educated bourgeois men, who were used to their liberties and privileges in civilian life, to serve in the army. Unaccustomed to obeying orders, humiliated by their duties, they were articulate enough to write of their experiences, thereby contributing to the rise of anti-patriotism.[52]

Etienne Lamy directed his ire against the bourgeois elite, specifically in the persons of antimilitarist writers. Their bourgeois vanity, he declared, had been humiliated by association with the poor classes. The danger of democracy, he believed, was the contradiction between its maxims and manners. In the name of equality, the bourgeoisie for the last one hundred years had eradicated all barriers separating it from the nobility while still maintaining all the barriers between itself and the people. Life in modern society only fortified the possessors of fortune, intelligence, and scientific knowledge of their own primacy. Only one institution challenged the bourgeoisie's vision of itself as superior. In the army, intelligence would be sterile without the devotion and courage of all; obedience, above all else, allowed the army to function. In the army, the possessors of fortunes realized how little they counted in the defense of the nation, especially in comparison to the poorer classes.[53]

While castigating bourgeois writers for their lack of understanding of the true meaning of democracy, Lamy also deplored the negative effects of democracy on the principle of authority. The principles of popular sovereignty and of universal manhood suffrage led individuals to believe in their own personal superiority vis-à-vis the leaders they elected. How could military authority remain intact in such a situation? Among the three traditional forces society used to discipline and educate men, only the army remained. The state was attempting to destroy the Catholic Church by exalting the grandeur and independence of human beings in the teachings of the school system. Instead of discipline and hierarchy, they learned intellectual rebellion.[54]

Lamy opposed the discipline of the army to "democratic pride," declaring that the abuse of reason had fomented intellectual anarchy,[55] a belief shared by Sully-Prudhomme, who felt that democracy promoted the individual desires and pride of each person.[56] The sole remedy lay in the army and its leaders, which could reestablish order. Only the army could illustrate that equality between men did not exist but rather a hierarchy of aptitudes.[57]

In "Après le procès," Ferdinand Brunetière noted that it was not with democracy that the army was incompatible but rather with the spirit of individualism and anarchy.[58] The army was not only a school for equality but also for hierarchy and discipline; inequality was acceptable if it was the result of individual merit rather than privilege.[59] In a talk he delivered for the Ligue de la Patrie française a year later, Brunetière argued that in a democracy, only an army was capable of national unity.[60]

The attitudes of these partisans of the army toward intelligence and learning all betray a certain defensiveness. Jules Lemaître valued intellectual qualities, calling for intelligence and humanity among officers.[61] He even claimed that there were intellectuals among soldiers.[62] Nevertheless, he lamented the fact that officers advanced in their careers because of their intellectual knowledge rather than for their martial qualities.[63]

Brunetière shared these beliefs. In the army, intellectuals would learn that intelligence was a quality like any other and that there were other qualities that were worth more.[64] Himself an intellectual, Brunetière seemed at times scornful of intellect, declaring that soldiers were perhaps not strong in paleography and organic science—he was deriding certain Dreyfusard intellectuals here—but possessed a spirit of sacrifice and abnegation.[65]

Although Lamy, too, deplored "intellectual anarchy," he did not juxtapose intelligence to obedience but rather attempted to reconcile the two. Commenting on the old army, Lamy declared that, previously, intelligence had not been a common characteristic among the mass of soldiers and officers. Within the new army, however, intelligence was a valued commodity. The soldier was no longer a brutal automaton; he had to use his judgment to understand the orders he was obeying. The new methods of instruction, far from destroying intelligence, as the enemies of the army claimed, required him to develop and extend his intelligence.[66]

The anonymous author of an article, "Du rôle social de l'officier," published in *La Revue des deux mondes*, himself an army officer, also recognized the advances made in the army as the result of the new emphasis on intelligence.[67] He, too, attempted to reconcile intelligence and reflection with action, deploring the traditional suspicion of "men of thought" with regard to "men of the sword."[68] At the same time, however, unlike Lamy, he felt that emphasis on intellectual ability and technocratic capacity created an automaton, well-versed in military techniques but lacking a civic and moral education.[69]

He believed that in light of the new law establishing universal military service, the army via the officer, had a duty to play a role in society as educator. Since all young men were obliged to spend time in the army, they offered great potential to the officer who could form them. The officer could create a sense of common purpose and harmony among soldiers, thereby contributing to national solidarity.[70]

The staff of the traditionalist *La Revue bleue* agreed. In an editorial entitled "L'Education morale dans l'armée," in which they praised the author of the *Revue des deux mondes* article, they declared that heretofore the typical officer had possessed military courage but had lacked civic courage; he had been a man of action but not of reflection. Moral education in the army could remedy this failing and contribute to both the renovation of the army and the renewal of the nation.[71] The role of the army, declared another *Revue bleue* collaborator René Vallery-Radot, was greater than ever, calling for a military manual that would expound on the role of the officer in peacetime.[72] It would be easy to caricature defenders of the army as rabid partisans of order, obedience, and hierarchy, opposed to the use of intelligence and conscience, but as these articles illustrate, this was not necessarily the case. Defenders of the army may have opposed "intellectual anarchy," a common accusation against one's enemies during this time, but they did not categorically oppose intelligence itself. Instead, they believed that intelligence must be reconciled with a sense of order and hierarchy and that it should be accompanied by a moral conscience. This belief in a moral conscience was shared by their opponents, albeit in defense of a different ideal. The texts I have examined also demonstrate that the battle lines pitting intelligence and independence of thought against hierarchy were not always clear-cut and moreover, that the question of intelligence in the army was itself part of a larger debate concerning the increasing importance of intelligence and learning in a democratic society.

For these defenders of the army, the majority of whom were anti-Dreyfusards (there were of course Dreyfusard defenders of the army—Péguy and Proust—to name the two most famous examples), the army represented authority and hierarchy and constituted the last bastion of traditional order. They feared an increasingly democratic society, which promoted mercantilism and mass culture. Mass culture was represented as feminine and therefore selfish and egotistical. The army, on the other hand, represented a scorn of money, a "disinterestedness." For others, the army was the last bulwark against "intellectual anarchy." They rejected a meritocratic society in which intelligence was measured by competitive exams and promoted by the state. In fact, they feared being left behind in a society in which intelligence increasingly represented power. Perhaps this is why certain anti-Dreyfusards sounded defensive when they claimed that soldiers could be intellectuals too. The opposition of the military hero to the intellectual hero would crystallize at the time of the Dreyfus Affair, in the person of Colonel Henry for the anti-Dreyfusards, and in Emile Zola and Colonel Picquart for the Dreyfusards.

The Intellectual Hero

Like his anti-Dreyfusard counterpart, the Dreyfusard hero was "disinterested" and sought to serve the common good. Naturally, the Dreyfusard vision of the common good differed radically from the anti-Dreyfusard notion. Although Dreyfusards sought to incorporate the contemporary ideal of the man of action into that of the intellectual, they valued above all intelligence and culture. The Dreyfusard hero, as the editorial staff of La Revue blanche noted, obeyed not men but rather abstract ideals.[73] His conscience compelled him to sacrifice his person for truth and justice. He stood apart, indeed, above the crowd.

The first Dreyfusard hero was, of course, Emile Zola, who committed a "revolutionary act," to paraphrase Jules Guesde, by publishing "J'Accuse." His entry into battle forced intellectuals to take sides, for or against, and marked the full-fledged entry of intellectuals as a group into the life of the nation. Previously, lone figures like Voltaire and Hugo had entered the national arena. During the decade preceding the Affair, small groups of intellectuals, particularly of the avant-garde, had banded together in defense of a common cause. Intellectuals had thus already been politicized.

The Dreyfus Affair, however, was the first time intellectuals from a variety of different groups joined *en masse* into a national discussion, not only as individual citizens but as members of a sociological group, which had the right and indeed the duty to speak publicly. According to Alfred Vallette, Director of *Le Mercure de France*: "Monsieur Emile Zola had not only the right but also the duty—which is incumbent upon us all—to protest against illegality."[74] Similarly, fellow Dreyfusard Gabriel Séailles stated that the professional duty of intellectuals, in his case, of university professors, was to maintain the integrity of the national conscience.[75] This view was shared by anti-Dreyfusard intellectuals, although their vision of the nation differed radically from their Dreyfusard counterparts.

Although many Dreyfusard intellectuals felt that Zola was continuing in the great tradition of Voltaire, Hugo, and Lamartine, they clearly recognized, along with anti-Dreyfusards, the historical importance of Zola's act.[76] Gustave Geoffroy praised Zola for leaving the peace of his study to descend into the national arena. "Disinterestedness" and a love of truth had made him a "man of action." Geoffroy noted that Zola's intervention had surprised his opponents less than the fact that he had protested against the abuses of the army and the government. Had Zola published "J'Approuve," his opponents would have welcomed his involvement.[77]

In "Des Hommes d'action," published in *L'Aurore* on 28 February 1898, Henry Leyret declared that intellectuals, defined as "savants, *philosophes*, professors, artists, [and] writers," had abandoned the ivory tower to proclaim the inviolability of justice and reason against the tyranny of the sword. These "ideologues" had thus revealed themselves as "men of action," whereas previously, their role had been to serve as the honor and glory of the nation in a purely decorative sense.

Camille Mauclair stated that an intellectual revolution had been accomplished by Zola. Appealing to intellectuals to found an intellectual party and continue to fight, he recognized the entry of intellectuals in public life as a permanent state of affairs. He also spoke of a new moral Republic with intellectuals leading the way.[78]

Leyret praised intellectuals, naming not only Zola, but also savant Emile Duclaux, philosopher Gabriel Séailles, author Anatole

France, and artist Eugène Carrière. The only victories recognized by posterity, declared Leyret, were of the intellectual kind. Only through these intellectuals had France succeeded in maintaining its vitality.[79] This was a recurring theme in Dreyfusard discourse, as the responses to an *Enquête* "M. Zola et l'Opinion," published in the review *La Critique*, indicated.[80] One of the survey respondents Manuel Devaldès viewed Zola's "virile work" as an example to the "degenerates" of the period.[81] Respondent Edmond Fazy viewed Zola's heroism as a blow to bourgeois mediocrity, while another, Fernand Hauser praised Zola for an act of courage that stood out in an age of greed and cowardice.[82]

For Dreyfusards like Jean Ajalbert, Zola was a hero whose actions were the result of a life's work:

> I admire the attitude, the courage, the faith of Zola. It does not surprise me. It is the proud crowning of a life of work, of struggle and of honor. It is the inevitable culmination of an independent spirit impassioned by humanity.[83]

Dreyfusards praised not only his courage but also the beauty of his act. Armand Charpentier referred to the "act of courage and beauty accomplished by Zola," while poet René Ghil spoke of "Justice and Beauty."[84] Beauty, too, was an important theme in the Dreyfusard vision of the hero. Denying anti-Dreyfusards the ability to recognize true Beauty and Art, as did Laurent Tailhade, meant denying them honor and manhood as well.[85]

Dreyfusards celebrated not only the beauty of Zola's act, but also the fact that it was "so magnificently literary."[86] Moral action was clearly more important than physical deeds. A real man was one who obeyed his conscience, even if it meant defying authority. Accordingly, Leyret called Zola "a powerful writer" of "virile words" and contrasted his courage and strength to the pusillanimity of parliamentary politicians. Furthermore, he defined the protestation of intellectuals as an important weapon against error.[87]

For Tailhade, Zola was a "prince with the heart of a hero."[88] The greatest writers were those who lived their works: "Zola, deified in our eyes by his sublime gesture, is of this race of artists for whom the book is but one form of action."[89] Fernand Hauser called Zola's "J'Accuse" "an intellectual bomb," a view shared by Laurent Tailhade, who wrote that any book worth its name was also an act.[90] In the same vein, Gabriel Séailles indicated that one's teaching would be without authority if one were not prepared to back it up by actions, which he defined as obeying one's conscience.[91] Thus,

Dreyfusard intellectuals confronted the prevalent negative stereotype of intellectuals as weak and ineffectual. They valorized themselves by attaching the intellectual values of moral courage to the positive contemporary image of the man of action.

The pen was mightier than the sword, and the publication of "J'Accuse," which required moral courage, meant a great deal more than bravery in a military battle, as Octave Mirbeau noted:

> To rise up against the current of unleashed passions; to be the sole one to call for truth and justice, against an entire screaming mob, here is, I think, the most rare and beautiful act of courage that a man may accomplish.[92]

Mirbeau, like other Dreyfusard intellectuals, depicted the intellectual hero as a man who stood above the crowd. The editorial staff of the avant-garde journal *La Revue blanche* represented the Naturalist writer in similar terms: "It appears to us admirably dramatic, this lone writer standing proud against the droves provoked by be-ribboned military men and against the screaming mobs. . . ."[93] An intellectual hero was a rare individual who maintained a certain skepticism toward authority and an independence of thought rather than following the sheep-like crowd.

The juxtaposition of intellectuals and the crowd in Dreyfusard discourse is particularly striking and amply illustrated in the survey taken by *La Critique*. Henry D. Davray referred to intellectuals as "those alone who think and reason."[94] The crowd (*la foule*), on the other hand, was represented as brutal, stupid and unthinking. While intellectuals were "aware," the multitudes were "unaware." Jean Ajalbert worried about the effect of demagogues like Rochefort and Drumont on the crowd.[95] Other respondents feared the nefarious influence of the popular press in shaping public opinion, which was a cause of concern for intellectuals on the Right and the Left during the years preceding the Affair. *La Revue bleue* even published a lengthy survey on the press and public opinion in 1897.[96] Dreyfusard intellectuals feared the violence of the crowd and held on to an elitist ideal of the intellectual.

Intellectuals on both sides saw themselves as combatants in a major battle in which nothing less than the soul of France was at stake. Accordingly, one *Enquête* respondent called Zola both a hero and a patriot.[97] In a similar vein, Tailhade felt that "J'Accuse" represented the triumph of the "blues," that is, the republicans, against the "whites," the monarchists.[98]

Through the course of the Affair, Lieutenant-Colonel Picquart, who refused to condone the cover-up of the army, too, assumed heroic proportions for Dreyfusards.[99] Along with Zola, he stands out as an icon in Dreyfusard mythology. Zola and Picquart represent two sides of the same coin. Yet portraits of the two men depict them as complete individuals. Zola the intellectual was a man of action and Picquart the man of action was also an intellectual. While Alfred Dreyfus was viewed as a passive victim of the misfortune that had befallen him and therefore not as a hero, Georges Picquart became the avenger (*justicier*.)[100] He was represented as one of two inventors of Dreyfusism, much to the disappointment of the first Dreyfusards, notably, Bernard Lazare.[101]

Picquart, like Dreyfus himself, was an Alsatian, whose family had chosen French nationality in 1872. In common with Dreyfus, he was an ardent patriot, "doubly French," in the words of Francis de Pressensé, vice-president of the Ligue des Droits de l'Homme.[102] A graduate of the prestigious Saint-Cyr, Picquart advanced quickly and became the head of counter espionage in 1895. Picquart does not appear to have been someone who would defy military authority in the name of the rights of man.[103] Yet despite his brilliant army career, he was in some ways extremely different from the typical army officer. Picquart was an agnostic; moreover, unlike a number of army officers in the military bureaucracy, he was firmly attached to republican values. Since he wished to modernize the army, he was seen as a representative of the new technocratic type of officer.

Picquart became an object of controversy not only because he violated the army code of strict obedience, but also because within the army itself, he represented the new, republican, intellectual soldier. He did not come from a military family; his mother was an amateur musician and one of his cousins was a graduate of the Ecole Normale. What distinguished Picquart from the majority of army officers was his erudition and culture. He frequented salons and attended plays and concerts. A Germanist who appreciated German philosophy and culture, he was a friend of Austrian composer Gustave Mahler. Finally, Piquart never married, thereby fueling rumors regarding his sexual preference.[104]

Dreyfusard accounts of Picquart celebrate him not as a military man but rather as a man of culture and above all, as a man of conscience. In his Preface to the *Hommage des artistes à Picquart*, an album which included lithographs by various artists, along with lists of those who signed the petition protesting the charges brought against "the heroic artisan of the revision," Octave Mirbeau wrote of a visit with Colonel Picquart during which the two men discussed a variety of subjects, including Nietzsche, Plato, Rembrandt, Carlyle, and Wagner.[105]

Dreyfusard iconography of Picquart further reinforces this portrait. One of the most striking images in the *Hommage des artistes à Picquart* represents Picquart in prison, surrounded by books. Also depicted are two women, Truth and Justice, one of whom is holding a mirror, the other a sword. In a note at the end of the album, Henri Rainaldy declared that the editors of the volume sought to glorify in Picquart not the soldier, but rather to render homage to "He who, in spite of the imprint of a passive education, found the strength to rebel against Injustice and Lies and who had the courage to remain an *honnête homme*, underneath the golden braids of the [military] uniform." Here, military education, defined as passive, was depicted as an obstacle to be overcome. Furthermore, the act of revolt against unjust authority was celebrated. As in other Dreyfusard accounts, Picquart was described as an "honnête homme," a man of honor, who had fulfilled his duty as a man, not betrayed it.

Similarly, Joseph Reinach's work on Picquart referred to the Colonel as a "conscience" and a "hero":

> He has refused to prostitute his conscience: he has spoken. . . . He was but a loyal soldier, an *honnête homme*. Here he is a hero, a martyr, the hero of Right, the martyr of Truth.[106]

For Reinach, Picquart became a hero the moment he defied authority in the name of what he felt was right. He did not succumb to hierarchy but rather followed the more difficult path of his own conscience, thereby exposing himself to great danger: "Here at this precise moment, when Picquart invokes his conscience in front of the superior officer who has two or three more stripes than he, is born the hero."[107]

For Pressensé, Picquart was also *Un Héros*, the title of his book. Like Reinach, Pressensé spoke of the need for heroes in contemporary society,[108] as did Octave Mirbeau, who saw Picquart not only as a hero but also as a symbol:

> In the rout of our beliefs and our energies, in the ruins of ourselves, has risen up, all of a sudden, like an image of duty, of the spirit of sacrifice and of conscience that is in

him, by all the tranquility of male will that emanates from him, it is he who has rallied our courage, and has given a noble and precise form to our vague desires for justice, to our obscure love of humanity.[109]

In common with Zola, Picquart was held up as an example in a time of decadence. His "masculine will" (*mâles vouloirs*) was juxtaposed to the decline in national energies. It is evident in both Dreyfusard and anti-Dreyfusard discourse that Max Nordau's analysis of the degeneration of French society had made a great impact on the contemporary imagination.

To this end, Picquart was valorized by Dreyfusards as a man of action, not because he was a soldier—the passivity of the soldier, according to some Dreyfusards, belied the ideal of action—but because of his moral courage. Pressensé felt that moral courage was more rare than its physical counterpart:

> This great *honnête homme* . . . this soldier who has displayed a civic courage a thousand times more rare and noble than military courage . . . two times a hero, because along with the courage, in truth, facile, of the field of battle, he has displayed a sublime simplicity of courage in the battle for right.[110]

Moreover, Picquart, in choosing the army, did not abdicate the dignity of his conscience and the independence of his soul.[111]

A true hero in the Dreyfusard tradition had to suffer. Zola amply fit this bill. Faced with imprisonment, he was forced to flee to England. Furthermore, his possessions were seized and put up for auction. Without the generosity of such Dreyfusard friends as Mirbeau and editor P.-V. Stock, Zola would have lost all his material goods. Moreover, by writing "J'Accuse," Zola had renounced forever his lifelong quest to enter the Académie française. Finally, he was threatened and calumnied for his stance. For Dreyfusard Armand Charpentier, Zola was pilloried by his enemies, like Christ on the cross: "by the size of the Gesture, by the energy of the Word, Zola has transformed himself into a modern-day Christ."[112]

Picquart was represented in similar terms. Octave Mirbeau declared: "with our dear Zola, he is the martyr and the hero." He spoke of the plots against Picquart's honor and life and contrasted his fate—he was condemned "to the worst of tortures" for having cried out the truth—to that of traitors like Colonel Henry, who were glorified by the opposition.[113] Pressensé called him "this martyr of right" and affirmed that his persecution "was the rule," speaking of Picquart's "Via Dolorosa" and his "Calvary."[114] Thus, the Dreyfusard hero had to suffer and moreover suffer with dignity to prove his worth. Various accounts of Picquart mention his "firm and tranquil courage." He faced adversity calmly and even with joy.[115]

Although he had referred to Picquart as a hero earlier, in the final analysis, Mirbeau praised Picquart not as a hero but rather as a man who had honored humanity. Heroes in the traditional sense, after all, had contributed to human brutality and destruction:

> I extend my apologies to my dear and noble companion in battle [Pressensé], but I, who do not like heroes, I who know what blinded and bloody brutes are, throughout history, these nefarious beings, most often military men, that one calls heroes, I will state that Colonel Picquart is a man. . . . Humanity dies from having too many heroes; it comes to life from having men.[116]

For Dreyfusards, honoring humanity was a primary concern. They eschewed violence and attempted to resolve problems in a peaceful manner. The Ligue des Droits de l'Homme was founded at the height of the Affair not only to resolve the issues of the Affair peaceably, but also to combat forces that interfered with the march of progress and humanity.[117]

Colonel Henry or the Simple Soldier

The anti-Dreyfusard hero was a brave solider who sacrificed himself for the nation. Commandant Esterhazy could by no stretch of the imagination be represented in such terms. Salvation, however, came in the form of Colonel Henry, who by dying (he ostensibly committed suicide by slitting his throat with a razor), offered anti-Dreyfusards the perfect opportunity to acclaim a martyr for their cause. In his *Souvenirs sur l'Affaire Dreyfus*, Léon Blum remarked on the Dreyfusards' shock at this surprising turn of events.[118] They had naively assumed that Henry's death would mark the end of the Affair and the revision of the case, but they had not reckoned with the powerful rhetoric of Charles Maurras, whose article "Le Premier Sang," published in *La Gazette de France* on 6 and 7 September 1898, succeeded in reviving anti-Dreyfusard spirits. This article launched the apotheosis of Henry, a process which was completed by the subscription lists launched in *La Libre Parole* for Henry's widow.

Maurras ascribed disinterested motives to Henry, depicting him as a hero and as "this great man of honor," who had invented "le faux patriotique" to save France. Maurras's article, dedicated to Henry's memory, began with a funeral oration designed to appeal to the emotions of his readers:

> While the party followers of Dreyfus were displaying all over the signs of an obscene satisfaction, a great many patriots were cutting out . . . the portrait of Lieutenant-Colonel Henry and were placing this image, based on a rough and hurried sketch, with an eye to the sacred, in the most visible place in their homes. While awaiting that Justice renders to him the public honors he so deserves, the French people have dedicated a domestic cult to this good citizen, to this brave soldier, to this heroic servant of great national interests.

Whereas Dreyfusards were described as "party followers," that is, an interest group, even a political party, anti-Dreyfusards were patriots above politics who had established a sacred cult in Henry's honor.

Maurras described Henry as a martyr who had sacrificed himself for the public good, thereby justifying his falsification. In other words, for Maurras, the ends justified the means, if the honor of the nation were at stake.[119] Furthermore, Henry was represented as a victim of the betrayal of his army superiors and of the dangers of democracy and public opinion. Maurras, like some Dreyfusards, feared the crowd, which he described as childlike and in need of guidance.

Henry, as Maurras, Drumont, and other anti-Dreyfusards were careful to note, had served the nation literally with his blood. He had risen through the ranks because of his war experience. Moreover, he had paid the ultimate price by shedding his "generous blood" for the good of the nation. Like the Dreyfusard hero, the anti-Dreyfusard hero was also destined to suffer. Maurras lamented the fact that Henry's enemies would spread lies about him. Heroes, concluded Maurras, sometimes shared the destiny of poets.

In an article published in *La Libre Parole* shortly after Henry's death, Edouard Drumont described him as a simple soldier, "a simple soul, an intellect without much culture."[120] Drumont described Henry's falsification as a clumsy error, but a mere "childishness," in comparison with the machinations of Dreyfusards. Drumont asked his readers to pity the "poor devil," who had committed suicide because he was horrified to finish his hitherto blameless life in dishonor. Although Henry was often described as a heroic solider, a man of action, by both his supporters and detractors, rarely did the former proclaim his intellectual attributes. What they valued above all in Henry was his physical bravery, his dedication to the army, and his sense of loyalty and obedience. This emphasis on obedience was somewhat ironic given that some believed he had deceived his superiors for a higher good in falsifying "proof" of Dreyfus's guilt.[121]

In the wake of the criticisms leveled against Henry, particularly in response to Joseph Reinach's articles in *Le Siècle*,[122] which claimed that Henry was not only a forger, but also an accomplice of Esterhazy, Drumont rushed to defend the fallen soldier. *La Libre Parole* launched a subscription drive in December 1898 to collect money so that Henry's widow could sue Reinach for libel. Drumont and his colleagues succeeded in collecting 131,000 francs.[123] The donations, often accompanied by short statements, were published in *La Libre Parole* and represent the anti-Dreyfusard equivalent to the Dreyfusard petitions in favor of Zola and Picquart. The lists, which provide a fascinating glimpse into the mindset of anti-Dreyfusards, celebrate Henry as a martyr and hero.[124]

Not unnaturally, the highest incidence by profession of subscribers to the "Monument Henry," as it was dubbed by Dreyfusard Pierre Quilllard, was the military, although a public declaration of this sort constituted a radical departure from the traditional military ideal of silence with regard to political matters.[125] Most expressed solidarity with a fellow officer and the "honor of the army," venting their frustrations against representatives of the new army, whom they equated with Jews.

In the subscription lists of *La Libre Parole*, Henry was described as a "great patriot, an impoverished but real Frenchman." One subscriber asked when a statue would be erected to the "noble victim of duty."[126] Other subscribers called Henry a martyr.[127] Yet another described him as a hero dirtied by Reinach.[128] In these lists, it is evident that subscribers saw Henry as well as themselves as victims of a new society that sought to disenfranchise them. Like Henry, they were "weak" and "poor" but all the more noble as a result. They did not possess money, but they clung tightly to their honor.

The man on horseback served as a model not only for members of the military profession, but for civilians too. The anti-Dreyfusard cosmos, as Stephen Wilson notes, was made up of the trinity of the

Nation, the Church, and the Army.[129] Thus, several subscribers called for a coup d'état, with one even calling for a "Morny or a Saint-Arnaud to save the nation."[130]

Professors of Energy: Déroulède, Morès, and Marchand

Although the anti-Dreyfusard hero, par excellence, was the man on horseback, this ideal did not exclude the presence of intellectual qualities. Maurice Barrès's heroes combined thought and action, not surprising given that he felt that the two greatest forces in life were the "sword" and the "idea."[131] In *Les Déracinés*, the first novel of a trilogy of "romans de l'énergie nationale," Napoleon, the man on horseback, and Victor Hugo, the national poet, were celebrated as "professors of energy" whose contact had the power to revive the nation.[132]

In both Napoleon and Hugo, Barrès celebrated not the real men but rather the mythic, abstract figures—"the Napoleon of the soul," on the one hand, and "the mystical leader," "the modern visionary," on the other.[133] In a chapter dedicated to the Napoleonic legend, Barrès spoke of the impact of Napoleon on the seven young Lorrainers who had left their homes to find their fortunes in Paris. Gathered around the Emperor's tomb, they felt their hero's energy, which in turn gave them strength: "The tomb of the Emperor, for Frenchmen twenty-years old. . . . It is the crossroads of all the energies known as audacity, will and appetite."[134]

Napoleon was a man of destiny, as was his counterpart Hugo, the "Master of words."[135] Through the power of words, he made one feel not only the mystery and grandeur of human existence, but also of the origins of the national community: "by the disposition and the power of his word, Hugo expands in us the ability to feel the secrets of the past and the enigmas of the future. . . . It is the genius of our race that seeks refuge in its own recesses."[136] Barrès, like other anti-Dreyfusard intellectuals, sought "an intellectual Bonaparte"—a man with powerful words whose dreams could be translated into action.[137] He thought he had found such a hero in Boulanger but was sorely disappointed, searching until his death to find such a contemporary ideal.[138]

Other anti-Dreyfusards were influenced by Barrès's model. In an article entitled "Professeurs d'énergie," Edouard Drumont used Barrès's expression not only to talk about the cult of Napoleon as it was depicted in *Les Déracinés*, but also to decry the degeneration of modern society, the decline of energies, and to praise such "professors" of energy as Jean-Baptiste Marchand (1863–1934), the

Marquis de Morès (1858–1896), and Paul Déroulède (1846–1914).[139] These heroes, the first a general, the second an adventurer, and the third a nationalist poet, were often compared favorably to politicians and Dreyfusard intellectuals.

The author of "Soldats et politiciens" contrasted the sacrifice and deprivation of Marchand and his men, "civilizing the savages" in the French Congo, to the machinations and baseness of France's politicians.[140] Similarly, the author of an article published in a special supplement to *La Libre Parole* devoted to Marchand, lamented the fact that politicians had forced this "man of destiny," who represented the energy and ideal of the French race, to give Fashoda up to the English.[141]

In his funeral oration of the Marquis de Morès in 1896, Barrès described him as a "heroic thinker" who took into account the psychological conditions of the society in which he lived and acted to further the interests of the nation.[142] In "Morès," Drumont depicted the Marquis as a male, energetic figure and praised his physical and civic courage, along with his sacrifice for the nation. Morès, who had given his life for his country, had suffered horribly. Ambushed and outnumbered, he had been shot in the back, the act of cowards. Until the very end, however, he had managed to kill several of his attackers.[143]

Although the civic courage of heroes was lauded, the shedding of blood seemed to be of primordial importance to anti-Dreyfusards. Indeed, the virility and energy of these heroes was contrasted to the femininity not only of politicians, but also of Dreyfusard intellectuals and Jews.[144] In "Déroulède et Reinach," Drumont juxtaposed Déroulède's probity, humanity, and loyalty to Reinach's treachery.[145] Unlike Jews, who sucked the nation's lifeblood, Déroulède had given his blood to serve his country.[146] This ultimate gift established a link between the individual and the nation; the blood of these heroes mingled with the earth of their ancestors. Indeed, Barrès praised Marchand and Morès as two French heroes who were rooted in French soil.[147] The physical bond forged between anti-Dreyfusard heroes and the nation distinguished them from their Dreyfusard counterparts, who viewed the nation less as a physical entity than as an idea.

In a similar vein, Drumont explained that the anti-Semitic artist Forain became "strong and virile" the moment he became an anti-Dreyfusard and moreover that other artists who were Dreyfusards were dissipating their energies.[148] "Dissipating one's energies" was another way of speaking of masturbation, which was considered unmanly. Here, Drumont spoke in figurative terms;

Dreyfusard intellectuals were wasting their energies by not contributing to the life of the nation.

Despite the emphasis on the physical, it should be obvious that anti-Dreyfusards were not anti-intellectual in the broader sense of the term. According to Barrès, there was nothing that intelligence could not examine. He did not contest the right of Dreyfusards to speak and express their opinions, merely the content of their opinions: "But whether it is the right of men of thought, who, ordinarily, live outside the world of politics, to question authority, this is incontestable. . . . Thus, we have contested not their right to speak, but their words themselves."[149] Drumont agreed, expressing his belief in the liberty of expression: "To be an intellectual is to have a just and profound vision of the world, a lofty conception of the functioning of the social order, a clear notion of the role filled by each one according to his kind and his duties."[150] Drumont implored writers to be intellectual in the real sense of the word, that is, to accept that even if Dreyfus had been condemned illegally, civilians should not intervene.[151] For Drumont, a real intellectual was "a scientific, positive, empirical, and reasoning intellect."[152] Such a definition does not seem too different from that of certain Dreyfusard intellectuals.

Drumont's collaborator Gallus at *La Libre Parole* placed the poet Chateaubriand above the politician Talleyrand, even though the latter might have provided a more useful service to France. The poet, however, was a visionary capable of inspiring his countrymen in a way the politician never could. Gallus celebrated Chateaubriand as the "liberator of intelligence," and also placed Hugo, Vigny, and Lamartine in this category, along with anti-Dreyfusards François Coppée and Jules Lemaître and indeed Drumont himself.[153] In an article on Michelet, Drumont called him a national historian equaled only by Hugo and Balzac in terms of influence on contemporaries. Drumont was not shocked by Zola's intervention but rather horrified that the place of France's intellectual heroes should be taken over by the Naturalist writer.[154] Among respondents to *La Critique*'s survey, even those who disagreed with Zola's stance like Henri Mazel, former director of *L'Ermitage*, recognized the right of intellectuals to speak.[155]

Anti-Heroes and Other Effeminate Figures

Just as both sides believed in the right and duty of intellectuals to speak on national issues, so, too, did they lay exclusive claim to honor and manhood, describing their opponents as effeminate.

Anti-Dreyfusards were particularly adept in this area, and they singled
out Zola and Picquart, especially the latter, for vilification. Zola, described as a pornographer, was often represented in scatological terms.
This image was linked to fears of "abnormal" sexuality, which was
ascribed to Jews and intellectuals.[156] Sexual promiscuity—any kind of
"abnormal" sexuality—was feared as a sign of modernity.

While Picquart was described by Dreyfusards as honorable and
manly, he was described by anti-Dreyfusards as the effeminate
"Georgette," reader of "perfumed novels."[157] Gyp's *Les Femmes du
Colonel* satirized "Colonel Flamand"—who was never seen in her
novel—and his followers, among them such "esthetic" men as
Lancelot des Algues and women like Mme. Dampyré, who saw in
him a "saint" and a "gentle hero." For the anti-Dreyfusards in the
novel, however, Flamand was a cold, ambitious officer, described as
"unbalanced" and "unwholesome." Gyp never explicitly stated that
Flamand was a homosexual, but she certainly implied it, underlin-
ing the irony of his massive feminine following.

In "Les Izolâtres," published in *La Libre Parole* on 3 March
1898, Gyp referred to Picquart as "the beautiful Jewish blond," who
ingratiated herself with the Dreyfusards with her kittenish manners. Gyp, whose ideas regarding her own femininity were ambivalent to say the least, lumped silly women, esthetes, and homosexuals
together; all were lacking in honor and substance.[158] Gyp's ideal hero
was a rough and ready solider like the anti-Dreyfusard General
Belpogne of the novel, represented as a man's man.

In a series of drawings for the anti-Dreyfusard illustrated journal
Psst!, caricaturist Caran d'Ache mocked not only Picquart but also the
Dreyfusards' hero-worship of the Colonel, representing both intellectuals and Picquart as effeminate esthetes. The Oscar Wilde trial had
reinforced the association of estheticism with homosexuality. In a
drawing entitled "La Cellule smart," Picquart is represented in his
prison cell, which is decorated with Liberty furnishings, a hallmark of
the English esthetes. Picquart asks a lady friend, who is in the cell
with him, where she buys her corsets.[159] In "Le Grand Match," Picquart
is depicted as a queen on a chessboard whose chesspieces bear the
faces of various prominent Dreyfusards.[160] Not only was Picquart seen
as effeminate, so, too, were intellectuals described as mere "pawns."
Controlled by others, they were not real men.

Still other illustrations were even more explicit. In "Flagrant
délit," Picquart, dressed as a woman, is depicted in the arms of a
judge. A gendarme with "Loi" written on his sleeve, arrives, announcing "caught" (*pincés*).[161] Another drawing "Magistrature
nouvelle," also shows Picquart with a judge. Picquart's suspenders

are undone and the judge is removing his robes; the caption reads "Alone, at last!"[162] Both these drawings illustrate anti-Dreyfusards' fears that Picquart and other Dreyfusards were in cahoots with the magistrature, but more importantly, they serve to cast doubt on Picquart's manliness.

Yet this image of Picquart as a homosexual was also accompanied by another of him as a seducer of women, as he was portrayed in Gyp's *Les Femmes du Colonel*. In a drawing entitled "Une dame rédactrice," a woman journalist, looking thrilled at the prospect, asks a policeman if Colonel Picquart rapes women.[163] The woman journalist obviously referred to the Dreyfusard Séverine and also to reporters for the feminist, Dreyfusard newspaper *La Fronde*. Once again, frivolous women and effeminate men were lumped together. The images of Picquart as a seducer of women and as a homosexual are not necessarily contradictory. Both were representations of what was viewed as abnormal, excessive sexuality.

The image of an effeminate male was associated with cowardice and the loss of honor. In a 22 July 1899 *Psst!* illustration entitled "Sabre d'honneur," Picquart is shown with his fingers in his ears. Referring to the abandoned sword lying on the table next to him, Picquart asks "Not loaded, I hope?" Picquart is a coward, having forsaken his sword, the soldier's badge of honor. The phallic symbolism of an uncharged/unloaded sword should have been quite obvious to contemporary readers.

In contrast to soldiers who were represented as the repository of national honor, Jews and intellectuals were denied the claim to honor, the former because they were associated with money, the latter because they were seen as "eunuchs," who "reasoned badly" or who had "lost their reason."[164] A number of entries in *Le Monument Henry* defined intellectuals as "incoherent and unbalanced,"[165] and as "decadent," describing them as cowards and fomenters of anarchy.[166] Yet another entry accused intellectuals of "perverting our beautiful country."[167] Reason was claimed as a valuable trait, not only by Dreyfusards, with whom it has long been associated, but also by their opponents. In both cases, a loss of reason implied a loss of honor and manhood. As they themselves were careful to note, these anti-Dreyfusards did not oppose intelligence itself—one even signed himself an "intelligent intellectual"[168]—but rather Dreyfusard intellectuals, whom they associated with the republican state. This allowed them to overcome their own feelings of inferiority in an increasingly literate society and assert their own superiority vis-à-vis official, professional intellectuals, promoted through the republican university.[169]

Such depictions of effeminacy or perversion were not exclusively the province of anti-Dreyfusards. In Octave Mirbeau's novel *Le Journal d'une femme de chambre*, written at the height of the Affair, the anti-Semitic, anti-Dreyfusard Joseph was a brutal child rapist and murderer. Like the female journalist who admired Picquart, Célestine, the chamber maid of the book's title, was titillated by what she learned about Joseph, whom she eventually married.

In *Tout le Crime*, Joseph Reinach mocked Du Paty du Clam as a decadent litterateur who painted watercolors, liked music, and enjoyed the works of Symbolist poet Maurice Maeterlinck and playwright Henrik Ibsen.[170] Like Picquart, he was described as "unbalanced."[171] Reinach denounced the "elegant" and "diabolic" machinations of Du Paty, whom he viewed as a classic villain in a boulevard melodrama.[172] Estheticism had thus become a code word for homosexuality by this time, and it was used by individuals on both sides to denigrate the manhood and honor of their opponents. In the same vein, Reinach described the collection of false documents, the secret dossier against Dreyfus as "this foul correspondence of Lesbos and of Gomorrha."[173] Finally, Dreyfusards criticized chauvinistic patriots of not reasoning.[174]

Particularly adept at casting aspersions on the manliness of his opponents was anarchist litterateur Laurent Tailhade, who wrote for the Dreyfusard newspaper *Les Droits de l'Homme*. Special targets were anti-Dreyfusards Jean Lorrain and Pierre Loti, both of whom were homosexual. A poem entitled "Troisième Sexe," published years before the Affair, targeted Lorrain.[175] In other poems written during the Affair, Lorrain was repeatedly described as a "queen" who slept with the army, both literally and figuratively.[176] Other anti-Dreyfusards were also frequent targets. Urbain Gohier dismissed anti-Dreyfusard intellectuals Coppée, Lemaître, and Rochefort as old men who wished to play at soldiers. When they were young, their gaucherie and ugliness had deprived them of women, their physical deformities of military service. Thus, in their old age, they were prey to both "sexual and patriotic sadism."[177] Finally, in a poem entitled "La Prière pour tous," Tailhade had anti-Dreyfusards chanting that they were "without talent, honor and manhood" (*sexe*).[178]

As these attacks delivered by both sides indicate, Dreyfusards and anti-Dreyfusards, alike, shared a strong belief in honor and manhood, which was subsumed in conflicting ideals of the nation. The best way of targeting one's enemies was to define them as effeminate and thereby deny them the right to honor and manliness. The final insult was to accuse them of betraying the nation. Both sides not only denigrated female qualities, thereby illustrating the deep-rooted misogyny of French fin-de-siècle culture, they also valorized men of action and opposed them to politicians, who represented the decadent state of French society. The vocabulary used to describe the Dreyfusard hero and the anti-Dreyfusard hero is remarkably similar. Defined by reason, a manly trait par excellence, both heroes were honorable men of action. They exhibited courage, physical as well as moral, and had suffered for the good of the nation.

Yet behind the vocabulary were very real differences between the two ideals. The Dreyfusard hero was above all a man of conscience, who respected ideas not hierarchy. Moral courage was valued over physical courage. Significantly, Picquart's military exploits and the fact that he was a soldier were played down. Indeed, he was explicitly depicted as a man of culture rather than as a man of the sword. Zola, the writer, was naturally valued for his ideas, but great care was made to indicate that he, too, was a man of action. The real man acted through his words, and the pen was mightier than the sword. Physical force, viewed as a mark of bestiality, was frowned upon and even feared. In keeping with a fear of violence was a mistrust of the masses. The Dreyfusard hero stood alone, far above the crowd.

Like his Dreyfusard counterpart, the anti-Dreyfusard hero was a man of action, but in a much more literal way. Physical courage and the sacrifice of blood joined him with the body of the nation. The exaltation of physical force was a major point of difference between Dreyfusards and anti-Dreyfusards. While Dreyfusards eschewed violence, certain anti-Dreyfusards like Drumont and Barrès were fascinated by it and, indeed, by the potential for violence of the crowd.

There was a certain defensiveness in Dreyfusard discourse with regard to the manliness and virility of intellectuals. After all, Dreyfusard intellectuals were combating the contemporary portrait of the physically weak, unmanly intellectual. Laying claim to virility was yet another way of valorizing themselves and justifying their new place in society. Moreover, many found attack the best form of defense, by accusing soldiers of being unmanly since they obeyed orders blindly. Despite their antipathy to violence, they still subscribed to contemporary codes of honor and manhood and felt it all the more necessary to defend themselves in duels. Thus, Laurent Tailhade criticized anti-Dreyfusards who violated the principles of the honorable duel by fighting their opponents and insulting them afterward.[179] Tailhade denounced "the dandies of Boulangism [who] ignore the most elementary forms of civility," describing them as "these esthetes."[180] Tailhade, along with Clemenceau and others, fought countless duels during the Affair, thereby upholding the "honor" of the Dreyfusard side.

Anti-Dreyfusards were defensive too, albeit in a different way. They were fascinated with the man on horseback. This was a weakness that Dreyfusards like Gohier and Tailhade picked up on, mocking "impotent" intellectuals who worshipped all they were not. For them, the ultimate irony was that effete dandy Barrès dreamed of an "intellectual Bonaparte."

While the fascination of authoritarian intellectuals for military men is unquestionable, it should also be noted that these intellectuals looked to other intellectuals as role models too. Barrès, for instance, sought to combine the ideals of the military and intellectual heroes.

Dreyfusard and anti-Dreyfusard intellectuals alike believed in the right and duty of intellectuals to speak out on national issues. Both Drumont and Barrès acknowledged the other side's right to its own opinion. Furthermore, as the *Enquête* published in *La Critique* on Zola amply illustrates, many of those who disagreed with Zola envisaged an important role for intellectuals in society. For both sides, the intellectual was a voice of the national conscience. While Dreyfusard intellectuals tended to see a new role in society for themselves as national arbiters, replacing the traditional authority of the Catholic Church and the army, anti-Dreyfusards tried to reconcile this new role with a respect for traditional authority. The anti-Dreyfusard intellectual subordinated himself to the needs of the nation. As Drumont observed, he knew his place in society. The Dreyfusard intellectual, on the other hand, felt that the needs of the nation were best served by individuals who stood above the crowd and eschewed respect for authority. The place of the individual in society and the nature of society itself was a topic of great discussion during the Affair.

This examination of Dreyfusard and anti-Dreyfusard heroes should illustrate the need to examine the Dreyfus Affair not only in sociological and political terms, but also in terms of gender. Conflicting ideals of the nation at the fin de siècle became embedded in gender discourse on manhood and virility. The fear of a loss of French manhood, exacerbated by the French defeat in the Franco-Prussian War, a declining birthrate, and the changes wrought by modern society led to the apotheosis of the hero. While both Dreyfusards and anti-Dreyfusards believed in the power of intellectuals, it was the first group that offered a new alternative to the traditional military hero. In the wake of the Dreyfus Affair, however, disappointment and frustration with this model would lead to criticism from former Dreyfusards like Charles Péguy and Georges Sorel. Nevertheless, the image of the intellectual hero was to haunt both the Left and the Right during the years to come.

Figure 6.1 "Vox populi," *Le Sifflet,* 17 February 1898. "As a single voice . . . against a lone man." Illustration by Hermann Paul. Reproduced courtesy of the Trustees of the Boston Public Library, Rare Books.

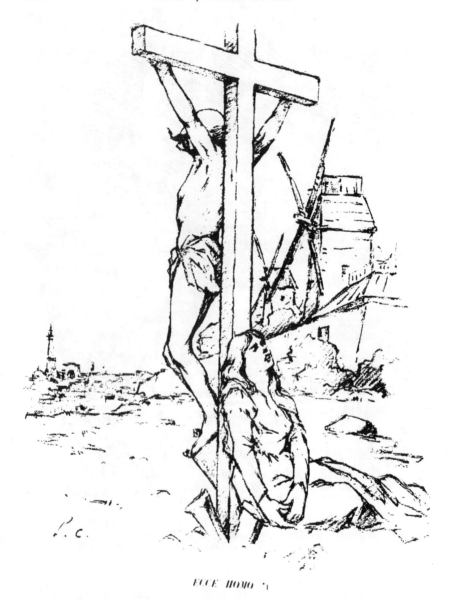

ECCE HOMO

Figure 6.2　"Ecce Homo," *Le Sifflet,* 10 March 1899. "Behold the Man."
Illustration by Louis Chevalier.　Reproduced courtesy of the Trustees of
the Boston Public Library, Fine Arts.

Le Maître interviewé

— Ce qui m'a le plus manqué en Angleterre, c'est mes cabinets.

Figure 6.3 "Le Maître interviewé," *Psst!* 24 June 1899. "What I missed the most in England was my water closet." Illustration by Caran d'Ache. Reproduced courtesy of the Trustees of the Boston Public Library, Print Department.

Projet de monument

Figure 6.4 "Projet de monument," *Psst!* 23 July 1898. Monsieur Zola: "Add: 'and King of Rome.'" Illustration by Caran d'Ache. Reproduced courtesy of the Trustees of the Boston Public Library, Print Department.

Religion nouvelle

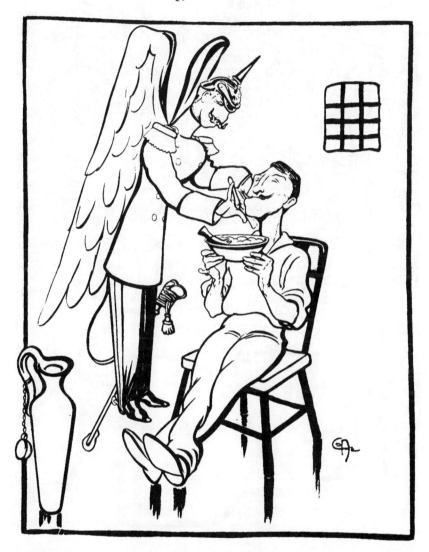

Figure 6.5 "Religion nouvelle," *Psst!* 15 October 1898. "Saint-Picquart and the Archangel von Schwartzkoppen." Illustration by Caran d'Ache. Reproduced courtesy of the Trustees of the Boston Public Library, Print Department.

Figure 6.6 "La Cellule smart," *Psst!* 4 March 1899. Picquart is speaking to the woman: "Where do you buy your corsets?" Illustration by Caran d'Ache. Reproduced courtesy of the Trustees of the Boston Public Library, Rare Books.

Figure 6.7 "Le Grand match," *Psst!* 13 May 1899. "Chess match. At stake: France." Illustration by Caran d'Ache. Reproduced courtesy of the Trustees of the Boston Public Library, Rare Books.

Figure 6.8 "Flagrant délit," *Psst!* 11 February 1899. "Caught!" Illustration by Caran d'Ache. Reproduced courtesy of the Trustees of the Boston Public Library, Rare Books.

Figure 6.9 "Magistrature nouvelle," *Psst!* 18 February 1899. "Alone, at last!" Illustration by Caran d'Ache. Reproduced courtesy of the Trustees of the Boston Public Library, Rare Books.

APRÈS LA COUR D'ASSISES

Figure 6.10 "Après la Cour d'Assises," *Le Sifflet*, 7 April 1898. "Alone at last!" Illustration by Louis Chevalier. Reproduced courtesy of the Trustees of the Boston Public Library, Fine Arts.

Une dame rédactrice

Figure 6.11 "Une dame Rédactrice," *Psst!* 17 June 1899. "Is it true, officer, that Colonel Picquart rapes ladies at Armenonville?" Illustration by Caran d'Ache. Reproduced courtesy of the Trustees of the Boston Public Library, Print Department.

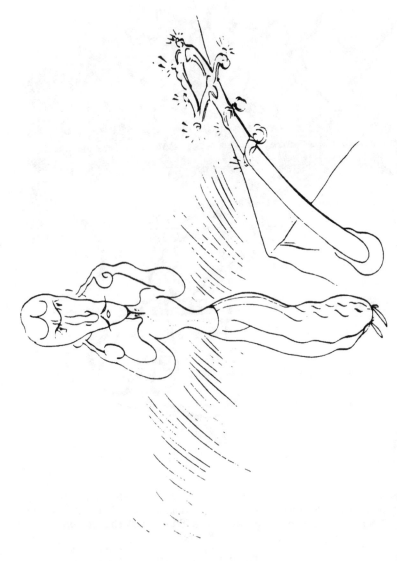

Figure 6.12 "Sabre d'honneur," *Psst!* 22 July 1899. "Not loaded, I hope?" Illustration by Caran d'Ache. Reproduced courtesy of the Trustees of the Boston Public Library, Rare Books.

Figure 6.13 "Enquête sur l'Esprit français," *Psst!* 9 July 1898. The man with the mustache is a journalist who asks the intellectual, who is depicted with glasses, a pointy beard, and a flower at his side, the following: "What do you think of the French mood?" The intellectual replies: "Know, sir, that all that is French disgusts me!" Illustration by Caran d'Ache. Reproduced courtesy of the Trustees of the Boston Public Library, Rare Books.

Figure 6.14 "L'Aristocratie de demain," *Psst!* 1 April 1899. This intellectual is a sloppy, unkempt man; he is wearing slippers on his feet, on one of the slippers is the image of Zola, on the other that of Picquart. Next to him, is a statue bearing the name "Vérité en Marche," a reference to an article by Zola. On his desk is a sheaf of papers. The caption reads: "The aristocracy of tomorrow? Well, it is us!" Illustration by Caran d'Ache. Reproduced courtesy of the Trustees of the Boston Public Library, Rare Books.

Salons intellectuels

Figure 6.15 "Salons intellectuels," *Psst!* 10 December 1898. Chorus of ladies: "My kingdom for a lieutenant of the dragons!" Illustration by Caran d'Ache. Reproduced courtesy of the Trustees of the Boston Public Library, Print Department.

Extase intellectuelle

« J'entends des voix qui me disent : C'est tout
de même toi, obscur et pauvre écrivain, qui a créé
ce mouvement qui sauvera la France. »

Libre Parole, 31 mai.

Figure 6.16 "Extase intellectuelle," *Le Sifflet,* 26 May 1899. "Be careful,
M. Drumont, you could hurt yourself." Illustration by H.-G. Ibels. Reproduced courtesy of the Trustees of the Boston Public Library, Fine Arts.

7

—◦◦◦—

"Individualism and Solidarity: Organicist Discourse in the Dreyfus Affair"

The Dreyfus Affair was a debate about ideas as well as a struggle for power between new and old elites in French society. Moreover, it was to a large extent a *sociological* debate concerning the role of the individual in society and by extension, of a certain type of individual, the intellectual. The relationship of the individual to society was certainly not a new issue in France. Like the question of elites, it took on a certain urgency during the fin de siècle, in light not only of the establishment of a parliamentary republic, but also of the rise of its challengers, on both the Left and the Right.[1] Indeed, during the Dreyfus Affair, arguably the most celebrated civil rights case in French history, the relationship of the individual and society became a key element of the debate between two groups which propagated different visions of national identity.

Traditional historical accounts of the Dreyfus Affair have depicted the two sides as monolithic *blocs*, each devoted to a set of immutable ideals. Thus, Dreyfusards have been represented as "individualist" and anti-Dreyfusards as "organicist."[2] More recent research has attempted to divide intellectuals along sociological lines, pitting established disciplines (anti-Dreyfusard) against newer ones (Dreyfusard); the republican university (Dreyfusard) against the world of letters (anti-Dreyfusard).

Both types of accounts neglect the diversity within each group as well as the common beliefs—or at the very least—common vocabulary—shared by both sides. Dreyfusards and anti-Dreyfusards alike used organicist discourse. Furthermore, "individualism," along with "solidarity," was a fluid term without fixed meaning.[3] Dreyfusards and their opponents both believed in individualism and solidarity, although they defined them in different ways. Anti-Dreyfusard Gustave Le Bon saw himself as an individualist as did Dreyfusard Octave Mirbeau, who was closely associated with the anarchist movement. Similarly, both Dreyfusard Emile Durkheim and anti-Dreyfusard Ferdinand Brunetière spoke of solidarity.

In this chapter, I shall first place the debate surrounding the individual and society during the Dreyfus Affair within the broader context of contemporary discussions on the topic and then study the writings of leading spokesmen on both sides of the Affair, including Dreyfusards Emile Durkheim and Jean Jaurès and anti-Dreyfusards Maurice Barrès and Ferdinand Brunetière, to determine the points of commonality in their vocabulary, if not in their visions of national identity. New light can be shed on intellectual life in France by concentrating on the beliefs shared by Dreyfusard and anti-Dreyfusard intellectuals.

Writing in the inaugural issue of *L'Ermitage* in April 1890, editor Henri Mazel proclaimed the dawning of a new era in which the "social question" was of primary importance. The laissez-faire attitudes of the Manchester school, he declared, had been supplanted by socialism and theologians by sociologists.[4] Mazel's observations were accurate. Among the most important developments of the late nineteenth century was the replacement of a liberalism based on metaphysical philosophy by one based on sociology.[5] As a result, French liberals moved away from laissez-faire individualism to theories which accentuated both the individual and the social and which accorded an important role to the state.[6] In any case, French liberals had never gone to the individualist extremes of a Herbert Spencer or a Max Stirner; nor had they wholeheartedly adopted Social Darwinist ideas, which were much more influential in England and the United States.[7]

The terms "individualism" and "solidarity" are words whose fortunes are linked. Just as eighteenth-century France had witnessed the emergence of the idea of personal liberty, along with the institution of civil and political justice for the defense of individual rights, the nineteenth century promulgated the idea of solidarity to counteract excessive individualism as represented by laissez-faire by introducing a measure of social and economic justice.[8]

The first uses of the term individualism in France were born of the reaction to the Revolution and to its alleged sources in

Enlightenment thought.[9] For conservative thinkers, the tragic results of the Revolution were "proof" of the danger of exalting individual wills. The individual should be subordinate to the organic whole of the nation, a part of a hierarchical and stable order. Conservative thinkers like Joseph de Maistre and Louis de Bonald equated individualism with anarchy; the former even claimed that individualism was the product of Protestant thought.[10] Such sentiments were echoed by conservative thinkers during the fin de siècle, among them Charles Maurras and Ferdinand Brunetière.

Conservatives, however, were not the only ones to criticize the individualism of the Revolutionaries; so, too, did the Saint-Simonians, who were the first to use "individualism" systematically in the 1820s.[11] Saint-Simonians also criticized the exaltation of the individual, which they felt had led to social atomization and anarchy. In general, the term individualism in the French context acquired negative connotations. It was viewed as the source of social dissolution, although a number of thinkers, ranging from anarchist Pierre Proudhon to laissez-faire economists, adopted the label by mid-century.[12]

Given that Roman Catholic social theologians were among the initial opponents of the individualism of the French Revolution, it is not surprising that they should be the first to appeal to its opposite—solidarity, juxtaposing the Christian ideal of charity with the "godless" principle of laissez-faire.[13] It was largely through the efforts of socialist thinkers, however, that the notion of solidarity was widely spread in the mid-nineteenth century, disseminated by Saint-Simonian Pierre Leroux, credited by some as having coined the term, along with Charles Fourier, Louis Blanc, and Pierre Proudhon.[14]

Like the conservatives, the Saint-Simonians also desired an organic, stable social order, conceiving of solidarity not only in spatial but also in temporal terms, with the present linked to the past and the future to the present.[15] Unlike the conservatives, however, they dreamed of an industrial order rather than a feudal one.[16] During the early part of the nineteenth century, solidarism was viewed as the opposite of individualism, but by the end of the century, it came to be seen as a bridge between individualism and socialism.[17]

Certain socialist leaders tried to reconcile these principles, among them Louis Blanc and Charles Fourier, who declared that no opposition existed between the two.[18] Their heirs at the turn of the century, Radical-Socialist minister Léon Bourgeois and Socialist leader Jean Jaurès concurred, with the former defining himself as a liberal socialist and the latter stating that socialism was the logical completion of individualism.[19]

By the turn of the century, the term solidarity had been in use for some time. Léon Bourgeois, who helped to popularize the notion at the fin de siècle, noted approvingly that the word was widely used and by a variety of different groups.[20] Indeed, solidarity was the most talked about ideal of the 1890s. Whereas solidarity earlier in the century had been promulgated largely by socialist thinkers, by the end of the century its proponents were mostly members of the middle classes, who attempted to establish a halfway house between individualist liberalism and collectivist socialism. Inspired simultaneously by a fear of socialism and by the recognition that extreme individualism was inadequate for the needs of modern industrial society, they sought to address social problems on both a moral and scientific basis.[21]

Darwinian principles made a great impact on European thought in the nineteenth century. While most French thinkers rejected the racist implications of Social Darwinism, along with the model of conflict inspired by the notion of survival of the fittest, they, too, sought to apply biological principles to human society. In France, such a desire led primarily to a search for models of cooperative organization.[22] French zoologist Henri Milne-Edwards argued that a living organism was made up of large numbers of cells working together and that the law of nature was therefore cooperation rather than competition.[23] His ideas, along with those of sociobiologists Jean Izoulet and Alfred Espinas, were cited approvingly by solidarists to justify their thinking.

Others who spoke of solidarity included economist Charles Gide (uncle of André) and philosopher Alfred Fouillée, who sought to combine aspects of voluntarist social contract theory with those of biological organicism. While Fouillée warned against overuse of biological analogies, he did believe, like Auguste Comte himself, that society was an organism which was nonetheless distinct from biological organisms. Moreover, society, while it could not exist apart from individuals, was composed of more than the sum of its parts.[24] The individual was a social being, dependent on other human beings, not only biologically, but also as a result of a voluntary contract. Fouillée thus spoke of the "organic and voluntary solidarity of individuals in the group," developing the idea of the quasi-contract. The quasi-contract was a way of justifying legislation which obliged the individual to make sacrifices for the collective good without falling into the trap of the tyranny of the majority.[25]

Léon Bourgeois used these ideas, along with those of other thinkers, including sociologist Emile Durkheim, to develop the political doctrine of Solidarism, which by 1900 had become the

semiofficial ideology of the Third Republic.[26] Bourgeois first published a series of articles in *La Nouvelle Revue* in 1895; these were
collected and published in book form the following year under the
title *Solidarité*. In his writings, Bourgeois postulated the interdependence of human beings.[27] Man was not an abstract being, seen
as an individual entity, but the product of society.[28] For Bourgeois
and other Solidarists, there was no contradiction between the law
of solidarity and the law of individual development. The association of individual actions was a mode of individual liberation as
well as a condition of human development and progress:

> Personal liberty of man, that is, the ability to develop one's
> *self* freely, is as necessary to the development of society as
> to the development of the individual.[29]

Thus, society evolved as a result of cooperation rather than
competition.[30]

Solidarists rejected Rousseau's notion of a voluntary contract
for mutual benefit and replaced it with solidarity, which was viewed
as a moral imperative.[31] Man, born a debtor to human society, owed
a debt to his ancestors, who had contributed to the amelioration of
society.[32] His duty therefore consisted of working toward human
progress for the good of future generations. The recognition of this
debt among members of society resulted in the idea of the quasi-
social contract, borrowed from Fouillée, which formed the basis for
their obligations.

Bourgeois sought to replace the Christian ideal of charity, which
was voluntary, with the "scientific" notion of solidarity, which was
compulsory. He also attempted to transcend the overly abstract
republican notion of fraternity with the idea of social solidarity,
which implied not only the rights outlined in the Declaration of the
Rights of Man, but also the obligations of the individual to society.
Bourgeois wrote, "*Solidarity* first, then *equality* or *justice*, which, in
truth, are the same thing; finally, *liberty*. This seems to be the
necessary order of the three ideas in which the Revolution sums up
social truth."[33] In effect, he was applying the republican principle
of fraternity to the social and economic spheres.[34]

Solidarists believed in the sanctity of private property and felt
that it promoted the freedom of the individual. While they accepted
natural inequalities, they felt that justice required that they not be
compounded by inequalities of social origin and inherited wealth.[35]
To that end, they declared that the privileged owed a debt to help
those less fortunate than themselves and proposed a program of

social welfare, which included free education, a progressive income tax, a minimum wage, and unemployment insurance.

While Solidarists placed their main hopes on voluntary mutual benefit societies, they also believed in state action when needed, thereby antagonizing both liberal economists, who felt that the Solidarists had gone too far in justifying state intervention, and socialists, who felt the Solidarists did not go far enough. For many socialists, Solidarist legislation, which was piecemeal, did not seek to remake bourgeois society but rather to correct its most glaring abuses. In addition, they and others suspected that Solidarists spoke of social reform in order to neutralize their socialist rivals and minimize class conflict.

Solidarism, however, did initially succeed in raising the hopes of many left-wing liberals and reformist socialists seeking to implement significant social reform in France. In 1895, socialists supported Bourgeois's first entirely Radical Cabinet, and in 1902, the policy of "no enemies on the left," inspired by Bourgeois, led to the victory of the *bloc des gauches*, but ultimately, cooperation between the two groups proved unfruitful. In pursuit of the goal of Socialist unity, Jaurès was obliged to abandon cooperation with "bourgeois" parties. As for the aptly named Bourgeois, he was much too timid about pushing his reforms through parliament. Although Solidarism accomplished much in beginning programs in national and municipal welfare, it did not succeed in permanently uniting the Left.[36]

Discussions of the individual in society prevailed not only in liberal circles of the time, but also among liberalism's opponents. Furthermore, these discussions were not limited to political circles but were also present in literary ones. Anarchist leader Jean Grave developed his views on individualism in a series of books, including *La Société mourante et l'anarchie* (1893), *La Société future* (1895), and *L'Individu et la société* (1897); so, too, did Maurice Barrès, beginning with the *culte du moi* trilogy (1888–1891) and culminating in *Les Déracinés* (1897).

The attraction of anarchism for a number of young litterateurs was predicated on a misunderstanding of individualism as defined by such anarcho-communists as Grave and Kropotkin. This confusion was the hallmark of the 1893 *Ermitage* referendum on the social question. Many of those attracted to anarchism valued it only for its narrowly individualist aspects, without concerning themselves with the accompanying sense of social responsibility. A similar confusion existed among its opponents, who dismissed it as an overly individualist and anarchical (as opposed to anarchist) doctrine.[37] Yet even among those one could find individuals like Henri Mazel and Henry Bérenger, who exalted individual rights.

In common with the Solidarists, Bérenger opposed both anarchism, which he defined as an extreme individualism, and collectivist socialism, which he viewed as destructive of the individual.[38] Like Fouillée and Izoulet, he believed in solidarity in nature as well as the Solidarist idea of a quasi-contract.[39] Bérenger, who felt that solidarity presupposed individualism, cited sociologist Gabriel Tarde's laws of imitation approvingly, stating that the superior individual was the motor of human progress.[40]

Bérenger believed that an intellectual aristocracy was needed to reconcile democracy's aim of steering a middling course between individualism and solidarity.[41] Bérenger went on to become a Dreyfusard and even entered politics, serving as the Radical-Socialist Senator from Guadeloupe between 1912 and 1940.[42]

Criticism of laissez-faire individualism was to be found along the entire length of the political spectrum. Supporters of anarchism like André Veidaux celebrated their own "refined, generous individualism," while denigrating the egotistical individualism of others, in this case, that of the bourgeoisie.[43] Striking a slightly different note, Grave himself associated bourgeois individualism with the individualist anarchism of certain avant-garde litterateurs.[44]

Although Grave, along with all anarchists, called for the abolition of the state, he certainly did not reject the idea of man as a social being. In La Société mourante et l'anarchie, he proclaimed the interdependence of the individual and society, declaring that individuality could only develop in the community.[45] In L'Individu et la société, Grave represented his ideas as a compromise between extreme individualism and collectivism:

> The individual's goal is his own happiness; he must sacrifice it to no one, nor to an entity; however, because he is not self-sufficient . . . his efforts should be associated with those of his peers.[46]

Just as it was absurd to sacrifice the individual to society, so, too, was it ridiculous to deny the collectivity in favor of an individual seen as an entity in and of itself.[47]

Nevertheless, he was careful to distinguish himself from Social Darwinists who sought to oblige the individual to submit to society by likening the former to a cell subordinate to the latter, represented as an organism. He even employed their organicist imagery to derail their claims, "Every living organism . . . is made up of cells; . . . it is not the organism that preceded the cell. The latter is anterior to the organism. . . ."[48]

While man was a social being, this did not mean that one could cite social cohesion to justify the violation of an individual's rights. Such a view eventually led Grave to a Dreyfusard stance.

In common with a variety of thinkers of different political perspectives, Grave called for a society based on solidarity.[49] In his view, solidarity consisted of voluntary cooperative associations:

> We maintain that there may exist a society in which individuals will know how to organize themselves in groups, producers or consumers, without needing masters, leaders or overseers.[50]

Much of his thinking, from the moral basis of his beliefs to his faith in progress and science, linked him to many reformist liberal thinkers of the period, although Grave, unlike the liberals, believed in the abolition of private property and opposed the authority of the state.[51]

While Grave was rather contemptuous of anarchism à la Barrès, such was the intellectual and linguistic confusion of the time that some of his pronouncements seem to resemble those of the future anti-Dreyfusard. Writing in *La Cocarde* on 5 September 1894, Barrès declared: "An individualism that is both free and profound, together with social solidarity—these are the twin concerns from which our ideal is formed."[52] Although he continued to define himself as an individualist, subsequently, he would use the term solidarity much less often, after it was increasingly identified with the Solidarists.

This brief examination illustrates that the terms individualism and solidarity were ubiquitous during the fin de siècle and that many of those who used them spoke at cross purposes. It is against this confusing backdrop that we must situate the debate concerning the individual and society during the Dreyfus Affair.

No one article, with the obvious exception of Zola's "J'Accuse," elicited as many responses during the Affair as Ferdinand Brunetière's "Après le procès," published in *La Revue des deux mondes* on 15 March 1898.[53] A member of the Académie française, Brunetière had rejected positivism for Catholicism a few years earlier, proclaiming the bankruptcy of science. In "Après le procès," Brunetière expounded on the importance of the army in a democracy. He also elaborated therein a scathing critique of "individualism" and intellectuals, accusing them of setting themselves up as an aristocracy of intelligence, above the law:

[The intellectual] is the "superman" of Nietzsche or even
the "enemy of laws," who is not made for these laws [note
the reference to Barrès's book of the same title], but for
placing himself above them . . . when intellectualism and
individualism reach this degree of self-infatuation they simply are or have become anarchy.[54]

This article has been cited by some historians as "proof" that
anti-Dreyfusards rejected the involvement of intellectuals in public
life. While anti-Dreyfusards criticized their opponents' ideas, they
either implicitly or explicitly accepted the intervention of intellectuals in public life. Brunetière's diatribe against Dreyfusard intellectuals must be viewed in this light. By the very writing of this
piece, his actions belied his words.[55]

Brunetière criticized Dreyfusard intellectuals as the enemies
of France, accusing them of fomenting cultural, political, and social
anarchy through their individualist doctrines:

It is not democracy that is the enemy, it is individualism
and it is anarchy . . . "intellectuals," without knowing it
perhaps, and certainly without wanting to—are the worst
enemies of democracy itself and of the army.[56]

Brunetière's use of the word "anarchie" in this text and elsewhere is muddled. He not only used it to denote the political doctrine of anarchism but also as a general term implying disorder.
Part of the overlap is of course the result of his equating the two.
For Brunetière, anarchism was an extreme version of individualism. He viewed it only in terms of the principle of negative liberty,
without regard to its positive aspects. Like the litterateurs of the
1893 *Ermitage* Referendum, he sought to separate anarchism and
socialism:

Today, we confuse the most contrary things in the world:
collectivism with anarchy, socialism with individualism . . .
what is anarchy, if not the most acute form of individualism.[57]

Brunetière, unlike many other conservative commentators, feared
individualism more than socialism or parliamentarianism, declaring: "*Individualism* . . . is the great illness of the present time, not
parliamentarianism, nor socialism, nor collectivism. . . ."[58] Noting that
individualism was an ill inherited from the French Revolution, he

equated it with the rise of an industrial, mercantile culture and with laissez-faire economic principles. All anarchist theoreticians, he believed, had been inspired by Englishman Herbert Spencer, whom he described as "the greatest theoretician of anarchy of the last half-century."[59] This was, of course, a gross misrepresentation of the political doctrine of anarchism. Jean Grave opposed laissez-faire economics as much as the Catholic Brunetière.

In his presentation, "Les Ennemis de l'âme française," delivered on 15 March 1899, Brunetière exhorted his audience to combat France's internal enemies, the individualists, whom he feared more than France's external enemies.[60] Individualists were destroying the French "spirit" by breaking with the French tradition of solidarity, as represented by the nation and by Catholicism.[61] Brunetière blamed the French Revolution for promoting individualism not only in economic and social life, but also in art and literature, castigating the Romantics and their heirs. French literature, up to the Revolution, he claimed, had been social.[62] Under the banner of individualism, Brunetière could attack all of the "enemies" of France, uniting political, social, and cultural criticism.[63]

If Brunetière opposed socialism less than anarchism, it was because he felt the former, unlike the latter, promoted a type of human solidarity, although it was one that Brunetière rejected.[64] For Brunetière, true solidarity was to be found in "the nation, which of all associations, is the most natural, and is equally the most beautiful, the most generous, and also the most sweeping."[65] Some Dreyfusards may have been surprised that Brunetière quoted Jaurès approvingly on this point, but he did recognize that both he and the Socialist leader believed in the ideal of the nation and sought to preserve it, albeit in very different ways.[66] They were undoubtedly more shocked that he quoted Kant to justify the preservation of the nation through war and his claim that Kant was not the exclusive property of the Dreyfusards.[67] In a certain sense, Brunetière is the anti-Dreyfusard counterpart of Dreyfusard Henry Bérenger; the former was an anti-Dreyfusard admirer of Kant, the latter, a Dreyfusard opponent of the philosopher.

For Brunetière, France did not suffer from a lack of individualism but rather an excess; the primary goal of contemporary Frenchmen was to subordinate the individual to society as represented by the nation. Declaring that the conservation of the French race was the fundamental aim of solidarity, he celebrated such traditional institutions as the army, the Catholic Church, and the family, all of which contributed to both spatial and temporal solidarity.[68]

While Brunetière employed the term solidarity frequently during the height of the Affair, by 1900, in a talk to Catholic university students in Toulouse, he spoke of solidarity mostly to criticize its use by liberal Solidarists.[69] Pointing to the origins of the term among conservative, Catholic thinkers like Bonald and de Maistre, he claimed that solidarity, divested of the Christian moral ideal of charity, lost its very meaning.[70] Brunetière felt that Solidarists Fouillée and Bourgeois confused the solidarity of human beings with association and dependence in nature.[71] Humans, he claimed, were not organisms, similar to other animals and that basing human behavior on the natural sciences was erroneous. In this sense, Brunetière may be seen as anti-organicist, although he certainly saw society as an organic whole. While it is true that many conservative writers at the fin de siècle were using Social Darwinism to justify their thinking just as their opponents had earlier in the century, Brunetière clearly was not among their number.[72]

If Brunetière's attack on individualism in "Après le procès" has become one of the most cited of texts published during the Dreyfus Affair, so, too, has Emile Durkheim's response "L'Individualisme et les intellectuels," published in La Revue bleue on 2 July of the same year.[73] In responding to Brunetière, Durkheim essentially turned his anti-Dreyfusard opponent's arguments on their head, accusing Brunetière and anti-Dreyfusards of betraying French traditions and thereby contributing to cultural, political, and social anarchy. Both Brunetière and Durkheim agreed on social malaise and anarchy in society, although they disagreed on its sources.

Durkheim began his article with a reference to Brunetière, agreeing with his foe that the question of Dreyfus's innocence or guilt had become the touchstone for a far-reaching debate concerning the nature of French society:

The question which, for six months now, has so grievously divided the country is in the process of transformation; having begun as a simple question of fact, it has become more and more general in scope. The recent intervention of a well-known litterateur has contributed greatly to this development. . . . We too believe that the controversies of yesterday were only superficial expressions of a deep disagreement; and that men's minds have been divided much more over a question of principle than over a question of fact. Let us therefore leave to one side the minutely detailed arguments which have been exchanged from side to side; let us forget the Affair itself and the melancholy scenes we have witnessed. The problem confronting us goes infinitely beyond the current events and must be disengaged from them.[74]

He accused Brunetière of misunderstanding individualism by confusing it with the narrow utilitarianism and utilitarian egoism of Spencer and the economists. Such individualism, he declared, was outmoded and had scarcely any admirers. There existed, however, another individualism, which was much less easily dismissed: of Kant and Rousseau, the *spiritualistes*, and the Declaration of the Rights of Man, "that which is currently taught in our schools and which has become the basis of our moral catechism."[75] Such "moral" individualism, "far from making personal interest the object of human conduct . . . sees in all personal motives the very source of evil."[76]

Although he felt that Kant and Rousseau had not fully understood the relationship between the individual and society,[77] Durkheim emphatically asserted that for both thinkers, a notion of the good of the collectivity was a part of their individualism:

> The only ways of acting that are moral are those which are fitting for all men equally, that is to say, which are implied in the notion of man in general . . . duty consists in averting our attention from what concerns us personally, from all that relates to our empirical individuality, so as uniquely to seek that which our human condition demands, that which we hold in common with all our fellow men.[78]

Thus, Durkheim argued that individualism was not immoral and self-interested, but a moral doctrine based on the collective interest.

He also declared that such individualism was "religious" in nature, with man as its object—undoubtedly a blasphemous thought for Brunetière and his fellow Catholics.[79] Individualism, according to Durkheim, was:

> The glorification not of the self, but of the individual in general. Its motive force is not egoism but sympathy for all that is human, a wider pity for all sufferings, for all human miseries, a more ardent desire to combat and alleviate them, a greater thirst for justice. Is this not the way to achieve a community of all men of good will?[80]

Such moral individualism was the basis of national solidarity: "Not only is individualism distinct from anarchy; but it is henceforth the only system of beliefs which can ensure the moral unity of the country."[81] Furthermore, it was perfectly in keeping with French tradition: "And if there is one country among all others in which the individual cause is truly national, it is our own; for there is no other whose fate has been so closely bound with the fate of these ideas."[82] Inherited not only from the Revolution, it was also rooted in Christian morality. Here, Durkheim was contesting Brunetière on his own terms, although his vision of Christianity, with its emphasis on its individualist spirit, was more Protestant than Catholic.[83] This "Protestant" morality would not be lost on anti-Dreyfusards, who lumped Dreyfusards, Protestants, and Jews in the same category, as the enemies of Catholic France.[84]

Durkheim also challenged Brunetière's claim that Dreyfusard intellectuals had used their specialized training as a justification for their intervention. While Durkheim was willing to bow to the authority of others, he was only prepared do so if that authority were rationally based and could prove a special competence to judge the issue at hand. A discussion of the guilt or innocence of Dreyfus, however, required no special expertise and was thus a "problem of practical morality concerning which every man of good sense is competent and about which no one ought to be indifferent."[85] Indeed, to acquiesce to the judgment of the military court was contrary both to reason and duty.[86]

Rather than members of an "intellectual aristocracy" who set themselves above the law as Brunetière charged, Dreyfusard intellectuals were acting as responsible citizens:

> If, therefore, in these recent times, a certain number of artists, but above all of scholars, have believed that they ought to refuse to assent to a judgment whose legality appeared to them to be suspect, it is not because, as chemists or philologists, philosophers or historians, they attribute to themselves any special privileges, or any exclusive right of exercising control over the case in question. It is rather that being men, they seek to exercise their entire right as men to keep before them a matter which concerns reason alone. It is true that they have shown themselves more jealous of this right than the rest of society; but that is simply because, as a result of their professional activities, they have it nearer to heart. Accustomed by the practice of scientific method to reserve judgment when they are not fully aware of the facts, it is natural that they give in less readily to the enthusiasms of the crowd and to the prestige of authority.[87]

Durkheim not only accused his opponents of shirking their duty but of contributing to the disintegration of national unity. Institutions like the army were only a means to an end, not an end in itself. Those who would argue for *la raison d'état* by denying an individual's rights thus betrayed the end itself.[88] It was the anti-Dreyfusards who were traitors to French society. Durkheim dismissed them as literary dilettantes, thereby betraying his professorial disdain for litterateurs:

> They are neither apostles who allow themselves to be overwhelmed by their anger or their enthusiasm, nor are they scholars who bring us the product of their research and their deliberations. They are literary men seduced by an interesting theme. It seems therefore impossible that these games of dilettantes should succeed in keeping hold for long of the masses. . . .[89]

His suspicions were the counterpart to Brunetière's literary prejudices against professors.

To understand fully the implications of this article with regard to the discussion of individualism and solidarity during the Affair, it is necessary to examine further Durkheim's writings and then to compare his thoughts with those of other contemporary thinkers, both fellow Dreyfusard Jean Jaurès and anti-Dreyfusard Maurice Barrès. Not surprisingly, Durkheim and Jaurès shared numerous ideas; more striking are the parallels between Durkheim and Barrès, especially in the way in which they viewed the problems besetting modern French society.

Although he saw himself as an heir of Kant, Rousseau, and Spencer, Durkheim believed it impossible to conceive of an abstract individual existing prior to society. For Durkheim, the individual was not an atomistic entity but rather, "a social institution," inseparable from society.[90] Durkheim rejected both the ideas of laissez-faire thinkers, who thought that state intervention would lead to the diminution of individual liberties, and of contemporaries like Barrès and Brunetière, who believed in a "mystical" state, which subordinated the individual to the glory of society.[91] For Durkheim, the growth of the state was not incompatible with the growth of individualism but rather the opposite; the stronger the state, the more the individual was respected. In common with the Solidarists, he felt that the fundamental duty of the state was moral. Indeed, it was the "very organ of social thought."[92]

Although Durkheim rejected the application of simplistic analogies drawn from biology to human society, he may be seen as an organicist, in metaphoric, if not in literal terms.[93] For Durkheim, society resembled a biological organism in that its institutions resembled biological organs and its individual members biological cells. Unity in society was determined by the functioning of every institution and individual working toward the collective goal of the common interest or health of the social organism. Thus, Durkheim spoke of the "organic" solidarity of modern, industrial societies, which resulted from increasing differences among individuals, contrasting it to the older "mechanistic" solidarity of traditional societies, which was based on their similarities.[94] In the same vein, he viewed the sociologist as a diagnostician of the ills of society.[95]

Durkheim's vision of the individual in society was similar to that of Jaurès, who argued that socialism was a logical extension of individualism in an article entitled "Socialisme et liberté," published in La Revue de Paris on 1 December 1898.[96] This article may be viewed not only as another response to Brunetière, but also as a companion piece to Durkheim's "L'Individualisme et les intellectuels." Like Durkheim and the Solidarists, Jaurès sought to reconcile the individual's rights with responsibility to the collectivity. He distinguished his brand of "collectivist" or "communist" socialism from what he called "State Socialism" (le Socialisme d'Etat). While state socialism was essentially a state capitalism which promoted class warfare, collectivist socialism, by abolishing private property, created a new society in which it was not necessary to pit one class against another, all classes having been absorbed by the unity of the nation.[97] In his vision of the socialist order, liberty would be sovereign:

> Socialism is the supreme affirmation of individual rights. Nothing is superior to the individual . . . universal education, universal suffrage, universal property, here is . . . the real postulate of the individual human being. Socialism is logical and complete individualism. In expanding it, it perpetuates revolutionary individualism.[98]

Jaurès, again like the Solidarists and Durkheim, believed that the exaltation of the individual was not contrary to the ideal of solidarity: "But this exaltation of the individual . . . is contrary neither to the ideal, nor to solidarity, nor to sacrifice."[99] Not only was the individual the centerpiece of socialism, so, too, was the

nation, since national unity was the condition of the unity of production and of property. In common with both fellow Dreyfusards
and anti-Dreyfusards, Jaurès viewed the nation as an organic
whole.[100] Unlike anti-Dreyfusards, however, Jaurès felt that the
nation was not a goal in and of itself but rather a means to justice
and liberty.[101] Referring to the Affair, Jaurès declared that the nation
was not

> above conscience . . . above man. The day she turned against
> liberty and the dignity of the individual, would be the day
> she would lose her titles. Those who would make of her
> some sort of monstrous idol which has the right to sacrifice
> even an innocent man, work toward her demise. . . . She is
> and will remain legitimate only to the extent that she guar-
> antees individual rights.[102]

Like Durkheim, he opposed anti-Dreyfusards who argued that
revision of the Dreyfus case would lead to the destruction of the
nation and of the social order. National unity, he argued, would in
fact be destroyed by injustice. Thus, it was the anti-Dreyfusards
who were betraying the nation, not the Dreyfusards, who were true
patriots. Finally, along with Durkheim, he spoke of humanity in
religious terms, describing the coming of socialism as a great religious revelation.[103]

When the writings of Barrès are compared to those of Durkheim
and Jaurès, it becomes clear that Dreyfusards and anti-Dreyfusards
used remarkably similar vocabulary to say different things.
Brunetière and Maurras, notwithstanding, spokesmen for both sides
could lay claim to a certain type of "individualism." It is therefore
much too simplistic to designate Dreyfusards as "individualists"
and anti-Dreyfusards as "anti-individualists."

Maurice Barrès has often been represented as "anti-individualist"
by scholars who feel that there was a break between his early *culte
du moi* period and the period that began with *Les Déracinés*.[104]
Barrès, however, always claimed his nationalism was a logical
extension of his cult of the self:

> To think by oneself is to move towards thinking in common
> with others, . . . All in all, the work of my ideas boils down
> to having recognized that the individual self was entirely
> supported and nourished by society. . . . You will see that
> there is no opposition between the diverse phases of a pro-
> cess that is so easy, so logical.[105]

In his justification of the *culte du moi*, he declared that patriotism and individualism were not opposed; in fact, patriotism was nothing more than "national egoism."[106] For Barrès, as for Durkheim, the individual was a product of society, although the sociologist Durkheim certainly would have contested the physiological and deterministic explanations given by Barrès to explain national solidarity:

> We are not the masters of the thoughts which are born in us. They do not spring from our intelligence; they are ways of reacting which reflect very old physiological dispositions . . . we are the continuation of our parents. . . . They think and speak through us. An entire line of descendants comprises in reality one and the same being.[107]

Like Durkheim, Barrès believed it impossible to conceive of an abstract individual existing prior to society:

> Thus the individual seems to me to be linked to all of his dead ancestors by the work of individuals and of the sacrificed who have preceded him, like the stone is joined to the mass by mortar formed by the work of successive layers.[108]

Barrès believed that in finding the self, individuals would eventually discover the authentic tradition of their culture, as David Carroll notes in his recent book on French literary fascism. Discovering the true individual self was a starting point for building a new sense of morality and politics and a new feeling of national unity.[109]

In this vein, Barrès accused Dreyfusards, many of whom were his former disciples, of learning only the first part of his teachings:

> Here is the incomplete reasoning of those who are called "Intellectuals." These people are capable of attaining the first level of culture: they know that an individual should first know himself and should take possession, in order to make use of it, of his Self. But they do not go far enough, in order to determine how the self . . . destroys itself to leave behind it the collectivity that produced it.[110]

Other similarities may also be found between Durkheim and Barrès. Both men worried about the isolation of individuals, the former speaking of *anomie*, the latter of dispersed energies.[111] They viewed the nation as an organic whole and believed in the necessity of education to achieve national solidarity.[112] Both Durkheim and Barrès also spoke in religious terms. For Barrès, nationalism was a new religion, while Durkheim referred to a religion of humanity. Barrès, however, rejected the republican university of which Durkheim was a product as well as a spokesman. Furthermore, Barrès, unlike Durkheim, defined such solidarity in function of its rejection of foreign influences, whether represented by internal enemies or external ones.[113] Durkheim's nationalism, like that of Jaurès, was more inclusive, less defensive and inward looking than Barrès's "integral" nationalism.[114] While Barrès continued to respect Jaurès, even after the Affair had separated them, he denigrated the Socialist leader's vision of the nation as an idea, opposing it to his own view of it as a product of blood and soil.

Durkheim, Jaurès and other Dreyfusards, on the other hand, undoubtedly viewed Barrès's cult of the nation as a collective egoism. For Durkheim, anti-Semitism, which for Barrès was a means by which to forge national unity, was a symptom of a "social malaise" that endangered the health, indeed, the organic solidarity of the nation.[115] For Durkheim, society progressed in function of an increase in individual differences; thus he viewed Barrès's vision of a homogeneous France which attempted to rid herself of "foreign influences" as retrograde.[116] In his respectful but critical review of *Les Déracinés*, Dreyfusard Léon Blum stated that nothing falsified the development of individual energies more than Barrès's communities of the family and the commune:

> These are the most dangerous collectivities because we love them and because they have a hold on us. What I fear is most opposed to the free development of the individual is not constraint or misery, but the ties of shared affection and mediocre happiness.[117]

For Blum, as for Durkheim, individuals were truly free only in a centralized nation.[118] In "Socialisme et liberté," Jaurès went even farther, stating: "To decentralize without transforming property is to reestablish the supremacy of old land-owning influences, it is to return to the past."[119]

Their vision of the nation was the crux of differences between Dreyfusards and anti-Dreyfusards. It was clearly a question of ends and means. For Durkheim, Jaurès and Blum, the nation was not an end in and of itself but rather a means of achieving greater justice and liberty for the individual. Violating an individual's rights was tantamount to betraying the *raison d'être* of the state. Barrès and Brunetière, on the other hand, placed the state in the form of the nation above all else; it was an end in itself.[120]

To further illustrate the complexity of the issues involved, I would like to examine briefly anti-Dreyfusard Gustave Le Bon's views on individualism and solidarity, as expressed in his *Psychology of Socialism*, published in 1898 (the English edition was published in 1899) at the height of the Affair. Like Dreyfusard Gabriel Tarde, Le Bon saw himself as an individualist, in large part, because he saw the individual as the motor of human progress: "All that has gone to make the greatness of civilizations . . . has been the work of individuals. . . ."[121] For Le Bon, societies which valued individualism were more advanced than those that favored the collectivity; thus, he viewed socialism as a retrograde doctrine. Furthermore, both Le Bon and Tarde, unlike Barrès and Durkheim, viewed the individual as superior to the collectivity and based their sociology on individual psychology. Le Bon, in common with Barrès, criticized the French Revolution for depriving France of intermediary, corporatist bodies and replacing them with a centralized state.[122]

Unlike such anti-Dreyfusards as Brunetière and Maurras, however, he did not criticize the Revolution's excessive "individualism," but rather praised it. In keeping with classical laissez-faire liberals, he instead lauded the Anglo-Saxon model, citing Herbert Spencer as a positive example, since the English thinker sought to liberate the individual and simultaneously limit the power of the state.[123] Tarde, it should be noted, did not oppose state intervention to individual liberty.[124]

With regard to solidarity, Le Bon once again disagreed with fellow anti-Dreyfusard Brunetière, who sang the praises of the Christian ideal of solidarity. For Le Bon, as for Barrès, solidarity merely implied association, not charity or altruism.[125] In fact, charity was noxious and antisocial since it discouraged its receivers from hard work. Although Le Bon's pronouncements seem to resemble those of the Solidarists, they were in actuality quite different.[126] Le Bon, too, spoke of solidarity in nature, yet for him, unlike for the Solidarists, such solidarity was based on the defense by the weak against the strong.[127] For Le Bon, the ultimate aim of association was to struggle against other interests: "Solidarity is only a particular form of the universal conflict of classes and individuals."[128] Solidarists, of course, rejected the Social Darwinist principle of conflict. Again, like the Solidarists, Le Bon spoke of mutual societies and associations, among them trade unions, yet his rejection of state intervention in the social and economic spheres separated him from the Solidarists, even if on occasion he quoted Bourgeois approvingly.

According to Le Bon and other anti-Dreyfusards, solidarity was based on similarity of interests. Such similarity was dismissed as "mechanical," "primitive" solidarity by Durkheim. In common with Barrès, Le Bon's solidarity was the replacement of "impotent egoism of the individual by a collective and powerful egoism by which everyone profits."[129] Such egoism, whether individual or collective, was rejected by Solidarists, as well as by Dreyfusards like Jaurès and Durkheim.[130] Moreover, the solidarity of Barrès and Le Bon was based on a biological determinism, which was rejected not only by Jaurès and Durkheim but also by Tarde.

This brief examination of Dreyfusard and anti-Dreyfusard discourses reveals the striking parallels between the two sides, as well as the diverging positions within each camp. The complexities of the issues involved should illustrate the limited usefulness of such simplistic categories as "individualist" and "organicist." Individualism meant a variety of things to different people. While Brunetière rejected "individualism" as a selfish doctrine, Durkheim, the Solidarists, anarcho-communists like Grave, and Jaurèsian socialists all proudly laid claim to a generous individualism. The word was so fluid that anti-Dreyfusards Le Bon and Barrès, too, could define themselves as individualists, extending the cult of the self to the collective cult of the nation.

Even more contested was the notion of solidarity—especially up to 1900, by which time it had been assimilated by the Solidarists. Solidarity was conceived in a variety of ways; for some it was voluntary, for others, involuntary. Solidarity could be based on biology, sociology, psychology, or even economics. Furthermore, different individuals sought to implement solidarity on a variety of levels, among them the family, the commune, the trade union, the nation, and the international association.[131]

Both sides were "organicist" if we are to define "organicism" as the belief in French society as an integrated whole rather than a conglomeration of atomized individuals, even Tarde and Brunetière, both of whom emphatically rejected all biological applications to human society.[132] Biological analogies, whether of the Darwinian or Lamarckian variety, were so widespread at the fin de siècle that one could find commentators who used organicist imagery, either literally or metaphorically, to speak of human society, on both sides. Some chose to emphasize conflict in nature and in society while others emphasized cooperation. Use of biological analogies could lead to very different social theories and political positions.[133] Even similar views could lead to different positions—Dreyfusard Gabriel Tarde's brand of individualism had more in common with anti-Dreyfusard Gustave Le Bon's view of the individual than it did with the individualism of fellow Dreyfusard Durkheim.

Given such diversity within each camp, it is no wonder that the fragile Dreyfusard coalition fell apart by 1902 and that in the anti-Dreyfusard camp, Barrès, along with those who went on to form the Action française, increasingly distanced themselves from the founding members of the Ligue de la Patrie française. Both groups proved the old adage that it is much easier to unite against a common enemy than it is to stay united after battle.

Even if their definitions of individualism and solidarity led them in different directions, the fact that Dreyfusards and anti-Dreyfusards shared a common vocabulary meant that both sides agreed that contemporary French society suffered a malaise caused by the emergence of mass democracy and industrialization. Modernity had contributed to the destruction of the organic whole of the nation. Dreyfusards and anti-Dreyfusards generally agreed on the terms of the debate launched by the Affair, as Durkheim noted in his response to Brunetière. Contemporaries realized that the Affair was much more than a question of the guilt or innocence of one man. It was nothing less than a discussion about the nature of society and the future of France.

Conclusion: From "Mystique" to "Politique"

"Tout commence en mystique et finit en politique," (Everything begins in mystique and ends in politics) lamented Charles Péguy in *Notre Jeunesse* (1910).[1] In September 1899, when Alfred Dreyfus accepted a presidential pardon, after again being found guilty at the Rennes trial—this time with "extenuating" circumstances—the "heroic" period of the Affair was already over.[2] During the three years that followed, the Dreyfusard coalition and its anti-Dreyfusard counterpart came unraveled.

Inside each camp, there were tensions between the radicals and the moderates. Maurras and Barrès, frustrated with the middle-of-the-road views of the leaders of the Ligue de la Patrie française, took their distance from the movement. In 1898, Maurras founded the Action française, which he viewed as a more "muscular" formation.[3]

On the Dreyfusard side, cracks in the coalition had already formed during the Rennes trial, with disagreements between Dreyfus's lawyers, the flamboyant Labori against the more cautious Demange. The acceptance by Dreyfus of President Loubet's pardon further contributed to the disintegration of the Dreyfusard camp. Despite the 1902 victory of the *bloc des gauches*, the unification of the Socialist Party in 1905, which now rejected cooperation with "bourgeois" parties, contributed to the rift, which was finally cemented by former Dreyfusard Clemenceau's brutal treatment of striking workers during his tenure as prime minister, between 1906 and 1909.[4]

The two camps also witnessed tensions that pitted literary intellectuals against political leaders and political groups. Anti-Dreyfusard Ferdinand Brunetière and others left the Ligue de la Patrie française, when its intention to engage in parliamentary politics became clear.[5] Among the Dreyfusards, some intellectuals, like those associated with André Gide, withdrew from the political arena to the realm of "pure" literature by founding *La NRF*. A good number of their colleagues, especially among those who had been associated with the anarchist movement, drew closer to Jaurèsian socialism, which they viewed in esthetic and ethical, rather than political, terms. When the socialist newspaper *L'Humanité* was founded in 1904, it could boast the presence of numerous intellectuals among its contributors, including Octave Mirbeau, Jules Renard, Léon Blum, and Tristan Bernard.[6] This association also suffered from the unification of the Socialist Party. Some intellectuals withdrew because they, like their anti-Dreyfusard counterparts, were wary of the party's parliamentary strategy.[7]

While the tensions within the anti-Dreyfusard camp were largely generational, the tensions within the Dreyfusard camp opposed literary intellectuals against their university colleagues. Although literary intellectuals participated alongside university professors in the founding of the *Universités populaires*, the traditional suspicion of each group for the other re-emerged quickly, as various *enquêtes* of the period, among them a survey by *La Revue blanche* and another, by *La Revue bleue*, illustrate.[8] In the *Revue blanche* survey, for example, a number of literary intellectuals denounced the state-run educational system. By 1902, the brief moment in time, which Léon Blum likened to the experience of the Revolution and the Great War, was over, leaving behind a legacy and a legend for both the Left and the Right, not just in France but the world over.

Through an exploration of the cultural milieu of the fin de siècle, it becomes evident that the literary avant-garde played a key role in the emergence of the intellectual in France. This origin marked indelibly in the popular imagination the image of the French intellectual as an outsider, a rebel—even when intellectuals were no longer outsiders but very much a part of the establishment. Moreover, the intellectual was born during the years just preceding the Affair. While modern-day intellectuals are in many ways the heirs of the eighteenth-century *philosophes*, they represent new players in French cultural life.

It may be argued that France, which possesses a long literary tradition, one that values highly literature and those who create it, was especially predisposed to the early emergence of the intellectual. Furthermore, France was also the home of the first democratic regime in Europe, a prerequisite for the emergence of the modern intellectual. Intellectuals are the product of mass democracy not only because freedom of the press is required for them to express their opinions, but also because they need a large, literate public to receive those opinions. The wide circulation of ideas—whether expressed in books or newspapers—is not possible in a country without the aforementioned conditions, not to mention modern printing methods and a system of rapid transport.

It is ironic, though of fundamental importance, to recognize that these very same political and economic conditions that allowed an independent intellectual class to emerge soon became causes of strain and self-questioning within this burgeoning milieu. While intellectuals are the product of a democratic society, indeed, of a crisis of nascent democracy, they have been remarkably wary, even hostile, to its manifestations. The emergence of popular culture and of mass politics and political parties led in the 1890s to the self-realization of intellectuals as a group. The writings of avant-garde intellectuals, along with *enquêtes* and other surveys of the period, reflect a growing awareness of themselves as a group and moreover as a group with a role to play in the new democratic society. The nature of this role, particularly their relationship to political formations, divided them more fundamentally than the more obvious disagreements that separated Dreyfusard and anti-Dreyfusard intellectuals during the Affair. The Dreyfus Affair did not produce such divisions but merely exposed already existing tensions.

My examination of the literary avant-garde illustrates that despite the seemingly insurmountable divide of the Affair, Dreyfusard and anti-Dreyfusard intellectuals shared common values that put them at odds with themselves and the prevailing political, social, and cultural structures of their time. Both sets of intellectuals were products of a common culture and education—not surprising in a nation such as France, where cultural institutions, in particular, educational ones, are centralized. The two groups shared a similar way of looking at the world and its problems, even if they did not agree on solutions to those problems.

Fin-de-siècle intellectuals, especially of the avant-garde, feared for their status in a modern, democratic society. Alienated from both the literary and political establishments, they deplored the effects of modernization on the traditional elitist culture of the nation. They reacted with apprehension to the rise of the masses and the emergence of popular culture and tastes—even those who purported to express anarchist or socialist views. Almost all of them disdained the newly founded Third Republic, a regime which they viewed as both corrupt and inefficient. While some opposed all forms of democracy, others objected specifically to the type of democracy represented by this new parliamentary regime.

These literary intellectuals reacted with hostility not only to politicians, who increasingly wielded power in the new society, but also to university intellectuals, a product of the republican state, denigrating them as an "intellectual proletariat." In opposition to these groups, avant-garde intellectuals banded together in the 1880s and 1890s. Defining themselves as an "intellectual aristocracy," they proposed to restore the grandeur and dignity of the writer in France, lost with the rise of the marketplace.

For some avant-garde intellectuals, this fear lured them into the trap of anti-Semitism, since a significant number of Jews had risen to positions of prominence under the new republican regime. Anti-Semitism ultimately contributed to the split which occurred in the avant-garde camp during the Affair. Some avant-garde intellectuals, chief among them Maurras and Barrès, spearheaded the campaign against Jews in France, while others, like the intellectuals of *La Revue blanche*, both Jewish and Gentile, broke with their former comrades-in-arms to come to the defense not only of Dreyfus but also of the Rights of Man. Each group laid claim to honor and to representing the "true" vision of the French nation. Moreover, both sides believed in the power of words and ideas, along with the right and responsibility of the intellectual to serve as the nation's conscience. But what was the true nature of the French nation and who had the right to be its conscience?

At the very heart of the birth of the intellectual in France lies then the question of national identity. These intellectuals, who made it their cause to define the national identity, were simultaneously faced with the equally challenging task of defining their own nature. In the wake of the loss of the Franco-Prussian War and the decline of France's role on the European stage, intellectuals deplored the country's "decadence" and called for a regeneration of the country. Moreover, they felt they were ideally suited to lead France to such regeneration. Like their contemporaries, they equated the loss of national honor with a loss of French manhood, a view exacerbated by the decline of the national birthrate. These fears were further fueled by the entry into public life of increasing numbers of women. Intellectuals of the avant-garde shared with their establishment opponents not only common views of women but also of honor and manhood.

The line between future Dreyfusards and their opponents was by no means clearly delineated, as the avant-garde's common, but troubled defense of Oscar Wilde illustrates. Already fearful of being labeled effeminate, writers of the avant-garde nevertheless came to Wilde's defense, although they distanced themselves from his sexual proclivities. Instead, through Wilde, they defended the avant-garde ideal of art, which exalted emotion and sensitivity, and proclaimed Wilde's artistic right to freedom of expression. As such, their defense of Wilde presaged the avant-garde's less than unanimous defense of Emile Zola three years later. The Wilde Affair also revealed heightened tensions surrounding notions of honor and manhood. While some progressive intellectuals like Max Nordau viewed avant-garde art as effeminate, other intellectuals, especially of the literary avant-garde, viewed the "excessive intellectualism" of university professors as equally effeminate. Some of these individuals included future Dreyfusards, who are generally associated with a defense of reason.

By the time of the Dreyfus Affair, however, two opposing visions of the hero had emerged, each embedded in a different vision of the nation. For Dreyfusards, the hero was represented by the intellectual, a man of moral courage, who stood above the crowd in defiance of both public opinion and the government. For anti-Dreyfusards, on the other hand, the hero was represented by the soldier, who obeyed orders, respected hierarchy, and exhibited physical courage. Intellectual heroes for these anti-Dreyfusards were those who defended an ordered vision of the nation and society. Despite such fundamental differences, however, Dreyfusards and anti-Dreyfusards shared a common vocabulary to express their ideals. This shared vocabulary also shaped their different understandings of the individual in society. The two groups feared the breakdown of an "organic" French society by the forces of modernity. Intellectuals on both sides of the Affair thus rejected laissez-faire individualism and called for some form of social solidarity. Yet once again, they were unable to reach a workable compromise between their own sense of individual identity and their vision of the nation.

Many of the issues raised by fin-de-siècle intellectuals were to remain unresolved up through the tragedy of the Vichy experience. Whether all of these fundamental questions are resolved even now in our own fin de siècle is perhaps debatable. Ironically, however, it may be in their own difficult birth that intellectuals have left their legacy both to France and the rest of the world. Their, at times, uncertain but ultimately unmistakable participation in the life of the city has become a fundamental aspect of French national identity. During the twentieth century, the French intellectual has emerged not only as a national icon, but also as an international symbol whose currency is as rich as the complex history of its origin.

Appendix of Intellectuals of the Literary Avant-Garde of the Generation of 1890

Compiled by Venita Datta and Stefanie Diaz

Adam, Paul (1862). Beginning his career as a Naturalist with the publication of *Chair molle* (1885), he later collaborated on two Symbolist novels with Jean Moréas, ran for public office as a Boulangist candidate from Nancy, and then moved on to anarchism. Focusing on social commentary, he contributed to numerous avant-garde journals: *La Revue indépendante, La Vogue, Le Symboliste,* which he helped found, *Les Entretiens politiques et littéraires,* and *La Revue blanche,* along with the anarchist publication *L'Endehors.*

Ajalbert, Jean (1863). Poet, novelist, journalist, and lawyer, Ajalbert was a contributor to the anarchist publication *L'Endehors* and was one of the first writers to join the Dreyfusard camp.

Andler, Charles (1866). *Normalien* and a close friend of Lucien Herr, he was a noted Germanist and socialist, frequently collaborating on such reviews as *La Revue blanche.*

Barrès, Maurice (1862). One of the major theoreticians of "integral nationalism," Barrès was a writer and politician. He served briefly as editor of *La Cocarde* (September 1894 to March 1895), a formerly Boulangist publication whose staff included both future Dreyfusard and anti-Dreyfusard intellectuals. In 1889, he was elected Deputy from Nancy on the Boulangist ticket, publishing at the same time the first volumes of his *culte de moi* trilogy on individualism, which earned him the title "Prince of Youth." A notable anti-Dreyfusard, he presented his ideas on nationalism in another trilogy *Le Roman de l'énergie nationale* (1897-1902), which included *Les Déracinés* (1897).

In 1906, he was elected to the Académie française and also reelected to Parliament as a Deputy from Paris.

Barrière, Marcel (1868). Former secretary to the Duc d'Orléans, he served as editor of *La Revue blanche* for a short period.

Barrucand, Victor (1866). One of the writers most closely associated with the anarchist movement, he wrote for *L'Endehors* and collaborated on *La Revue blanche*, publishing articles on social issues therein. A playwright, he also had a number of his plays presented in Lugné-Poë's avant-garde Théâtre de l'Oeuvre.

Beaubourg, Maurice (1866). A literary anarchist, he was associated with a variety of avant-garde reviews, among them *La Revue blanche*.

Benda, Julien (1867). Essayist and critic, he proclaimed himself a "Dreyfusard by reason," publishing articles in *La Revue blanche*. He was briefly associated with Charles Péguy and collaborated on the *Cahiers de la quinzaine*. Later collaborating on *La Nouvelle Revue française*, he published *La Trahison des clercs* (1927), a criticism of the intellectuals' descent into the corrupt political arena.

Bérenger, Henry (1867). Author of both novels (*L'Effort*, 1895; *La Proie*, 1897)) and essays (*L'Aristocratie intellectuelle*, 1895), he also contributed to a number of avant-garde journals, including Pujo's *L'Art et la vie* and Mazel's *L'Ermitage*. In addition, he published a number of *enquêtes* for the established *La Revue bleue*. A proponent of an "intellectual aristocracy," he went on to become a Dreyfusard and later served in public office as a Radical Senator.

Bernard, Tristan (1866). Playwright and frequent collaborator on *La Revue blanche*, his witty dramatic works were featured in Lugné-Poë's avant-garde Théâtre de l'Oeuvre, among other avant-garde and boulevard theaters.

Bizet, Jacques (1872). Writer, he cofounded *Le Banquet* with a group of friends from the Lycée Condorcet, later joining *La Revue blanche*.

Blum, Léon (1872). Graduate of the Ecole Normale Supérieure, this essayist and journalist contributed to *La Revue blanche* as a literary and drama critic, and later became a renowned Socialist leader, founding *Le Populaire*, a socialist daily newspaper. He became Prime Minister in 1936, during the Popular Front.

Boylesve, René (born Tardiveau, 1867). A novelist, who wrote on provincial life, he was a member of the *Ermitage*'s editorial committee.

Coolus, Romain (born René-Max Weil, 1868). A former *normalien*, this author of light comedies collaborated on *La Revue blanche* as drama critic.

Darien, Georges (1862). Associated with the anarchist movement, he was the author of *Biribi*, a novel which dealt with the hardships of soldiers in the colonial army.

Descaves, Lucien (1861). This novelist, dramatist, and critic, who wrote for *L'Endehors*, is best-known for his antimilitarist novel *Les Sous-offs* (1889), which led both to his being tried for defamation of the army and his defense by his peers in a petition published in *Le Figaro*.

Deschamps, Léon (1863). As director of *La Plume*, a review characterized by its mixture of generations, literary movements, and political views, he featured diverse works by the Symbolists and Naturists, and by members of the Ecole romane, along with those of older writers.

Ducoté, Edouard (1870). A journalist, he succeeded Mazel as director of *L'Ermitage* in 1895.

Fénéon, Félix (1861). Writer and literary critic, he founded *La Revue indépendante* (1884), then collaborated on Zo d'Axa's anarchist publication *L'Endehors* and on the Natanson brothers' *La Revue blanche*. He later served as the *Revue blanche*'s long-time editorial secretary until the review's demise in 1903, launching the careers of many writers and artists. Associated with the anarchist movement, he was also employed at the War Ministry. In 1894, he was acquitted during the notorious *Procès des Trente*, in which anarchist litterateurs and theoreticians were brought to trial.

Geoffroy, Gustave (1855). Critic and journalist, he was a collaborator of Georges Clemenceau. Associated with the anarchist and socialist movements, he was an ardent Dreyfusard.

Ghéon, Henri (born Vanglon, 1875). Essayist and critic, he helped to found *La Nouvelle Revue française* with André Gide and later converted to Catholicism.

Ghil, René (1862). Symbolist poet and theorist, his work was much influenced by Mallarmé.

Gide, André (1869). Novelist, dramatist, and essayist, he served as literary critic for *La Revue blanche* and later cofounded *La Nouvelle Revue française* (1909) with Henri Ghéon. Among his works emphasizing themes of introspection and social and political morality, *Corydon* (1911; 1920; 1924) addresses the theme of homosexual masculinity. In 1947, he received the Nobel Prize for Literature.

Gourmont, Remy de (1858). Born of a noble Norman family, this Symbolist writer and critic was one of the cofounders of *Le Mercure de France*. In 1891, he was fired from his position at the Bibliothèque Nationale for the publication of his article "Le Joujou patriotisme." He was an ardent literary anarchist whose anarchism was more individualist and aristocratic than social.

Gregh, Fernand (1874). Critic and poet, he headed the *Humanisme* movement in reaction against the Symbolists and the Parnassians. In collaboration with classmates from the Lycée Condorcet, he founded the short-lived review *Le Banquet* and later contributed to *La Revue blanche*. An ardent Dreyfusard, he helped to collect signatures for the petitions requesting the revision of Dreyfus's trial.

Halévy, Daniel (1872). Part of the Lycée Condorcet group, he helped to the found *Le Banquet* and later contributed to *La Revue blanche*. A social historian and friend of Charles Péguy, he collaborated on *Les Cahiers de la quinzaine*.

Hermant, Abel (1862). His early novel *Le Cavalier miserey* (1887) presented a criticism of army life, while his later works depicted Parisian life. A great anglophile, he was an admirer of Oscar Wilde and of London fashions.

Herr, Lucien (1864). Graduate, then librarian of the Ecole Normale Supérieure, he converted many generations of *normaliens* to socialism. In 1898, members of the editorial staff of *La Revue blanche* asked him to write a letter in the review, "excommunicating" Barrès, who had joined the anti-Dreyfusard camp. In 1904, he was one of the cofounders, along with Jean Jaurès, of the socialist daily *L'Humanité*.

Huret, Jules (1863). A prolific journalist, he published "L'Enquête sur l'évolution littéraire" (1891), one of the first notable *enquêtes* of the fin-de-siècle period, in *L'Echo de Paris*.

Jarry, Alfred (1873). Playwright, he published the satirical farce *Ubu roi* in 1896, which was staged at Lugné-Poë's Théâtre de l'Oeuvre. He also served as drama critic for *La Revue blanche*.

Kahn, Gustave (1859). Symbolist poet, he was a cofounder with Jean Moréas of the reviews *La Vogue* and *Le Symboliste*. He later contributed to *La Revue blanche* as poet-in-residence.

Lazare, Bernard (born Lazare Bernard in 1865). A principal collaborator on *Les Entretiens politiques et littéraires*, he was a critic of the Parnassian and Naturalist movements and a defender of the Symbolists. In 1893, he founded his own briefly lived journal *L'Action* (later *L'Action sociale*), a product of his increased interest in anarchism as a social and political movement. He published in both avant-garde journals, among them *La Revue blanche*, and mainstream newspapers. In addition, Lazare, who was a vigorous critic of anti-Semitism, is known as the first Dreyfusard outside the Dreyfus family.

Le Blond, Maurice (1877). A leader of the Naturist group, which called for a return to natural values and a celebration of daily life.

Louÿs, Pierre (born Pierre Louis, 1870). A Symbolist poet, he was a founder of the little magazine *La Conque.*

Lugné-Poë (born Aurélien Lugné, 1869). Actor and director, he founded the Théâtre de l'Oeuvre, which featured foreign and French plays and presented Alfred Jarry's *Ubu roi* in 1896.

Mauclair, Camille (born Séverin Faust in 1872). Poet, literary and art critic, he contributed to the anarchist publication *L'Endehors*, to Maurice Barrès's *La Cocarde*, along with such avant-garde journals as *Le Mercure de France* and *La Plume.*

Maurras, Charles (1868). The major proponent of "integral nationalism," along with Barrès, he was a classicizer who rejected the foreign, "Germanic" influences of the Romantics and their Symbolist heirs. He began his career in letters, serving as the chief critic for the Ecole romane, which called for a return to France's "true" roots in classical Greco-Roman culture. As a literary critic, he contributed to a number of newspapers: *La Gazette de France* and *Le Soleil*, along with *La Cocarde*, as well as such avant-journals as *L'Ermitage*. An ardent anti-Semite and a vocal anti-Dreyfusard, he took up the defense of Colonel Henry, thereby contributing to the apotheosis of Henry by anti-Dreyfusards. He founded the royalist Action française at the height of the Dreyfus Affair.

Mazel, Henri (1864). Writer and critic, he was the founder and director of *L'Ermitage* (1890), while employed as a civil servant at the Naval Ministry, where he worked until his retirement in 1929. He contributed a regular column on social issues to *Le Mercure de France.*

Merrill, Stuart (1863). Symbolist poet and graduate of the Lycée Condorcet, he briefly served as editorial secretary at *L'Ermitage* and also contributed to *La Plume.*

Moréas, Jean (1856). Initially a Symbolist poet, he later separated from the movement to form his own group, the neoclassicist Ecole romane, with Charles Maurras and Ernest Raynaud.

Muhlfeld, Lucien (1870). He served as *La Revue blanche*'s first literary critic and editorial secretary. His position as literary critic was later occupied by Léon Blum and André Gide.

Natanson, Alexandre (1866), Alfred (1873), and Thadée (1868). Graduates of the Lycée Condorcet, the Natanson brothers were the directors of the avant-garde journal *La Revue blanche*, which became an important *centre dreyfusard* during the Affair. With Alfred as drama critic and Thadée as art critic, *La Revue blanche* also devoted special attention to poetry and theater. The Natanson family also owned *Le Cri de Paris.*

Péguy, Charles (1873). Essayist and poet, he engaged in the Dreyfus Affair as an anticlerical socialist. An ardent Dreyfusard, he wrote numerous articles in *La Revue blanche*. Breaking with the socialist movement, he founded *Les Cahiers de la quinzaine* in 1900. Increasingly concerned over the perceived menace of an aggressive Germany, he became a staunch patriot and a fervent, almost mystical (but not practicing) Catholic. In *Notre jeunesse* (1910), he lamented that the "mystique" of the Affair had soon degenerated into "politique."

Péladan, Joséphin (1859). Novelist and playwright, he was involved in a revival of Rosicrucianism and founded Le Théâtre de la Rose-Croix, in opposition to the Naturalism of Le Théâtre Libre.

Proust, Marcel (1871). Novelist known for his multivolumed work *A la recherche du temps perdu* (1913–1927), he was educated at the Lycée Condorcet and co-founded *Le Banquet*. He also contributed to such avant-garde reviews as *La Revue blanche* and mainstream newspapers. An ardent Dreyfusard, he, along with former *Le Banquet* colleagues, collected signatures for the revision of the Dreyfus case.

Pujo, Maurice (1872). Director of *L'Art et la vie*, he was later an anti-Dreyfusard and also a founding member of the Action française.

Quillard, Pierre (1864). Graduate of the Lycée Condorcet, this Symbolist writer contributed to *La Pléiade*, the precursor of *Le Mercure de France*, as well as to Vielé-Griffin's *Les Entretiens politiques et littéraires* and Zo d'Axa's *L'Endehors*. A Dreyfusard, he compiled *Le Monument Henry* (1899), a series of subscription lists for Henry's widow, accompanied by anti-Semitic rhetoric, orginally published in *La Libre Parole*.

Rachilde (born Marguerite Eymery, 1860). Novelist and wife of *Le Mercure de France*'s director, Alfred Vallette, she served as the review's literary critic for novels from 1892 to 1926. Her own, seemingly daring novels, which depicted a reversal of male/female relationships, appealed to rather than criticized male fantasies.

Raynaud, Ernest (1864). Poet, he began his career as a Symbolist, serving as one of the co-founders of *Le Mercure de France*. He also was associated with the Ecole romane group.

Rebell, Hugues (born Georges Grassal, 1867). Born of a pious Catholic family, he execrated Christianity while praising Catholicism and the Catholic Church. A self-styled paganist and admirer of Nietzsche, this writer of poetry and novels was a member of the Ecole romane, later joining the Action française. Author of *Union des trois aristocraties* (1894), he was also closely involved with avant-garde journals, in particular, *L'Ermitage*, but also *La Plume*, *La Revue blanche*, and *Le Mercure de France*.

Régnier, Henri de (1864). Symbolist poet, he contributed to *La Pléiade*, the precursor of *Le Mercure de France*, and also frequently collaborated on *Les Entretiens politiques et littéraires*. He was elected to the Académie française in 1911.

Renard, Jules (1864). Writer, he collaborated to establish *Le Mercure de France* and also contributed to *La Revue blanche*. Usually associated with Symbolism, his writing incorporated characteristics of Naturalism and other movements.

Retté, Adolphe (1863). Beginning his career as a Symbolist poet (*Le Thulé des brumes*, 1891), he served as an editor at *L'Ermitage*. He then turned to anarchism and rejected the Symbolist esthetic to espouse Naturist ideals. During this period, he published anticlerical works, only to convert to Catholicism in 1906.

Rolland, Romain (1866). Writer, historian, and critic of fine arts, he graduated from the Lycée Louis-le-Grand in Paris and the Ecole Normale Supérieure, where he later taught history and music history. A friend of Charles Péguy, he collaborated for a period on *Les Cahiers de la quinzaine*. In 1916, he received the Nobel Prize for Literature.

Saint-Georges de Bouhélier (1876). Poet and leader of the Naturist movement.

Séverine (born Caroline Rémy, 1855). Journalist, she was one of the most widely known woman writers of the period. She directed *Le Cri du peuple*, after the death of Jules Vallès. A controversial socialist and feminist, she was one of the first intellectuals to engage as a Dreyfusard in the Affair, writing for the feminist newspaper *La Fronde*.

Simiand, François (1873). Sociologist and economist, he graduated from the Ecole Normale Supérieure and belongs to the group influenced by the socialist ideas of Lucien Herr. A disciple of Durkheim, he is noted for his work in economic and social theory.

Tailhade, Laurent (1854). Writer, he published several collections of poems inspired by the Parnassian movement; his later works were influenced by anarchist ideas. He also contributed to a variety of avant-garde journals, including *La Pléiade*, the precursor of *Le Mercure de France*. A Dreyfusard, he wrote a number of works questioning the honor and manhood of his anti-Dreyfusard opponents.

Valéry, Paul (1871). Poet and essayist, he was initially influenced by Symbolism and Mallarmé, occasionally publishing in such small reviews as *La Conque*. During the Dreyfus Affair, he contributed to *Le Monument Henry*. Abandoning his public service career, he devoted himself to his writing. He was elected to the Académie française in 1925 and later taught at the Collège de France.

Vallette, Alfred (1858). Printer by profession, he collaborated to establish *Le Mercure de France* and subsequently served as its director.

Veber, Pierre (1869). A playwright, he served as drama critic at *La Revue blanche*.

Vielé-Griffin, Francis (1864). A Symbolist poet, he became editor of *Les Entretiens politiques et littéraires*, a polemical literary and political review that featured the work of both literary anarchists and anarchist theoreticians.

Zo d'Axa (born Gallaud, 1864). This journalist directed the anarchist publication *L'Endehors*.

Artists

Blanche, Jacques-Emile (1861). Painter, writer, and art critic, he was influenced by the Impressionists and became known as a portraitist. Apart from writing novels, he also contributed articles to *La Revue blanche*.

Bonnard, Pierre (1867). Painter, he is known for the numerous posters that he created for *La Revue blanche* and for the sets he constructed for Lugné-Poë's Théâtre de l'Oeuvre.

Caran d'Ache (born Emmanuel Poiré in 1859). A major contributor, along with Forain, to the illustrated anti-Dreyfusard journal *Psst!*

Denis, Maurice (1870). Painter, decorator, and writer, he contributed artwork to *La Revue blanche* and set decorations to the Théâtre de l'Oeuvre.

Forain, Jean-Louis (1852). Painter and engraver, this artist frequented the social circles of such writers as Verlaine and Rimbaud and associated with the Impressionists. He became known as a caricaturist and founded the anti-Dreyfusard illustrated journal *Psst!* with Caran d'Ache (1898).

Ibels, Henri-Gabriel (1867). Featured in a special issue of *La Plume* on the history of the French illustrated poster, this artist went on to contribute numerous drawings to the Dreyfusard cause, in particular, *Le Sifflet*, the Dreyfusard response to *Psst!*

Ranson, Paul (1864). Painter, engraver, and writer, he created color lithographs for *La Revue blanche*.

Roussel, Ker-Xavier (1867). Painter, he graduated from the Lycée Condorcet with Vuillard. Along with Vuillard and friends from the Académie Julian: Bonnard, Denis, and Ranson, he contributed to *La Revue blanche*.

Signac, Paul (1863). Painter and watercolorist, he rejected the salon world to participate in the 1884 Exposition des artistes indépendants, thereafter developing the style of Neo-Impressionism. He also contributed art criticism to *La Revue blanche*.

Toulouse-Lautrec, Henri-Marie de (1864). Painter and lithographer, he graduated from the Lycée Condorcet and developed his craft in Paris, influenced by Impressionists. He is known for his depictions of Parisian life and his popular posters. A regular contributor to *La Revue blanche* and to Lugné-Poë's Théâtre de l'Oeuvre, he was featured in a special issue of *La Plume* on the history of the French illustrated poster.

Vallotton, Félix (1865). Painter, engraver, and writer, he was a student at the Académie Julian and regularly contributed his work to *La Revue blanche*. His illustration "L'Age du papier," published in *Le Cri de Paris*, vividly depicts the explosion of the press during the Dreyfus Affair.

Vuillard, Edouard Jean (1868). Painter, decorator, and engraver, he met Roussel, who later became his brother-in-law, at the Lycée Condorcet. Vuillard, who subsequently attended the Académie Julian, created sets for Lugné-Poë's Théâtre de l'Oeuvre and contributed illustrations to *La Revue blanche*.

Willette, Adolphe (1857). One of the best-known illustrators of the Belle Epoque, he depicted scenes of Bohemian life in Montmartre, contributing to a variety of illustrated journals, including *Le Chat noir* and *Le Courrier français*. An ardent anti-Semite, he ran as an anti-Semitic candidate in the 1889 legislative elections.

Notes

Introduction

1. The term "lieu de mémoire" refers to people, places, and events that have been incorporated into collective memory. For example, De Gaulle, the Eiffel Tower, and Vichy are all *lieux de mémoire*. Pierre Nora, ed. *Les Lieux de mémoire*, 7 vols. (Paris: Gallimard, 1984–92). The term has even entered *Le Grand Robert de la langue française*.

2. A few years ago, a journal devoted solely to the study of the literary review was founded in Paris: *La Revue des revues*.

3. See Jacques Juilliard's introduction to a special issue of *Les Cahiers Georges Sorel* on "Le Monde des revues au début du siècle" 5 (1987):3–9. Christophe Prochasson's recent *Les Intellectuels, le socialisme et la guerre, 1900–1938* (Paris: Seuil, 1993), 43, examines the link between the cultural avant-garde and the political avant-garde immediately after the Affair until 1938. Prochasson, rightly so, cites the importance of the avant-garde literary journal in French cultural history. As he notes: "Among the various forms of communication, intellectuals have always privileged journals, an incontestable site of their legitimate expression."

4. See Prochasson, *Les Intellectuels, le socialisme et la guerre*, 17–19 and "Histoire intellectuelle/histoire des intellectuels: le socialisme français au début du XXè siècle," *Revue d'histoire moderne et contemporaine* 39, no. 3 (July–September 1992):423–448.

5. Jacques Julliard, "Le Fascisme en France," *Annales, économies, sociétés, civilisations* 39, no. 4 (July–August 1984):855.

6. Victor Brombert, *The Intellectual Hero: Studies in the French Novel: 1880–1955* (Philadelphia: J. B. Lippincott, 1961), 32.

7. Louis Bodin and Jean Touchard's "Les Intellectuels dans la société française contemporaine: définitions, statistiques et problèmes," *Revue française de science politique* 9 (December 1959): 835–859; and Louis Bodin's *Les Intellectuels* (Paris: Presses Universitaires de France), published in 1964, are among the first scholarly works on intellectuals published in France. Victor Brombert's *The Intellectual Hero* is another pioneering work in the field.

8. See Max Gallo's editorial "Les Intellectuels, la politique et la modernité," in *Le Monde*, 26 July 1983, in which he asked where all the intellectuals had gone.

9. I hasten to add that this in no way denies the quality of their work.

10. Among the numerous publications of these authors, see especially Michel Winock, "Les Intellectuels dans le siècle," *Vingtième Siècle*, no. 2 (April–June 1984):3–14; Pascal Ory and Jean-François Sirinelli, *Les Intellectuels en France, de l'Affaire Dreyfus à nos jours* (Paris: Armand Colin, 1986); Jean-François Sirinelli, *Intellectuels et passions françaises: manifestes et pétitions au XXème siècle* (Paris: Fayard, 1990); Pascal Ory, ed. *Dernières Questions aux intellectuels* (Paris: Olivier Orban, 1990); Jean-Pierre Rioux and Jean-François Sirinelli, eds. *La Guerre d'Algérie et les intellecuels français* (Paris: Editions Complexe, 1991); Christophe Prochasson, *Les Intellectuels, le socialisme et la guerre, 1900–1938*; Christophe Charle, *Naissance des "intellectuels": 1880–1910* (Paris: Editions de Minuit, 1990).

11. Robert Wohl, *The Generation of 1914* (Cambridge, Mass.: Harvard University Press, 1979), and Alan Spitzer, *The French Generation of 1820*, (Princeton, NJ: Princeton University Press, 1987) both examine the intellectual via the trope of "intellectual generation." Tony Judt, *Past Imperfect: French Intellectuals, 1944–1956* (Berkeley, Calif.: University of California Press, 1992). I would also like to mention Martha Hanna's *The Mobilization of Intellect: Scholars, Writers, and the French War Effort, 1914–1918* (Cambridge, Mass.: Harvard University Press, 1996) and a work in progress by Paul Mazgaj on intellectuals of the 1930s.

12. Charle's writings provide a notable exception as do the works of American scholars Jerrold Seigel, *Bohemian Paris: Culture, Politics, and the Boundaries of Bourgeois Life, 1830–1930* (New York: Viking, 1986; Penguin, 1987), and Richard D. Sonn, *Anarchism and Cultural Politics in Fin-de-siècle France*, (Lincoln, Neb.: University of Nebraska Press, 1989).

13. I am thinking in particular of Régis Debray's *Le Pouvoir intellectuel en France*, translated by Francis Mulhern into English as *Teachers, Writers, Celebrities* (London, Eng.: New Left Books, 1981). Debray elaborates three overlapping stages of intellectual power since the Dreyfus Affair. The first period is the "University cycle," from 1880–1920, then the "editorial cycle," from 1920 to 1960, and finally, the "media cycle," from 1968 to the

present. As Pascal Ory and Jean-François Sirinelli have noted, such a schematic analysis ignores the importance of both the newspapers and avant-garde "little magazines" in the emergence of the intellectual: *Les Intellectuels en France, de l'Affaire Dreyfus à nos jours*, 30.

14. George L. Mosse, *Nationalism and Sexuality: Middle-Class Morality and Sexual Norms in Modern Europe* (Madison, Wis.: University of Wisconsin Press), 1985, and Robert Nye, *Masculinity and Male Codes of Honor in Modern France* (New York: Oxford University Press, 1993). See also Karen Offen, "Depopulation, Nationalism, and Feminism in Fin-de-Siècle France," *American Historical Review* 89, no. 3 (June 1984):648–676; Edward Berenson, *The Trial of Madame Caillaux* (Berkeley, Calif.: University of California Press, 1992); Michelle Perrot, "The New Eve and the Old Adam: Changes in French Women's Condition at the Turn of the Century," in Margaret Higonnet, ed. *Behind the Lines: Gender and the Two World Wars,* (New Haven, Conn.: Yale University Press, 1987), 51–60, and Annelise Maugue, *L'Identité masculine en crise au tournant du siècle, 1871–1914* (Paris: Editions Rivages, 1987).

15. The concepts of "habitus" and "field" are essential components of Pierre Bourdieu's writings. The former refers to the structures and ways of thinking that condition the way an individual sees the world through his or her entire life, even outside the *habitus* itself. For example, someone of a working-class *habitus* would view the world differently than another person of an upper-middle-class *habitus*. As for the field, this refers to the space in which agents operate, in an economic field, for instance, or in a literary field. In the literary field, competition often concerns authority inherent in recognition or consecration. This is symbolic capital; cultural capital refers to forms of cultural knowledge, which can often be more important in the literary field than economic capital. See Randal Johnson, "Pierre Bourdieu on Art, Literature and Culture," Introduction to Pierre Bourdieu, *The Field of Cultural Production: Essays on Art and Literature*, ed. Randal Johnson (New York: Columbia University Press, 1993), 6–7.

16. First in Christophe Charle, "Les Ecrivains et l'Affaire Dreyfus," *Annales, économies, sociétés, civilisations* 32, no. 2 (March–April 1977):240–264 and most recently in *Naissance des "intellectuels."*

17. Debray, *Teachers, Writers, Celebrities*, 50–51.

18. A fact noted by Eric Cahm in his review of Charle's book: "Intellectuals, the Elite and the Dreyfus Affair: Further Work from Christophe Charle," *Modern and Contemporary France* 42 (1990):68–170.

19. Bourdieu, *The Field of Cultural Production*. For an interesting discussion of Bourdieu's desire to steer a middle ground between objectivist and subjectivist analysis, see the editor's introduction, pgs. 3–4.

20. As Priscilla Clark puts it: "Every country, every literature has politically committed writers, but only France has a tradition of writers

who transmute those commitments into an encompassing identification with country. Only France has a literary culture that elects the writer as spokesman and invests literature with such powers. Priscilla Parkhurst Clark, *Literary France: The Making of a Culture* (Berkeley, Calif.: University of California Press, 1987), 4. See also Daniel Lindenberg, "L'intellectuel est-il une spécialité française?" in *Dernières Questions aux intellectuels*, Pascal Ory, ed. 155–205.

21. Michel Winock, "Les Intellectuels dans le siècle," *Vingtième Siècle*, 3–5.

22. For the genealogy of the term, see G. Idt, " 'L'Intellectuel' avant l'Affaire Dreyfus," *Cahiers de lexicologie* 15, no. 2 (1969):35–46. As she notes, whether positive or negative, the word intellectual was used whenever individuals of different professions felt they shared a common mission and an *esprit de corps*, if not a class consciousness, 40. See also William Johnston, who reminds us about the role of the now forgotten writer Henry Bérenger in helping to popularize the term during the 1890s: "The Origin of the Term 'Intellectuals' in French Novels and Essays of the 1890s," *Journal of European Studies* 4 (1974):43–56, and Trevor Field, "Vers une nouvelle datation du substantif 'intellectuel,'" *Travaux de linguistique et de littérature* 14, no. 2 (1976):159–167. For the ways in which the image of the intellectual has been contested, see Shlomo Sand, "Mirror, Mirror on the Wall, Who Is the True Intellectual of Them All? Self-Images of the Intellectual in France," in *Intellectuals in Twentieth-Century France: Mandarins and Samurais*, Jeremy Jennings, ed. (New York: St. Martin's Press, 1993), 33–58.

23. See Barrès's article in *Le Journal*: "La Protestation des intellectuels!" published on 1 February 1898.

24. "A. M. Maurice Barrès," *La Revue blanche* 15 (15 February 1898):241.

25. See Pascal Ory, "Qu'est-ce qu'un intellectuel?" in *Dernières Questions aux intellectuels*, 9–50. Jeremy Jennings also summarizes this discussion in his "Introduction: Mandarins and Samurais: The Intellectual in Modern France," to *Intellectuals in Twentieth-Century France: Mandarins and Samurais*, 1–32.

26. Winock, "Les Intellectuels dans le siècle," 5.

27. Ory, "Qu'est-ce qu'un intellectuel?" 27–29; Jacques Julliard and Michel Winock, eds. *Dictionnaire des intellectuels français* (Paris: Seuil, 1996), 11–12.

28. Cited by John Lough, *Writer and Public in France: From the Middle Ages to the Present* (Oxford, Eng.: Clarendon Press, 1978), 245.

29. Ibid., 240–245.

30. On this period, see Alain Viala, *Naissance de l'écrivain: sociologie de la littérature à l'âge classique* (Paris: Editions de Minuit, 1985). I would like to thank Stephen C. Bold for sharing his observations on seventeenth-century cultural life with me.

31. Among the many works on the Enlightenment and Revolutionary period, I list here Robert Darnton, *The Literary Underground of the Old Regime* (Cambridge, Mass.: Harvard University Press, 1982); Paul Bénichou *Le Sacre de l'écrivain, 1750–1830* (Paris: José Corti, 1985); and Roger Chartier, *The Cultural Origins of the French Revolution*, trans. Lydia G. Cochrane (Durham, North Carolina: Duke University Press, 1991).

32. Some of the *philosophes*, including Voltaire, also made a great amount of money in England.

33. Both men had earlier traded insults at the Comédie Française in order to impress the current and past mistress of Voltaire and his noble rival, respectively.

34. See Richard Holmes' article, "Voltaire's Grin" in the 30 November 1995 issue of the *New York Review of Books*, 49–50. John Lough also describes this incident (238–239) and cites a work published in Paris in 1858 by V. Fournel, entitled *Du Rôle des coups de bâton dans les relations sociales dans l'histoire littéraire*.

35. Lough, 241–242.

36. Arthur Young, *Travels in France,* Cited by Lough, 243.

37. This was in keeping with a counterrevolutionary tradition inaugurated by Joseph de Maistre and others.

38. Lough, 245.

39. Christophe Charle, "Le Champ de la production littéraire," in *Histoire de l'édition française,* edited by Roger Chartier and Henri-Jean Martin, *vol. 3, Le temps des éditeurs: du romantisme à la Belle Epoque* (Paris: Promodis, 1985; Fayard/Promodis, 1990), 140.

40. See Christophe Charle, *Naissance des "intellectuels,"* for a presentation of the ancestors of the modern-day intellectual, 20–38.

41. Lough, 238.

42. Ibid., 197–8.

43. Ibid., 314–317.

44. Charle, "Le Champ de la production littéraire," 137–175.

45. Lough, 286.

Chapter 1

1. 'Following the examples of Alan Spitzer and Robert Wohl, first references to individuals, especially those of the generation of 1890, will be followed by a birthdate.

In his introduction to a special issue of *Les Cahiers Georges Sorel* on "Le Monde des revues au début du siècle," 5 (1987):3–9, Jacques Julliard states: "A real review is a family . . . In the literal and figurative sense, the family review is a meeting place. . . ." pg. 6. Similarly, Jean-François Sirinelli notes that the review represents "a first-rate observatory for the study not only of the movement of ideas, but also for the sociability of the intellectual milieu," "Le Hasard ou la nécessité? une histoire en chantier: l'histoire des intellectuels," *Vingtième Siècle*, no. 9 (Jan–March 1986):104. Madeleine Rebérioux, "Avant-garde esthétique et avant-garde politique: le socialisme français entre 1890 et 1914," in *Esthétique et Marxisme* (Paris: Editions 10/18, 1974), 33, refers to the "crossroads review" (revue carrefour).

2. Within the "generation enclosed by the revolutions of 1830 and 1848," writes Renato Poggioli, *The Theory of the Avant-Garde*, trans. Gerald Fitzgerald (Cambridge, Mass.: Belknap Press of Harvard University Press, 1968), 10.

3. Ibid., 35.

4. Léon Blum, "Chronique des revues," *La Revue blanche* 6 (January 1894), reprinted in *L'Oeuvre de Léon Blum*, vol. 1 (Paris: Albin Michel, 1954), 2.

5. Elisabeth Parinet, "L'Edition littéraire, 1890–1914," in *Histoire de l'edition française*, edited by Roger Chartier and Henri-Jean Martin, *vol. 4, Le Livre concurrencé, 1900–1950* (Paris: Promodis, 1986; Fayard/Promodis, 1991), 165; Christophe Charle, *La Crise littéraire à l'époque du naturalisme: roman, théâtre, politique* (Paris: Presses de l'Ecole Normale Supérieure, 1979), 41–54. Unlike Zola, Georges Ohnet (1848–1918) wrote snobbish, sentimental novels popular with society ladies.

6. Parinet, "L'Edition littéraire," 171–173.

7. Ibid., 174–175.

8. The most successful being *Le Mercure de France* and to a lesser extent, *La Revue blanche*. In addition, of the most important avant-garde journals, *La Plume* and *L'Ermitage* also published books: Claire Lesage, "Des avant-gardes en travail, "*Revue des sciences humaines* 95, no. 219 (July–September 1990):85–105. The avant-garde of the fin de siècle made a unique contribution to the history of the avant-garde in that it carried one of the external signs most characteristically avant-garde to the highest development: the founding of periodicals: Poggioli, *Theory of the Avant-Garde*, 21.

9. Francis Vielé-Griffin, "Le plus grand poète," *Les Entretiens politiques et littéraires*, no. 8 (1 November 1890):277; Henri Mazel, *Aux beaux temps du symbolisme, 1890–1895* (Paris: Mercure de France, 1943), 9. Barrès, writing in 1888 in *La Revue indépendante*, spoke of the independence of the collaborators of this journal and of a "limited public," "M. le Général Boulanger et la nouvelle génération" 8 (April 1888):55.

10. Lesage, "Des avant-gardes en travail," 87, and Anna Boschetti, "Légitimité littéraire et stratégies éditoriales," *Histoire de l'édition française* 4:514–515.

11. See Barrès's response to Jules Huret's inquiry *L'Enquête sur l'évolution littéraire*, 47. This *enquête* was subsequently published in book form, most recently in 1982 by Les Editions Thot in Vanves, France. Barrès indicated that sober publications like *Le Temps* and *Les Débats* would refuse publication. The Symbolist manifesto was published in *Le Figaro*, as were the manifestoes for the Ecole romane and the Naturistes. See Bonner Mitchell: *Les Manifestes littéraires de la Belle Epoque, 1886–1914* (Paris: Seghers, 1966).

12. Thomas Ferenczi, *L'Invention du journalisme en France: naissance de la presse moderne à la fin du XIXème siècle* (Paris: Plon, 1993), 237.

13. Similarly, banquets that honored their own—Barrès referred to the Banquet Moréas—were a means by which to create publicity for themselves: Huret, *L'Enquête sur l'évolution*, 48.

14. The *Revue blanche Enquête* on Scandinavian letters was published on 15 February 1897, the inquiry on the Commune on 15 March 1897, the *Enquête* on education on 1 June 1902. The *Mercure de France Enquêtes* on Germany were published in April 1895 and in November–December 1902. Even the venerable *Revue bleue* devoted a series of *enquêtes* in the 1890s to the role of the university, the role of the press, and finally the role of elites in a democracy. The famous *Enquêtes* on the generation of 1914, of which the Agathon inquiry is the best known, marked the apogee of the genre. Precursors of modern opinion polls, *enquêtes*, which target an elite group of intellectuals and politicians, continue to flourish in France today, even in an age of mass media.

15. The work was reedited in 1900 by the *Mercure de France* press. For Remy de Gourmont, the most successful, those that served as models for all the rest, were *Le Mercure de France, La Revue blanche, L'Ermitage*, and *La Plume* (Preface).

16. Benoît Lecoq, "Les revues," *Histoire de l'édition française* 4:355.

17. Ibid., 352–354.

18. Boschetti, "Légitimité littéraire," 516.

19. On Mazel, see Victor Nguyen, "Elites, pouvoir et culture sur une correspondance entre Charles Maurras et Henri Mazel à la veille de la crise dreyfusienne," *Etudes maurrassiennes*, no. 4 (1980):144–145.

20. Maurras's article was published on 13 January 1894, pg. 54, and Mazel's reply, entitled "Chroniques pro domo," in *L'Ermitage* 8 (January 1894):40–42.

21. *L'Ermitage 11* (December 1895):311.

22. Adolphe Retté, *Le Symbolisme: anecdotes et souvenirs* (Paris: Léon Vanier, 1903), 113.

23. *L'Ermitage* (December 1895):311–314.

24. Richard D. Sonn, *Anarchism and Cultural Politics in Fin-de-siècle France* (Lincoln, Neb.: University of Nebraska Press, 1989), 202–209; Retté speaks of his emergence as a Naturist and his political development in his memoirs: *Le Symbolisme: anecdotes et souvenirs*, 1–13.

25. A number of writers, in particular, Retté, Maurice Barrès, and Paul Adam, moved from Boulangism to anarchism after the fall of Boulanger.

26. The destructive impulse associated with the avant-garde can be associated with the Left or Right: Poggioli, *Theory of the Avant-Garde,* 96; 99. Furthermore, during the 1890s, Left and Right were confused. On Rebell, see Auriant, *Hugues Rebell à "L'Ermitage" (1892–1900): avec dix lettres à Henri Mazel,* (Reims: Editions "A l'Ecart," 1988), and Mazel's *Aux beaux temps du symbolisme,* 115–127.

27. *L'Ermitage* (December 1895):313.

28. For information on the beginnings of *Le Mercure de France,* see two articles by Edith Silve published in *La Revue des revues,* entitled "Rachilde et Alfred Vallette et la fondation du *Mercure de France,*" and "Les premières heures du *Mercure de France,*" published in Nos. 2, and 3, November 1986 and spring 1987: 13–16, and 12–17, respectively. See also a special issue of *Revue d'histoire littéraire de la France,* no. 1 (January–February 1992):3–72, in particular, an article by Michel Décaudin, "*Le Mercure de France*: filiations et orientations," 7–15, as well as the memoirs of Ernest Raynaud: *La Mêlée symboliste: portraits et souvenirs (1870–1910)*(Paris: 1900; reprint: Nizet, 1983), 467–482. Although Raynaud was a police commissioner, his profession does not seem to have interfered with his participation in avant-garde enterprises. Another valuable source for information on all the avant-garde journals of the period is an inquiry published by the review *Belles-Lettres* in 1924 on "Les Revues d'avant-garde (1870–1914)." Members of the various avant-garde journals were asked to talk about their experiences in founding the journals in question. This inquiry was republished recently by Olivier Corpet and Patrick Fréchet (Paris: Ent'revues, Editions Jean-Michel Place, 1990).

29. *Le Mercure de France* 1 (January 1890):4

30. Décaudin, *"Le Mercure de France,"* 13.

31. Silve, "Rachilde et Alfred Vallette et la fondation du *Mercure de France*," 14–15.

32. See an article by Claude Dauphiné in the special issue of *Revue d'histoire littéraire de la France*: "Rachilde et *Le Mercure*," 17–28.

33. Grudging being the operative word in Remy de Gourmont's article on Rachilde in *Le Livre des masques*, première série, 109–111. Originally published in 1896 by the press of *Le Mercure de France*, this volume, along with the second book of the series, was republished in 1963.

34. As Poggioli notes, an aristocratic stance is perfectly in keeping with an avant-garde position, *Theory of the Avant-Garde*, 99.

35. On *La Plume*, see Guy de Grosbois, "Il y a 100 ans, les agapes de *La Plume*," *La Revue des revues*, no. 8 (Winter, 1989–1990):21–24; a special issue of the review *A Rebours* devoted to *La Plume*, no. 47 (1989), and Ernest Raynaud, *La Mêlée symboliste*, 129–149.

36. Raynaud, *La Mêlée*, 137.

37. Phillip Dennis Cate, " 'La Plume' and its 'Salon des cent': Promoters of posters and prints in the 1890s," *Print Review* 8 (1978):61–68.

38. On the founding of *Les Entretiens*, see Henri de Paysac, *Francis Vielé-Griffin, poète symboliste et citoyen américain* (Paris: Nizet, 1976), 121–135.

39. On Lazare, see Jean-Denis Bredin's recent biography: *Bernard Lazare: de l'anarchiste au prophète* (Paris: Editions de Fallois, 1992), and Nelly Wilson, *Bernard Lazare: Anti-Semitism and the Problem of Jewish Identity in Late-Nineteenth-Century France* (New York: Cambridge University Press, 1978).

40. See J. Ann Duncan, *Les Romans de Paul Adam: du symbolisme littéraire au symbolisme cabalistique* (Berne: Peter Lang, 1977).

41. See my *"La Revue blanche (1889–1903): Intellectuals and Politics in Fin-de-Siècle France"* (Ph.D diss. New York University, 1989).

42. The earlier manifesto was published in *La Revue blanche*'s Belgian series, vol. 1 (1 December 1889):1. The second declaration of principles appeared in the first Parisian issue (15 October 1891), vol. 1:1. *La Revue blanche*'s first editorial secretary Lucien Muhlfeld was an ardent admirer of Barrès as his correspondence with the older writer, located in the Fonds Barrès at the Bibliothèque Nationale (Salle des Manuscrits), illustrates.

43. André Dinar, *La Croisade symboliste* (Paris: Mercure de France, 1943), 165.

44. See Joan Halperin's *Félix Fénéon: Aesthete and Anarchist in Fin-de-Siècle Paris* (New Haven, Conn.: Yale University Press, 1988).

45. The question of circulation for nearly all the avant-garde magazines is difficult, given the absence of review archives. Based on an entry from Gide's journal, A. B. Jackson, the author of *La Revue blanche (1889–1903): origine, influence, bibliographie* (Paris: Minard, 1960), estimates a figure as high as fifteen thousand copies for *La Revue blanche* (page 138), while art historian Fritz Hermann, the author of a thesis entitled *Die Revue blanche und die Nabis* (Munich, 1959), places the figure at seven to eight thousand copies (Letter to the author, September 1986).

46. Urbain Gohier, *L'Armée contre la nation, édition augmentée des notes du "Procès L'Armée contre la nation"* (Paris: Editions de la Revue blanche, 1899).

47. There were around six thousand to seven thousand holders of the baccalaureate degree per year from 1873 to 1891, estimates Jean-Marie Mayeur: *Les Débuts de la IIIème République, 1871–1898* (Paris: Seuil, 1973), 145–146.

48. Sonn, *Anarchism and Cultural Politics,* 194.

49. The memoirs of Annette Vaillant, the daughter of Alfred Natanson, are a precious source of information on the private lives of the Natanson brothers: *Le Pain polka* (Paris: Mercure de France, 1974).

50. On the social geography of Montmartre, see Sonn, *Anarchism and Cultural Politics,* chapter 3, "The Social and Symbolic Space of Parisian Anarchism," 49–94 as well as a more general essay on the social geography of the literary milieu of the fin de siècle: Christophe Charle, "Situation spatiale et position sociale: essai de géographie sociale du champ littéraire à la fin du 19e siècle," *Actes de la recherche en sciences sociales,* no. 181 (13 February 1977):45–58.

Chapter 2

1. Maurice Barrès, *Un Homme libre: Le Culte du moi* (Paris: Union Générale d'Editions, 10/18, 1986), 127.

2. Léon Blum, "Les Nouvelles Conversations de Goethe avec Eckermann," *L'Oeuvre de Léon Blum,* vol. 1 (Paris: Albin Michel, 1954), 198.

3. Léon Blum, "Chronique des revues," *La Revue blanche* 6 (January 1894), reprinted in *L'Oeuvre de Léon Blum,* 1:2.

4. Henri Mazel, "Au lecteur," *L'Ermitage* 11 (December 1895):311.

5. Adolphe Retté, "Une Année de combat," *La Plume* 4, no. 112 (15 December 1893):527–528.

6. As did Francis Vielé-Griffin in "Le plus grand poète," *Les Entretiens politiques et littéraires* 1, no. 8 (1 November 1890):277–278.

7. "Pour clore une polémique," *Les Entretiens politiques et littéraires* 1, no. 7 (1 October 1890):201–209; Bernard Lazare, "Une Lettre," *Les Entretiens politiques et littéraires* 3, no. 19 (October 1891):142–145. See also Paul Adam's diatribe against the older generation: "Au vieillard," *Les Entretiens politiques et littéraires* 2, no. 11 (1 February 1891):45–48, and Henri Mazel's "Le Règne des vieux," *Les Entretiens politiques et littéraires* 2, no. 10 (1 January 1891):20–25. Léon Blum, however, seemed to find it natural that one should be ignored by one's elders: "Chronique des revues," *La Revue blanche* 6 (January 1894) in *Oeuvre*, 1:2.

8. Vielé-Griffin, "Le plus grand poète," 278. Bernard Lazare even encouraged young artists to be intolerant: "De la nécéssité de l'intolérance," *Les Entretiens politiques et littéraires* 3, no. 21 (December 1891):208–211.

9. "The only intellectuals of our murky times," Retté, "Une Année de combat," *La Plume*: 527.

10. See Alan Spitzer, "The Historical Problem of Generations," *American Historical Review* 78, no. 5 (December 1978):1353–1385; Jean-François Sirinelli, "Le Hasard ou la nécessité? une histoire en chantier: l'histoire des intellectuels," *Vingtième Siècle*, no. 9 (January–March 1986):97–108, both of whom are favorable to the use of generation in historical study. Raoul Girardet, "Du concept de génération à la notion de contemporanéité," *Revue d'histoire moderne et contemporaine* 30 (April–June 1983):257–270, and Annie Kriegel, "Le Concept politique de génération: apogée et déclin," *Commentaire*, no. 7 (Autumn 1979):390–399 have serious reservations about the usefulness of the generational concept.

11. See the special issue of *Vingtième Siècle* on intellectual generations: no. 22 (April–June 1989), especially Michel Winock, "Les Générations intellectuelles," 17–38. See also in the same issue: Jean-Pierre Azéma, "La Clef générationnelle," 3–10, and Marc Devriese, "Approche sociologique de la génération," 11–16. In "Le Hasard ou la nécessité?" Jean-François Sirinelli proposes three "tools" for the study of intellectuals: the charting of itineraries, the observation of structures of sociability, and the generational concept. "Le Hasard," 98. See also his *Intellectuels et passions françaises, manifestes et pétitions au XXe siècle*, (Paris: Fayard, 1990), 14.

12. Robert Wohl, *The Generation of 1914* (Cambridge, Mass.: Harvard University Press, 1979), 5.

13. Pierre Nora, "La Génération," *Les Lieux de mémoire*, ed. Pierre Nora, vol. 3, part 1 (Paris: Gallimard, 1992), 940.

14. Ibid., 952–954.

15. As Nora observes: "There is no generation without conflict, nor without a declaration of its self-consciousness, thus making politics and literature the preferred fields for the manifestation of the generational phenomenon," Ibid., 947.

16. Ibid., 954. See also Renato Poggioli, who notes that the avant-garde is the product of modern liberal democracy: *The Theory of the Avant-Garde*, trans. Gerald Fitzgerald (Cambridge, Mass.: Belknap Press of Harvard University Press, 1968), 106.

17. Karl Mannheim, "The Problem of Generations," *Essays on the Sociology of Knowledge* (London: Routledge and Kegan Paul, 1959), 276–322.

18. Henri Peyre speaks of a double generation grouped around two different dates but emphasizes their continuity. According to Peyre, the first wave was born between 1860 to 1862 and the second, between 1867 and 1870. Henri Peyre, *Les Générations littéraires* (Paris: Boivin, 1948), 149. Like Albert Thibaudet, he states that these men came of age from roughly 1885 to 1895. Albert Thibaudet, *Histoire de la littérature française de Chateaubriand à Valéry* (Paris: Stock, 1936; reedition, Marabout, 1983), 411–425.

19. Winock, "Les Générations intellectuelles," 18, and Azéma, "La Clef générationnelle," 6.

20. Winock, "Les Générations intellectuelles," 19.

21. Devriese, "Approche sociologique de la génération," 13. Alan Spitzer has admirably illustrated this principle in his work *The French Generation of 1820* (Princeton, NJ: Princeton University Press, 1987). See especially "Introduction: The Generation as Social Network," 3–34.

22. The *Enquête* was first published in the daily *L'Opinion* in 1912 and subsequently published as *Les Jeunes gens d'aujourd'hui* (Paris: Plon, 1913). On the Agathon inquiry, see Wohl, *Generation of 1914*, 5–41 and Philippe Bénéton, "La Génération de 1912–1914: image, mythe et réalité?" *Revue française de science politique* 21, no. 5 (October 1971):981–1009. On Massis and his cultural generationalism, see Paul Mazgaj, "Defending the West: The Cultural and Generational Politics of Henri Massis," *Historical Reflections/Réflexions historiques* 17, no. 2 (1991):103–123.

23. Paul Lachance, "The Consciousness of the Generation of 1890 at Maturity: An Alternative Reading of the Image of French Youth in 1912–1914," *Journal of Interdisciplinary Studies* 2, no. 1 (Fall 1978):67–81, and "The Nature and Function of Generational Discourse in France on the Eve of World War I," in *Political Symbolism in Modern Europe: Essays in Honor of George L. Mosse*, eds. Seymour Drescher, et al. (New Brunswick, NJ: Transaction Books, 1982), 239–255.

24. Lachance, "The Generation of 1890 at Maturity," 77, and "The Nature and Function," 241.

25. Claude Digeon, *La Crise allemande de la pensée française, 1870–1914* (Paris: Presses Universitaires de France, 1959; reedition, 1992), 1–8. One could easily extend the time period through World War II.

26. The overwhelming question of the period was thus not only "Where are we going?" *(Où allons-nous?)*, the title of a *Figaro Enquête* published in September and October 1898, but also "What are we?"

27. Debora L. Silverman, *Art Nouveau in Fin-de-Siècle France: Politics, Psychology and Style* (Berkeley, Calif.: University of California Press, 1989), 66. As Silverman notes, the French birthrate declined at this time. From 1872 to 1911, the French population increased by 10 percent while the German population increased by 58 percent: Robert A. Nye, Crime, *Madness and Politics in Modern France: The Medical Concept of National Decline* (Princeton, NJ: Princeton University Press, 1984), 134.

28. Nye, *Crime, Madness and Politics*, 133.

29. Susanna Barrows comments that "it is no simple coincidence that the Golden Age of Science was viewed by intellectuals as the apogee of anxiety and anomie," *Distorting Mirrors: Visions of the Crowd in Late-Nineteenth-Century France* (New Haven, Conn.: Yale University Press, 1981), 2.

30. See Silverman, *Art Nouveau in Fin-de-Siècle France*, 79–83.

31. Nye, *Crime, Madness and Politics*, 132.

32. Léon Bélugou characterized Taine, along with Renan, as "the great flame that lights and dominates an entire century," "Chronique philosophique: une oeuvre posthume de H. Taine," *La Revue blanche* 10, no. 67 (March 1896):280.

33. Robert Nye observes that this represented a break from earlier positivists whose faith in science had accompanied an optimism about man's future: *The Origins of Crowd Psychology: Gustave Le Bon and the Crisis of Mass Democracy in the Third Republic* (Beverly Hills, Calif.: Sage Publications, 1975), 22.

34. In Maurras, *Bon et Mauvais Maîtres, Oeuvres capitales*, vol. 3 (Paris, Flammarion, 1954), 499–504. Although he disagreed with the idea of an excess of the classical spirit being responsible for the Revolution.

35. Blum, "Nouvelles conversations," *L'Oeuvre*, 1:212–213.

36. Although he rejected Renan's idea of the nation as an "esprit." See Zeev Sternhell, *Maurice Barrès et le nationalisme français* (Paris: Editions Complexe, 1985), 284–285. Barrès wrote a highly disrespectful *Huit jours chez M. Renan* (1888), which is reproduced in *L'Oeuvre de Maurice Barrès*, vol. 2 (Paris: Au Club de L'Honnête Homme, 1965), 309–340.

37. Barrows, *Distorting Mirrors*, 73–92. In her conclusion, Barrows notes that crowd psychology explained the failure of an intellectual aristocracy. Writers, and not only of the Right, could affirm their own superiority and explain their impotence in the areas of politics and public opinion, pg. 192. I shall explore this topic at length in the next chapter.

38. Maurras, *Bons et Mauvais Maîtres, Oeuvres capitales*, 3:505–517.

39. Barrès in *Enquête*: "Quelques opinions sur l'oeuvre de H. Taine," *La Revue blanche* 13, no. 101 (15 August 1897):263–295. Various individuals who were representative of their generation were polled on Taine's influence, among them Barrès, Henri Mazel, and Emile Durkheim of the young generation; among their elders, sociologist Gabriel Tarde and historian Gabriel Monod.

40. See Blum's discussion of *Les Déracinés* in "Nouvelles Conversations," *L'Oeuvre*, 1:219. See Mazel's answer in the *Revue blanche* inquiry on Taine: 280–282.

41. "And surely nothing is less scientific than this belief," wrote Blum. See "Premiers paradoxes sur Renan," *La Revue blanche* 3, no. 13 (November 1892): 242. See Barrès, *Mes Cahiers*, vol. 1:1896–1898 (Paris: Plon, 1929), 153–154.

42. H. Stuart Hughes, *Consciousness and Society: The Reorientation of European Social Thought, 1890–1930* (New York: Vintage Books, revised edition, 1977), 37, and 41.

43. Blum, "Nouvelles Conversations," *L'Oeuvre*, 1:304–305.

44. Barrès, *L'Oeuvre de Maurice Barrès*, 1:451. The excerpt comes from an article published in *Les Taches d'encre*.

45. Hughes, *Consciousness and Society*, 58. See also Blum, "La Prochaine Génération littéraire," *La Revue de Paris* 20 (1 February 1913):519–536. In this article, Blum makes a case for the continuity between his generation and that of 1914 with regard to the revolt against positivism.

46. Huret first polled the partisans of the newer literary schools, the "Psychologues" in prose and the Symbolists in poetry. He then questioned their rivals, the proponents of the established literary schools: Naturalist novelists and Parnassian poets. Since the *Enquête* was published in serial form, the latter group had read the answers of the first group before responding themselves.

47. Huret, *L'Enquête sur l'évolution*, 45.

48. In an article entitled "L'Individualisme," *Les Entretiens politiques et littéraires* 1, no. 5 (1 August 1890):137–142, Emile Goudeau (1850) called on members of the young generation to work together as friends, despite their different literary tendencies.

49. Huret, *L'Enquête sur l'évolution*, 99.

50. See Remy de Gourmont's "L'Idéalisme," *Les Entretiens politiques et littéraires* 4, no. 25 (April 1892):145–148. See also Jean Pierrot, *L'Imaginaire décadent, 1880–1900* (Paris: Presses Universitaires de France, 1977), 84–101 for a detailed discussion of idealism.

51. Huret, *L'Enquête sur l'évolution*, 95.

52. Maurice Barrès, "Examen des trois romans idéologiques," *Le Culte du moi*, 16–17.

53. *Le Mercure de France* and *La Revue blanche* were both founded under the aegis of Barrès. See the opening statements for *Le Mercure* 1 (January 1890):1–4, and for *La Revue blanche* 1 (1 October 1891):1. As for *La Plume*, it even devoted an entire issue in April 1892 to Barrès and his theories. On the impact of Barrès on his peers, Léon Blum writes: "He was for me, as he was for the majority of my colleagues, not only the master, but the guide; we formed a school around him, even a court." *Souvenirs sur l'Affaire* (Paris: Gallimard, 1935; reedition 1981), 84.

54. Huret, *L'Enquête sur l'évolution*, 131. Such feelings were echoed by Francis Vielé-Griffin, who in an article published in *Les Entretiens politiques et littéraires*, referred to the "repulsion" and the "disdain" that young writers felt for Zola: "Encore de M. Zola" 4, no. 24 (March 1892):97.

55. Huret, *L'Enquête sur l'évolution*, 224–227. Hermant also separated himself from the Symbolists, who, he felt, were preaching a crusade against science and modernity.

56. Vielé-Griffin, "Encore de M. Zola," 99. See Susanna Barrows on Zola's depiction of crowds, *Distorting Mirrors*, 93–113. Despite Zola's sympathy for the striking miners, he depicted the crowd as brutal.

57. Vielé-Griffin, "Encore de M. Zola," 98. His colleague on *Les Entretiens*, Gabriel Mourey (1865) continued the assault on Zola by criticizing both his esthetics and his ethics: "Here in its entirety is bourgeois morality, in the lesser sense of the word, the morality of platitudes and of egoism, of serene indifference and of the full stomach, the stifling of all energy, of all generosity, of all grandeur." He was defending the young generation against Zola's admonition that they were dreamers and idlers who rejected truth and reality: "Pour la foi," *Les Entretiens politiques et littéraires* 7, no. 46 (10 July 1893):31.

58. Writing shortly after Zola's death in 1902, Pierre Quillard expressed his regret at not having realized the value of Zola during his youth: "Emile Zola," *Le Mercure de France* 44, no. 155 (November 1902):383–390.

59. Eugen Weber, "The Endless Crisis," *France Fin de Siècle* (Cambridge, Mass.: Belknap Press of Harvard University Press, 1986), 105–129.

60. Barrès, who categorically denounced the previous political generation, summed up their feelings, referring to politicians as the "failures" of literature, medicine, or law in "M. le Général Boulanger et la nouvelle génération," *La Revue indépendante* 8 (April 1888):58.

61. Boulanger gained wide publicity for army reforms he instituted while serving as Minister of War in 1886. His popularity was so great that

he obtained unsolicited support in special elections to the Chamber of Deputies in 1887. When he was transferred to an obscure military post, Boulanger resigned his commission in order to campaign seriously. His victories in a succession of special legislative elections in the spring and summer of 1888 transformed his personal popularity into a political plebiscite, which culminated in his victory in a legislative election in Paris in January 1889. When his enemies in the government, fearing a possible coup d'état, took measures to pursue him, he fled the country for Belgium. Boulanger later committed suicide on the grave of his mistress. The scandal that served as a catalyst for the development of Boulangism as a mass movement was the Wilson affair. In 1887, President Grévy's son-in-law Daniel Wilson was caught selling military decorations. In the wake of the scandal, Grévy was forced to resign.

62 Romain Rolland, *Le Cloître de la rue d'Ulm* (Paris: Albin Michel, 1952), 214–215. Léon Blum felt that intellectuals were attracted to Boulangism for esthetic reasons. See "Le Progrès de l'apolitique en France," *La Revue blanche* 3, no. 10 (July 1892):13–14.

63. On nationalism, see Raoul Girardet, *Le Nationalisme français: 1871–1914* (Paris: Seuil, 1983); on the "revolutionary right," Zeev Sternhell, *La Droite révolutionnaire: les origines françaises du fascisme, 1885–1914* (Paris: Seuil, 1978); on Boulangism, William D. Irvine, *The Boulanger Affair Reconsidered: Royalism, Boulangism and the Origins of the Radical Right in France* (New York: Oxford University Press, 1989).

64. Directors of the Panama Company, finding the firm in grave financial difficulties, sought to raise funds through a public lottery. To secure parliamentary approval, they bribed a number of deputies. Although only one politician was formally charged, several leading politicians were swept out of office in the anti-Panama wave, including Georges Clemenceau (1841).

65. Trade unions were legalized in 1884 and their numbers grew steadily during the next few years, although striking workers had no protection against dismissal.

66. Blum, who expressed reservations with regard to anarchism, announced that it was a result of the disjunction between the individual and society: "Le Progrès de l'apolitique en France," *La Revue blanche*, pgs. 19–20. Blum, of course, would soon become a Socialist, but even an intellectual foe like Charles Maurras would have agreed that apathy had dissolved the links between the individual and society.

67. This declaration accompanied Ludovic Malquin's article "L'Anarchie," published in *La Revue blanche* 1, no. 2 (November 1891):97.

68. Retté, "Une Année de combat," *La Plume*, pg. 527. Mazel agreed with Retté on the importance of this development, but did not agree with the consequences of this change, instead describing anarchism as an "epidemic," and a "smallpox," "Au lecteur," *L'Ermitage* (December 1895):311–312.

69. "Référendum artistique et social," *L'Ermitage* 7 (July 1893):1–24.

70. Christophe Charle, *Naissance des "intellectuels": 1880–1910* (Paris: Editions de Minuit, 1990), 116.

71. On Blum, see Louis Lévy, *Comment ils sont devenus socialistes* (Paris: Editions du Populaire, 1931), 21. See Maurras, "Les jeunes revues II," *La Revue bleue* (13 January 1894):52–54, and *Le Mont de Saturne* (Paris: Les Quatre Jeudis, 1950), 26.

72. On anarchism, see George Woodcock, *Anarchism: A History of Libertarian Ideas and Movements* (New York: Penguin Books, 1986); James Joll, *The Anarchists* (Cambridge, Mass.: Harvard University Press, 1980); Jean Maitron, *Histoire du mouvement anarchiste en France*, vol. 1: *Les origines à 1914* (Paris: Gallimard, 1975). On anarchism and intellectuals, the most complete work is Richard D. Sonn, *Anarchism and Cultural Politics in Fin-de-siècle France* (Lincoln, Neb.: University of Nebraska Press, 1989). See also my "Passing Fancy?: The Generation of 1890 and Anarchism," *Modern and Contemporary France*, no. 44 (January 1991):3–11.

73. See Richard D. Sonn: "The Early Political Career of Maurice Barrès: Anarchist, Socialist, or Protofascist?" *Clio* 21, no. 1 (Fall 1991):41–60.

74. Ludovic Malquin, "L'An-archie," *La Revue blanche* 1, no. 2 (November 1891):97–106.

75. ——, "Notes sur obéir," *La Revue blanche* 2, no. 7 (25 April 1892): 193–201.

76. Lucien Muhlfeld, "Chronique de la littérature," *La Revue blanche* 2, no. 9 (June 1892):357.

77. Even the word individualism possessed multiple meanings. For many, it meant complete freedom of the individual, for others, it meant "disinterested" individualism, which included a sense of responsibility to society.

78. "We believed in good faith that these men vanquished by the society of pleasure-seeking capitalists . . . were martyrs of individualism," wrote Camille Mauclair in his memoirs, *Servitude et grandeur littéraires* (Paris: Ollendorff, 1922), 115.

79. Adam, "Eloge de Ravachol," *Les Entretiens politiques et littéraires* 5, no. 28 (24 July 1892):27–30; Barrucand, *L'Endehors*, no. 64 (24 July 1892).

80. Symbolism, he stated, "translates literally by the word Liberty and for the violent ones, by the word Anarchy," *La Revue blanche* 2, no. 9 (25 June 1892):322.

81. Paul Adam, "Critique du socialisme et de l'anarchie," *La Revue blanche* 4, no. 19 (25 May 1893):371.

82. Adolphe Retté, "Une Année de combat," *La Plume*, 527–528.

83. Henri Mazel and Hugues Rebell, "Un Référendum," *L'Ermitage*, 21–24.

84. Hugues Rebell, *Union des trois aristocraties* (Paris: Bibliothèque artistique et littéraire, 1894).

85. A transplanted American who had attended the Lycée Condorcet, Stuart Merrill was a Symbolist poet, who became a Dreyfusard, while Rebell became an anti-Dreyfusard and subsequently joined the Action française. Incidentally, Merrill was a follower of Jean Grave and therefore should have been grouped with the anarchists.

86. "Contrainte et liberté," *L'Ermitage* 4, no. 11 (November 1893): 257–265.

87. As the response of Hugues Rebell, one of the authors of the *Enquête*, illustrates: "The socialist state toward which the crowd today turns its gaze . . . will realize, under the hypocritical banner of liberty, a tyranny more frightening than those of the past. . . .", 17. Christophe Prochasson has remarked on the irony of the fact that intellectuals, a product of democracy, have traditionally had great difficulty in accepting the mechanisms of its functioning since they might conflict with their own authority and liberty: "Histoire intellectuelle/histoire des intellectuels," *Revue d'histoire moderne et contemporaine* 39, no. 3 (July–September 1992):430.

88. See for example an article "Philosophie de l'anarchie" by André Veidaux in a special issue of *La Plume* on anarchism. Veidaux claimed that if he had to choose between the rule of the bourgeoisie and the scientific materialism of the socialists, he would choose the former: *La Plume* 4 (1 May 1893):192.

89. "Un Référendum," *L'Ermitage:* Beaubourg, 3.

90. Compare the answer of Remy de Gourmont, listed as "indifferent": "Sure to always be crushed by the social machinery, the artist must be wary of—everything (10) to that of Rachilde, classified as a partisan of "art for art's sake": "the artist should admit that outside of artistic questions, he has no preference (16).

91. Gustave Kahn, "L'Art social et l'art pour l'art," *La Revue blanche* 11 (1 November 1896):416.

92. Xavier Durand, "L'Art social au théâtre: deux expériences (1893, 1897)," *Le Mouvement social*, no. 91 (April–June 1975):14.

93. See both Gourmont's "Le Symbolisme," *La Revue blanche* 2, no. 9 (June 1892):321–325, and "L'Idéalisme," *Les Entretiens politiques et littéraires* 4, no. 25 (April 1892):142–148. Gourmont represented idealism

as the relativity of all knowledge, concluding that idealism led naturally to a complete disinterest in society. If the only reality was that of the self, then why should the idealist need to involve him or herself with the outside world, with society and politics? Furthermore, if each individual constituted his or her own world and one hundred individuals created one hundred worlds, each as legitimate as the next, then, concluded Gourmont, idealism could lead to only one form of government: anarchy. "L'Idéalisme," 146–47.

94. Adolphe Retté, "Du rôle des poètes," *La Plume* 4 (1 November 1893):455.

95. Retté, "L'Art et l'anarchie," *La Plume* 4 (1 February 1893):45.

96. Barrès, "Lettre à la *Plume,*" *La Plume* 4 (15 mars 1893):116.

97. Vielé-Griffin, "Entretiens sur le mouvement poétique," *Les Entretiens politiques et littéraires* 6, no. 39 (25 March 1893):246–247.

98. Gustave Kahn, "L'Art social et l'art pour l'art," 418–419.

99. Ibid., 418.

100. While Kahn and a number of his colleagues no doubt viewed the intellectual as an inspirer, they were not prepared to serve as political propagandists. In 1896, when Kahn wrote about the artist and political action, he did not at all have in mind the type of active engagement of intellectuals in the Dreyfus Affair. As he noted later, his first impulse during the Dreyfus Affair had been to reject active involvement in politics but that subsequent events, notably the publication of Zola's "J'Accuse," had changed his mind. See Kahn's "Zola," *La Revue blanche* 15, no. 100 (15 February 1898):270–271. The Affair thus did not launch intellectuals into the public arena so much as it obliged them to serve as propagandists and enter the thick of the fray.

101. Bernard Lazare, "Les Livres," *Les Entretiens politiques et littéraires* 6, no. 43 (25 May 1893):476.

102. Ibid., 478.

103. Three years later, Lazare reiterated his position in favor of "social art," defined as "universal art," but this time, he was much less conciliatory and roundly condemned the Symbolists for creating hermetic art suited only for small coteries: "L'Ecrivain et l'art social," (Paris: Bibliothèque du Groupe de l'Art Social, 1896). This eleven page text, which was presented as a talk on 4 April 1896, may be found in the archives of the Alliance Israélite in Paris.

104. Rebell published the aforementioned *Union des trois aristocraties* and Mazel guest edited a July 1894 issue of *La Plume* on "L'Aristocratie," and devoted the entire November 1894 issue of *L'Ermitage* to the same topic.

105. "Une Enquête franco-allemande," *Le Mercure de France* 14, no. 64 (April 1895):1–65. Henceforth cited as *Mercure Enquête 1895*.

106. Remy de Gourmont, "Le Joujou patriotisme," *Le Mercure de France* 2, no. 16 (April 1891):192–198.

107. Ibid. Most critics could not get past Remy de Gourmont's bluster, in particular, the phrase "I would not give, in exchange for the lost lands [the lost provinces], neither the little finger of my right hand . . . nor the little finger of my left hand. . . .", 194.

108. The second inquiry was conducted in November and December of 1902: nos. 155–156. See my "Germany Revisited: The *Mercure de France* Surveys of 1895 and 1902," *Proceedings of the Annual Meeting of the Western Society for French History* 18 (1991):381–387.

109. *Mercure Enquête 1895*: 1–2.

110. Ibid., 2.

111. Of the twenty-four Frenchmen (no women) polled, only four were what could loosely be called "political types." Although this survey was biased in favor of anti-establishment intellectuals, even Maurras admitted the representativity of the sample as far as his own generation was concerned: *Quand les Français ne s'aimaient pas, chronique d'une renaissance, 1895–1905* (Paris: Nouvelle Librairie nationale, 1916), 1–15.

112. *Mercure Enquête 1895*: Gourmont, 11; Lazare, 16–17.

113. Ibid., Lazare, 17; Grave, 12–13.

114. Ibid., Gourmont, 11; Péladan, 21.

115. Ibid., Tailhade, 25.

116. Ibid.

117. Ibid., Péladan, 22.

118. Gourmont, "Le Joujou," 196.

119. *Mercure Enquête 1895*: Adam, 3; Barrès, 7.

120. Ibid., Lazare, 16; Barrès, 8.

121. Ibid., Kahn, 15.

122. Gourmont, "Le Joujou patriotisme," 198.

123. Ibid., 195.

124. Téodor de Wyzewa was an exception as was the conservative writer and critic Eugène-Melchior de Vogüé (1848).

125. *Mercure Enquête 1895*: Adam, 5; Lazare, 16–17. Some of the avant-garde writers, like Gustave Kahn, made clear that such exchanges should

take place between young writers of the avant-garde, rather than between official, establishment intellectuals, 15.

126. Ibid., Kahn, 16.

127. "Enquête sur l'influence allemande," *Le Mercure de France*, no. 155 (November 1902): Henceforth cited as *Mercure Enquête 1902*. On the "nationalist revival," see Eugen Weber, *The Nationalist Revival in France, 1905–1914* (Berkeley, Calif.: University of California Press, 1986).

128. *Mercure Enquête 1902:* (November): Barrès, 301.

129. "Enquête sur l'influence des lettres scandinaves," *La Revue blanche* 12, no. 89 (15 February 1897): Gourmont, 156; *Mercure Enquête 1902*, (November): Gourmont, 336–337.

130. *Mercure Enquête 1895*: Péladan, 22; Wyzewa, 31.

131. "Enquête sur l'influence des lettres scandinaves," 153–166. The survey asked writers if French literature had recently been subject to influence by foreign literatures, specifically Scandinavian ones, and whether this development was to be favored or combated.

132. I shall explore this issue more fully in chapter 7. I would like to suggest that the opponents of Kant or more precisely of neo-Kantians did not represent a uniform, monolithic *bloc*. Barrès opposed Kantianism for its universalist principles; Maurras because it attempted to substitute a lay morality (seen as Protestant) for a Catholic, French morality. Remy de Gourmont, on the other hand, opposed Kantianism because it was too "religious." Barrès and others even used the subjective aspects of idealist thought to combat the universalism of Kantianism.

133. Blum, *Souvenirs sur l'Affaire*, 35. Charles Maurras, *Pour un jeune français* (Paris: Amiot-Dumont, 1949), 101.

Chapter 3

1. With the possible exception of the period of the French Revolution.

2. Gambetta and other republicans viewed universal suffrage as a framework for a democratic regime in which an elite of talent would actually rule: Fritz Ringer, *Fields of Knowledge: French Academic Culture in Comparative Perspective, 1890–1920* (New York: Cambridge University Press, 1992), 209.

3. The set of articles on the "intellectual proletariat" was eventually collected and published in book form: *Les Prolétaires intellectuels en France* (Paris: Editions de la Revue, 1901). Among the contributors were Henry Bérenger, Paul Pottier, and Marius-Ary Leblond. In the preface to the book, the authors wrote that the problem of an intellectual proletariat had

become a global one. They spoke also of the "grandeur of the one-sided duel" which opposed "Intelligence" and "Money." Bérenger, who established a reputation as an expert on the topic, testified in 1899 before the Ribot commission, whose task it was to conduct an investigation of French secondary education. The articles on an intellectual elite and democracy were published in the 21 May, 28 May, and 4 June 1904 issues.

4. Christophe Charle states that the split between official republican rhetoric concerning a meritocratic society and the reality of the limitations of such a discourse served to alienate intellectual elites from political ones. He also argues that intellectual elites were more broadly recruited socially than economic ones, with the political elite occupying a middle position. Through the course of the 1880s and 1890s, political and administrative elites managed to form close associations with economic elites, thereby further isolating intellectual elites: *Naissance des "intellectuels": 1880–1910* (Paris: Editions de Minuit, 1990), 11–13. The alienation of university intellectuals from the political regime began around 1890, after a period of very close relations. Charle explains that this division resulted from an increasing desire for independence from the regime on the part of such intellectuals as Lucien Herr and Charles Andler, both of whom turned to socialism, 82–92. This would help to explain the ties between the literary and university avant-gardes during the Affair.

5. On writers and politics during this time, see Eugenia Herbert, *The Artist and Social Reform: France and Belgium, 1885–1898* (New Haven, Conn.: Yale University Press, 1961). Among the Symbolists, Decadents and Naturists, only 15 percent came from the middle classes; those of aristocratic birth and lowly origins were overrepresented. Richard Sonn suggests that this social composition made them more prone to anarchism: "Anarchism found its supporters among the rich as well as the poor, but few among the solid middle classes," *Anarchism and Cultural Politics in Fin-de-siècle France* (Lincoln, Neb.: University of Nebraska Press, 1989), 192–193.

6. On *La Cocarde*, see Victor Nguyen, "Un Essai de pouvoir intellectuel au début de la Troisième République," *Etudes maurrassiennes* 1 (1972): 145–155, and Henri Clouard, *La "Cocarde" de M. Barrès* (Paris: Nouvelle Librairie nationale, 1910).

7. Maurice Barrès, ed., "La Nouvelle Cocarde," *La Cocarde*, 5 September 1894.

8. For a general discussion of the writer in society, see John Lough, *Writer and Public in France: From the Middle Ages to the Present* (Oxford, Eng.: Clarendon Press, 1978). For writers during the nineteenth century, see Paul Bénichou, *Le Sacre de l'écrivain, 1750–1830* (Paris: José Corti, 1985), and Christophe Charle, "Le Champ littéraire," *Histoire de l'édition française*, vol. 3, *Le temps des éditeurs: du Romantisme à la Belle Epoque* (Paris: Promodis, 1985; Fayard/Promodis, 1990), 137–175, as well as Charle's *La Crise littéraire à l'époque du naturalisme: roman, théâtre, politique* (Paris: Presses de l'Ecole Normale Supérieure, 1979).

9. Stephen Wilson, *Ideology and Experience: Antisemitism in France at the Time of the Dreyfus Affair* (East Brunswick, NJ: Associated University Press, 1982), 607.

10. Retté, "Du rôle des poètes," *La Plume* 4 (1 November 1893):454–455.

11. Alphonse Germain, "Aux intellectuels," *Les Entretiens politiques et littéraires* 2, no. 11 (1 February 1891):40–44.

12. In 1880, after much discussion, republican leaders finally agreed on 14 July as a national holiday—1889 marked the Centennial of the Revolution and 1893 of the Terror; the anarchist bomb-throwing incidents of 1893 undoubtedly intensified the debate over the legacy of 1793. In the midst of such enormous changes, contemporaries were self-conscious about their place in history.

13. Henry Bérenger, *L'Aristocratie intellectuelle* (Paris: Armand Colin, 1895), 65–66.

14. On Bérenger, see William M. Johnston, "The Origin of the Term 'Intellectuals' in French Novels and Essays of the 1890s," *Journal of European Studies* 4 (1974):43–56.

15. Bérenger's *La Proie* was reviewed in *La Revue bleue* by another founding member of the Action française: Gabriel Syveton (19 February 1898):245–248. Charles Maurras also contributed to *La Revue bleue*, notably his series on "young" reviews in 1894.

16. I am thinking especially of the intellectuals who wrote for *La Revue blanche*. In fact, Bérenger himself dubbed them a group of "sorbonnards" in an article quoted in *Le Mercure de France* 21 (January 1897):229. The *Revue blanche* group also had close ties through Léon Blum and others with the Ecole Normale. Bérenger is listed in *L'Ermitage's* "Livre d'or" of collaborators, along with Charles Maurras. Bérenger was one of those polled for the Referendum of 1893; he was also quoted in Mazel's special issue of *La Plume* on aristocracy.

17. In his *Livre des masques*, Remy de Gourmont referred to Rebell as both a pagan and an aristocrat, stating that his aristocratic ideas led him to a "liberty of manners." (Paris: Mercure de France, 1896 and 1898; 1963), 163.

18. Hugues Rebell, *Union des trois aristocraties* (Paris: Bibliothèque artistique et littéraire, 1894). See especially pages 11; 47–48. Rebell called equality "a deadly lie" (47). Although both he and Maurras deplored the "individualism" of the Revolution, as represented by "laissez-faire," Rebell was himself an "individualist" of sorts, exalting as he did the rights of the superior man and of the artist.

19. Ibid., 28. "Miserable revolution! Your only beneficial effect was to augment in us the hatred of the baseness that you represent.... Revolution, malady of humanity!... Enemy of Beauty and of Thought...." (48).

20. Ibid., 35–36. Rebell felt that the man of genius could advance more easily under the Ancien Régime than under the parliamentary republic since its bureaucracy had replaced the arbitrage of intelligent and cultivated men: 25. Rebell had dire predictions for aristocracies that kept intelligence at bay, 29.

21. Ibid., 15, and 44. Of significance here is the fact that while he decried the advent of democracy and the industrialization of literary production, Rebell did not oppose the accumulation of wealth, in particular, by Jews. This would become a point of contention with his future colleagues of the Action française, in particular, Charles Maurras, as expressed in his review of Rebell's book: "Le Privilège des meilleurs," *La Gazette de France*, 4 December 1894.

22. Henri Mazel, "Quelques notes sur les Vicissitudes de l'esprit d'aristie en France depuis un siècle," *L'Ermitage*, no. 11 (November 1894):306–308.

23. Henri Mazel, "L'Aristocratie," 247–248, and "Qu'est-ce que l'aristocratie?" 249, both in *La Plume*, no. 124 (15 June 1894).

24. "The French Revolution is the height of stupidity and of horror; no epoch is more dishonoring for humanity.... No explosion of the passions of envy and hatred was more infernal. It is against all superior moral and social values, against all nobility—more so of the heart, of the mind, and of character, than of birth—that Jacobin satanism hurled itself." *La Synergie sociale* (Paris: Armand Colin, 1896), 124–125.

25. Mazel, "L'Aristocratie," *La Plume*, 247. Mazel believed that a domination by any type of elite was preferable to the despotism of the collectivity. He even claimed that there existed a hierarchy of civilizations based on the role they had given to "individual pride." In such a schema, Christian societies were superior to non-Christian ones: "Qu'est-ce que l'aristocratie?," and "Civilisation et aristocratie," *La Plume*, 249, and 252. In *Synergie*, 343, Mazel noted: "In democracy what is odious is not the numbers it represents, it is the baseness of spirit." Mazel also admitted that the Revolution for one brief moment at its beginnings had sprung from a love of justice; he deplored, however, its immediate degeneration into envy and hatred: "Qu'est-ce que l'aristocratie?" *La Plume*, 249.

26. Mazel, *Synergie*, 107. He disagreed then with Rebell, who called for a revolution against 1789: "We must become revolutionaries—revolutionaries it is true, of a new kind. We do not seek to destroy, but to restore...." *Union*, 10.

27. Mazel, *Synergie*, 103, and 112: "All revolution is criminal when evolution is possible" (112).

28. Ibid., 108. Like Taine, he believed that the excesses of the Revolution were peculiarly French, a product of the French tendency for absolutes, 108–109.

29. Although Mazel disassociated himself with those who called themselves liberals, referring to them as "libérâtres," who combated injustices and inequalities out of hatred and jealousy: "Qu'est-ce que l'aristocratie?" *La Plume*, 249. See also a letter dated 7 January 1930 to Auriant in which Mazel explained that he was a "republican liberal" in 1895: Auriant, *Hugues Rebell à "L'Ermitage"(1892–1900): avec dix lettres à Henri Mazel* (Reims: Editions "A l'Ecart," 1988), 52. Mazel's discussion of regimes of the nineteenth century points to his sympathies with both the Restoration and the Second Empire. He admired Napoleon as a man of action, but claimed that his Empire was doomed to failure since a true aristocracy was pluralist, not rule by one man: "Quelques notes sur les vicissitudes de l'esprit d'aristie en France depuis un siècle," *L'Ermitage*, 304–307.

30. Particularly the excesses of the Terror: "De Chateaubriand à Barrès," *La Revue bleue* (30 January 1897):130. On the Revolution, see especially chapter 8 of Bérenger's book *L'Aristocratie intellectuelle*: "L'Aristocratie intellectuelle et les principes de 1789," 191–225.

31. Bérenger, *L'Aristocratie intellectuelle*, 205; "the great error of the Revolution . . . was to affirm in effect the absolute equality of all men and to deny by this very declaration the necessity of a social aristocracy."(239). Because the Revolution attempted to do away with all forms of hierarchy, the aristocracies of money and of politics emerged, 241.

32. See chapter 9 of *L'Aristocratie intellectuelle*: "Socialisme et aristocratie," 227–273, especially 249–251. Like Maurras and Mazel (but not Rebell), Bérenger deplored the pernicious influence of Rousseau, whom he viewed as the predecessor of Vaillant and Henry, 197, and 206.

33. Henry Bérenger, "De Chateaubriand à Barrès," *La Revue bleue*, 131–132; 135.

34. On the Revolution, see Bérenger, *L'Aristocratie intellectuelle*, 208; on universal suffrage, 269.

35. In an entry of 1896 from his *Cahiers*, Barrès quoted Pascal: " 'Plurality is the best way, because it is visible and it has the strength to make itself obeyed. Nevertheless, it is the expression of the least clever.'" Barrès commented: "this is why the cause of democracy is henceforth indisputable. It is strength; we must accord it, against our aristocratic predilections, against our taste for high culture, the quality of justice." *Mes Cahiers*, vol. 1:1896–1898 (Paris: Plon, 1929), 96–97. Barrès also spoke in his *Cahiers* of a conversation on the Revolution with Mazel; while he may have agreed with Mazel with regard to his criticisms of the Revolution, unlike Mazel, Barrès felt that one must accept it as one did Catholicism, 95.

36. Mazel, "L'Aristocratie," *La Plume*, 247; Rebell, *Union*, 9, and 28.

37. Bérenger, *L'Aristocratie intellectuelle*, 251–252.

38. Ibid., 253. "the real end of a Democracy is in a reconciliation between individualism and solidarity....", 182. Barrès spoke in similar terms in an editorial in *La Cocarde* entitled "Réflexions: individualisme et socialisme, 5 September 1894: "An individualism that is both free and profound, together with social solidarity—these are the twin concerns from which our ideal is formed."

39. Bérenger, *L'Aristocratie intellectuelle*, 241–242.

40. Ibid., 254–255.

41. Fritz Ringer, *Fields of Knowledge*, 28.

42. William Logue, *From Philosophy to Sociology: The Evolution of French Liberalism, 1870–1914* (Dekalb, IL, Northern Illinois University Press, 1983), 75.

43. Linda L. Clark, *Social Darwinism in France* (Tuscaloosa, AL: University of Alabama Press, 1984), 56.

44. Logue, *From Philosophy to Sociology*, 80.

45. Ringer, Fields of Knowledge, 50.

46. See George Weisz, *The Emergence of Modern Universities in France, 1863–1914* (Princeton, NJ: Princeton University Press, 1983), especially "The Creation of the French Universities," 134–161; and Ringer, *Fields of Knowledge*, 43–50.

47. Weisz, *Emergence of Modern Universities*, 228.

48. Weisz indicates that the students enrolled in the university numbered 11, 200 in 1876; in 1914, 42,000 were enrolled: 225. See also Ringer, *Fields of Knowledge*, 50–51.

49. Mazel, *Synergie*, 209.

50. Barrès, *Les Déracinés* (Paris: Union Générale d'Editions, 10/18, 1986), 114.

51. Léon Blum, "Les Livres," *La Revue blanche* 14 (15 November 1897):292–294.

52. While Barrès was speaking of a proletariat of "bacheliers," Bérenger was talking about university students.

53. The page references to Bérenger's article refer to the reprint included in the book *Les Prolétaires intellectuels en France*, cited in an earlier footnote, 3–6.

54. Ibid., 25–32.

55. Ibid., 34–35.

56. Ibid., 42.

57. Ibid., 44.

58. Ibid., 24.

59. Mazel, too, deplored this 1891 law, stating that those exempted should be farmers, industrialists, and colonists. These men were much more needed by France than more doctors and lawyers: Mazel, *Synergie*, 208.

60. Bérenger, *Les Prolétaires intellectuels*, 44–45.

61. Ibid., 50–51.

62. Mazel: "L'Aristocratie," *La Plume*, 247; Rebell: Introduction to Rebell's translation of Nietzsche's "De l'homme supérieur," *L'Ermitage* 6 (April 1893):263.

63. "Thus the hero is the superior soul of democracy; he only combats it in order to make it better." Bérenger, *L'Aristocratie intellectuelle*, 144–145.

64. Adolphe Retté, "L'art et l'anarchie," *La Plume* 4, no. 91 (1 February 1893):45–46. This view was echoed by Alphonse Germain, who lumped the proletariat and the bourgeoisie together, claiming that rule by either would amount to the same thing: the destruction of "Intellectuality," "Aux intellectuels," *Les Entretiens*, 43.

65. In "Du rôle des poètes," *La Plume*, Retté declared that the poet's purpose was to present "the Beautiful, the True, the Just," 454.

66. Ibid., 455.

67. Vielé-Griffin, "Entretiens sur le mouvement poétique," *Les Entretiens politiques et littéraires* 6, no. 39 (25 March 1893): 247; Adam, "Un Référendum artistique et social," *L'Ermitage* 7 (July 1893):1.

68. Charle, *Naissance des "intellectuels,"* 65–66.

69. See Barrès's *Cahiers*, 1, "We admire . . . in Leconte de Lisle the aristocracy of his art. It is not good for art to be vulgar. . . ." (in an entry dated 1897):159.

70. Commenting on the ideas of Leconte de Lisle, Barrès wrote: "What is inexact . . . is that intellectuals constitute an aristocracy in humanity. . . . But even if I do not see the means by which to establish a hierarchy based on varying occupations, it remains true that individuals are born for different functions, and some of these having been born with the gift for giving a moving expression to ideals for which humanity combats, care not a bit for such battles. They create parties by the ideas and the emotions they bring into the world, and how would they join the ranks of a party that represents merely the tail end of their work," "Réflexions: l'intellectuel et la politique," *La Cocarde*, 24 February 1895.

71. Charles Maurras, "Le Privilège des meilleurs," *La Gazette de France*.

72. Henri Mazel, "Qu'est-ce que l'aristocratie?" *La Plume*, 248. Among the *"aristes* of will" included Vercingétorix and Joan of Arc; among the *"aristes* of love," Saint Louis and Saint Theresa, and among the *"aristes* of intellect," Darwin, Pasteur, along with the poets Lamartine, Hugo, and Balzac, as well as such thinkers as Kant, Hegel, and Pascal.

73. Ibid. Mazel further defined the "ariste" in a tautological manner: "the superior man is one who is conscious of his superiority," 248.

74. Bérenger, too, dismissed the traditional aristocracies of birth and wealth as completely out of step with the times but thought there might still be hope for the religious aristocracy since the Church recruited openly. *L'Aristocratie intellectuelle*, 80–81.

75. Ibid., 79.

76. Ibid., 256. Bérenger made clear that a closed aristocracy such as Renan's caste of savants who ruled by force was antithetical to his beliefs; he preferred the domination of the collectivity to a tyranny by an elite. Rebell and Mazel, on the other hand, preferred the domination of any kind of elite rather than the rule of the masses. I would question the strength of Mazel's conviction since he deplored Rebell's vision of three aristocracies which dominated by force.

77. Camille Mauclair, "Chronique: un projet d'association artistique," *La Cocarde*, 24 September 1894. During the Affair, leading anti-Dreyfusard Ferdinand Brunetière would write that an "intellectual aristocracy" was unacceptable because it could not be adequately proved or defined: "Après le Procès," *La Revue des deux mondes* 146 (March 1898):428–446.

78. Alphonse Germain, "Aux intellectuels," 40.

79. Barrès, "Réflexions: le problème est double," 8 September 1894. Mazel echoed these sentiments, quoting Andrew Carnegie: "man does not live by bread alone," Mazel, *Synergie*, 318.

80. "A new ideal that guides our behavior, dominates our thought and leads an entire people." Rebell, *Union*, 30–31. See also Barrès: "Réflexions: il faut un idéal," *La Cocarde*, 13 September 1894, "The people want us to propose a model of social perfection. They want an ideal."

81. Mazel, *Synergie*, 332–333; Bérenger, *L'Aristocratie intellectuelle*, 163. In addition, Bérenger wanted to reconcile science and religion (78). He encouraged the Catholic Church to reconcile itself with modernity by accepting the Republic (he approved of Pope Leon XIII); moreover, like other intellectuals of this time, he looked back to the Medieval Catholic Church and exalted the ideals of the Gospel. Rebell, who saw himself as a pagan, accepted Catholicism but detested the spirit of the Gospel, which, he felt, was the basis of inspiration for Marx and his disciples, *Union*, 21–22, note.

82. Rebell, *Union*, 31.

83. Camille Mauclair, "L'Art en silence," *La Cocarde*, 13 February 1895.

84. Barrès, "La Question des 'Intellectuels'," *La Cocarde*, 20 September 1894. Although he is coy, in the following passage from "Réflexions: il faut un idéal," *La Cocarde*, Barrès is undoubtedly speaking of intellectuals who exalted socialism because it allowed them to play a role in society:

> A great many socialists labelled as such would reject the immediate and complete application of the doctrines that they approve. What pleases them in socialism, other than the fact that they find it logical and generous, is that it gives them an important role in the history of the universe; it allows them to view themselves as a moment in a sublime evolution, like workers in a great and definitive social harmony: it brings them closer to the ideal.

85. Retté, "Du rôle des poètes," *La Plume*, 455.

86. Bérenger, *L'Aristocratie intellectuelle*, 130.

87. Ibid., 102.

88. Henri Mazel, "Sursum Corda," *La Plume*, no. 124 (15 June 1894):254.

89. Mauclair, "Chronique: un projet d'association artistique," *La Cocarde*, 24 September 1894.

90. See Maurras's series on "Les Jeunes Revues," published in *La Revue bleue* in late 1893 and early 1894, especially the 13 January issue; Bérenger, *L'Aristocratie intellectuelle*, 37–39, and "De Chateaubriand à Barrès," *La Revue bleue*, 134.

91. Mauclair, "Chronique: un projet d'association artistique," *La Cocarde*.

92. In order to defend themselves against exploitation by the masses and the bourgeoisie: Alphonse Germain, "Aux intellectuels," *Les Entretiens*, 44.

93. Rebell, *Union*, 38; 42; Retté, "Du rôle des poètes," *La Plume*, 455.

94. Bérenger, "De Chateaubriand à Barrès," *La Revue bleue*, 130.

95. Bernard Lazare, "L'Ecrivain et l'art social," (Paris: Bibliothèque de l'"Art Social,' 1896), 1.

96. The article, entitled "Les Littérateurs à la Chambre," was originally published in *Le Figaro* on 31 July 1893; it is included in a collection of Jules Huret, *Interviews de littérature et d'art* (Vanves: Editions de Thot, 1984), 35–39.

97. Barrès, "Réflexions: la leçon des scandales," *La Cocarde*, 17 February 1895.

98. Barrès, L'Intellectuel et la politique," *La Cocarde*, 24 February 1895.

99. Mauclair, "L'Art en silence," *La Cocarde*.

100. Bernard Lazare, "Anarchie et littérature," *La Révolte*, supplément littéraire, no. 24, (24 February–3 March 1894), cited by Charle, *Naissance des "intellectuels,"* 115.

101. These articles, which were part of a *Figaro* series on "Les Littérateurs et la politique," are also included in Huret's *Interviews de littérature et d'art*. Zola's interview was originally published on 4 August 1893, pgs. 41–45; Adam's on 6 September 1893, pgs. 49–53.

102. Barrès, "Réflexions: les frères de Bernadette de Lourdes," *La Cocarde*, 1 February 1895.

103. Henry Fèvre, "Indications politiques," *Les Entretiens politiques et littéraires* 7, no. 48 (10 August 1893):97–100.

104. Lazare, "L'Ecrivain et l'art social," 1.

105. Bérenger, *L'Aristocratie intellectuelle*, 78.

106. Rebell, *Union*, 36–37. Just as the aristocracies of birth and wealth needed the intellectual to survive, so, too, did he feel that the intellectual needed to create an aristocratic public for his art.

107. Mazel, *Synergie*, 342–343; Maurras, "Le Privilège des meilleurs."

108. Bérenger, "La Science, la démocratie et le christianisme" of *L'Aristocratie intellectuelle*, chapter 3, 59–76.

109. Régis Debray, *Teachers, Writers, Celebrities*, trans. Francis Mulhern (London, Eng.: New Left Books, 1981), 50–51.

110. Charle does mention the parallels between "dominants-dominés," that is, anti-Dreyfusards from the avant-garde; and the "dominés-dominés," the Dreyfusards who came from the avant-garde, but his analysis is not sufficiently developed. Charle, *Naissance des "intellectuels,"* 213–214.

111. Worth noting is that university intellectuals laid claim to scientific method, even in literature; witness the case of Gustave Lanson. Their disdain of litterateurs was linked to a view of literature as "effeminate" and therefore subversive. Christopher Forth, "Intellectual Anarchy and Imaginary Otherness: Gender, Class, and Pathology in French Intellectual Discourse, 1890–1900," *Sociological Quarterly* 37, no. 4 (Fall 1996):662–663.

112. Unlike university professors and established litterateurs who possessed institutional backing, avant-garde intellectuals could point only to their artistic "purity."

113. Pascal Ory and Jean-François Sirinelli, *Les Intelllectuels en France, de l'Affaire Dreyfus à nos jours* (Paris: Armand Colin, 1986), 8.

114. Retté, "L'Art et l'anarchie," *La Plume*, 46.

115. Therefore, concludes Eugen Weber, Barrès could afford to see himself as a "socialist," since he had less to fear from the proletariat than from the lower-middle classes. "Inheritance, Dilettantism, and the Politics of Maurice Barrès," in *My France: Politics, Culture, Myth* (Cambridge, Mass.: Belknap Press of Harvard University Press, 1991), 226–243.

116. Proletarians, declared Germain, were not the only "damned of the social order." So, too, were intellectuals, who had been humiliated both by the public's rejection and by the need to earn a living. Indeed, the plight of the intellectual was more serious because without "l'intellectif" a nation would destroy itself, "Aux intellectuels," *Les Entretiens*, 41.

117. See Susanna Barrows, *Distorting Mirrors: Visions of the Crowd in Late-Nineteenth-Century France* (New Haven, Conn.: Yale University Press, 1981) and Robert A. Nye, *The Origins of Crowd Psychology: Gustave Le Bon and the Crisis of Mass Democracy in the Third Republic* (Beverly Hills, Calif.: Sage Publications, 1975).

Chapter 4

1. Stephen Wilson, *Ideology and Experience: Antisemitism in France at the Time of the Dreyfus Affair* (East Brunswick, NJ: Associated University Press, 1982), 606–610.

2. On the construction of French national and cultural identity during the second half of the Third Republic, see Herman Lebovics, *True France: the Wars over Cultural Identity, 1900–1945* (Ithaca, NY: Cornell University Press, 1992; 1994).

3. Pierre Birnbaum, *Anti-Semitism in France: A Political History from Léon Blum to the Present*, trans. Miriam Kochan (Cambridge, Mass.: Basil Blackwell, 1992). See especially "Introduction: Assessing Anti-Semitism in France," 1–25. Both types of anti-Semitism could and did coexist. Birnbaum feels that Drumont and Barrès represent the older, economic tradition of anti-Semitism, whereas Maurras truly inaugurates the newer, political anti-Semitism. I am not sure that I would draw as sharp a line between Barrès and Maurras. See Birnbaum, *Anti Semitism*, 89, and 95.

4. In establishing this paradigm, I do not mean to oversimplify an extremely complex problem. Not only were a number of assimilated Jewish intellectuals inspired by Barrès's writings to return to their own Jewish roots, similarly, the Action française had a broad appeal, attracting—for however brief a time—such intellectuals as André Gide and Jewish intellectuals as

Daniel Halévy. On Gide and the Action française, see Martha Hanna, "What did André Gide see in the Action française?" *Historical Reflections / Réflexions historiques* 17, no. 1 (1991):2–22; on Halévy and the Action française, see Stephen Wilson, "The 'Action française' in French Intellectual Life," *The Historical Journal* 12, no. 2 (1969):346–348. I would like to point out, however, that most assimilated Jewish intellectuals attempted to reconcile their Jewish heritage and their ideal of Frenchness by appealing to such universal attributes.

5. Gobineau and Vacher de Lapouge notwithstanding; both these racial theorists were more influential in Germany than in their own native France. See Robert Byrnes, *Anti-Semitism in Modern France, vol. 1, The Prologue to the Dreyfus Affair* (New Brunswick, NJ: Rutgers University Press, 1950), 79, and George Mosse, *The Crisis of German Ideology: Intellectual Origins of the Third Reich* (New York: Howard Fertig, 1981), 91, and 99. Stephen Wilson speaks of Maurras's distaste for racial theories: "History and Traditionalism: Maurras and the Action française," *Journal of the History of Ideas* 29, no. 3 (July–September 1968):371.

For a comparative perspective on anti-Semitism, see Léon Poliakov, *The History of Anti-Semitism, vol. 3, From Voltaire to Wagner*, trans. Miriam Kochan (New York: Vanguard Press, 1975), and Albert S. Lindemann, *The Jew Accused: Three Anti-Semitic Affairs (Dreyfus, Beilis, Frank, 1894–1915)*; (New York: Cambridge University Press, 1991). Worth noting is the fact that German anti-Semites associated anti-Semitic sentiments with anti-French ones just as French anti-Semites associated their anti-Semitic prejudices with anti-German ones. In both countries, the Jew was not only the other, but also was linked to what was seen as the very antithesis of national identity: French qualities in one case and Germanic ones in the other.

6. According to Stephen Wilson, "Assimilationism, in effect, by denying Jewish particularity, by linking antisemitism to that particularity, and by treating both as phenomena that would simply fade away in the course of time, tended to negate the very idea of a Jewish reaction to antisemitism," *Ideology and Experience*, 693.

7. Byrnes, *Anti-Semitism in Modern France*, 285. See also 269.

8. Stephen Wilson, *Ideology and Experience*, 609–610.

9. Rebell, *Union des trois artistocraties* (Paris: Bibliothèque artistique et littéraire, 1894). Rebell cited this as a trend of the nineteenth century, 40.

10. Charles Maurras, *L'Avenir de l'intelligence*, published in *Romantisme et Révolution* (Paris: Nouvelle Librairie nationale, 1925), 62.

11. Maurras, *Avenir*, 43. See also Rebell, *Union*, 34.

12. Barrès, *Mes Cahiers*, vol. 1:1896–1898 (Paris: Plon, 1929), 158–159.

13. Edouard Drumont *La France juive*, vol. 2, (Paris: Editions du Trident, La Librairie française, 1986), 191–192. In the same volume of *La*

France juive, he quoted the often repeated story of Marie Antoinette correcting an intendant who dared to refer to a writer simply by his last name: "When the King or I speak of a writer, we always say Monsieur Sedaine," 193–194.

14. "... the new generation no longer respects the written idea, the notion of the writer's true right of expression," Edouard Drumont, *Testament d'un antisémite* (Paris: Editions du Trident, La Librairie française, 1988), 80.

15. Edouard Drumont, *La Dernière Bataille* (Paris: Editions du Trident, La Librairie française, 1986), 316–317.

16. See Christophe Charle, *La Crise littéraire à l'époque du naturalisme: roman, théâtre, politique* (Paris: Presses de l'Ecole Normale Supérieure, 1979).

17. Maurras, *Avenir*, 81.

18. Drumont, *Testament d'un antisémite*, 58.

19. Drumont, *La France juive*, 2:191–192.

20. Rebell, *Union*, 7 (footnote).

21. See Richard D. Sonn, *Anarchism and Cultural Politics in Fin-de-siècle France* (Lincoln, Neb.: University of Nebraska Press, 1989), 31–48.

22. Rebell did not believe that writers—he mentioned Henri de Régnier as an example—should deliberately isolate themselves from the public, but he could not blame them given the current state of literary affairs, *Union*, 7–8.

23. Maurras, *Avenir*, 63.

24. Drumont, *La France juive*, 2:82, and 149.

25. Rebell, *Union*, 9. Rebell believed that democracy was based on a false premise—egalitarianism—and therefore proposed a union of three aristocracies: of intellect, money, and birth to renew French society. He included such wealthy Jews as the Rothschilds and the Péreires in the second group. Here he differed from some of his colleagues of the *Cocarde* and of the Action française in that he was not an anti-Semite. Rebell saved his ire for anarchists and socialists, whom he viewed as enemies of all civilizations. Indeed, he blamed anti-Semitism on the advent of democracy: "Democracy hates all rich men, Christians and Jews alike" (24), whereas Maurras claimed that the democratic spirit was the product of Jews and Protestants: "The democratic spirit is Protestant or Jewish, it is Semitic or German, it does not come from us," *Quand les Français ne s'aimaient pas, chronique d'une renaissance, 1895–1905* (Paris: Nouvelle Librairie nationale, 1916), 124. Rebell revised his text after the Affair for publication in *L'Action française* (15 August and 1 September 1905). He regretted especially that

the "Jewish aristocracy" had thrown its lot in with the socialists during the Affair. See Victor Nguyen, "Note sur le problème de l'antisémitisme maurrassien," *L'Idée de la race dans la pensée politique française contemporaine*, eds. Pierre Guirard and Emile Temime (Paris: Editions du CNRS, 1977), 155.

26. Rebell, *Union,* 28.

27. Maurras, *Avenir,* 45–46.

28. Ibid., 39.

29. Ibid., 78. He developed this idea more fully in *Quand,* 73.

30. Maurras, *Avenir,* 39–40.

31. Barrès, *Mes Cahiers.* As the following entry from 1898 illustrates: vol. 2:54.

32. Pierre Lasserre, *La doctrine officielle de l'Université,* 4th ed. (Paris: Garnier Frères, 1913).

33. Maurras, *Quand,* 270. Maurras spoke often of the disorganization of intellects characterized by an excess of individualism brought on by the Revolution and vulgarized by Romanticism: *Au signe de Flore: souvenirs de vie politique* (Paris: Les Oeuvres représentatives, 1931), 61. He developed this theme in a number of works, but most explicitly in *Trois Idées politiques.* See *Romantisme et Révolution,* which contains *Trois Idées,* 243–289. As Richard Sonn has pointed out to me, it is ironic that the German philosopher Kant was identified with individualism and anarchy rather than the more usual association of Germany with statism and collectivism à la Marx and Hegel. The use of Kantian theories for universalist ends by modernist intellectuals in France also offers an interesting point of comparison with the interpretation of Kant by certain German Volkish politicians and writers. Such anti-Semites as Houston Stewart Chamberlain used Kant to postulate the existence of intrinsic German racial values. Mosse, *The Crisis of German Ideology,* 88–89; 94–95.

34. Barrès, *Scènes et doctrines du nationalisme* (Paris: Editions du Trident, La Librairie française, 1987), 65.

35. Cited in Barrès, *Cahiers,* 1:94.

36. Barrès, *Cahiers,* 2:83.

37. Ibid., 59.

38. Ibid., 84. See also 123: "there are many truths." This idea of Truth(s) was developed more fully in *Scènes et doctrines du nationalisme,* under the heading "Qu'est-ce que la vérité?" in which Barrès spoke of French justice and French truth, pg. 15.

39. Barrès, *Cahiers,* 2:84. Barrès expanded this theme in *Scènes et doctrines,* 30.

40. *Cahiers*, 1:147, and 174, respectively.

41. Maurras, *Quand*, 29. Maurras traced this decline to the French admiration for Fichte (Barrès, by the way, was an admirer of Fichte), "Democracy is an abominable upheaval. . . . Romanticism seemed to us a great error, the Revolution an act of profound stupidity," 126. On the Revolution, Maurras wrote, "The ideas of the so-called French Revolution (against which all of our greatest traditions protest in horror) have completely disfigured the Latin world," 143.

42. Ibid., 36, 95.

43. Ibid., 269. Indeed, Kantian lay morality had succeeded the cathechism, becoming the basis for popular morality, 269–270. See also 95.

44. Barrès, *Scènes et doctrines*, 46. A caveat by Barrès—he did not wish to be confused with "Congregationists," who saw their Catholic schools as rivals of the state schools. He specifically opposed the Kantianism of the republican university, page 45 (note 2).

45. Maurras, *Quand*, 217. He had developed this theme of "métèques" in his earlier writings. See Stephen Wilson, "L'Action française et le mouvement nationaliste français entre les années 1890 et 1900," *Etudes maurrassiennes*, no. 4 (1980):309–322.

46. Maurras, *Quand*, 219–220.

47. Barrès, *Scènes et doctrines*, 39.

48. Maurras, *Au signe de Flore*, 54.

49. Drumont, *Testament d'un antisémite*, 61. Drumont saw the influence of Jews everywhere—especially in the press, where he felt that they had taken over. He claimed that even journalists who were sympathetic to anti-Semitism were afraid to manifest their beliefs for fear of having all doors to the press in France closed to them.

50. Michael Marrus, *The Politics of Assimilation: A Study of the French Jewish Community at the Time of the Dreyfus Affair* (Oxford, Eng.: Clarendon Press, 1971), 29, and 31.

51. Ibid., 29.

52. Paula Hyman, *From Dreyfus to Vichy: The Remaking of French Jewry, 1906–1939* (New York: Columbia University Press, 1979), 20.

53. Thibaudet states that they brought to the literary world of that time "a precocious, succinct, brilliant, ardent," and "urban intellect." *Histoire de la littérature française de Chateaubriand à Valéry* (Paris: Stock, 1936; Marabout 1981), 415–416.

54. Hyman, *From Dreyfus to Vichy*, 22.

55. Durkheim expressed this opinion in *Suicide*, cited by Stephen Lukes, *Emile Durkheim: His Life and Work* (New York: Harper and Row,

1972), 208. Durkheim, like other assimilated Jews, manifested a certain hostility to practicing Jews, for he claims in the same passage that Jews did not learn to replace their prejudices by ideas based on reflection, but simply to better confront their enemies.

56. Salomon and Théodore Reinach: the first was a philologist and archaeologist and the second was a historian who later taught at the Collège de France.

57. Marrus, *The Politics of Assimilation,* 42. This era also witnessed the arrival of Jewish immigrants from the East who discomfited their assimilated coreligionists as much as they did anti-Semites.

58. Robert Byrnes, *Anti-Semitism in Modern France,* 155.

59. Wilson, *Ideology and Experience,* 256–57.

60. Byrnes, *Anti-Semitism in Modern France,* 262.

61. Cited in English by Arthur Gold et Robert Fizdale, *The Life of Misia Sert* (New York: Alfred Knopf, 1980), 30. The entry is dated 26 January 1896. Léon Daudet noted at the time of the Affair that Jews had "infiltrated" the press, singling out the "Jewish" *Revue blanche*: *Au temps de Judas,* (Paris: Grasset, 1933), 111.

62. When *La Revue blanche* broke with Barrès over Dreyfus, his response was: "A Jewish review, which defends its own. What could be more natural?" Cited in Stephen Wilson, *Ideology and Experience,* 717. The *Revue blanche*'s editors deliberately chose Lucien Herr, the librarian of the Ecole Normale, to excommunicate the former "Prince of Youth." His article "A M. Barrès," published in the 15 February 1898 issue, bid adieu to Barrès on behalf of the review's members. Not only did Herr exert a moral influence on the members of their generation, but he was also a Gentile.

63. Brunetière, "Après le procès," *La Revue des deux mondes* 146 (15 March 1898):430.

64. Maurras, *Quand,* 83. Maurras dedicated an entire chapter of the book to Monod, "Sentinelle allemande dans l'Université," 71–104. He also developed a long diatribe against the entire Monod family in *Au signe de Flore.*

65. Maurras, *Quand,* 269.

66. Ibid., 113.

67. Both Benda and Maurras were positivist rationalists, each in his own way. On the attacks against Bergson by the Action française by Benda, see Romeo Arbour, *Bergson et les lettres françaises* (Paris: José Corti, 1955), 198–207.

68. In seeing Bergson strictly as an "anti-intellectualist," both sides misinterpreted his ideas. On Bergson and the French university milieu,

see Phyllis H. Stock, "Students versus the University in Pre-World Paris," *French Historical Studies* 7, no. 2 (Spring 1971):93–110, and Paul M. Cohen, "Reason and Faith: The Bergsonian Catholic Youth of Pre-War France," *Historical Reflections/Réflexions historiques* 13, nos. 2–3 (1986):473–497 for Bergson's influence in Catholic circles.

69. Given the fact that Bergson was known to favor a broad, classical education, which was also favored by Action française critic Pierre Lasserre, how does one explain Lasserre's following assertion: "I fear that the language of Bérénice and of Antigone, which is anything but fluid or amorphous, but rather possesses a vital energy and a great coherence, will not be able to sing to the soul of M. Bergson." Cited in French by Arbour, *Bergson et les lettres françaises*, 202. This sounds suspiciously close to Barrès's contention that a peasant could understand Pascal and Corneille in a way that a "foreign" Jew never could.

70. As H. Stuart Hughes notes in *Consciousness and Society: The Reorientation of European Social Thought, 1890–1930* (New York: Vintage Books; 1961; 1977), 58.

71. Maurras, *Trois Idées*, 269–270; Barrès, *Scènes et doctrines*, 47–51.

72. The anti-Semitism of Maurras and Barrès predate the Affair. On Maurras and anti-Semitism, see Victor Nguyen, "Note sur le problème de l'antisémitisme maurrassien," in *L'Idée de la race*, 139–155. See also Nguyen, *Aux origines de l'Action française: intelligence et politique à l'aube du XXème siècle* (Paris: Fayard, 1991). On Barrès, see Zeev Sternhell, "Le Déterminisme physiologique et racial à la base du nationalisme de Maurice Barrès et de Jules Soury," *L'Idée de la race*, 117–138.

73. Barrès, *Scènes et doctrines*, 50. In the same passage, Barrès quoted Jules de Gaultier who stated that Protestantism was less dangerous as a religion than in its lay form which gave the appearance of being free thinking.

74. Maurras, *Quand*, 104.

75. *Cahiers*, 1:216, and 232, respectively.

76. In a letter dated 14 November 1897, *La République ou le roi: correspondance inédite, 1888–1923: Maurice Barrès-Charles Maurras* (Paris: Plon, 1970), 150.

77. Barrès, *Cahiers*, 2:140. In another passage of the same volume of his *Cahiers*, Barrès observed that priests said "je crois" (I believe) whereas he said "je sais" (I know), 141. Similarly, like his mentor Jules Soury, he noted that Jews "believed" while Aryans "knew," 118.

78. Cited in Barrès, *Cahiers* 2:151.

79. This is not to say that Barrès denied instinct, for as his writings abundantly show, he firmly believed instinct to be the basis of all thought.

He even criticized the excessive "rationality" of Maurras, saying he had elaborated a theory that was in accordance with his instincts. Barrès, *Cahiers*, 2:177. Indeed, Maurras himself claimed the positivist heritage of rationality. See Maurras on Auguste Comte, included in *Romantisme et Révolution*, 91–127.

80. Birnbaum, "Grégoire, Dreyfus, Drancy et Copernic," ed. Pierre Nora, *Les Lieux de mémoire*, vol. 3, *Les France*, part 1, *Conflits et Partages* (Paris: Gallimard, 1992), 561–613.

81. Fritz Stern, *The Politics of Cultural Despair: A Study in the Rise of Germanic Ideology* (Berkeley, Calif.: University of California Press, 1961).

82. In *Quand*, Maurras wrote "Letters have led us to politics. . . ." Préface, XV. On the links between Maurras's literary theories and his political ones, see Stephen Wilson, "History and Traditionalism," 376–377. See also David Carroll for the relationship of the esthetic and the political in Maurras's writings, *French Literary Fascism: Nationalism, Anti-Semitism, and the Ideology of Culture* (Princeton, N.J.: Princeton University Press, 1995), especially chapter 3, "The Nation as Artwork," 71–96.

83. George L. Mosse and Carl E. Schorske have spoken eloquently of the estheticization of politics in Germany and Austria, respectively. See Mosse's *The Crisis of German Ideology* and *The Nationalization of the Masses: Political Symbolism and Mass Movements in Germany from the Napoleonic Wars through the Third Reich* (Ithaca, NY: Cornell University Press, 1991), and Schorske's *Fin-de-Siècle Vienna: Politics and Culture* (New York: Vantage Books, 1981). In the first book, Mosse describes the esthetic aspects of the racism of Volkish politicians, some of whose ideas were rooted in Romanticism. In his book on Vienna in the chapter, "Politics in a New Key: An Austrian Trio," 116–180, Schorske speaks of the estheticism of anti-Semitic politicians Georg von Schönerer and Karl Lueger, as well as of the Zionist Theodor Herzl. In addition, he quotes Herzl referring to Drumont as an "artist," 157.

84. Priscilla Parkhurst Clark, *Literary France: The Making of a Culture* (Berkeley Calif.: University of California Press, 1987), 4–5.

85. This declaration was made in the National Assembly at the time of Jewish emancipation. Cited by Hyman, *From Dreyfus to Vichy*, 5.

86. Hyman, *From Dreyfus to Vichy*, 5–6.

87. See Philip Nord, *The Republican Moment: Struggles for Democracy in Nineteenth-Century France*, especially chapter 4, "Republican Judaism," (Cambridge, Mass.: Harvard University Press, 1995).

88. It is surely no accident, observes Stephen Wilson, that the number of prominent Jewish intellectuals involved in Dreyfusard organizations, particularly in the Ligue des Droits de l'Homme, was high. Similarly, almost no specifically Jewish Dreyfusard organizations existed. Wilson,

Ideology and Experience, 715–716. Among Jewish Dreyfusards were Joseph Reinach and Paul Meyer, both of whom served on the national committee of the Ligue. Meyer later became vice president, Victor Basch, president. Durkheim was a founding member. The *Revue blanche*'s director, Thadée Natanson, sank the family fortune in the Ligue to the extent that he was later obliged to liquidate the review and sell its publishing house to Fasquelle. That is not to say that no Jews were involved in the anti-Dreyfusard movement, but they were the exception rather than the rule. At the *Revue blanche*, Lucien Muhlfeld was anti-Dreyfusard as was the humorist Pierre Veber, whose fellow *Revue blanche* member and brother-in-law Tristan Bernard was an ardent Dreyfusard. Bergson, of course, is one of the most important exceptions to the involvement of Jewish intellectuals in the Affair, maintaining a strict neutrality. One must therefore not assume that allegiance to Dreyfus was automatic or natural for assimilated Jews.

89. Bergson was also a graduate of Condorcet.

90. Bernard Lazare, "L'Antisémitisme au Moyen Age," *La Revue blanche* 6 (April 1894):318–332. Parts of Lazare's article were incorporated into his book *L'Antisémitisme, son histoire et ses causes historiques*.

91. The references in this chapter are to the most recent edition of Lazare's book, published by Les Editions 1900 in 1990 with a preface by Jean-Denis Bredin. Muhlfeld's comments on the book are somewhat puzzling. The review was much too short for a book of such importance, and Muhlfeld barely addressed the issues it presented. He wrote at the beginning of his review that Lazare's book was as "amusing as a novel," yet observed that the topic was a worthy, indeed, timely one. A point worth noting: Muhlfeld concluded that if he had the time, he would prove that the underlying cause of contemporary anti-Semitism was not Jewish exclusivity, as Lazare claimed (a misrepresentation of Lazare's ideas—Lazare stated that this was one cause of anti-Semitism), but increased assimilation—a perspicacious comment. Muhlfeld, an anti-Dreyfusard, subsequently disassociated himself from the *Revue blanche*, in part because the review assumed an increasingly politicized stance, specifically, a Dreyfusard stance. In addition, his newfound position as drama critic of *L'Echo de Paris* undoubtedly made him more cautious and conservative than his *Revue blanche* peers. Whether he was a Jewish anti-Semite is not altogether clear, for he maintained a prudent silence during the Affair. Muhlfeld's career came to an abrupt end with his premature death in 1902.

92. A. B. Jackson estimates that about half of its collaborators were Jewish: *La Revue blanche: (1889–1903): origine, influence, bibliographie* (Paris: Minard, 1960), 16. I would add that the proportion of those who comprised the review's inner circle was even higher.

93. Henry Bérenger, *Le Mercure de France* 21 (January 1897):208–209. This word "bilatéralité" is striking. It could easily be used by anti-Semites,

who claimed that Jews could never be truly French because of their dual allegiance.

94. Durkheim came from a family of rabbis. The Rabbi of Epinal, his father was also the Chief Rabbi of the Vosges and Haute Marne. Steven Lukes, *Durkheim*, 39–40. There is reason to believe that the combined influence of his Ecole Normale classmates Jaurès and Bergson led to Durkheim's final break with Judaism, 44.

95. Léon Blum, "Les Nouvelles Conversations de Goethe avec Eckermann," published originally in the *Revue blanche* during the time of the Affair, were later revised and pubished in book form and are included in the *Oeuvre de Léon Blum*, vol. 1 (Paris: Albin Michel, 1954), 266. Michael Marrus, Pierre Birnbaum, and others have defined Franco-Judaism as a secular and civic adaptation to living in a Christian world. Jewish identity and practice in such a context were private matters. Birnbaum, *Anti-Semitism in France*, 32, and Marrus, *The Politics of Assimilation,* 100–101.

96. Julien Benda, *La Jeunesse d'un clerc* (Paris: Gallimard, 1936), 47. Nelly Wilson describes a similar situation in the case of Bernard Lazare: *Bernard Lazare: Anti-Semitism and the Problem of Jewish Identity in Late-Nineteenth-Century France* (New York, NY: Cambridge University Press, 1978), 6. Other Jews at the *Revue blanche* testify to a similar upbringing, among them Tristan Bernard.

97. Georges Davy, cited by Lukes, *Durkheim*, 40.

98. Benda, *La Jeunesse d'un clerc*, 34; 36–37; 42.

99. Benda claims that he was somewhat shocked by his father's statement, in large part because the gains of the Revolution were a given for those of his generation, but also because he did not believe in gratitude, preferring instead what he calls an "independence of spirit." Ibid.

100. Response to Henri Dagan, *Enquête sur l'antisémitisme* (Paris: Stock, 1899), 60.

101. Blum, "Nouvelles Conversations," 262. This entry is dated 11 April 1899.

102. Benda, *La Jeunesse d'un clerc*, 45.

103. Blum, "Nouvelles Conversations," 263. Anti-Semitism was thus seen as part of a battle between clerical and anticlerical forces.

104. Gustave Kahn, "L'Idée nationaliste," *La Revue blanche* 20 (15 Novembre 1899):401–405.

105. Benda, *La Jeunesse d'un clerc*, 42–43.

106. Ibid., 43.

107. Blum, "Nouvelles Conversations," 263–264.

108. Blum published a number of articles pertaining to controversial political matters under the pseudonym of "un juriste." "Le Procès [Zola]," "Les Lois scélérates," and "L'Article 7." These articles, first published in *La Revue blanche*, are reproduced in Blum, *Oeuvre*, 1:343–390.

109. Blum continues: "Let us rejoice then for young Jews . . . if even as the result of annoying acts and despicable passions, they are set on the right path. Their real nature will be preserved. . . ." "Nouvelles Conversations," 264.

110. In *La Jeunesse d'un clerc*, Benda writes with distaste and irritation of fellow Jews who told him that as Jews, they were proud of his books. He also claims that although he was successful in his studies, he felt no need to succeed in order to "honor his race," 44.

111. Hyman, *From Dreyfus to Vichy*, 11–12.

112. Blum, "Nouvelles Conversations," 267. Such a statement seems naive and inconsistent with other statements by Blum. At the very least, it indicates a temporary confusion about the challenge of anti-Semitism.

113. Cited by Dagan, *Enquête sur l'antisémitisme*, 62–63.

114. Durkheim valued corporate bodies but he did not envision them as territorial units, as did Maurras and Barrès, but based on a division of labor. Many anarchists and socialists recognized that Barrès's version of decentralization merely involved a devolution of power to localities rather than a real sharing of power with those governed and that local governments could suppress individual liberty just as well as national ones. See Georges Dalbert, "Fédéralisme et provincialisme," *La Revue blanche* 9 (15 July 1895):91–93.

115. Blum, "Les Livres," *La Revue blanche* 14 (15 November 1897): 293; Birnbaum, *Anti-Semitism In France*, 38–39.

116. The state was the "very organ of social thought." Quoted by Steven Lukes, *Durkheim*, 269; Birnbaum, *Anti-Semitism in France*, 234–235.

117. Cited by Lukes, *Durkheim*, 46.

118. William Logue, *From Philosophy to Sociology: The Evolution of French Liberalism, 1870–1914* (DeKalb, IL: Northern Illinois University Press, 1983), 176.

119. Bernard Lazare, "Juifs et Israélites," *Les Entretiens politiques et littéraires* 1 (September 1890). For a discussion of this article, see Nelly Wilson, *Bernard Lazare*, 74–82.

120. "La solidarité juive," *Les Entretiens politiques et littéraires* 1 (October 1890), cited by Nelly Wilson, *Bernard Lazare*, 76; Benda, *La Jeunesse d'un clerc*, 50.

121. *La Revue blanche* 15 (1 February 1898):165.

122. As Stephen Wilson has noted, "Jewish anticlerical antisemitism, motivated by hostility to the Judaic religion and the ghetto mentality which it helped to foster, was not uncommon, especially among intellectuals. . . ." (708).

123. Tristan Bernard, *Souvenirs et anecdotes* (Paris: Le Cherche Midi, 1992), 22–23.

124. Dagan, *Enquête sur l'antisémitisme*, 60.

125. Stephen Wilson, *Ideology and Experience*, 692–725.

126. Benda, for example, spoke not only of the "Jewish race," but also of the "race" of intellectuals, 202–203. See Marrus, *The Politics of Assimilation*, 10–27.

127. Durkheim, "L'Individualisme et les intellectuels," *La Revue bleue* (2 July 1898). Although I have consulted the original text, I will be referring to the translation published by Steven Lukes in *Political Studies* 17 (1969):14–30, referred to hereafter as Lukes, *Political Studies*.

128. Lukes, *Political Studies*, 26.

129. This theme was, of course, an embarrassment for many French Jews. See Marrus, *The Politics of Assimilation*, 185–186.

130. James Darmesteter was Ernest Renan's student: Marrus, *The Politics of Assimilation*, 100–110. Although Lazare disagreed with Renan on several points (in particular, with his racial theories), he did build on Renan's view of Jews as agents of change. See the chapters "L'Esprit révolutionnaire dans le judaïsme" and "Les Juifs et les transformations sociales," Bernard Lazare, *L'Antisémitisme*, 303–362. See also Nelly Wilson, *Bernard Lazare*, 275–277, n. 16.

131. Lazare concludes that anti-Semitism would be defeated by the forces of social revolution in his book, "Les Destinées de l'antisémitisme," *L'Antisémitisme*, 389–409. He came to a different conclusion later. For proof of the continuity of Lazare's thoughts concerning the revolutionary legacy of Judaism, see "La Conception sociale du judaïsme et du peuple juif," *La Grande Revue*, 1 September 1899, cited by Marrus, *The Politics of Assimilation*, 190. Nelly Wilson and others have pointed to the dichotomy of the book. The first part is a historical account of anti-Semitism from Greco-Roman times to the French Revolution. Written largely before 1892, it reflects Lazare's early anti-Semitic notions. The second part of the book, which examines anti-Semitism during modern times, was written between 1893 and 1894. It was conceived in a different spirit, in order to combat anti-Semitism. The chapter on the revolutionary spirit of Judaism, which I examine at length in this chapter, is part of the second part of the book. See N. Wilson, *Bernard Lazare*, 90–107. See also Jean-Denis Bredin's re-

cent biography of Lazare, *Bernard Lazare: de l'anarchiste au prophète* (Paris: Editions de Fallois, 1992), 116–131.

132. Lazare criticized "pusillanimous" Jews in "Contre l'antisémitisme," *Le Voltaire*, 20 May 1896, cited by Marrus, *The Politics of Assimilation*, 182.

133. Blum, "Nouvelles Conversations," 263–264.

134. Blum, *Souvenirs sur l'Affaire* (Paris: Gallimard 1935, reedition 1981), 34. As we have seen, Blum himself nearly advocated the course of behavior he is criticizing here. He was writing in the 1930s with the benefit of hindsight.

135. Blum, "Nouvelles Conversations," 265.

136. Ibid.

137. Kahn, "L'Idée nationaliste," 404. See also Lazare, *L'Antisémitisme*, 343; and Blum, "Nouvelles Conversations," 267.

138. Blum, "Nouvelles Conversations," 266. Blum points out that this "force" was not merely destructive but led Jews to rebuild as well.

139. Lazare, *L'Antisémitisme*, 304.

140. Benda tells us that as a "rationaliste absolu," he believed in Truth more than in Justice, which he found to be a less clearly defined concept and which, moreover, was imbued with romantic overtones, 198. Blum speaks of the "rational faith" of Jews in "Nouvelles Conversations," 266–267. Lazare tells us that the Talmud is impregnated with rationalism and that this spirit of "libre examen" is destructive: *L'Antisémitisme*, 330–331.

141. Blum, "Nouvelles Conversations," 267.

142. Lazare, *L'Antisémitisme*, 310.

143. Ibid., 314–317.

144. Ibid., 319–320. In a later work, Lazare spoke of the universal applicability of Jewish consciousness, calling Jews "soldiers of justice and human fraternity" for all humankind. *Le Nationalisme juif*, originally published in 1898, has been included in a recent collection of Lazare's essays, *Juifs et antisémites* (Paris: Editions Allia, 1992), edited by Philippe Oriol, 161.

145. Excerpt in Raoul Girardet, *Le Nationalisme français, 1871–1914* (Paris: Seuil, 1983), 143.

146. Blum, "Nouvelles Conversations," 264.

147. Nelly Wilson, *Bernard Lazare*, 98.

148. Benda, *La Jeunesse d'un clerc*, 48–49. Lazare in his later writings associated his concept of Jewish consciousness with universalism,

thereby distinguishing it from the "national exclusiveness" of such anti-Dreyfusards as Barrès.

149. Blum stated that socialists were even more wary of anti-Semites than the Jews. "Nouvelles Conversations," 262. While this was true during the Affair, it was not the case previously. Lazare in his early writings saw anti-Semitism in terms of a conflict between Jewish and Catholic capitalism.

150. This phenomenon has been described by both Jean-Paul Sartre and Albert Memmi; see Sartre's *Anti-Semite and Jew*, trans. George J. Becker (New York: Schocken Books, 1948), and Memmi's *Portrait d'un juif* (Paris, Gallimard, 1962).

151. Lazare was alone in depicting himself as a Jew coming to the aid of another Jew: "I want people to say that I was the first to speak out, that the first to rise up for the Jewish martyr was a Jew" ("Lettre ouverte à M. Trarieux," cited by Nelly Wilson, *Bernard Lazare,* 160).

152. Lazare, too, believed before the Affair that anti-Semitism would disappear. In the wake of the Affair, however, he came to the conclusion that there was no solution to anti-Semitism: "Lettre ouverte à M. Trarieux," *L'Aurore,* 7 June 1899 and "Nécessité d'être soi-même," *Zion,* (30 April 1897), cited by Marrus, *The Politics of Assimilation,* 188.

153. Dominick Lacapra, *Emile Durkheim: Sociologist and Philosopher* (Ithaca, NY: Cornell University Press, 1972), 75.

154. Blum, *Souvenirs sur l'Affaire,* 35.

155. These "guerres franco-françaises" escalated during the 1930s when former Dreyfusard, Socialist and Jew Léon Blum became Prime Minister. Seen in this light, Vichy may be viewed as the revenge of the anti-Dreyfusards; indeed, Maurras referred to Vichy's downfall as the "revenge of Dreyfus." See the special issue of *Vingtième Siècle,* no. 5 (January–March 1985), specifically Michel Winock's article "Les Affaires Dreyfus," reprinted in *Nationalisme, antisémitisme et fascisme en France* (Paris: Seuil, 1990), 157–185.

156. In an essay entitled "Reflections on the Jews in France," Eugen Weber argues that the Jewish question in France was strictly a Jewish question, *The Jews in Modern France,* eds. Frances Malino and Bernard Wasserstein (Hanover, NH: University Press of New England, 1985), 8.

Chapter 5

1. This chapter is greatly indebted to my reading of the works of Robert Nye, George Mosse, Edward Berenson, and Karen Offen whose pathbreaking efforts on nationalism and sexuality have shaped my own thinking on the topic. I have also found the works of Joan Scott, *Gender*

and the Politics of History (New York: Columbia University Press, 1988); Debora Silverman and Susanna Barrows extremely useful. All works, unless otherwise listed here, are cited in subsequent footnotes.

2. On the crisis of male identity in France at this time, see Annelise Maugue, *L'Identité masculine en crise au tournant du siècle, 1871–1914* (Paris: Editions Rivages, 1987).

3. Edward Berenson, *Trial of Madame Caillaux* (Berkeley, Calif.: University of California Press, 1992), 169, and 183.

4. Berenson, *Trial of Madame Caillaux,* 169. Robert Nye observes that "honor was embodied in bourgeois men as a set of normative sexual characteristics that reflected the strategies of bourgeois social reproduction." *Masculinity and Male Codes of Honor in Modern France* (New York: Oxford University Press, 1993), 9.

5. Nye, *Masculinity and Male Codes of Honor,* 86.

6. Berenson, *Trial of Madame Caillaux,* 170.

7. Ibid., 170, and Elaine Showalter, *Sexual Anarchy: Gender and Culture at the Fin de Siècle* (New York, Viking, 1990), 6.

8. George L. Mosse, *Nationalism and Sexuality: Middle-Class Morality and Sexual Norms in Modern Europe* (Madison, Wis.: University of Wisconsin Press, 1985), 13. Mosse notes that sexual perversion was thought to be as threatening to middle class life as the restlessness of the lower classes, 25.

9. Ibid., 9.

10. Cited by Berenson, *Trial of Madame Caillaux,* 117.

11. Ibid., 115.

12. Max Nordau, *Degeneration*, introduction by George L. Mosse (New York: Howard Fertig, 1968), 25. See Christopher Forth, "Intellectual Anarchy and Imaginary Otherness: Gender, Class, and Pathology in French Intellectual Discourse, 1890–1900," *Sociological Quarterly* 37, no. 4 (Fall 1996):645–671.

13. Remy de Gourmont, as cited by Nye, *Masculinity and Male Codes of Honor,* 94.

14. Victor Joze, "Le Féminisme et le bon sens," *La Plume*, no. 154 (15 September 1895):391. The equation of sex and sexuality is clearly present in this article. Joze declared that women only existed in function of their ovaries.

15. Ibid., 392.

16. Mirbeau was lamenting the arrival of a woman on the steering committee of la Société des Gens de Lettres. "Propos galants sur les femmes"

was first published in *Le Gaulois* and was later reprinted in *Les Ecrivains (1895–1910)* deuxième série (Paris: Flammarion, 1926), 190–191.

17. Jose, "Le Féminisme et le bon sens," 392.

18. Showalter, *Sexual Anarchy,* 8.

19. Mosse, *Nationalism and Sexuality,* 25.

20. Showalter, *Sexual Anarchy,* 6–9 and Forth, *Intellectual Anarchy,* 649–653.

21. Susanna Barrows, *Distorting Mirrors: Visions of the Crowd in Late-Nineteenth-Century France* (New Haven, Conn.: Yale University Press, 1981), and Debora Silverman, *Art Nouveau in Fin-de-Siècle France: Politics, Psychology and Style* (Berkeley, Calif.: University of California Press, 1989), 73.

22. Christopher Forth, *Intellectual Anarchy,* 659–663.

23. Steven C. Hause and Jennifer Waelti-Walters, eds. *Feminisms of the Belle Epoque: A Historical and Literary Anthology* (Lincoln, Neb.: University of Nebraska Press, 1994), 2. See also Maïté Albistur and Daniel Armogathe, *Histoire du féminisme français,* 2 vols. (Paris: Editions des Femmes, 1977).

24. Jennifer Birkett, *The Sins of the Fathers: Decadence in France 1870–1914* (London: Quartet Books, 1986), 161–162.

25. Cited by Willa Z. Silverman, *The Notorious Life of Gyp: Right-Wing Anarchist in Fin-de-Siècle France* (New York: Oxford University Press, 1995), 67.

26. Julie Sabiani, "Féminisme et dréyfusisme," in *Les Ecrivains et l'Affaire Dreyfus,* edited by Géraldi Leroy, (Orléans: Presses Universitaires de France, 1983), 199–206. During the Dreyfus Affair, anti-Dreyfusards would use the presence of Séverine and other reporters of *La Fronde* in the Dreyfusard camp to designate their opponents as effeminate. Dreyfusards themselves did not necessarily valorize the presence of these women and some found it embarrassing. Indeed, they themselves attacked anti-Dreyfusards as effeminate.

27. G. Idt, " 'L'Intellectuel' avant L'Affaire Dreyfus," *Cahiers de lexicologie* 15 (1969): 35–36. Intelligence, states Idt, was viewed as a "noble faculty," but the intellectual was seen as a "monster."

28. Ibid., 38–42.

29. Nordau, *Degeneration,* 35–36.

30. Léon Blum and Tristan Bernard, "Chronique du Sport," *La Revue blanche* 6 (January 1894):87.

31. Octave Mirbeau, "Le Duel," originally published in *La Révolte* (supplément littéraire), no. 44 (30 July 1892):274, was reprinted in *L'Echo de Paris.*

32. Mosse, *Nationalism and Sexuality*, 13, and 23.

33. Berenson, *Trial of Madame Caillaux*, 170, and 182, and Nye, *Masculinity and Male Codes of Honor*, 155.

34. Mirbeau, "Le Duel," 274–275.

35. Barrès, *Les Déracinés* (Paris: Union Générale d'Editions, 10/18, 1986), 153.

36. Cited by Maugue, *L'Identité Masculine*, 73.

37. Bérenger, *Les Prolétaires intellectuels en France* (Paris: Editions de la Revue, 1901), 27–28. Bérenger, who, like Barrès, feared an "intellectual proletariat," used similar organicist metaphors. He spoke of the rise of this "intellectual proletariat" as an "infection," a "leprosy," and a "social malady." The militarism, which was partly responsible for this state of affairs, was likened to "an armor of the Middle Ages, rusty, infected with vermin [which] would crush, sully the delicate body of a modern woman." The "delicate body" in this case would be that of France, pg. 50.

38. Barrès, *Les Déracinés*, 39.

39. Ibid., 41–42.

40. Ibid., 49, and 51.

41. Ibid., 48.

42. Ibid., 304.

43. Bérenger, *L'Effort* (Paris: Armand Colin, 1895), preface, viii.

44. Ibid., xv.

45. Ibid., xix–xx.

46. Ibid., xxi.

47. Ibid., xxiii–xxix.

48. Charles Maurras, "Le Romantisme féminin," *Romantisme et Révolution* (Paris: Nouvelle Librairie nationale, 1925), 189.

49. The novelist and polemicist Léon Daudet, who was a member of the Action française, shared these ideas on Romanticism. See *Le Stupide 19ème Siècle* in *Souvenirs et polémiques* (Paris: Laffont, 1992), 1183–1331.

50. Nordau, *Degeneration*, 20.

51. Eve Sedwick, as cited by Showalter, *Sexual Anarchy*, 14.

52. Nye, *Masculinity and Male Codes of Honor*, 99–100, and Mosse, *Nationalism and Sexuality*, 27. Robert Nye tells us that the medicalization and pathologization of sexual identity was more widely and deeply developed in France than elsewhere in Europe at the fin de siècle, pg. 102. It

was at this time that homosexuality emerged as a type rather than as an incidental behavior.

53. Nye, *Masculinity and Codes of Honor,* 102–103.

54. Ibid., 108.

55. Ibid., 112–116.

56. See Martha Hanna, "Natalism, Homosexuality, and the Controversy over *Corydon*," in *Homosexuality in France,* edited by Jeffrey Merrick and Bryant T. Ragan Jr. (New York: Oxford University Press, 1996), 202–224.

57. Cited by Mosse, *Nationalism and Sexuality,* 44. Homosexuality, indeed, any type of "perverse" sexuality, was an important theme in Decadent literature. It could be found in the works not only of Huysmans, but also in those of Rachilde, Joséphin Péladan, Remy de Gourmont and others. Such depictions served both to "illustrate" and criticize the excesses of the materialist society of the fin de siècle. See Jennifer Birkett, *The Sins of the Fathers: Decadence in France 1870–1914.* Depictions of homosexuals exist in French literature prior to the fin-de-siècle period. Citing the novels of Balzac and Théophile Gautier among others, Victoria Thompson notes that during the July Monarchy "ambiguous gender and sexual identity functioned as a metaphor for a society in which social and economic boundaries were perceived as permeable." Later, under the Second Empire, same sex sexuality, in particular, lesbianism, which became more negative and pessimistic, was used to condemn the excessive materialism of contemporary bourgeois society [in the novels of Zola, for example] as well as the violent underside of bourgeois rule—a theme further developed by Decadent writers: "Creating Boundaries: Homosexuality and the Changing Social Order in France, 1830–1870," in *Homosexuality in France,* pgs. 105, and 119, respectively.

58. Richard Dellamora, quoted in Showalter, *Sexual Anarchy,* 3.

59. Schwob, too, challenged Huret to a duel but both sets of seconds settled it. See *L'Echo de Paris* for 15 and 17 April, along with *Le Figaro* of 16 and 17 April, as well as Henry Bauër's "Chronique" in *L'Echo de Paris* for 20 April 1895.

60. André Gide, *Oscar Wilde: In Memoriam*, trans. Bernard Frechtman (New York: Philosophical Library, 1949), 13.

61. "Effeminacy," Sinfield writes, "was still flexible, with the potential to refute homosexuality, as well as to imply it." (New York: Columbia University Press, 1994), 93. See also Ed Cohen, "Writing Gone Wilde: Homoerotic Desire in the Closet of Representation," *PMLA* 103 (October 1987):801–813, and Ed Cohen, *Talk on the Wilde Side: Toward a Genealogy of a Discourse on Male Sexualities* (New York: Routledge, 1993).

62. Nordau, *Degeneration*, 317.

63. Ibid., 320.

64. Gaston Jollivet, "L'Affaire Wilde," *Le Gaulois*, 7 April 1895.

65. Gaston Jollivet, "La Police des moeurs," *Le Gaulois*, 15 April 1895.

66. Ibid.

67. Nestor condemned the barbarity of Wilde's sentence while denouncing the Irish writer's behavior, "La Barbarie," *L'Echo de Paris*, 30 May 1895.

68. Octave Mirbeau, "A propos du 'Hard Labour,'" was subsequently published in *Les Ecrivains (1895–1910)* deuxième série, 39–44. Bauër's article "Chronique" was published in *L'Echo de Paris* on 3 June 1895.

69. Octave Mirbeau, "Sur un livre," *Les Ecrivains*, deuxième série, 45, and Henry Bauër, "Chronique," *L'Echo de Paris* of 3 June 1895, as well as "Chronique," 20 April 1895.

70. Henry Bauër, "Chronique," *L'Echo de Paris*, 20 April 1895.

71. Louis Lormel, "A M. Oscar Wilde," *La Plume*, no. 144 (10 April 1895):165.

72. Adolphe Retté, "Chronique des livres: *Le Portrait de Dorian Gray*," *La Plume*, no. 156 (15 October 1895):474–475.

73. Lormel, A M. Oscar Wilde, 165, and Hugues Rebell, "Défense d'Oscar Wilde," *Le Mercure de France* 15 (August 1895):183. This distinction between public and private is an important point of difference between French and "Anglo-Saxon" attitudes.

74. Hugues Rebell, "Défense d'Oscar Wilde," *Le Mercure de France*, 185.

75. Paul Adam, "L'Assaut malicieux," *La Revue blanche* 8 (15 May 1895):458.

76. Ibid., 459–461.

77. Ibid., 462.

78. Lord Alfred Douglas, "Une Introduction à mes poèmes, avec quelques considérations sur l'affaire Oscar Wilde," *La Revue blanche* 10 (1 June 1896):485.

79. Ibid., 486–487.

80. Rebell, "Défense d'Oscar Wilde," *Le Mercure de France*, 187.

81. Stuart Merrill, "Pour Oscar Wilde," *La Plume*, no. 161 (1 January 1896):8. Lormel also referred to Wilde as a madman, not necessarily for his sexual preferences, but because he had actually attempted to prosecute Queensberry, thereby leaving himself vulnerable to prosecution: "A M. Oscar Wilde," *La Plume*, 165.

82. Retté, "Chronique des livres," *La Plume*, 474.

83. Hugues Rebell, "No more than the Puritans, certainly! I have no intention of defending acts of perversity. . . ." "Défense d'Oscar Wilde," *Le Mercure de France*, 185.

84. Louis Lormél, "A M. Oscar Wilde," *La Plume*, 165.

85. Rebell, "Défense d'Oscar Wilde," *Le Mercure de France*, 186.

86. Stuart Merrill, "Pour Oscar Wilde," *La Plume*, 8.

87. Rebell, "Défense d'Oscar Wilde," *Le Mercure de France*, 187–188.

88. Camille Mauclair, "Les Livres," *Le Mercure de France* 15 (August 1895):238.

89. Retté, "Chronique des livres," *La Plume*, 474.

90. See "Tribune libre," in *La Plume*, 15 November, no. 158, and 1 December 1895, no. 159:508–509, and 559–560, respectively.

91. Merrill, "Pour Oscar Wilde," *La Plume*, 10.

92. For a discussion of various "dress rehearsals" for the Dreyfus Affair, see Christophe Charle, *Naissance des "intellectuels": 1880–1910* (Paris: Editions de Minuit, 1990), 126–136.

93. Cited by Mosse, *Nationalism and Sexuality*, 42.

94. Bernard Lazare, "Anarchie et littérature," *La Révolte*, supplément littéraire, no. 24, (24 February–3 March 1894), cited by Charle, *Naissance des "intellectuels,"* 115.

95. The article was subsequently published in *La France intellectuelle* (Paris: Armand Colin, 1899), 119.

96. Karen Offen states that the fascination for military men among neo-traditionalist intellectuals like Barrès is a reassertion of their masculinity, "Depopulation, Nationalism, and Feminism in Fin-de-Siècle France," *American Historical Review* 89, no. 3 (June 1984):648–676.

Chapter 6

1. Paul Gerbod, "L'Ethique héroïque en France (1870–1914)," *La Revue historique*, no. 268 (1982):409–429.

2. Ibid., 424.

3. Ibid., 424–425.

4. Robert A. Nye, *Masculinity and Male Codes of Honor in Modern France* (New York: Oxford University Press, 1993), 225, and Edward

Berenson, *The Trial of Madame Caillaux* (Berkeley, Calif.: University of California Press, 1992), 186–198.

5. The term "intellectual hero" comes from Victor Brombert's seminal work on the topic, *The Intellectual Hero: Studies in the French Novel, 1880–1955* (Philadelphia: J. B. Lippincott, 1961). This hero is largely ignored in the work of Christophe Charle, who concentrates on the sociological aspects of the birth of the intellectual: *Naissance des "intellectuels": 1880–1910* (Paris: Editions de Minuit, 1990). In attempting to demythologize intellectuals and their origins, Charle has fallen into the opposite trap of neglecting their sincere belief and vision of themselves as heroes. The crusading aspects of the Affair are prominent in the works of Léon Blum and Charles Péguy on the Dreyfusard side, and in the works of Maurice Barrès and Charles Maurras on the anti-Dreyfusard side. See John J. Cerullo, "Truth and Justice? Honor and Manhood! Toward a Gendered Interpretation of Intellectuals and the Dreyfus Affair." Paper presented at the French Historical Studies Conference, Atlanta, March 1995.

6. Paul Déroulède, *De l'éducation militaire*, cited by Jean-Denis Bredin, *L'Affaire* (Paris: Julliard, 1983), 26.

7. Cited by Raoul Girardet, *La Société militaire dans la France contemporaine (1815–1939)* (Paris: Plon, 1953), 165.

8. Eugen Weber, *Peasants into Frenchmen: The Modernization of Rural France, 1870–1914* (Stanford, Calif.: Stanford University Press, 1976), 293–294. In 1905, the term of service was reduced to two years but it returned to three years in 1913.

9. Girardet, *La Société militaire*, 162.

10. Ibid., 165.

11. See Raoul Girardet, *Mythes et mythologies politiques* (Paris: Seuil, 1986).

12. Fourcaud, "Nos Petits Pioupious," *Le Gaulois*, 15 March 1895.

13. Jérôme Hélie, "L'Arche sainte fracturée," in *La France de l'affaire Dreyfus*, ed. Pierre Birnbaum (Paris: Gallimard, 1994), 226–250. Hélie feels that World War I, often represented as the end of the difficulties between civil society and the army, was only an interlude and that the Affair inaugurated a crisis that culminated with the putsch of the generals during the Algerian War.

14. Bredin, *L'Affaire*, 23; Michael Burns, *Dreyfus: A Family Affair, 1789–1945* (New York: Harper Collins, 1991), 76.

15. Hélie, "L'Arche sainte," 232–233.

16. Whereas the number of Jews in the Army before 1870 was roughly two per thousand, roughly equal to the proportion of Jews in French society,

this figure increased to ten per thousand by 1892. William Serman, *Les Officiers français dans la nation (1848–1914)* (Paris: Aubier Montaigne, 1982), 101; Hélie, "L'Arche sainte," 232.

17. Hélie, "L'Arche sainte," 230–231.

18. Serman, *Les Officiers,* 8.

19. Ibid., 18.

20. Hélie, "L'Arche sainte," 234–235.

21. Serman, *Les Officiers,* 98.

22. Fourcaud, "Nos Petits Pioupious," *Le Gaulois,* 15 March 1895.

23. Jean Rabaut, *L'Antimilitarisme en France, 1810–1975* (Paris: Hachette, 1975), 9–12.

24. Cited by Rabaut, *L'Antimilitarisme,* 28.

25. Lucien Descaves, *Les Sous-offs: roman militaire* (Paris: Tresse and Stock, 1890).

26. Ibid., 435.

27. Ibid.

28. Christophe Charle, *Naissance,* 112–113. Oscar Wilde's homosexuality precluded such a united defense on his behalf several years later.

29. Dated 20 January 1898, published in *Imbéciles et gredins* (Paris: Maison d'Art Moderne, 1900), 134.

30. Published in *Plaidoyer pour Dreyfus,* ed. Gilles Picq (Paris: Séguier, 1994), 151.

31. Laurent Tailhade, "Conscrits," *Imbéciles et gredins,* 135.

32. Urbain Gohier, "Les Femmes," *L'Aurore,* 27 March 1898.

33. Laurent Tailhade, "La Tache noire," was published originally in *Les Droits de l'homme* on 25 November 1898, and is included in *Plaidoyer pour Dreyfus,* 160.

34. Gohier, "Les Femmes," *L'Aurore,* 27 March 1899.

35. Ibid., *L'Aurore,* 20 July 1899.

36. Etienne Lamy, "Les Ennemis de l'armée," *La Revue des deux mondes* 122 (15 March 1894):425–455. Lamy was a Catholic who "rallied" to the republican regime.

37. Ibid., 443–444.

38. Ibid., 433.

39. Ibid., 448.

40. In an article entitled "La Caserne," published on 25 February 1895. The author deplored the new national pastime of denigrating the army, although he understood that universal military service meant that every mother henceforth had a personal stake in the soldier's quality of life.

41. René Vallery-Radot, "L'Esprit militaire en France depuis cent ans," published in *La Revue bleue* 45 (8 February 1890):172.

42. Lamy, "Les Ennemis," 432.

43. Fourcaud, "Nos Petits Pioupious," *Le Gaulois*, 15 March 1895.

44. 8 December 1898. The article was written by "Gallus."

45. Brunetière, "Après le procès," *La Revue des deux mondes* 146 (15 March 1898):434–435.

46. Jules Lemaître, *Opinions à répandre* (Paris: Société française d'imprimerie et de librairie, 1901). The article, which is dated 14 April 1898, is entitled "La Patrie et l'armée: le patriotisme," 88.

47. Lemaître, *Opinions à répandre*, "L'Armée et la paix," dated 12 September 1897, 97.

48. René-François-Armand Sully-Prudhomme, "Patrie, armeé, discipline," *La Revue des deux mondes* 147 (15 June 1898):730.

49. Ibid., 736–737.

50. Brunetière, "Après le procès," 438–439.

51. Ibid., 440.

52. See the entry "Armée," in *Dictionnaire politique et critique* 1 (Paris: Cité des Livres, 1932), 95.

53. Lamy, "Les Ennemis," 451–452.

54. Ibid., 453–454.

55. Ibid, 453.

56. Sully-Prudhomme, "Patrie," 740.

57. Lamy, "Les Ennemis," 454.

58. Brunetière, "Après le procès," 434. See also page 442.

59. Ibid., 442.

60. Ferdinand Brunetière, "La Nation et l'armée," delivered on 26 April 1899, published in *Discours de Combat*, première série 1 (Paris: Perrin, 1908):230.

61. Lemaître, "Sur l'armée," *Opinions à répandre*, 103.

62. Lemaître, "Le Rôle de l'officier," *Opinions à répandre*, 114.

63. Lemaître, "L'Armée et la paix," *Opinions à répandre*, 93.

64. Brunetière, "La Nation et l'armée," *Discours de combat*, 233.

65. Brunetière, "Après le procès," 440.

66. Lamy, "Les Ennemis," 439.

67. Anon., "Du rôle social de l'officier," *La Revue des deux mondes* 104 (15 March 1891):443–459.

68. Ibid., 446.

69. Ibid., 455.

70. Ibid., 457–459.

71. "L'Education morale dans l'armée," *La Revue bleue* 47 (16 May 1891):609–610.

72. René Vallery-Radot, "L'Esprit militaire depuis cent ans," *La Revue bleue*, 172.

73. "Protestation," *La Revue blanche* 15 (1 February 1898):166.

74. Alfred Vallette's reply was included in an *enquête* on "M. Emile Zola et l'opinion," published in *La Critique*, no. 71 (February 1898):25. Hereafter referred to as *La Critique Enquête*.

75. Gabriel Séailles, "Pourquoi j'ai signé," *L'Aurore*, 20 February 1898.

76. See the responses by Jean Ajalbert (25), Chavenon (26), and Edgar Baès (29) in *La Critique Enquête*.

77. Gustave Geoffrey, "Le motif de Zola," *L'Aurore*, 17 February 1898.

78. See Camille Mauclair, "L'Opposition française," *L'Aurore*, 28 March 1898, and "La Médaille usée," *L'Aurore*, 7 March 1898.

79. Henry Leyret, "Des Hommes d'action," *L'Aurore*, 28 February 1898.

80. The pages of the *Enquête* are: 25–35.

81. Manuel Devaldès, *La Critique Enquête*, 27.

82. Ibid., 28.

83. Ibid., 25.

84. Ibid., Armand Charpentier, 26; René Ghil, 32.

85. Tailhade, "Littérature antisémite," originally published in *Les Droits de l'homme*, 19 October 1899, republished in *Plaidoyer pour Dreyfus*, 179.

Such a view is echoed by the editorial staff of *La Revue blanche* in "Protestation," the article that launched their Dreyfusard campaign; they, too, accused their opponent of lacking artistic and esthetic sense, 166.

86. In the words of *Enquête* respondent Victorien du Saussay, 27.

87. Leyret, "Des hommes d'action," *L'Aurore*, 28 February 1898.

88. Tailhade, "Ballade touchant les aboyeurs antisémites," *Plaidoyer pour Dreyfus*, 140. This poem was originally published in *L'Aurore* on 24 January 1898.

89. Tailhade,"Bleus et Blancs," *Plaidoyer pour Dreyfus*, 166, originally published in *Les Droits de l'homme* on 8 December 1898.

90. Fernand Hauser, *La Critique Enquête*, 28; Tailhade, "Valets de Picque," originally published in *Les Droits de l'homme* on 22 May 1898, reprinted in *Plaidoyer pour Dreyfus*, 151.

91. Gabriel Séailles, "Pourquoi j'ai signé," *L'Aurore*, 20 February 1898.

92. Octave Mirbeau, *La Critique Enquête*, 33.

93. "Protestation," *La Revue blanche* 15 (1 February 1898), 166.

94. Henry D. Davray, *La Critique Enquête*, 26. René Ghil, among others, distinguished between anti-Dreyfusard intellectuals and "real" Dreyfusard intellectuals; the latter were the only ones that thought, pg. 32.

95. Jean Ajalbert, *La Critique Enquête*, 25.

96. "Enquête sur les responsabilités de la presse," *La Revue bleue* (December 1897, and January 1898). See also E. Spuller's article "La Presse et la démocratie," *La Revue bleue* (21 April 1894):481–486.

97. *La Critique Enquête*, 26.

98. Tailhade, "Bleus et Blancs," *Plaidoyer pour Dreyfus*, 167.

99. See Christophe Prochasson's article "Le Colonel Georges Picquart ou la vertu cachée," in *Mil neuf cent: Revue d'histoire intellectuelle*, special issue "Comment sont-ils devenus dreyfusards ou antidreyfusards?" 11, (1993):15–20.

100. Joseph Reinach, *L'Affaire Dreyfus: Tout le Crime*, vol. 3 (Paris: Stock, 1900), 13.

101. Christophe Prochasson, "Le Colonel Picquart," 15.

102. Francis de Pressensé, *Un Héros: Le Lieutenant-Colonel Picquart* (Paris: Stock, 1898), xv.

103. Prochasson, "Le Colonel Picquart," 17.

104. Ibid., 19.

105. "Hommage des artistes à Picquart: derrière un grillage," reproduced in Octave Mirbeau, *Combats politiques*, eds. Pierre Michel and Jean-François Nivet (Paris: Séguier, 1990), 215. The album itself was published in 1899 by the Société libre d'Edition des gens de lettres (Houghton Collection, Harvard University).

106. Joseph Reinach, *L'Affaire Dreyfus: une conscience: le Lieutenant-Colonel Picquart* (Paris: Stock, 1898), 6–7.

107. Ibid., 12.

108. Reinach, *Une Conscience*, 36; Pressensé, *Un Héros*, v–vi.

109. "Le Festin des sauvages," originally published in *L'Aurore*, 24 November 1898, collected in Octave Mirbeau, *L'Affaire Dreyfus*, eds. Pierre Michel and Jean-François Nivet (Paris: Séguier, 1991), 168–169.

110. Pressensé, *Un Héros,* xv.

111. Ibid., xii.

112. Armand Charpentier, *La Critique Enquête*, 26. Zola, too, was depicted as Christ on the cross.

113. Octave Mirbeau, "Derrière un grillage," *Combats politiques*, 211–217.

114. Pressensé, *Un Héros,* xv, and xiii.

115. Mirbeau, "Derrière un grillage," *Combats politiques*, 213.

116. Ibid., 216.

117. See Emmanuel Naquet, "La Ligue des Droits de l'Homme au tournant du siècle," *L'Affaire Dreyfus au tournant du siècle*, 164–168.

118. Léon Blum, *Souvenirs sur l'Affaire* (Paris: Gallimard, 1935; reedition 1981), 141–143. Even if they had not reckoned with Maurras's rehabilitation of Henry, for Dreyfusards the heroic phase of the Affair was over, pg. 143.

119. Although Maurras praised Henry, "our energetic plebian," another anti-Dreyfusard, Fernand Xau, publisher of *Le Journal*, deplored Henry's actions and expressed surprise that such an unsuitable man, devoid of intellectual attributes, had been appointed to head the intelligence service, "Le Suicide du Colonel Henry," *Le Journal*, 2 September 1898.

120. Edouard Drumont, "La Fin d'un soldat," *La Libre Parole*, 3 September 1898. See also "Le Prisonnier," in the 1 September 1898 issue. In "Le Colonel Henry et Reinach," published on 27 January 1899, Drumont described Henry as the representative of "our military democracy."

121. This was an inconsistency pointed out by Dreyfusards. If Henry were clever, he could have deceived his superiors. But if one lauded him as a simple, naive soldier, he would have been incapable of ruse and therefore had to have been following orders.

122. Published as *Tout le Crime*.

123. See Stephen Wilson, *Ideology and Experience: Antisemitism in France at the time of the Dreyfus Affair* (East Brunswick, NJ: Associated University Press, 1982), "The Henry Subscriptions 1898–1899," 125–165.

124. As Dreyfusard Pierre Quillard noted in his introduction to the lists, which he entitled *Le Monument Henry* (Paris: Stock, 1899).

125. Wilson, *Ideology and Experience,* 137.

126. Quillard, *Le Monument Henry,* 576.

127. Ibid., 577.

128. Ibid., 584.

129. Wilson, *Ideology and Experience,* 154.

130. Quillard, *Le Monument Henry,* 24–25.

131. Maurice Barrès, "Les Intellectuels et l'armée," *Le Journal,* 11 November 1898.

132. Barrès, *Les Déracinés* (Paris: Union Générale d'Editions, 1986). Writing of Napoleon in *Les Déracinés,* Barrès stated that "contact with him had the power to expand souls," 169.

133. Barrès, *Les Déracinés,* 167 (Napoleon), and 332 (Hugo).

134. Ibid., 165.

135. Ibid., 173–175.

136. Ibid., 334.

137. On Barrès's heroes, see David Carroll, *French Literary Fascism: Nationalism, Anti-Semitism, and the Ideology of Culture* (Princeton, NJ: Princeton University Press, 1995), chapter 1, "The Use and Abuse of Culture: Maurice Barrès," 19–41.

138. Ibid., 36.

139. Edouard Drumont, "Professeurs d'énergie," *La Libre Parole,* 8 February 1899. There were internal rivalries among the anti-Semites, between Drumont and Morès, for example. Having cooperated closely with him in the first Ligue Antisémitique, Drumont broke with Morès in 1893 and thereafter had no contact with him until he attended his funeral. Drumont was also on bad terms with Rochefort and Barrès. As for relations

with Déroulède, they, too, were problematic. According to Raphael Viau, although Déroulède came frequently to the offices of *La Libre Parole*, he did not appear to like Drumont much, in part, because the latter had made fun of him in his books. In addition, Déroulède professed not to be an anti-Semite.

The case of Marchand is even more interesting; although he was celebrated by the nationalists as a hero, he proved to be solidly behind the Republic. See Stephen Wilson, *Ideology and Experience,* pp. 199, 385, and 79.

140. Intérim, "Soldats et politiciens," *La Libre Parole,* 4 February 1898.

141. The issue was published on 29 May 1899.

142. Barrès, *Scènes et doctrines du nationalisme* (Paris: Editions du Trident, 1987), 232.

143. Drumont, "Morès," *La Libre Parole,* 9 June 1898.

144. In "L'Acquittement de Déroulède," published in *La Libre Parole* on 1 June 1899, Drumont claimed that Déroulède's acquittal meant that virile energy was not quite dead in France.

145. Drumont, "Déroulède et Reinach," *La Libre Parole,* 28 February 1899. Treachery, it should be noted, was viewed as a "feminine" characteristic.

146. Drumont, "Gloire à Déroulède," *La Libre Parole,* 21 December 1899. In an article on Marchand "De l'Ile du Diable à Fachoda," published in *La Libre Parole* on 9 November 1898, Drumont contrasted Marchand's heroism and exploits to the treachery of Jews in Paris.

147. Barrès, "Marchand et Morès," *Le Journal,* 28 October 1898. On courage and national revival, see Robert A. Nye, *Masculinity and Male Codes of Honor,* 220.

148. Drumont, "L'Horrible Campagne des infâmes," *La Libre Parole,* 25 November 1898.

149. Barrès, "Les Intellectuels et l'armée," *Le Journal,* 11 November 1898.

150. Drumont, "Les Intellectuels et l'Affaire Dreyfus," *La Libre Parole,* 29 January 1898. Nevertheless, he felt that a military man had special rights and if one accepted the protection of the army, one had no right to question an internal military decision.

151. Ibid.

152. Drumont, "La Lessive nécessaire," *La Libre Parole,* 25 February 1898.

153. Gallus, "Le Parti nationaliste," *La Libre Parole,* 13 May 1898. See also an article commemorating the fiftieth anniversary of Chateaubriand's death: Gallus, "Le Cinquantenaire de Chateaubriand et la tradition nationale," *La Libre Parole,* 28 May 1899.

154. Drumont, "Michelet," *La Libre Parole*, 28 June 1898. These three men were "remueurs d'idées."

155. Henri Mazel, *La Critique Enquête*, 26.

156. Wilson, *Ideology and Experience*, 587.

157. "Picquart au Cherche-Midi," *La Libre Parole*, 23 September 1898. The article is unsigned.

158. Willa Z. Silverman, *The Notorious Life of Gyp: Right-Wing Anarchist in Fin-de-Siècle France* (New York: Oxford University Press, 1995), 142.

159. "La Cellule smart," 4 March 1899; the *Psst!* drawings are located in the Boston Public Library. I would like to thank John Cerullo for pointing these drawings out to me.

160. "Le Grand Match," 13 May 1899.

161. "Flagrant délit," 11 February 1899.

162. "Magistrature nouvelle," 18 February 1899. Dreyfusards would turn this image on its head in an illustration for *Le Sifflet*.

163. "Une dame rédactrice," 17 June 1899.

164. Quillard, *Le Monument Henry*, 635–636. See also Wilson, *Ideology and Experience*, 149–151.

165. One entry defines intellectuals as follows: "Intellectual means incoherent, unbalanced." Another entry describes them as "deranged" (636).

166. "Intellectuals are cowards." "Intellectuals are professional consultants for anarchism." Quillard, *Le Monument Henry*, 636.

167. Ibid., 637.

168. Ibid.

169. Wilson, *Ideology and Experience*, 151–152.

170. Reinach, *Tout le Crime*, 52, 122, and 218–219.

171. Ibid., 51.

172. Ibid., 381.

173. Ibid., 349.

174. Henry Leyret, "L'Ecole des grands mots," *L'Aurore*, 30 January 1898.

175. Tailhade, "Troisième Sexe," originally published in *Le Décadent* on 1 August 1888, *Plaidoyer pour Dreyfus*, 110.

176. Tailhade, "Vieille Dame," was originally published in *Les Droits de l'homme* on 11 January 1899, *Plaidoyer pour Dreyfus*, 39–40.

177. Urbain Gohier, "Les Femmes," *L'Aurore*, 27 March 1898.

178. Tailhade, "La Prière pour tous," *Plaidoyer pour Dreyfus*, 27. In another article "Amuseur des cannibales," Barrès and Bourget were referred to as "eunuchs," 143.

179. Such manners contradicted the essence of the duel, which was the mutual respect that both adversaries had for each other, "Les Duels," *Imbéciles et gredins*, 172.

180. Ibid., 171–172.

Chapter 7

1. In his study of the evolution of French liberalism during the nineteenth century, William Logue notes that determining the proper balance between the individual and the community was not only one of the most difficult problems of liberal political philosophy, but also one of the most pressing issues of the fin de siècle. It dominated the political life of the period. *From Philosophy to Sociology: The Evolution of French Liberalism, 1870–1914* (De Kalb IL: Northern Illinois University Press, 1983), 2, and 11.

2. Michel Winock, "Les Affaires Dreyfus," *Nationalisme, antisémitisme et fascisme en France* (Paris: Seuil, 1990), 165–166.

3. Along with the term "liberalism," which was defined in a variety of ways, as Logue notes, 5. Moreover, there were liberals on both sides of the Dreyfus Affair, 7.

4. Henri Mazel, "Au lecteur," *L'Ermitage* 1 (April 1890):4.

5. Logue, *Philosophy to Sociology*, 2.

6. Ibid., 2.

7. On Social Darwinism in France, see Linda L. Clark, *Social Darwinism in France* (Tuscaloosa, AL: University of Alabama Press, 1984).

8. J. E. S. Hayward, "Solidarity: The Social History of an Idea in Nineteenth Century France," *International Review of Social History* 4 (1959):264.

9. Steven Lukes, *Individualism* (New York: Harper and Row, 1973), 3.

10. Ibid., 3–5.

11. Ibid., 6.

12. Ibid., 8–9.

13. Hayward, "Solidarity," 274–275.

14. Ibid., 277. The term solidarity was initially a juridical term which first appeared in the *Dictionnaire de l'Académie Française* in 1694. It also appeared in the Napoleonic Code, pg. 269. Socialist Georges Renard saw Leroux as the "initiator" of solidarism: Hayward, "The Official Social Philosophy of the French Third Republic: Léon Bourgeois and Solidarism," *International Review of Social History* 6 (1961):22.

15. Hayward, "Solidarity," 275.

16. Lukes, *Individualism*, 5–6.

17. Hayward, "Solidarity," 269.

18. Lukes, *Individualism*, 11–12.

19. See Jaurès's "Socialisme et liberté," which was first published in *La Revue de Paris* on 1 December 1898, and Aaron Noland, "Individualism in Jean Jaurès's Socialist Thought," *Journal of the History of Ideas* 22 (1961):63–80. On Bourgeois, see J. E. S. Hayward, "Léon Bourgeois and Solidarism," 32–33.

20. Léon Bourgeois, *Solidarité* (1896; 7th edition, Paris: Armand Colin, 1912), 1–2.

21. Logue, *Philosophy to Sociology*, 139.

22. Ibid., 96.

23. Theodore Zeldin, *France 1848–1945, Politics and Anger* (New York: Oxford University Press, 1979), 292.

24. Logue, *Philosophy to Sociology*, 142.

25. Ibid., 142–3. Among Fouillée's two most important contributions to French liberal thought were his attempt to give it a scientific basis, in order to counter the scientific claims of Marxists and Social Darwinist individualists, and the elaboration of a theory of state action.

26. Born in 1851, Bourgeois was a jurist by training. Elected Deputy to the Marne in 1888, he eventually served as prime minister, from 1 November 1895 to 21 April 1896. In 1899, he declined the president's offer to form a government, instead suggesting Waldeck-Rousseau. He preferred to serve the cause of international "solidarity" by representing France at the International Conference on Arbitration at the Hague, in 1899 and again in 1907. Bourgeois was elected president of the National Assembly in 1902, along with Jaurès who was elected vice president. Elected senator in 1905, Bourgeois served as foreign minister in 1906 and 1914. In 1920, he was awarded the Nobel Peace Prize. Hayward, "Léon Bourgeois and Solidarism," 21.

27. Bourgeois, *Solidarité*, 6.

28. Ibid., 38.

29. Ibid., 69–70. See also page 28.

30. Ibid., 28–29.

31. Ibid., 45–46, and Zeldin, *France 1848–1945*, 293.

32. Bourgeois, *Solidarité*, 54.

33. Ibid., 105.

34. Zeldin, *France 1848–1945*, 291–293.

35. Bourgeois, *Solidarité*, 52.

36. Hayward notes that had Léon Bourgeois and Jean Jaurès actively joined forces for an extended period of time, they might have succeeded in implementing far-reaching social legislation, exceeding even that of the Liberal Governments of Britain during the early years of the twentieth century: "Léon Bourgeois and Solidarism," 35.

37. On the use of the term "anarchy" by a variety of groups to denigrate their opponents, see Christopher E. Forth, "Intellectual Anarchy and Imaginary Otherness: Gender, Class, and Pathology in French Intellectual Discourse, 1890–1900," *Sociological Quarterly* 37, no. 4 (Fall 1996):645–671.

38. Bérenger, *L'Aristocratie intellectuelle* (Paris: Armand Colin, 1895), 249–50.

39. Ibid., 228.

40. Ibid.

41. Ibid., 182. "The real ends of a Democracy is the reconciliation of individualism and solidarity."

42. William M. Johnston, "The Origin of the Term 'Intellectuals' in French Novels and Essays," *Journal of European Studies* 4 (1974):55.

43. André Veidaux, "Philosophie de l'anarchie," *La Plume* 4, no. 97 (1 May 1893): 192.

44. Jean Grave, *L'Individu et la société* (Paris: Stock, 2nd edition, 1897), 84. See K. Steven Vincent, "Jean Grave and French Communist Anarchism." Paper presented at the WSFH Conference, Las Vegas, Nov. 8–11, 1995, 9.

45. Jean Grave, *La Société mourante et l'anarchie* (Paris: Stock, 1893), 3; Vincent, 8.

46. Jean Grave, *L'Individu*, 187.

47. Ibid., 187–188, and 195.

48. Ibid., 62.

49. Jean Grave, *La Société future* (Paris: Stock, 1895), 147.

50. Grave, *L'Individu*, 238.

51. Ibid., 236; see also Vincent, "Jean Grave," 13–14.

52. The article was entitled "Réflexions: individualisme et socialisme."

53. Brunetière, "Après le procès," *La Revue des deux mondes* (15 March 1898), 146:428–446.

54. Ibid., 445.

55. Indeed, in a presentation delivered the following year, Brunetière cited France's great writers, Corneille, Racine, Molière among them, as the sources of French energy and action. "Les Ennemis de l'âme française," *Discours de combat* (première série, Paris: Perrin, 1908), 188–189. Anti-Dreyfusards and Dreyfusards alike invoked a long French literary tradition, thereby illustrating the profoundly literary nature of French culture.

56. Brunetière, "Après le procès," 442.

57. Ibid., 434.

58. Ibid., 445.

59. Ibid., 434. In "Les Ennemis de l'âme française," *Discours de combat* [première série], he holds individualism responsible for all the ills attributed to capitalism, 208.

60. Brunetière, "Les Ennemis," 163–164.

61. "It is solidarity which is old in France, and individualism which is new. Solidarity and union through independence, such was, in past times, the motto of our country," Ibid., 209.

62. Ibid., 208.

63. As did fellow anti-Dreyfusard Charles Maurras.

64. Brunetière, "Après le procès," 434.

65. Brunetière, "Les Ennemis," 169.

66. Ibid., 170.

67. Ibid., 166–167.

68. Ibid., 206–207.

69. Brunetière, "L'Idée de solidarité," published in *Discours de combat* (nouvelle série, Paris: Perrin, 1903), 51–83.

70. Ibid., 59.

71. Ibid., 61.

72. See chapter 6 "Social Darwinism and the Right" in Linda L. Clark's *Social Darwinism in France*, 90–105.

73. I will be referring to the English translation published by Steven Lukes in *Political Studies* 17 (1969):14–30.

74. Lukes, *Political Studies*.

75. Ibid., 20–21.

76. Ibid., 21.

77. Ibid., 28.

78. Ibid., 21. For a detailed analysis of Durkheim's thinking on Kant and Rousseau in this article, see Mark S. Cladis, "Durkheim's Communitarian Defense of Liberalism," *Soundings* 72. 2–3 (Summer/Fall, 1989):281–283.

79. Lukes, Political Studies, 21–22.

80. Ibid., 24.

81. Ibid., 25.

82. Ibid., 28.

83. Ibid., 26; Cladis, "Durkheim's Communitarian," 287–288.

84. As did Brunetière in "Après le procès," 430.

85. Lukes, *Political Studies,* 25.

86. Ibid., 24–25.

87. Ibid., 25.

88. Ibid., 28.

89. Ibid., 30. Such prejudices would surface against his own Dreyfusard allies in the wake of the Affair.

90. Ibid., 28. See also Lukes, *Emile Durkheim: His Life and Work* (New York: Harper and Row, 1972), 270.

91. Lukes, *Durkheim*, 270.

92. Cited by Lukes, *Durkheim*, 269.

93. He shared Spencer's view of society as an organism, along with socio-biologist Espinas's belief that social phenomena could be studied as analogous but not identical to organs performing functions within societies: Lukes, *Durkheim*, 84–85, and 140. I have found the question of Durkheim's "organicism" a problematic one. Both William Logue and Linda Clark emphasize Durkheim's rejection of biological sociology, while Jennifer M. Lehmann emphasizes the "organicist" aspects of his thought, stating that

organicism structures Durkheim's entire theoretical system, *Durkheim and Women* (Lincoln, Neb.: University of Nebraska Press, 1994), 75. I do not think that these approaches are necessarily contradictory. While Durkheim may have seen society as an organism, he believed that human society was subject to social laws which were different than those in biology.

94. Emile Durkheim, *The Division of Labor in Society*, trans. George Simpson (Glencoe, IL: The Free Press, 1933), see chapters 2, and 3 of book 1.

95. Lukes, *Durkheim*, 76.

96. It was later published in a collection of Jaurès's essays, *Pages choisies de Jean Jaurès* (Paris: Rieder, 1928), 208–244.

97. Ibid., 209–210.

98. Ibid., 224–226.

99. Ibid., 233.

100. Ibid. "An entire race of beings, an entire organic whole."

101. Ibid., 231.

102. Ibid., 232.

103. Ibid., 234.

104. Robert Soucy, *Fascism in France: The Case of Maurice Barrès* (Berkeley, Calif.: University of California Press, 1972). See especially chapter 3: "Conversion to Rootedness," 69–115. Note, however, that his contemporary Léon Blum continued to see him as individualist, even after the publication of *Les Déracinés*. In his review of the book, Blum declared, "Monsieur Barrès who was the theoretician of the self and who has remained an individualist. . . ." "Les Livres," *La Revue blanche* 14 (15 November 1897):293.

105. Barrès, *Scènes et doctrines du nationalisme* (1902; Paris: Editions du Trident, 1987), 17.

106. Barrès, "Examen des trois romans idéologiques," published in *Le Culte du moi* (Paris: Union Générale d'Editions, 10/18 1986), 18–19.

107. Barrès, *Scènes et doctrines du nationalisme*, 18.

108. Ibid., 20.

109. David Carroll, *French Literary Fascism: Nationalism, Anti-Semitism, and the Ideology of Culture* (Princeton, N.J.: Princeton University Press, 1995), 22–24. This is also the position of Zeev Sternhell, *Maurice Barrès et le nationalisme français* (Paris: Editions Complexe, 1985), 48, and 54–57.

110. Barrès, *Scènes et doctrines du nationalisme*, 136.

111. Durkheim, in Lukes, *Durkheim*, 207–210; Barrès, *Scènes et doctrines du nationalisme*, 76–77.

112. Barrès, *Scènes et doctrines du nationalisme*, 72–73; Durkheim, *L'Education morale*, quoted in Marco F. Diani, "Metamorphosis of Nationalism: Durkheim, Barrès, and the Dreyfus Affair," *The Jerusalem Journal of International Relations* 13, no. 4 (1991):91.

113. Barrès wrote of the French need to understand themselves: *Scènes et doctrines du nationalisme*, 20, and 67.

114. As Lucien Herr stated in his letter "excommunicating" Barrès in the name of an entire generation: "The French soul was truly great and strong only when it was both welcoming and giving. You wish to bury it in the tetanus-ridden straightjacket where it has been confined by rancor and hatred." "A M. Maurice Barrès," *La Revue blanche*, 15 (15 February 1898):244. On integral nationalism, see Raoul Girardet, *Le Nationalisme français: 1871–1914* (Paris: Seuil, 1983).

115. In his response to Henri Dagan's *Enquête sur l'antisémitisme* (Paris: Stock, 1899), 59–63.

116. Ibid. I should point out that Durkheim's discussion does not refer to Barrès specifically, but given the context of the Affair, it was clear to contemporary readers that he was referring to Barrès, among others in his discussion.

117. Léon Blum, "Les Livres," *La Revue blanche*, 293.

118. Blum, "Les Livres," 293; Durkheim, *The Division of Labor*, 195.

119. Jaurès, *Page Choisies*, 244.

120. In his thought-provoking article "Metamorphosis of Nationalism: Durkheim, Barrès, and the Dreyfus Affair," Marco F. Diani examines the similarities between the nationalism of Durkheim and Barrès. While I agree that there are parallels in that they both "invoked nationalism as a remedy that was to be diffused through society by a system of moral education" (72), I disagree strongly with Diani's conclusion that for both men "the desire for justice was replaced by the desire for social solidarity" (91). Such a reading misrepresents Durkheim's concept of the individual in society. Durkheim, to my mind, clearly argues in "L'Individualisme et les intellectuels," (Individualism and the Intellectuals) that injustice toward one individual is contrary to the idea of social solidarity. Moreover, I disagree with Diani's analysis of Barrès as an "anti-individualist" (83).

121. Gustave Le Bon, *Psychology of Socialism* (New York: Macmillan, 1899), 25.

122. Ibid.

123. Ibid., 26, and 36. Unlike Brunetière, who deemed Spencer an "anarchist," Le Bon saw him as a socialist.

124. Logue, *Philosophy to Sociology*, 125–127.

125. Le Bon, *Psychology of Socialism*, 342. He therefore also disagreed with Spencer on the issue of altruism. In *Scènes et doctrines*, Barrès speaks of "solidarity" as follows: "We've ruined it by adding to it what in Christian vocabulary is called 'charity.'" Barrès sought to define solidarity as an affinity: "When we wish to denote those instinctive sentiments of sympathy by which beings recognize each other, tend to associate and combine with one another, in time as well as in space, I propose that we speak of affinities.... This is how I understand the word affinity," pg. 17. Barrès had clearly read Le Bon.

126. Robert Nye points to the similarities between the Solidarists and Le Bon, *The Origins of Crowd Psychology: Gustave Le Bon and the Crisis of Mass Democracy in the Third Republic* (Beverly Hills, Calif.: Sage Publications, 1975), 90. I agree with Linda Clark that the two were quite different, *Social Darwinism in France*, 136.

127. Le Bon, *Psychology of Socialism*, 345.

128. Ibid., 344.

129. Ibid., 344.

130. In all fairness, it should be pointed out that some Dreyfusards adopted an egoistic, individualist stance.

131. Hayward, "Solidarity," 262.

132. Even Tarde used biological metaphors to criticize his opponents, Clark, *Social Darwinism in France*, 124–126.

133. Ibid., 75.

Conclusion

1. Charles Péguy, *Notre Jeunesse* (Paris: Gallimard, 1957), 31.

2. Blum, *Souvenirs sur l'Affaire* (Paris: Gallimard, 1935; reedition 1981), 145–147.

3. See Maurras's often disparaging comments about its leaders Lemaître and Coppée in *La République ou le Roi: Correspondance inédite, 1888–1923: Maurice Barrès-Charles Maurras* (Paris: Plon, 1970).

4. The decision to reject collaboration with bourgeois parties was reached at the Socialist Congress in Amsterdam in 1904.

5. Pascal Ory and Jean-François Sirinelli, *Les Intellectuels en France, de l'Affaire Dreyfus à nos jours* (Paris: Armand Colin, 1986), 23, and 25.

6. There were also several *normaliens* among its staff members.

7. Not all intellectuals felt this way. A number of intellectuals, particularly among the *normaliens*, drew closer to the socialist movement during the years preceding World War I. See Christophe Prochasson, *Les Intellectuels, le socialisme et la guerre, 1900–1938* (Paris: Seuil, 1993).

8. On the *Universités populaires*, see Ory and Sirinelli, *Les Intellectuels en France*, 24. The *enquêtes* in question were the "Enquête sur l'éducation," published in the 1 June 1902 issue of *La Revue blanche* and the survey on elites and democracy published in *La Revue bleue* on 21 May, 28 May, and 4 June 1904.

Selected Bibliography

Bibliography: Primary sources

I. JOURNALS & NEWSPAPERS:

Journals:

Les Entretiens politiques et littéraires, 1890–1894

L'Ermitage, 1890–1896

Le Mercure de France, 1890–1905

La Plume, 1889–1903

La Revue blanche, 1889–1903

La Revue bleue, 1890–1896

La Revue des deux mondes, 1889–1905

Newspapers:

L'Aurore, 1897–1899

La Cocarde, 1894–1895

Le Gaulois, 1894–1895

Le Journal, 1898–1899

La Libre Parole, 1897–1899

I. Books

Agathon. *Les Jeunes gens d'aujourd'hui*. Paris: Plon, 1913.

Auriant. *Hugues Rebell à "L'Ermitage" (1892–1900) avec dix lettres inédites à Henri Mazel*. Reims: Editions "A l'Ecart," 1988.

Barrès, Maurice. *Mes Cahiers*. Vols. 1, and 2. Paris: Plon, 1929.

———. *Ce que j'ai vu à Rennes*. Paris: Bibliothèque internationale d'édition, 1904.

———. *Le Culte du moi*. Paris: Union Générale d'Editions, 10/18, 1986.

———. *Les Déracinés*. Paris: Union Générale d'Editions, 10/18, 1986.

———. *L'Oeuvre de Maurice Barrès*. Vol. 2. Paris: Au Club de l'Honnête Homme, 1965.

———. *La République ou le roi: correspondance inédite, 1888–1923: Maurice Barrès-Charles Maurras*. Paris: Plon, 1970.

———. *Scènes et doctrines du nationalisme*. Paris: Editions du Trident, 1987.

Benda, Julien. *La Jeunesse d'un clerc*. Paris: Gallimard, 1936.

Bérenger, Henry. *L'Aristocratie intellectuelle*. Paris: Armand Colin, 1895.

———. *L'Effort*. Paris: Armand Colin, 1895.

———. *La France intellectuelle*. Paris: Armand Colin, 1899.

———. *La Proie*. Paris: Armand Colin, 1897.

———, et al. *Les Prolétaires intellectuels en France*. Paris: Editions de la Revue, 1901.

Bernard, Tristan. *Souvenirs et anecdotes*. Paris: Le Cherche Midi, 1992.

Blum, Léon. *L'Oeuvre de Léon Blum*. Vol. 1. Paris: Albin Michel, 1954.

———. *Souvenirs sur l'Affaire*. Paris: Gallimard, 1935; 1981.

Bourgeois, Léon. *Solidarité*. Paris: Armand Colin, 1896; 7th ed., 1912.

Brulat, Paul. *Violence et raison*. Paris: Stock, 1898.

Brunetière, Ferdinand. *Discours de combat*. 3 vols. Paris: Perrin, 1903; 1907; 1908.

Clemenceau, Georges. *Injustice militaire*. Paris: Stock, 1902.

———. *Justice militaire*. Paris: Stock, 1899.

Corpet, Olivier and Patrick Fréchet, eds. *Les Revues d'avant-garde (1870–1914), enquête de MM. Maurice Caillard et Charles Forot*. Paris: Ent'revues, Editions Jean-Michel Place, 1990.

Dagan, Henri. *Enquête sur l'antisémitisme*. Paris: Stock, 1899.

Daudet, Léon. *Souvenirs et polémiques*. Paris: Laffont, 1992.

———. *Au temps de Judas*. Paris: Grasset, 1933.

Descaves, Lucien. *Les Sous-offs: roman militaire*. Paris: Tresse et Stock, 1890.

Dinar, André. *La Croisade symboliste*. Paris: Mercure de France, 1943.

Drumont, Edouard. *La Dernière Bataille*. Paris: Editions du Trident, La Librairie française, 1986.

———. *La France juive*. Vols. 1, et 2. Paris: Editions du Trident, La Librairie française, 1986.

———. *Testament d'un antisémite*. Paris: Editions du Trident, La Librairie française, 1988.

Durkheim, Emile. *The Division of Labor in Society*. Translated by George Simpson. Glencoe, IL: The Free Press, 1933.

Gide, André. *Oscar Wilde: In Memoriam*. Translated by Bernard Frechtman. New York: Philosophical Library, 1949.

Gohier, Urbain. *L'Armée contre la nation, édition augmentée des notes du "Procès L'Armée contre la nation."* Paris: Editions de la Revue blanche, 1899.

Gourmont, Remy de. *Le Joujou patriotisme*. Edited by Jean-Pierre Rioux. Paris: Jean-Jacques Pauvert, 1967.

———. *Le Livre des masques, première et deuxième séries*. Paris: Mercure de France, 1896; 1898; reprint, 1963.

Grave, Jean. *L'Individu et la société*. 2nd ed. Paris: Stock, 1897.

———. *La Société future*. Paris: Stock, 1893.

———. *La Société mourante et l'anarchie*. Paris: Stock, 1893.

Gyp. *Les Femmes du colonel*. Paris: Flammarion, 1899.

Halévy, Daniel. *Regards sur l'Affaire Dreyfus*. Paris: Editions de Fallois, 1994.

Hermant, Abel. *Le Cavalier miserey*. Paris: Charpentier, 1887.

Huret, Jules. *L'Enquête sur l'évolution littéraire*. Vanves: Editions Thot, 1982.

———. *Interviews de littérature et d'art*. Vanves: Editions Thot, 1984.

Jaurès, Jean. *Pages choisies de Jean Jaurès*. Paris: Rieder, 1928.

Lasserre, Pierre. *La Doctrine officielle de l'Université*. 4th ed. Paris: Garnier Frères, 1913.

Lazare, Bernard. *L'Antisémitisme, son histoire et ses causes historiques*. Paris: Editions 1900, 1990.

———. *Juifs et antisémites*. Edited by Philippe Oriol. Paris: Editions Allia, 1992.

Le Bon, Gustave. *The Psychology of Socialism*. New York: Macmillan, 1899.

Lemaître, Jules. *Opinions à répandre*. Paris: Société française d'imprimerie et de librairie, 1901.

Mauclair, Camille. *Servitude et grandeur littéraires*. Paris: Ollendorff, 1922.

Maurras, Charles. *L'Avenir de l'intelligence*. Paris: Nouvelle Librairie nationale, 1909.

———. *Bon et Mauvais Maîtres, Oeuvres capitales*. Vol. 3. Paris: Flammarion, 1954.

———. *Dictionnaire politique et critique*. Vol. 1. Paris: Cité des Livres, 1932.

———. *Le Mont de Saturne*. Paris: Les Quatre Jeudis, 1950.

———. *Pour un jeune français*. Paris: Amiot-Dumont, 1949.

———. *Quand les Français ne s'aimaient pas, chronique d'une renaissance, 1895–1905*. Paris: Nouvelle Librairie nationale, 1916.

———. *Romantisme et Révolution, Oeuvre de Charles Maurras*. Paris: Nouvelle Librairie nationale, 1925.

———. *Au signe de Flore: souvenirs de vie politique*. Paris: Les Oeuvres représentatives, 1931.

Mazel, Henri. *Aux beaux temps du symbolisme, 1890–1895*. Paris: Mercure de France, 1943.

———. *La Synergie sociale*. Paris: Armand Colin, 1896.

Mikhail, E. H., ed. *Oscar Wilde: Interviews and Recollections*. Vol. 2. New York: Harper and Row, 1979.

Mirbeau, Octave. *L'Affaire Dreyfus*. Edited by Pierre Michel and Jean-François Nivet. Paris: Séguier, 1991.

———. *Combats politiques*. Edited by Pierre Michel and Jean-François Nivet. Paris: Séguier, 1990.

———. *Les Ecrivains* (1895–1910), deuxième série. Paris: Flammarion, 1926.

Nordau, Max. *Degeneration*. New York: Howard Fertig, 1968.

Pressensé, Francis de. *L'Affaire Dreyfus: un héros, le colonel Picquart*. Paris: Stock, 1898.

Quillard, Pierre, ed. *Le Monument Henry*. Paris: Stock, 1899.

Raynaud, Ernest. *La Mêlée symboliste: portraits et souvenirs (1870–1910)*. Paris: 1900; reprint: Nizet, 1983.

Rebell, Hugues. *Union des trois aristocraties*. Paris: Bibliothèque artistique et littéraire, 1894.

Reinach, Joseph. *L'Affaire Dreyfus: une conscience: le Lieutenant-Colonel Picquart*. Paris: Stock, 1898.

———. *L'Affaire Dreyfus: tout le crime*. Vol. 3. Paris: Stock, 1900.

Retté, Adolphe. *Le Symbolisme: anecdotes et souvenirs*. Paris: Léon Vanier, 1903.

Réville, Albert. *Les Etapes d'un intellectuel*. Paris: Stock, 1898.

Rolland, Romain. *Le Cloître de la rue d'Ulm*. Paris: Albin Michel, 1952.

Tailhade, Laurent. *Imbéciles et gredins*. Paris: Maison d'art moderne, 1900.

———. *Plaidoyer pour Dreyfus*. Edited by Gilles Picq. Paris: Séguier, 1994.

Tarde, Gabriel. *On Communication and Social Influence: Selected Papers*. Edited by Terry N. Clark. Chicago, IL: The University of Chicago Press, 1969.

Vaillant, Annette. *Le Pain polka*. Paris: Mercure de France, 1974.

Viau, Raphael. *Vingt ans d'antisémitisme, 1889–1909*. Paris, Bibliothèque Charpentier, 1910.

Secondary sources

I. Books

Angenot, Marc. *Ce que l'on dit des Juifs en 1889: antisémitisme et discours social*. Saint-Denis: Presses Universitaires de Vincennes, 1989.

Arbour, Romeo. *Bergson et les lettres françaises*. Paris: José Corti, 1955.

Aubéry, Pierre. *Milieux juifs de la France contemporaine à travers leurs écrivains*. Paris: Plon, 1957.

Barrows, Susanna. *Distorting Mirrors: Visions of the Crowd in Late-Nineteenth-Century France*. New Haven, Conn.: Yale University Press, 1981.

Bénichou, Paul. *Le Sacre de l'écrivain, 1750–1830*. Paris: José Corti, 1985.

Berenson, Edward. *The Trial of Madame Caillaux*. Berkeley, Calif.: University of California Press, 1992.

Birkett, Jennifer. *The Sins of the Fathers: Decadence in France 1870–1914*. London: Quartet Books, 1986.

Birnbaum, Pierre. *Anti-Semitism in France: A Political History from Léon Blum to the Present*. Translated by Miriam Kochan. Cambridge, Mass.: Basil Blackwell, 1992.

———. *La France aux Français: histoire des haines nationalistes*. Paris: Seuil, 1993.

———, ed. *La France de l'affaire Dreyfus*. Paris: Gallimard, 1994.

Bodin, Louis. *Les Intellectuels*. Paris: Presses Universitaires de France, 1964.

Bourdieu, Pierre. *The Field of Cultural Production: Essays on Art and Literature*. Edited by Randal Johnson. New York: Columbia University Press, 1993.

Bredin, Jean-Denis. *L'Affaire*. Paris: Julliard, 1983.

———. *Bernard Lazare: de l'anarchiste au prophète*. Paris: Editions de Fallois, 1992.

Brombert, Victor. *The Intellectual Hero: Studies in the French Novel: 1880–1955*. Philadelphia: J. B. Lippincott, 1961.

Burns, Michael. *Dreyfus: A Family Affair: 1789–1945*. New York: Harper Collins, 1991.

Byrnes, Robert. *Anti-Semitism in Modern France*. Vol. 1, *The Prologue to the Dreyfus Affair*. New Brunswick, NJ: Rutgers University Press, 1950.

Carr, Reginald. *Anarchism in France: The Case of Octave Mirbeau*. Montreal: McGill-Queen's University Press, 1977.

Carroll, David. *French Literary Fascism: Nationalism, Anti-Semitism, and the Ideology of Culture*. Princeton, NJ: Princeton University Press, 1995.

Charle, Christophe. *La Crise littéraire à l'époque du naturalisme: roman, théâtre, politique*. Paris: Presses de l'Ecole Normale Supérieure, 1979.

———. *Naissance des "intellectuels": 1880–1910*. Paris: Editions de Minuit, 1990.

Chartier, Roger. *The Cultural Origins of the French Revolution*. Translated by Lydia G. Cochrane. Durham, North Carolina: Duke University Press, 1991.

Chartier, Roger and Henri-Jean Martin. *Histoire de l'édition française*. Vols. 3, and 4. Paris: Promodis, 1985; 1986; Fayard/Promodis, 1990; 1991.

Clark, Linda L. *Social Darwinism in France*. Tuscaloosa, AL: University of Alabama Press, 1984.

Clark, Priscilla Parkhurst. *Literary France: The Making of a Culture*. Berkeley, Calif.: University of California Press, 1987.

Clark, Terry Nichols. *Prophets and Patrons: The French University and the Emergence of the Social Sciences*. Cambridge, Mass.: Harvard University Press, 1973.

Clouard, Henri. *La "Cocarde" de M. Barrès*. Paris: Nouvelle Librairie nationale, 1910.

Cohen, Ed. *Talk on the Wilde Side: Toward a Genealogy of a Discourse on Male Sexualities*. New York: Routledge, 1993.

Darnton, Robert. *The Literary Underground of the Old Regime*. Cambridge, Mass.: Harvard University Press, 1982.

Datta, Venita. *La Revue blanche* (1889–1903): Intellectuals and Politics in Fin-de-Siècle France. Ph.D. diss., New York University, 1989.

Debray, Régis. *Teachers, Writers, Celebrities: The Intellectuals of Modern France*. Translated by Francis Mulhern. London, Eng.: New Left Books, 1981.

Digeon, Claude. *La Crise allemande de la pensée française, 1870–1914*. Paris: Presses Universitaires de France, 1959; 1992.

Drouin, Michel, ed. *L'Affaire Dreyfus de A à Z*. Paris: Flammarion, 1994.

Duncan, J. Ann. *Les Romans de Paul Adam: du symbolisme littéraire au symbolisme cabalistique*. Berne: Peter Lang, 1977.

Ellmann, Richard. *Oscar Wilde*. New York: Knopf, 1988.

Ferenczi, Thomas. *L'Invention du journalisme en France: naissance de la presse moderne à la fin du XIXème siècle*. Paris: Plon, 1993.

Gervereau, Laurent and Christophe Prochasson, eds. *L'Affaire Dreyfus et le tournant du siècle (1894–1910)*. Paris: BDIC, 1994.

Gilman, Sander L. *Jewish Self-Hatred: Anti-Semitism and the Hidden Language of the Jews*. Baltimore, Maryland: Johns Hopkins University Press, 1986.

Girardet, Raoul. *Mythes et mythologies politiques*. Paris: Seuil, 1986.

———. *Le Nationalisme français: 1871–1914*. Paris: Seuil, 1983.

———. *La Société militaire dans la France contemporaine (1815–1939)*. Paris: Plon, 1953.

Gold, Arthur and Robert Fizdale. *The Life of Misia Sert*. New York: Alfred Knopf, 1980.

Griffiths, Richard. *The Use of Abuse: The Polemics of the Dreyfus Affair and its Aftermath*. New York: Berg, 1991.

Halperin, Joan U. *Félix Fénéon: Aesthete and Anarchist in Fin-de-Siècle Paris*. New Haven, Conn.: Yale University Press, 1988.

Hanna, Martha. *The Mobilization of Intellect: Scholars, Writers, and the French War Effort, 1914–1918*. Cambridge, Mass.: Harvard University Press, 1996.

Hause, Steven C. and Jennifer Waelti-Walters, eds. *Feminisms of the Belle Epoque: a historical and literary anthology*. Lincoln, Neb.: University of Nebraska Press, 1994.

Herbert, Eugenia. *The Artist and Social Reform: France and Belgium, 1885–1898*. New Haven, Conn.: Yale University Press, 1961.

Hughes, H. Stuart. *Consciousness and Society: The Reorientation of European Social Thought, 1890–1930*. New York: Vintage Books, 1961; 1977.

Hunt, Lynn, ed. *Eroticism and the Body Politic*. Baltimore, Maryland: Johns Hopkins University Press, 1991.

Hyman, Paula. *From Dreyfus to Vichy: The Remaking of French Jewry, 1906–1939*. New York: Columbia University Press, 1979.

Irvine, William D. *The Boulanger Affair Reconsidered: Royalism, Boulangism and the Origins of the Radical Right in France*. New York: Oxford University Press, 1989.

Jackson, A. B. *La Revue blanche (1889–1903): origine, influence, bibliographie*. Paris: Minard, 1960.

Jennings, Jeremy, ed. *Intellectuals in Twentieth-Century France: Mandarins and Samurais*. New York: Saint-Martin's Press, 1993.

Joll, James. *The Anarchists*. Cambridge, Mass.: Harvard University Press, 1980.

Judt, Tony. *Past Imperfect: French Intellectuals, 1944–1956*. Berkeley, Calif.: University of California Press, 1992.

Juillard, Jacques and Michel Winock, eds. *Dictionnaire des intellectuels français*. Paris: Seuil, 1996.

Kleeblatt, Norman L., ed. *The Dreyfus Affair: Art, Truth and Justice*. Berkeley, Calif.: University of California Press, 1987.

Lacapra, Dominick. *Emile Durkheim: Sociologist and Philosopher*. Ithaca, NY: Cornell University Press, 1972.

Lebovics, Herman. *True France: The Wars over Cultural Identity, 1900–1945*. Ithaca, NY: Cornell University Press, 1992; 1994.

Lehmann, Jennifer M. *Durkheim and Women*. Lincoln, Neb.: University of Nebraska Press, 1994.

Leroy, Géraldi, ed. *Les Ecrivains et l'Affaire Dreyfus*. Orléans: Presses Universitaires de France, 1983.

Lévy, Louis. *Comment ils sont devenus socialistes*. Paris: Editions du Populaire, 1931.

Lindemann, Albert S. *The Jew Accused: Three Anti-Semitic Affairs (Dreyfus, Beilis, Frank), 1894–1915*. New York: Cambridge University Press, 1991.

Logue, William. *From Philosophy to Sociology: The Evolution of French Liberalism, 1870–1914*. De Kalb, IL: Northern Illinois University Press, 1983.

Lough, John. *Writer and Public in France: From the Middle Ages to the Present*. Oxford, Eng.: Clarendon Press, 1978.

Lukes, Steven. *Emile Durkheim: His Life and Work*. New York: Harper and Row, 1972.

———. *Individualism*. New York: Harper and Row, 1973.

Maitron, Jean. *Histoire du mouvement anarchiste en France*. Vol. 1, *Les Origines à 1914*. Paris: Gallimard, 1975.

Malino, Frances and Bernard Wasserstein, eds. *The Jews in Modern France*. Hanover, NH: University Press of New England, 1985.

Marrus, Michael. *The Politics of Assimilation: A Study of the French Jewish Community at the Time of the Dreyfus Affair*. Oxford, Eng.: Clarendon Press, 1971.

Maugue, Annelise. *L'Identité masculine en crise au tournant du siècle, 1871–1914*. Paris: Editions Rivages, 1987.

Mayeur, Jean-Marie. *Les Débuts de la IIIème République, 1871–1898*. Paris: Seuil, 1973.

Mehlman, Jeffrey. *Legacies of Anti-Semitism in France*. Minneapolis, Minn.: University of Minnesota Press, 1983.

Memmi, Albert. *Portrait d'un juif*. Paris, Gallimard, 1962.

Merrick, Jeffrey and Bryant T. Ragan, Jr., eds. *Homosexuality in France*. New York: Oxford University Press, 1996.

Mitchell, Bonner. *Les Manifestes littéraires de la Belle Epoque, 1886–1914*. Paris: Seghers, 1966.

Mosse, George L. *The Crisis of German Ideology: Intellectual Origins of the Third Reich*. New York: Howard Fertig, 1981.

———. *Nationalism and Sexuality: Middle-Class Morality and Sexual Norms in Modern Europe.* Madison, Wis.: University of Wisconsin Press, 1985.

Nguyen, Victor. *Aux origines de l'Action française: intelligence et politique à l'aube du XXème siècle.* Paris: Fayard, 1991.

Nora, Pierre, ed. *Les Lieux de mémoire.* 7 vols. Paris: Gallimard, 1984–1992.

Nord, Philip. *The Republican Moment: Struggles for Democracy in Nineteenth-Century France.* Cambridge, Mass.: Harvard University Press, 1995.

Nye, Robert A. *Crime, Madness and Politics in Modern France: The Medical Concept of National Decline.* Princeton, NJ: Princeton University Press, 1984.

———. *Masculinity and Male Codes of Honor in Modern France.* New York: Oxford University Press, 1993.

———. *The Origins of Crowd Psychology: Gustave Le Bon and the Crisis of Mass Democracy in the Third Republic.* Beverly Hills, Calif.: Sage Publications, 1975.

Ory, Pascal and Jean-François Sirinelli. *Les Intellectuels en France, de l'Affaire Dreyfus à nos jours.* Paris: Armand Colin, 1986.

Ory, Pascal, ed. *Dernières Questions aux intellectuels.* Paris: Olivier Orban, 1990.

Pagès, Alain. *Emile Zola, un intellectuel dans l'Affaire Dreyfus.* Paris: Séguier, 1991.

Paysac, Henri de. *Francis Vielé-Griffin, poète symboliste et citoyen américain.* Paris: Nizet, 1976.

Peyre, Henri. *Les Générations littéraires.* Paris: Boivin, 1948.

Pierrot, Jean. *L'Imaginaire décadent, 1880–1900.* Paris: Presses Universitaires de France, 1977.

Poggioli, Renato. *The Theory of the Avant-Garde.* Translated by Gerald Fitzgerald. Cambridge, Mass.: Belknap Press of Harvard University Press, 1968.

Poliakov, Léon. *The History of Anti-Semitism.* Vol. 3, *From Voltaire to Wagner.* Translated by Miriam Kochan. New York: Vanguard Press, 1975.

Prochasson, Christophe. *Les Années éléctriques, 1880–1910.* Paris: Editions de la Découverte, 1991.

———. *Les Intellectuels, le socialisme et la guerre, 1900–1938.* Paris: Seuil, 1993.

Rabaut, Jean. *L'Antimilitarisme en France, 1810–1975.* Paris: Hachette, 1975.

Rémond, René, ed. *Pour une histoire politique.* Paris: Seuil, 1988.

Ringer, Fritz. *Fields of Knowledge: French Academic Culture in Comparative Perspective, 1890–1920.* New York: Cambridge University Press, 1992.

Rioux, Jean-Pierre. *Nationalisme et conservatisme: la Ligue de la patrie française, 1899–1904.* Paris: Editions Beauchesne, 1977.

Sartre, Jean-Paul. *Anti-Semite and Jew.* Translated by George J. Becker. New York: Schocken Books, 1948.

Schorske, Carl E. *Fin-de-siècle Vienna: Politics and Culture.* New York: Vantage Books, 1981.

Scott, Joan W. *Gender and the Politics of History.* New York: Columbia University Press, 1988.

Seigel, Jerrold. *Bohemian Paris: Culture, Politics, and the Boundaries of Bourgeois Life, 1830–1930.* New York: Viking, 1986; Penguin, 1987.

Serman, William. *Les Officiers français dans la nation (1848–1914).* Paris: Aubier Montaigne, 1982.

Showalter, Elaine. *Sexual Anarchy: Gender and Culture at the Fin de Siècle.* New York: Viking, 1990.

Silvera, Alain. *Daniel Halévy and his Times.* Ithaca, NY: Cornell University Press, 1966.

Silverman, Debora. *Art Nouveau in Fin-de-Siècle France: Politics, Psychology and Style.* Berkeley, Calif.: University of California Press, 1989.

Silverman, Willa Z. *The Notorious Life of Gyp: Right-Wing Anarchist in Fin-de-Siècle France.* New York: Oxford University Press, 1995.

Sinfield, Alan. *The Wilde Century: Effeminacy, Oscar Wilde and the Queer Movement.* New York: Columbia University Press, 1994.

Sirinelli, Jean-François. *Intellectuels et passions françaises: manifestes et pétitions au XXème siècle.* Paris: Fayard, 1990.

Sonn, Richard D. *Anarchism and Cultural Politics in Fin-de-siècle France.* Lincoln, Neb.: University of Nebraska Press, 1989.

Soucy, Robert. *Fascism in France: The Case of Maurice Barrès.* Berkeley, Calif.: University of California Press, 1972.

Spitzer, Alan. *The French Generation of 1820.* Princeton, NJ: Princeton University Press, 1987.

———. *Historical Truths and Lies about the Past: Reflections on Dewey, Dreyfus, de Man, and Reagan.* Chapel Hill, North Carolina: University of North Carolina Press, 1996.

Stern, Fritz. *The Politics of Cultural Despair: A Study in the Rise of Germanic Ideology.* Berkeley, Calif.: University of California Press, 1961.

Sternhell, Zeev. *La Droite révolutionnaire: les origines françaises du fascisme, 1885–1914.* Paris: Seuil, 1978.

————. *Maurice Barrès et le nationalisme français.* Paris: Éditions Complexe, 1985.

Stoekl, Alan. *Agonies of the Intellectual: Commitment, Subjectivity, and the Performative in the Twentieth-Century French Tradition.* Lincoln, Neb.: University of Nebraska Press, 1992.

Thibaudet, Alfred. *Histoire de la littérature française de Chateaubriand à Valéry.* Paris: Stock, 1936; Marabout 1981.

Viala, Alain. *Naissance de l'écrivain: sociologie de la littérature à l'âge classique.* Paris: Éditions de Minuit, 1985.

Weber, Eugen. *France Fin de Siècle.* Cambridge, Mass.: Belknap Press of Harvard University Press, 1986.

————. *My France: Politics, Culture and Myth.* Cambridge, Mass.: Belknap Press of Harvard University Press, 1991.

————. *The Nationalist Revival in France, 1905–1914.* Berkeley, Calif.: University of California Press, 1986.

————. *Peasants into Frenchmen: The Modernization of Rural France, 1870–1914.* Stanford, Calif.: Stanford University Press, 1976.

Weisz, George. *The Emergence of Modern Universities in France, 1863–1914.* Princeton, NJ: Princeton University Press, 1983.

Wilson, Nelly. *Bernard Lazare: Anti-Semitism and the Problem of Jewish Identity in Late-Nineteenth-Century France.* New York: Cambridge University Press, 1978.

Wilson, Stephen. *Ideology and Experience: Antisemitism in France at the Time of the Dreyfus Affair.* East Brunswick, NJ: Associated University Press, 1982.

Winock, Michel, *Nationalisme, antisémitisme et fascisme en France.* Paris: Seuil, 1990.

————. ed. *Histoire de l'extrême droite en France.* Paris: Seuil, 1993.

Wohl, Robert. *The Generation of 1914.* Cambridge, Mass.: Harvard University Press, 1979.

Woodcock, George. *Anarchism: A History of Libertarian Ideas and Movements.* New York: Penguin Books, 1986.

Zeldin, Theodore. *France 1848–1945, Politics and Anger.* New York: Oxford University Press, 1979.

II. Articles

Azéma, Jean-Pierre. "La Clef générationnelle." *Vingtième Siècle*, no. 22 (April–June 1989):3–10.

Bénéton, Philippe. "La Génération de 1912–1914: image, mythe et réalité." *Revue française de science politique* 21, no. 5 (October 1971):981–1009.

Byrnes, Robert. "Jean-Louis Forain: Antisemitism in French Art." *Jewish Social Studies* 12 (1950):247–56.

Cahm, Eric. "Les Débuts de l'Affaire Dreyfus revus et corrigés: le Général Mercier face à Drumont et à Rochefort en 1894." *Modern and Contemporary France* 40 (1990):3–15.

———. "Intellectuals, the Elite and the Dreyfus Affair: Further Work from Christophe Charle." *Modern and Contemporary France* 42 (1990):68–70.

Cate, Phillip Dennis. " 'La Plume' and its 'Salon des cent': Promoters of posters and prints in the 1890s." *Print Review* 8 (1978):61–68.

Cerullo, John J. "Truth and Justice? Honor and Manhood! Toward a Gendered Interpretation of Intellectuals and the Dreyfus Affair." Paper presented at the French Historical Studies Conference, Atlanta, March 1995.

Charle, Christophe. "Les Ecrivains et l'Affaire Dreyfus." *Annales, économies, sociétés, civilisations* 32, no. 2 (March–April 1977): 240–264.

———. "Situation spatiale et position sociale: essai de géographie sociale du champ littéraire à la fin du 19e siècle." *Actes de la recherche en sciences sociales*, no. 181 (13 February 1977):45–58.

Cladis, Mark S. "Durkheim's Communitarian Defense of Liberalism." *Soundings* 72, no. 2–3 (Summer/Fall 1989):275–295.

Cohen, Ed. "Writing Gone Wilde: Homoerotic Desire in the Closet of Representation." *PMLA* 103 (October 1987):803–813.

Cohen, Paul M. "Reason and Faith: The Bergsonian Catholic Youth of Pre-War France." *Historical Reflections / Réflexions historiques* 13, nos. 2–3 (1986):473–97.

Datta, Venita. "A Bohemian Festival in Montmartre: La fête de la vache enragée." *Journal of Contemporary History* 28 (1993):195–213.

———. "The Dreyfus Affair and Anti-Semitism: Jewish Identity at *La Revue Blanche*." Historical Reflections/Réflexions historiques 21, no. 1 (Winter 1995):113–130.

———. "Germany Revisited: The *Mercure de France* Surveys of 1895 and 1902." *Proceedings of the Annual Meeting of the Western Society for French History* 18 (1991):381–387.

———. "Passing Fancy?: The Generation of 1890 and Anarchism." *Modern and Contemporary France*, no. 44 (January 1991):3–11.

Décaudin, Michel. "Formes et fonctions de la revue littéraire au XXème siècle." *Situation et avenir des revues littéraires*, 13–22. Nice: Centre du XXème siècle, 1976.

Devriese, Marc. "Approche sociologique de la génération." *Vingtième Siècle*, no. 22 (April–June 1989):11–16.

Diani, Marco F. "Metamorphosis of Nationalism: Durkheim, Barrès, and the Dreyfus Affair." *The Jerusalem Journal of International Relations* 13, no. 4 (1991):72–94.

Field, Trevor. "Vers une nouvelle datation du substantif 'Intellectuel'." *Travaux de linguistique et de littérature* 14, no. 2 (1976):159–167.

Forth, Christopher. "Intellectual Anarchy and Imaginary Otherness: Gender, Class, and Pathology in French Intellectual Discourse, 1890–1900." *Sociological Quarterly* 37, no. 4 (Fall 1996):645–671.

Gerbod, Paul. "L'Ethique héroïque en France (1870–1914)." *La Revue historique*, no. 268 (1982):409–429.

Girardet, Raoul. "Du concept de génération à la notion de contemporanéité." *Revue d'histoire moderne et contemporaine* 30 (April–June 1983):257–270.

Grosbois, Guy de. "Il y a 100 ans, les agapes de *La Plume*." *La Revue des revues*, no. 8 (Winter, 1989–1990):21–24.

Hanna, Martha. "What did André Gide see in the Action Française?" *Historical Reflections/Réflexions historiques* 17, no. 1 (1991):2–22.

Hayward, J.E.S. "The Official Social Philosophy of the French Third Republic: Léon Bourgeois and Solidarism." *International Review of Social History* 6 (1961):19–48.

———. "Solidarity: The Social History of an Idea in Nineteenth-Century France." *International Review of Social history* 4 (1959):261–284.

Holmes, Richard. "Voltaire's Grin." *New York Review of Books* (30 November 1995):49–50.

Idt, G. "L' 'Intellectuel' avant l'Affaire Dreyfus." *Cahiers de lexicologie* 15, no. 2 (1969):35–46.

Johnston, William M. "The Origin of the Term 'Intellectuals' in French Novels and Essays of the 1890s." *Journal of European Studies* 4 (1974):43–56.

Juilliard, Jacques. "Le Fascisme en France." *Annales, économies, sociétés, civilisations* 39, no. 4 (July–August 1984):849–861.

———. "Le Monde des revues au début du siècle." *Les Cahiers Georges Sorel* 5 (1987):3–9.

Kriegel, Annie. "Le Concept politique de génération: apogée et déclin." *Commentaire*, no. 7 (Autumn 1979):390–399.

Lachance, Paul. "The Consciousness of the Generation of 1890 at Maturity: an Alternative Reading of the Image of French Youth in 1912–1914." *Journal of Interdisciplinary Studies* 2, no. 1 (Fall 1978):67–81.

———. "The Nature and Function of Generational Discourse in France on the Eve of World War I." In *Political Symbolism in Modern Europe: Essays in Honor of George L. Mosse*, edited by Seymour Drescher et al., 239–55. New Brunswick, NJ: Transaction Books, 1982.

Lesage, Claire. "Des Avant-gardes en travail." *Revue des sciences humaines* 95, no. 219 (July–September 1990):85–105.

Lukes, Steven. "Durkheim's Individualism and the Intellectuals." *Political Studies* 17, no. 1 (1969):14–30.

Mannheim, Karl. "The Problem of Generations." *Essays on the Sociology of Knowledge*, 276–322. London: Routledge and Kegan Paul, 1959.

Mazgaj, Paul. "Defending the West: The Cultural and Generational Politics of Henri Massis." *Historical Reflections / Réflexions historiques* 17, no. 2 (1991):103–123.

Nguyen, Victor. "Elites, pouvoir et culture sur une correspondance entre Charles Maurras et Henri Mazel à la veille de la crise dreyfusienne." *Etudes maurrasiennes*, no. 4 (1980):141–92.

———. "Un Essai de pouvoir intellectuel au début de la Troisième République." *Etudes maurrassiennes* 1 (1972):145–55.

———. "Note sur le problème de l'antisémitisme maurrassien." In *L'Idée de la race dans la pensée politique française contemporaine*, edited by Pierre Guirard and Emile Temime, 135–55. Paris: Editions du CNRS, 1977.

Nivet, Jean-François. "Octave Mirbeau et l'affaire Dreyfus." *Cahiers naturalistes* 64 (1990):79–102.

Noland, Aaron. "Individualism in Jean Jaurès's Socialist Thought." *Journal of the History of Ideas* 22 (1961):63–80.

Offen, Karen. "Depopulation, Nationalism, and Feminism in Fin-de-Siècle France." *American Historical Review* 89, no. 3. (June 1984):648–676.

Perrot, Michelle. "The New Eve and the Old Adam: Changes in French Women's Condition at the Turn of the Century." In *Behind the Lines: Gender and the Two World Wars*, edited by Margaret Higonnet, 51–60. New Haven, Conn.: Yale University Press, 1987.

Prochasson, Christophe. "Histoire intellectuelle/histoire des intellectuels: le socialisme français au début du XXème siècle." *Revue d'histoire moderne et contemporaine* 39, no. 3 (July–September 1992):423–448.

Rebérioux, Madeleine. "Zola, Jaurès et France: trois intellectuels devant l'Affaire." *Cahiers naturalistes* 26 (1989):266–281.

Silve, Edith. "Les premières heures du *Mercure de France*." *La Revue des revues*, no. 3 (Spring 1987):12–17.

———. "Rachilde et Alfred Vallette et la fondation du *Mercure de France*." *La Revue des revues*, no. 2 (November 1986):13–16.

Silverman, Willa Z. " 'Semitic Troubles': Author-Publisher Relations in Fin-de-Siècle France: The Case of Gyp and Calmann-Lévy." *Historical Reflections / Réflexions historiques* 19, no. 3 (1993):309–334.

Sirinelli, Jean-François. "Le hasard ou la nécessité? une histoire en chantier: l'histoire des intellectuels." *Vingtième Siècle*, no. 9 (January–March 1986):97–108.

Sonn, Richard D. "The Early Political Career of Maurice Barrès: Anarchist, Socialist, or Protofascist?" *Clio*, 21, no. 1 (Fall 1991):41–60.

Spitzer, Alan. "The Historical Problem of Generations." *The American Historical Review* 78, no. 5 (December 1978):1353–1385.

Sternhell, Zeev. "Le Déterminisme physiologique et racial à la base du nationalisme de Maurice Barrès et de Jules Soury." In *L'Idée de la race dans la pensée politique française contemporaine*, edited by Pierre Guirard and Emile Temime, 117–38. Paris: Editions du CNRS, 1977.

Stock, Phyllis H. "Students versus the University in Pre-World Paris." *French Historical Studies* 7, no. 2 (Spring 1971):93–110.

Suleiman, Susan Rubin. "L'Engagement sublime: Zola comme archétype d'un mythe culturel." *Cahiers naturalistes* 67 (1993):11–24.

Vincent, K. Steven. "Jean Grave and French Communist Anarchism." Paper presented at the WSFH Conference, Las Vegas, Nevada, Nov. 8–11, 1995.

Wesseling, H.L. "Reluctant Crusaders: French Intellectuals and the Dreyfus Affair." *Stanford French Review* 1 (1977):379–395.

Wilson, Stephen. "L'Action française et le mouvement nationaliste français entre les années 1890 et 1900." *Etudes maurrassiennes*, no. 4 (1980):309–22.

———. "The 'Action française' in French Intellectual Life." *The Historical Journal* 12, no. 2 (1969):328–50.

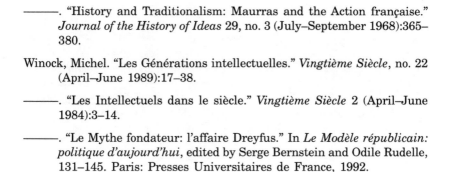
————. "History and Traditionalism: Maurras and the Action française." *Journal of the History of Ideas* 29, no. 3 (July–September 1968):365–380.

Winock, Michel. "Les Générations intellectuelles." *Vingtième Siècle*, no. 22 (April–June 1989):17–38.

————. "Les Intellectuels dans le siècle." *Vingtième Siècle* 2 (April–June 1984):3–14.

————. "Le Mythe fondateur: l'affaire Dreyfus." In *Le Modèle républicain: politique d'aujourd'hui*, edited by Serge Bernstein and Odile Rudelle, 131–145. Paris: Presses Universitaires de France, 1992.

Index